James Tift

The oration of Demosthenes on the crown

James Tift

The oration of Demosthenes on the crown

ISBN/EAN: 9783337273286

Printed in Europe, USA, Canada, Australia, Japan

Cover: Foto ©Suzi / pixelio.de

More available books at **www.hansebooks.com**

THE

ORATION

OF

DEMOSTHENES

ON

THE CROWN.

WITH NOTES,

BY J. T. CHAMPLIN,
PROFESSOR OF GREEK AND LATIN IN WATERVILLE COLLEGE.

"Cujus non tam vibrarent fulmina illa, nisi numeris contorta ferrentur." — CIC. Orator, c. 70.

NEW EDITION, REVISED.

BOSTON:
WILLIAM H. DENNET.
1867.

PREFACE

TO THE FIRST EDITION

The present edition of "The Crown" owes its existence to the conviction, that the ripening scholarship of our land calls for a new attempt to illustrate this great author. It would have been the choice of the editor, that the work should have been undertaken by some abler and more experienced hand; but as no such hand was put to it, he has, after much hesitation, ventured to attempt it himself The points upon which most attention has been bestowed, and in which the merits of the edition, if it have any, will be found principally to consist, are the following: —

1. An attempt has been made to furnish in the notes all necessary historical and archæological information. The need of such information is very much felt in reading this Oration, since it deals largely in the history, laws, and politics of Athens, and, indeed, of all Greece. Laws are quoted, measures cited, and historical events alluded to, which, though familiar to the audience to which they were addressed, require illustration in order to be understood at the present time. In such a discussion, too, there are necessarily many technical terms which need explanation. All needed aid of this kind, it is hoped, will be found in the notes. In furnishing information of this nature, I have derived great assistance, as will be seen by the references,

from Hermann's Manual of the Political Antiquities of Greece; a book full of the profoundest learning, presented in the clearest and most compressed form. I have also made free use of Thirlwall's History of Greece, an attentive perusal of which, but more particularly of Chapters XLI.–XLVII., I would recommend to all who read this Oration.

2. A good deal of attention has been bestowed upon the explanation of words, sentences, and grammatical constructions. Demosthenes is an unusually difficult author to translate; and hence an editor, who would adapt his labors to the attainments of students in our academic courses, has much to do in the way of removing difficulties of this kind. It has been with this end in view, that so many words, sentences, and, in a few instances, even long passages, have been translated. It has not been intended, however, to translate any word or sentence, the meaning of which it might be supposed to be within the power of our ordinary students fully to comprehend by a reasonable amount of study; except, perhaps, in a few cases, where the importance of a word or phrase to the understanding of what precedes or follows seemed to render it desirable to prevent all possibility of mistaking its meaning, by translating it. Generally, too, only those passages have been translated, which, in order to their full understanding, require, besides a translation, the introduction of certain explanatory words or phrases. In other words, I have translated but very little barely for the purpose of translation, but generally with a view to the introduction or addition of certain explanatory remarks. In doing this, however, I cannot deny that my object has been to make the task of reading the text easier. From my own experience, both as a student and a teacher of this author, I am convinced that there is need of something being done in this way to encourage the efforts of the beginner. Ripe scholars, who have an extensive and accurate knowledge of the Greek language,

and who, besides, have at hand the books which are necessary for a thorough original study of Demosthenes, need nothing but the bare text; but for mere learners, such as this book is designed for, I am satisfied that some assistance in the way of translating difficult words and passages is needed. This seems necessary, in order to prevent them from resorting to improper helps. Whatever objections, therefore, there may be, in ordinary cases, to so free a use of translation as has been made in the present instance, I hope it will be considered that there are weighty reasons in its favor, in this particular case, growing out of the nature of the author commented upon. After all the assistance that has been given in this way, it is believed that enough of difficulty remains to task the powers and stimulate the industry of the student in no ordinary degree. It should be added here, that the translations given in the notes have been made with the simple purpose of expressing, as clearly as possible, the meaning of the original.

3. Another point upon which no inconsiderable attention has been bestowed, is the development of the course of thought pursued by the orator. For this purpose, a very full and minute analysis has been prefixed to the Notes, and special pains have been taken to point out in the notes the meaning of those words and phrases which may be regarded as the *hinges* of the thought, to notice the transitions, to show the connection of consecutive ideas, and the relevancy of what, without explanation, might appear foreign to the subject. It has been my object to aid the diligent student in obtaining a clear and vivid conception of the stirring thoughts and sentiments contained in this masterpiece of the prince of orators; and should it be thought that I have succeeded in this to any good degree, I shall not feel that I have labored in vain.

In making up the *notes*, I have made free use of the comments of others, whenever they seemed to my purpose. I have designed that they should embody, in a compressed form, all that is truly valuable which has been contributed in the way of illustration, by the great editors of Demosthenes, such as Reiske, Wolf, Taylor, Schäfer, etc., and thus be a representative of the present state of the interpretation of this author. But on very many passages of no inconsiderable difficulty, I could find nothing satisfactory in any of the commentaries of others at my command, for the explanation of which, therefore, I have been obliged to draw upon my own reading and resources; so that I flatter myself it will be found that I have contributed something of my own towards the illustration of the text. Between what is original, therefore, and what is compiled, it is hoped that but few passages, which really need illustration, will be found unexplained; and that, whatever else may be said of the notes, it cannot be said of them, as Cecil said of commentaries on the Scriptures, that "they are very good, except on difficult passages." In thus meeting, rather than avoiding, the difficult questions, I am aware that I have laid myself open much more to criticism; but this consequence, however undesirable, I shall not regret, if I have really succeeded in throwing any light upon them.

This new edition has been as carefully revised as the time and circumstances of the editor would admit, and it is hoped will be found to contain all that the ordinary reader may desire.

ΔΗΜΟΣΘΕΝΟΥΣ

Ο ΠΕΡΙ ΤΟΥ ΣΤΕΦΑΝΟΥ ΛΟΓΟΣ.

Πρῶτον μέν, ὦ ἄνδρες Ἀθηναῖοι, τοῖς θεοῖς εὔχομαι 1
πᾶσι καὶ πάσαις, ὅσην εὔνοιαν ἔχων ἐγὼ διατελῶ τῇ
226 τε πόλει καὶ πᾶσιν ὑμῖν, τοσαύτην ὑπάρξαι μοι παρ'
ὑμῶν εἰς τουτονὶ τὸν ἀγῶνα, ἔπειθ', ὅ πέρ ἐστι μάλισθ'
ὑπὲρ ὑμῶν καὶ τῆς ὑμετέρας εὐσεβείας τε καὶ δόξης,
τοῦτο παραστῆσαι τοὺς θεοὺς ὑμῖν, μὴ τὸν ἀντίδικον
σύμβουλον ποιήσασθαι περὶ τοῦ πῶς ἀκούειν ὑμᾶς ἐμοῦ
δεῖ (σχέτλιον γὰρ ἂν εἴη τοῦτό γε), ἀλλὰ τοὺς νόμους 2
καὶ τὸν ὅρκον, ἐν ᾧ πρὸς ἅπασι τοῖς ἄλλοις δικαίοις
καὶ τοῦτο γέγραπται, τὸ ὁμοίως ἀμφοῖν ἀκροάσασθαι.
Τοῦτο δ' ἐστὶν οὐ μόνον τὸ μὴ προκατεγνωκέναι μηδέν,
οὐδὲ τὸ τὴν εὔνοιαν ἴσην ἀμφοτέροις ἀποδοῦναι, ἀλλὰ
καὶ τὸ τῇ τάξει καὶ τῇ ἀπολογίᾳ, ὡς βεβούληται καὶ
προῄρηται τῶν ἀγωνιζομένων ἕκαστος, οὕτως ἐᾶσαι
χρήσασθαι.

Πολλὰ μὲν οὖν ἔγωγ' ἐλαττοῦμαι κατὰ τουτονὶ τὸν 3
ἀγῶνα Αἰσχίνου, δύο δ', ὦ ἄνδρες Ἀθηναῖοι, καὶ με-
γάλα· ἓν μὲν ὅτι οὐ περὶ τῶν ἴσων ἀγωνίζομαι· οὐ

γάρ ἐστιν ἴσον νῦν ἐμοὶ τῆς παρ' ὑμῶν εὐνοίας διαμαρ-
τεῖν καὶ τούτῳ μὴ ἑλεῖν τὴν γραφήν, ἀλλ' ἐμοὶ μὲν—(οὐ
βούλομαι δὲ δυσχερὲς εἰπεῖν οὐδὲν ἀρχόμενος τοῦ λόγου),
οὗτος δ' ἐκ περιουσίας μου κατηγορεῖ. Ἕτερον δ', ὃ
φύσει πᾶσιν ἀνθρώποις ὑπάρχει, τῶν μὲν λοιδοριῶν καὶ
τῶν κατηγοριῶν ἀκούειν ἡδέως, τοῖς ἐπαινοῦσι δ' αὑτοὺς
3 ἄχθεσθαι· τούτων τοίνυν ὃ μέν ἐστι πρὸς ἡδονήν, τούτῳ
δέδοται, ὃ δὲ πᾶσιν ὡς ἔπος εἰπεῖν ἐνοχλεῖ, λοιπὸν ἐμοί.
Κἂν μὲν εὐλαβούμενος τοῦτο μὴ λέγω τὰ πεπραγμένα
ἐμαυτῷ, οὐκ ἔχειν ἀπολύσασθαι τὰ κατηγορημένα δόξω
οὐδ' ἐφ' οἷς ἀξιῶ τιμᾶσθαι δεικνύναι· ἐὰν δ' ἐφ' ἃ καὶ
πεποίηκα καὶ πεπολίτευμαι βαδίζω, πολλάκις λέγειν
ἀναγκασθήσομαι περὶ ἐμαυτοῦ. Πειράσομαι μὲν οὖν 221
ὡς μετριώτατα τοῦτο ποιεῖν· ὅ τι δ' ἂν τὸ πρᾶγμα
αὐτὸ ἀναγκάζῃ, τούτου τὴν αἰτίαν οὗτός ἐστι δίκαιος
ἔχειν ὁ τοιοῦτον ἀγῶνα ἐνστησάμενος.

Οἶμαι δ' ὑμᾶς, ὦ ἄνδρες Ἀθηναῖοι, πάντας ἂν ὁμο-
λογῆσαι κοινὸν εἶναι τουτονὶ τὸν ἀγῶνα ἐμοὶ καὶ Κτη-
σιφῶντι, καὶ οὐδὲν ἐλάττονος ἄξιον σπουδῆς ἐμοί· πάντων μὲν γὰρ ἀποστερεῖσθαι λυπηρόν ἐστι καὶ χαλεπόν,
ἄλλως τε κἂν ὑπ' ἐχθροῦ τῳ τοῦτο συμβαίνῃ, μάλιστα
δὲ τῆς παρ' ὑμῶν εὐνοίας καὶ φιλανθρωπίας, ὅσῳ περ
5 καὶ τὸ τυχεῖν τούτων μέγιστόν ἐστιν. Περὶ τούτων δ'
ὄντος τουτουὶ τοῦ ἀγῶνος, ἀξιῶ καὶ δέομαι πάντων
ὁμοίως ὑμῶν, ἀκοῦσαί μου περὶ τῶν κατηγορημένων
ἀπολογουμένου δικαίως, ὥσπερ οἱ νόμοι κελεύουσιν, οὓς
ὁ τιθεὶς ἐξ ἀρχῆς Σόλων, εὔνους ὢν ὑμῖν καὶ δημοτικός,

οὐ μόνον τῷ γράψαι κυρίους ᾤετο δεῖν εἶναι, ἀλλὰ καὶ
τῷ τοὺς δικάζοντας ὑμᾶς ὀμωμοκέναι· οὐκ ἀπιστῶν 7
ὑμῖν, ὥς γ' ἐμοὶ φαίνεται, ἀλλ' ὁρῶν ὅτι τὰς αἰτίας καὶ
τὰς διαβολάς, αἷς ἐκ τοῦ πρότερος λέγειν ὁ διώκων
ἰσχύει, οὐκ ἔνι τῷ φεύγοντι παρελθεῖν, εἰ μὴ τῶν δικα-
ζόντων ἕκαστος ὑμῶν τὴν πρὸς τοὺς θεοὺς εὐσέβειαν
φυλάττων καὶ τὰ τοῦ λέγοντος ὕστερον δίκαια εὐνοϊκῶς
προσδέξεται, καὶ παρασχὼν ἑαυτὸν ἴσον καὶ κοινὸν
ἀμφοτέροις ἀκροατήν, οὕτω τὴν διάγνωσιν ποιήσεται
περὶ ἁπάντων.

Μέλλων δὲ τοῦ τε ἰδίου βίου παντός, ὡς ἔοικε, λόγον 8
διδόναι τήμερον καὶ τῶν κοινῇ πεπολιτευμένων, βούλομαι πάλιν τοὺς θεοὺς παρακαλέσαι, καὶ ἐναντίον ὑμῶν
εὔχομαι πρῶτον μέν, ὅσην εὔνοιαν ἔχων ἐγὼ διατελῶ τῇ
228 τε πόλει καὶ πᾶσιν ὑμῖν, τοσαύτην ὑπάρξαι μοι παρ'
ὑμῶν εἰς τουτονὶ τὸν ἀγῶνα· ἔπειθ', ὅ τι μέλλει συνοίσειν καὶ πρὸς εὐδοξίαν κοινῇ καὶ πρὸς εὐσέβειαν
ἑκάστῳ, τοῦτο παραστῆσαι τοὺς θεοὺς πᾶσιν ὑμῖν περὶ
ταυτησὶ τῆς γραφῆς γνῶναι.

Εἰ μὲν οὖν περὶ ὧν ἐδίωκε μόνον κατηγόρησεν Αἰσχί- 9
νης, κἀγὼ περὶ αὐτοῦ τοῦ προβουλεύματος εὐθὺς ἂν
ἀπελογούμην· ἐπειδὴ δ' οὐκ ἐλάττω λόγον τἆλλα
διεξιὼν ἀνήλωκε καὶ τὰ πλεῖστα κατεψεύσατό μου,
ἀναγκαῖον εἶναι νομίζω καὶ δίκαιον ἅμα βραχέα, ὦ
ἄνδρες Ἀθηναῖοι, περὶ τούτων εἰπεῖν πρῶτον, ἵνα μηδεὶς
ὑμῶν τοῖς ἔξωθεν λόγοις ἠγμένος ἀλλοτριώτερον τῶν
ὑπὲρ τῆς γραφῆς δικαίων ἀκούῃ μου.

10 Περὶ μὲν δὴ τῶν ἰδίων ὅσα λοιδορούμενος βεβλασφήμηκε περὶ ἐμοῦ, θεάσασθε ὡς ἁπλᾶ καὶ δίκαια λέγω.
Εἰ μὲν ἴστε με τοιοῦτον οἷον οὗτος ᾐτιᾶτο (οὐ γὰρ
ἄλλοθί που βεβίωκα ἢ παρ' ὑμῖν), μηδὲ φωνὴν ἀνάσχησθε, μηδ' εἰ πάντα τὰ κοινὰ ὑπέρευ πεπολίτευμαι,
ἀλλ' ἀναστάντες καταψηφίσασθε ἤδη· εἰ δὲ πολλῷ
βελτίω τούτου καὶ ἐκ βελτιόνων, καὶ μηδενὸς τῶν μετρίων (ἵνα μηδὲν ἐπαχθὲς λέγω) χείρονα καὶ ἐμὲ καὶ
τοὺς ἐμοὺς ὑπειλήφατε καὶ γιγνώσκετε, τούτῳ μὲν μηδ'
ὑπὲρ τῶν ἄλλων πιστεύετε· δῆλον γὰρ ὡς ὁμοίως
ἅπαντ' ἐπλάττετο· ἐμοὶ δ', ἣν παρὰ πάντα τὸν χρόνον
εὔνοιαν ἐνδέδειχθε ἐπὶ πολλῶν ἀγώνων τῶν πρότερον,
11 καὶ νυνὶ παράσχεσθε. Κακοήθης δ' ὤν, Αἰσχίνη, τοῦτο
παντελῶς εὔηθες ᾠήθης, τοὺς περὶ τῶν πεπραγμένων
καὶ πεπολιτευμένων λόγους ἀφέντα με πρὸς τὰς λοιδορίας τὰς παρὰ σοῦ τρέψεσθαι. Οὐ δὴ ποιήσω τοῦτο·
οὐχ οὕτω τετύφωμαι· ἀλλ' ὑπὲρ μὲν τῶν πεπολιτευ- 225
μένων ἃ κατεψεύδου καὶ διέβαλλες ἐξετάσω, τῆς δὲ
πομπείας ταύτης τῆς ἀνέδην γεγενημένης ὕστερον, ἂν
βουλομένοις ἀκούειν ᾖ τουτοισί, μνησθήσομαι.
12 Τὰ μὲν οὖν κατηγορημένα πολλὰ καὶ δεινά, καὶ περὶ
ὧν ἐνίων μεγάλας καὶ τὰς ἐσχάτας οἱ νόμοι διδόασι
τιμωρίας· τοῦ δὲ παρόντος ἀγῶνος ἡ προαίρεσις αὕτη
ἐχθροῦ μὲν ἐπήρειαν ἔχει καὶ ὕβριν καὶ λοιδορίαν καὶ
προπηλακισμὸν ὁμοῦ καὶ πάντα τὰ τοιαῦτα, τῶν μέντοι
κατηγοριῶν καὶ τῶν αἰτιῶν τῶν εἰρημένων, εἴπερ ἦσαν
ἀληθεῖς, οὐκ ἔνι τῇ πόλει δίκην ἀξίαν λαβεῖν οὐδ'

ἐγγύς. Οὐ γὰρ ἀφαιρεῖσθαι δεῖ τὸ προσελθεῖν τῷ 13
δήμῳ καὶ λόγου τυχεῖν, οὐδ' ἐν ἐπηρείας τάξει καὶ
φθόνου τοῦτο ποιεῖν,—οὔτε, μὰ τοὺς θεούς, ὀρθῶς ἔχον
οὔτε πολιτικὸν οὔτε δίκαιόν ἐστιν, ὦ ἄνδρες Ἀθηναῖοι!
Ἀλλ' ἐφ' οἷς ἀδικοῦντά με ἑώρα τὴν πόλιν, οὖσί γε
τηλικούτοις ἡλίκα νῦν ἐτραγῴδει καὶ διεξῄει, ταῖς ἐκ
τῶν νόμων τιμωρίαις παρ' αὐτὰ τἀδικήματα χρῆσθαι,
εἰ μὲν εἰσαγγελίας ἄξια πράττοντά με ἑώρα, εἰσαγγέλ-
λοντα· καὶ τοῦτον τὸν τρόπον εἰς κρίσιν καθιστάντα
παρ' ὑμῖν, εἰ δὲ γράφοντα παράνομα, παρανόμων γρα-
φόμενον· οὐ γὰρ δήπου Κτησιφῶντα μὲν δύναται διώ-
κειν δι' ἐμέ, ἐμὲ δέ, εἴπερ ἐξελέγξειν ἐνόμιζεν, αὐτὸν
οὐκ ἂν ἐγράψατο. Καὶ μὴν εἴ τι τῶν ἄλλων ὧν νυνὶ 14
διέβαλλε καὶ διεξῄει, ἢ καὶ ἄλλ' ὁτιοῦν ἀδικοῦντά με
ὑμᾶς ἑώρα, εἰσὶ νόμοι περὶ πάντων καὶ τιμωρίαι καὶ
ἀγῶνες καὶ κρίσεις πικρὰ καὶ μεγάλα ἔχουσαι τἀπι-
230 τίμια, καὶ τούτοις ἐξῆν ἅπασι χρῆσθαι· καὶ ὁπηνίκα
ἐφαίνετο ταῦτα πεποιηκὼς καὶ τοῦτον τὸν τρόπον κε-
χρημένος τοῖς πρὸς ἐμέ, ὡμολογεῖτο ἂν ἡ κατηγορία
τοῖς ἔργοις αὐτοῦ.

Νῦν δ' ἐκστὰς τῆς ὀρθῆς καὶ δικαίας ὁδοῦ καὶ φυγὼν 15
τοὺς παρ' αὐτὰ τὰ πράγματα ἐλέγχους, τοσούτοις ὕστερον χρόνοις αἰτίας καὶ σκώμματα καὶ λοιδορίας συμφο-
ρήσας ὑποκρίνεται. Εἶτα κατηγορεῖ μὲν ἐμοῦ, κρίνει
δὲ τουτονί, καὶ τοῦ μὲν ἀγῶνος ὅλου τὴν πρὸς ἐμὲ
ἔχθραν προΐσταται, οὐδαμοῦ δ' ἐπὶ ταύτην ἀπηντηκὼς
ἐμοὶ τὴν ἑτέρου ζητῶν ἐπιτιμίαν ἀφελέσθαι φαίνεται.

16 Καίτοι πρὸς ἅπασιν, ὦ ἄνδρες Ἀθηναῖοι, τοῖς ἄλλοις οἷς ἂν εἰπεῖν τις ὑπὲρ Κτησιφῶντος ἔχοι δικαίοις, καὶ τοῦτ᾽ ἔμοιγε δοκεῖ καὶ μάλ᾽ εἰκότως ἂν λέγειν, ὅτι τῆς ἡμετέρας ἔχθρας ἡμᾶς ἐφ᾽ ἡμῶν αὐτῶν δίκαιον ἦν τὸν ἐξετασμὸν ποιεῖσθαι, οὐ τὸ μὲν πρὸς ἀλλήλους ἀγωνίζεσθαι παραλείπειν, ἑτέρῳ δ᾽ ὅτῳ κακόν τι δώσομεν ζητεῖν· ὑπερβολὴ γὰρ ἀδικίας τοῦτό γε.

Πάντα μὲν τοίνυν τὰ κατηγορημένα ὁμοίως ἐκ τούτων ἄν τις ἴδοι οὔτε δικαίως οὔτ᾽ ἐπ᾽ ἀληθείας οὐδεμιᾶς εἰρημένα· βούλομαι δὲ καὶ καθ᾽ ἓν ἕκαστον αὐτῶν ἐξετάσαι, καὶ μάλισθ᾽ ὅσα ὑπὲρ τῆς εἰρήνης καὶ τῆς πρεσβείας κατεψεύσατό μου, τὰ πεπραγμένα ἑαυτῷ μετὰ Φιλοκράτους ἀνατιθεὶς ἐμοί. Ἔστι δ᾽ ἀναγκαῖον, ὦ ἄνδρες Ἀθηναῖοι, καὶ προσῆκον ἴσως, ὡς κατ᾽ ἐκείνους τοὺς χρόνους εἶχε τὰ πράγματα ἀναμνῆσαι ὑμᾶς, ἵνα πρὸς τὸν ὑπάρχοντα καιρὸν ἕκαστα θεωρῆτε.

8 Τοῦ γὰρ Φωκικοῦ συστάντος πολέμου, οὐ δι᾽ ἐμέ, οὐ γὰρ δὴ ἔγωγε ἐπολιτευόμην πω τότε, πρῶτον μὲν ὑμεῖς οὕτω διέκεισθε, ὥστε Φωκέας μὲν βούλεσθαι σωθῆναι, 231
καίπερ οὐ δίκαια ποιοῦντας ὁρῶντες, Θηβαίοις δ᾽ ὁτιοῦν ἂν ἐφησθῆναι παθοῦσιν, οὐκ ἀλόγως οὐδ᾽ ἀδίκως αὐτοῖς ὀργιζόμενοι· οἷς γὰρ εὐτυχήκεσαν ἐν Λεύκτροις, οὐ μετρίως ἐκέχρηντο· ἔπειθ᾽ ἡ Πελοπόννησος ἅπασα διειστήκει, καὶ οὔθ᾽ οἱ μισοῦντες Λακεδαιμονίους οὕτως ἴσχυον ὥστε ἀνελεῖν αὐτούς, οὔθ᾽ οἱ πρότερον δι᾽ ἐκείνων ἄρχοντες κύριοι τῶν πόλεων ἦσαν, ἀλλά τις ἦν ἄκριτος καὶ παρὰ τούτοις καὶ παρὰ τοῖς ἄλλοις ἅπασιν

ἔρις καὶ ταραχή. Ταῦτα δ' ὁρῶν ὁ Φίλιππος (οὐ γὰρ
ἦν ἀφανῆ), τοῖς παρ' ἑκάστοις προδόταις χρήματα ἀνα-
λίσκων, πάντας συνέκρουε καὶ πρὸς αὑτοὺς ἐτάραττεν·
εἶτ' ἐν οἷς ἡμάρτανον οἱ ἄλλοι καὶ κακῶς ἐφρόνουν,
αὐτὸς παρεσκευάζετο καὶ κατὰ πάντων ἐφύετο. Ὡς δὲ
ταλαιπωρούμενοι τῷ μήκει τοῦ πολέμου οἱ τότε μὲν
βαρεῖς, νῦν δ' ἀτυχεῖς Θηβαῖοι φανεροὶ πᾶσιν ἦσαν
ἀναγκασθησόμενοι καταφεύγειν ἐφ' ὑμᾶς, ὁ Φίλιππος,
ἵνα μὴ τοῦτο γένοιτο μηδὲ συνέλθοιεν αἱ πόλεις, ὑμῖν
μὲν εἰρήνην, ἐκείνοις δὲ βοήθειαν ἐπηγγείλατο. Τί οὖν 20
συνηγωνίσατο αὐτῷ πρὸς τὸ λαβεῖν ὀλίγου δεῖν ὑμᾶς
ἑκόντας ἐξαπατωμένους; Ἡ τῶν ἄλλων Ἑλλήνων —
εἴτε χρὴ κακίαν εἴτ' ἄγνοιαν εἴτε καὶ ἀμφότερα ταῦτ'
εἰπεῖν, — οἵ, πόλεμον συνεχῆ καὶ μακρὸν πολεμούντων
ὑμῶν, καὶ τοῦτον ὑπὲρ τῶν πᾶσι συμφερόντων, ὡς ἔργῳ
φανερὸν γέγονεν, οὔτε χρήμασιν οὔτε σώμασιν οὔτ'
ἄλλῳ οὐδενὶ τῶν ἁπάντων συνελάμβανον ὑμῖν· οἷς καὶ
δικαίως καὶ προσηκόντως ὀργιζόμενοι ἑτοίμως ὑπηκού-
σατε τῷ Φιλίππῳ. Ἡ μὲν οὖν τότε συγχωρηθεῖσα
εἰρήνη διὰ ταῦτ', οὐ δι' ἐμέ, ὡς οὗτος διέβαλλεν, ἐπρά-
χθη· τὰ δὲ τούτων ἀδικήματα καὶ δωροδοκήματα ἐν
αὐτῇ τῶν νυνὶ παρόντων πραγμάτων, ἄν τις ἐξετάζῃ
δικαίως, αἴτια εὑρήσει.

Καὶ ταυτὶ πάνθ' ὑπὲρ τῆς ἀληθείας ἀκριβολογοῦμαι 21
καὶ διεξέρχομαι. Εἰ γὰρ εἶναί τι δοκοίη τὰ μάλιστα
ἐν τούτοις ἀδίκημα, οὐδέν ἐστι δήπου πρὸς ἐμέ, ἀλλ' ὁ
μὲν πρῶτος εἰπὼν καὶ μνησθεὶς περὶ τῆς εἰρήνης Ἀρι-

στόδημος ἦν ὁ ὑποκριτής, ὁ δ' ἐκδεξάμενος καὶ γράψας
καὶ ἑαυτὸν μετὰ τούτου μισθώσας ἐπὶ ταῦτα Φιλοκρά·
της ὁ Ἁγνούσιος, ὁ σός, Αἰσχίνη, κοινωνός, οὐχ ὁ ἐμός,
οὐδ' ἂν σὺ διαῤῥαγῇς ψευδόμενος, οἱ δὲ συνειπόντες,
ὅτου δήποτε ἕνεκα (ἐῶ γὰρ τοῦτό γ' ἐν τῷ παρόντι),
Εὔβουλος καὶ Κηφισοφῶν· ἐγὼ δ' οὐδὲν οὐδαμοῦ.
22 Ἀλλ' ὅμως, τούτων τοιούτων ὄντων καὶ ἐπ' αὐτῆς τῆς
ἀληθείας οὕτω δεικνυμένων, εἰς τοῦθ' ἧκεν ἀναιδείας,
ὥστ' ἐτόλμα λέγειν, ὡς ἄρα ἐγὼ πρὸς τῷ τῆς εἰρήνης
αἴτιος γεγενῆσθαι καὶ κεκωλυκὼς εἴην τὴν πόλιν μετὰ
κοινοῦ συνεδρίου τῶν Ἑλλήνων αὐτὴν ποιήσασθαι.
Εἶτ' ὦ — (τί ἂν εἰπών σέ τις ὀρθῶς προσείποι;) ἔστιν
ὅπου σὺ παρών, τηλικαύτην πρᾶξιν καὶ συμμαχίαν
ἡλίκην νυνὶ διεξῄεις ὁρῶν ἀφαιρούμενόν με τῆς πόλεως
ἠγανάκτησας, ἢ παρελθὼν ταῦτα ἃ νυνὶ κατηγορεῖς
23 ἐδίδαξας καὶ διεξῆλθες; Καὶ μὴν εἰ τὸ κωλῦσαι τὴν
τῶν Ἑλλήνων κοινωνίαν ἐπεπράκειν ἐγὼ Φιλίππῳ, σοὶ
τὸ μὴ σιγῆσαι λοιπὸν ἦν, ἀλλὰ βοᾶν καὶ διαμαρτύρεσθαι καὶ δηλοῦν τουτοισί. Οὐ τοίνυν ἐποίησας οὐδαμοῦ
τοῦτο, οὐδ' ἤκουσέ σου ταύτην τὴν φωνὴν οὐδείς· εἰκό-
τως· οὔτε γὰρ ἦν πρεσβεία πρὸς οὐδένας ἀπεσταλμένη
τότε τῶν Ἑλλήνων, ἀλλὰ πάλαι πάντες ἦσαν ἐξελη-
λεγμένοι, οὔθ' οὗτος ὑγιὲς περὶ τούτων εἴρηκεν οὐδέν.
24 Χωρὶς δὲ τούτων καὶ διαβάλλει τὴν πόλιν τὰ μέγιστα
ἐν οἷς ψεύδεται. Εἰ γὰρ ὑμεῖς ἅμα τοὺς μὲν Ἕλληνας
εἰς πόλεμον παρεκαλεῖτε, αὐτοὶ δὲ πρὸς Φίλιππον περὶ
εἰρήνης πρέσβεις ἐπέμπετε, Εὐρυβάτου πρᾶγμα, οὐ

πόλεως ἔργον οὐδὲ χρηστῶν ἀνθρώπων διεπράττεσθε.
Ἀλλ' οὐκ ἔστι ταῦτα, οὐκ ἔστιν· τί γὰρ καὶ βουλόμενοι μετεπέμπεσθ' ἂν αὐτοὺς ἐν τούτῳ τῷ καιρῷ;
Ἐπὶ τὴν εἰρήνην; Ἀλλ' ὑπῆρχεν ἅπασιν. Ἀλλ' ἐπὶ
τὸν πόλεμον; Ἀλλ' αὐτοὶ περὶ εἰρήνης ἐβουλεύεσθε.
Οὔκουν οὔτε τῆς ἐξ ἀρχῆς εἰρήνης ἡγεμὼν οὐδ' αἴτιος
ὢν ἐγὼ φαίνομαι, οὔτε τῶν ἄλλων, ὧν κατεψεύσατό
μου, οὐδὲν ἀληθὲς ὂν δείκνυται.

Ἐπειδὴ τοίνυν ἐποιήσατο τὴν εἰρήνην ἡ πόλις, ἐν- 25
ταῦθα πάλιν σκέψασθε τί ἡμῶν ἑκάτερος προείλετο
πράττειν· καὶ γὰρ ἐκ τούτων εἴσεσθε, τίς ἦν ὁ Φιλίππῳ
πάντα συναγωνιζόμενος καὶ τίς ὁ πράττων ὑπὲρ ὑμῶν
καὶ τὸ τῇ πόλει συμφέρον ζητῶν. Ἐγὼ μὲν τοίνυν
ἔγραψα βουλεύων ἀποπλεῖν τὴν ταχίστην τοὺς πρέσβεις
ἐπὶ τοὺς τόπους ἐν οἷς ἂν ὄντα Φίλιππον πυνθάνωνται,
καὶ τοὺς ὅρκους ἀπολαμβάνειν· οὗτοι δὲ οὐδὲ γράψαντος ἐμοῦ ταῦτα ποιεῖν ἠθέλησαν. Τί δὲ τοῦτ' ἠδύνατο,
ὦ ἄνδρες Ἀθηναῖοι; Ἐγὼ διδάξω. Φιλίππῳ μὲν ἦν 26
συμφέρον ὡς πλεῖστον τὸν μεταξὺ χρόνον γενέσθαι τῶν
ὅρκων, ὑμῖν δ' ὡς ἐλάχιστον. Διὰ τί; Ὅτι ὑμεῖς
234 μὲν οὐκ ἀφ' ἧς ὠμόσατε ἡμέρας μόνον, ἀλλ' ἀφ' ἧς
ἠλπίσατε τὴν εἰρήνην ἔσεσθαι, πάσας ἐξελύσασθε τὰς
παρασκευὰς τὰς τοῦ πολέμου, ὁ δὲ τοῦτο ἐκ παντὸς τοῦ
χρόνου μάλιστα ἐπραγματεύετο, νομίζων, ὅπερ ἦν ἀληθές, ὅσα τῆς πόλεως προλάβοι πρὸ τοῦ τοὺς ὅρκους
ἀποδοῦναι, πάντα ταῦτα βεβαίως ἕξειν· οὐδένα γὰρ
τὴν εἰρήνην λύσειν τούτων ἕνεκα. Ἃ ἐγὼ προορώμενος, 27

ὦ ἄνδρες Ἀθηναῖοι, καὶ λογιζόμενος, τὸ ψήφισμα τοῦτο γράφω, πλεῖν ἐπὶ τοὺς τόπους ἐν οἷς ἂν ᾖ Φίλιππος, καὶ τοὺς ὅρκους τὴν ταχίστην ἀπολαμβάνειν· ἵν᾽ ἐχόντων Θρᾳκῶν, τῶν ὑμετέρων συμμάχων, τὰ χωρία ταῦθ᾽ ἃ νῦν οὗτος διέσυρε, τὸ Σέῤῥιον καὶ τὸ Μύρτιον καὶ τὴν Ἐργίσκην, οὕτω γίγνοινθ᾽ οἱ ὅρκοι, καὶ μὴ προλαβὼν ἐκεῖνος τοὺς ἐπικαίρους τῶν τόπων κύριος τῆς Θρᾴκης κατασταίη, μηδὲ πολλῶν μὲν χρημάτων, πολλῶν δὲ στρατιωτῶν εὐπορήσας, ἐκ τούτων ῥᾳδίως τοῖς λοιποῖς ἐπιχειροίη πράγμασιν.

28 Εἶτα τοῦτο μὲν οὐχὶ λέγει τὸ ψήφισμα, οὐδ᾽ ἀναγιγνώσκει· εἰ δὲ βουλεύων ἐγὼ προσάγειν τοὺς πρέσβεις ᾤμην δεῖν, τοῦτό μου διαβάλλει. Ἀλλὰ τί ἐχρῆν με ποιεῖν; Μὴ προσάγειν γράψαι τοὺς ἐπὶ τοῦθ᾽ ἥκοντας, ἵν᾽ ὑμῖν διαλεχθῶσιν; Ἢ θέαν μὴ κατανεῖμαι τὸν ἀρχιτέκτονα αὐτοῖς κελεῦσαι; Ἀλλ᾽ ἐν τοῖν δυοῖν ὀβολοῖν ἐθεώρουν ἄν, εἰ μὴ τοῦτ᾽ ἐγράφη. Τὰ μικρὰ συμφέροντα τῆς πόλεως ἔδει με φυλάττειν, τὰ δ᾽ ὅλα, ὥσπερ οὗτοι, πεπρακέναι; Οὐ δήπου.

Λέγε τοίνυν μοι τὸ ψήφισμα τουτὶ λαβών, ὃ σαφῶς οὗτος εἰδὼς παρέβη. Λέγε.

ΨΗΦΙΣΜΑ.

9 Ἐπὶ ἄρχοντος Μνησιφίλου, Ἑκατομβαιῶνος ἕνῃ καὶ νέᾳ, φυλῆς πρυτανευούσης Πανδιονίδος, Δημοσθένης Δημοσθένους Παιανιεὺς εἶπεν· ἐπειδὴ Φίλιππος ἀποστείλας πρέσβεις περὶ τῆς εἰρήνης ὁμολογουμένας πεποίηται συνθήκας, δεδόχθαι τῇ βουλῇ καὶ τῷ δήμῳ τῷ Ἀθηναίων, ὅπως ἂν ἡ εἰρήνη ἐπιτελεσθῇ, ἡ ἐπιχειροτονηθεῖσα ἐν τῇ πρώτῃ ἐκκλησίᾳ, πρέσβεις ἑλέσθαι ἐκ πάντων Ἀθηναίων ἤδη

πέντε, τοὺς δὲ χειροτονηθέντας ἀποδημεῖν μηδεμίαν ὑπερβολὴν ποιουμένους, ὅπου ἂν ὄντα πυνθάνωνται τὸν Φίλιππον, καὶ τοὺς ὅρκους λαβεῖν τε παρ' αὐτοῦ καὶ δοῦναι τὴν ταχίστην ἐπὶ ταῖς ὡμολογημέναις συνθήκαις αὐτῷ πρὸς τὸν Ἀθηναίων δῆμον, συμπεριλαμβάνοντας καὶ τοὺς ἑκατέρων συμμάχους. Πρέσβεις ᾑρέθησαν Εὔβουλος Ἀναφλύστιος, Αἰσχίνης Κοθωκίδης, Κηφισοφῶν Ῥαμνούσιος, Δημοκράτης Φλυεύς, Κλέων Κοθωκίδης.

Ταῦτα γράψαντος ἐμοῦ τότε, καὶ τὸ τῇ πόλει συμφέρον, οὐ τὸ τοῦ Φιλίππου ζητοῦντος, βραχὺ φροντίσαντες οἱ χρηστοὶ πρέσβεις οὗτοι καθῆντο ἐν Μακεδονίᾳ τρεῖς ὅλους μῆνας, ἕως ἦλθε Φίλιππος ἐκ Θρᾴκης πάντα τἀκεῖ καταστρεψάμενος, ἐξὸν ἡμερῶν δέκα, μᾶλλον δὲ τριῶν ἢ τεττάρων, εἰς τὸν Ἑλλήσποντον ἀφῖχθαι καὶ τὰ χωρία σῶσαι, λαβόντας τοὺς ὅρκους πρὶν ἐκεῖνον ἐξελεῖν αὐτά· οὐ γὰρ ἂν ἥψατ' αὐτῶν παρόντων ἡμῶν, ἢ οὐκ ἂν ὡρκίζομεν αὐτόν, ὥστε τῆς
30 εἰρήνης ἂν διημαρτήκει καὶ οὐκ ἂν ἀμφότερα εἶχε, καὶ τὴν εἰρήνην καὶ τὰ χωρία.

Τὸ μὲν τοίνυν ἐν τῇ πρεσβείᾳ πρῶτον κλέμμα μὲν 31
Φιλίππου, δωροδόκημα δὲ τῶν ἀδίκων τούτων ἀνθρώπων καὶ θεοῖς ἐχθρῶν τοιοῦτον ἐγένετο, ὑπὲρ οὗ καὶ τότε καὶ νῦν καὶ ἀεὶ ὁμολογῶ πολεμεῖν καὶ διαφέρεσθαι τούτοις· ἕτερον δ' εὐθὺς ἐφεξῆς ἔτι τούτου μεῖζον κακούργημα θεάσασθε. Ἐπειδὴ γὰρ ὤμοσε τὴν εἰρήνην ὁ Φίλιπ- 32
πος, προλαβὼν τὴν Θρᾴκην διὰ τούτους τοὺς οὐχὶ πεισθέντας τῷ ἐμῷ ψηφίσματι, πάλιν ὠνεῖται παρ' αὐτῶν ὅπως μὴ ἀπίωμεν ἐκ Μακεδονίας, ἕως τὰ τῆς στρατείας τῆς ἐπὶ τοὺς Φωκέας εὐτρεπῆ ποιήσαιτο, ἵνα μή, δεῦρ' ἀπαγγειλάντων ἡμῶν ὅτι μέλλει καὶ παρα-

σκευάζεται πορεύεσθαι, ἐξέλθοιτε ὑμεῖς καὶ περιπλεύ-
σαντες ταῖς τριήρεσιν εἰς Πύλας ὥσπερ πρότερον κλεί-
σαιτε τὸν πορθμόν, ἀλλ' ἅμ' ἀκούοιτε ταῦτα ἀπαγγελ-
λόντων ἡμῶν κἀκεῖνος ἐντὸς εἴη Πυλῶν καὶ μηδὲν ἔχοιθ'
ὑμεῖς ποιῆσαι.

33 Οὕτω δ' ἦν ὁ Φίλιππος ἐν φόβῳ καὶ πολλῇ ἀγωνίᾳ,
μὴ καὶ ταῦτα προειληφότος αὐτοῦ, πρὸ τοῦ τοὺς Φωκέας ἀπολέσθαι ἀκούσαντες ψηφίσαισθε βοηθεῖν αὐτοῖς,
καὶ ἐκφύγοι τὰ πράγματ' αὐτόν, ὥστε μισθοῦται τὸν κατάπτυστον τουτονί, οὐκέτι κοινῇ μετὰ τῶν ἄλλων πρέσβεων, ἀλλ' ἰδίᾳ καθ' αὑτόν, τοιαῦτα πρὸς ὑμᾶς εἰπεῖν
34 καὶ ἀπαγγεῖλαι, δι' ὧν ἅπαντ' ἀπώλετο. Ἀξιῶ δέ,
ὦ ἄνδρες Ἀθηναῖοι, καὶ δέομαι, τοῦτο μεμνῆσθαι ὑμᾶς
παρ' ὅλον τὸν ἀγῶνα, ὅτι μὴ κατηγορήσαντος Αἰσχίνου
μηδὲν ἔξω τῆς γραφῆς οὐδ' ἂν ἐγὼ λόγον οὐδένα
ἐποιούμην ἕτερον, ἁπάσαις δ' αἰτίαις καὶ βλασφημίαις 237
ἅμα τούτου κεχρημένου, ἀνάγκη κἀμοὶ πρὸς ἕκαστα τῶν
35 κατηγορημένων μικρὰ ἀποκρίνασθαι. — Τίνες οὖν ἦσαν
οἱ παρὰ τούτου λόγοι τότε ῥηθέντες, καὶ δι' οὓς ἅπαντ'
ἀπώλετο; Ὡς οὐ δεῖ θορυβεῖσθαι τῷ παρεληλυθέναι
Φίλιππον εἴσω Πυλῶν· ἔσται γὰρ ἅπανθ' ὅσα βού-
λεσθ' ὑμεῖς, ἐὰν ἔχηθ' ἡσυχίαν, καὶ ἀκούσεσθε δυοῖν ἢ
τριῶν ἡμερῶν, οἷς μὲν ἐχθρὸς ἥκει, φίλον αὐτὸν γεγενημένον, οἷς δὲ φίλος, τοὐναντίον ἐχθρόν. Οὐ γὰρ τὰ
ῥήματα τὰς οἰκειότητας ἔφη βεβαιοῦν, μάλα σεμνῶς
ὀνομάζων, ἀλλὰ τὸ ταὐτὰ συμφέρειν· συμφέρειν δὲ
Φιλίππῳ καὶ Φωκεῦσι καὶ ὑμῖν ὁμοίως ἅπασι, τῆς

ἀναλγησίας καὶ τῆς βαρύτητος ἀπαλλαγῆναι τῆς τῶν
Θηβαίων. Ταῦτα δ᾽ ἀσμένως τινὲς ἤκουον αὐτοῦ διὰ 36
τὴν τόθ᾽ ὑποῦσαν ἀπέχθειαν πρὸς τοὺς Θηβαίους.

Τί οὖν συνέβη μετὰ ταῦτ᾽ εὐθύς, οὐκ εἰς μακράν;
Τοὺς μὲν ταλαιπώρους Φωκέας ἀπολέσθαι καὶ κα-
τασκαφῆναι τὰς πόλεις αὐτῶν, ὑμᾶς δ᾽ ἡσυχίαν ἀγα-
γόντας καὶ τούτῳ πεισθέντας, μικρὸν ὕστερον σκευα-
γωγεῖν ἐκ τῶν ἀγρῶν, τοῦτον δὲ χρυσίον λαβεῖν· καὶ
ἔτι πρὸς τούτοις τὴν μὲν ἀπέχθειαν τὴν πρὸς Θηβαίους
καὶ Θετταλοὺς τῇ πόλει γενέσθαι, τὴν δὲ χάριν τὴν
ὑπὲρ τῶν πεπραγμένων Φιλίππῳ. Ὅτι δ᾽ οὕτω ταῦτ᾽ 37
ἔχει, λέγε μοι τό τε τοῦ Καλλισθένους ψήφισμα καὶ
τὴν ἐπιστολὴν τὴν τοῦ Φιλίππου, ἐξ ὧν ἀμφοτέρων
ταῦθ᾽ ἅπανθ᾽ ὑμῖν ἔσται φανερά. Λέγε.

ΨΗΦΙΣΜΑ.

233 Ἐπὶ Μνησιφίλου ἄρχοντος, συγκλήτου ἐκκλησίας ὑπὸ στρατηγῶν,
καὶ πρυτάνεων καὶ βουλῆς γνώμῃ, Μαιμακτηριῶνος δεκάτῃ ἀπιόντος,
Καλλισθένης Ἐτεονίκου Φαληρεὺς εἶπε· μηδένα Ἀθηναίων μηδεμιᾷ
παρευρέσει ἐν τῇ χώρᾳ κοιταῖον γίγνεσθαι, ἀλλ᾽ ἐν ἄστει καὶ Πειραιεῖ,
ὅσοι μὴ ἐν τοῖς φρουρίοις εἰσὶν ἀποτεταγμένοι· τούτων δ᾽ ἑκάστους,
ἣν παρέλαβον τάξιν, διατηρεῖν μήτε ἀφημερεύοντας μήτε ἀποκοιτοῦν-
τας. Ὃς ἂν δ᾽ ἀπειθήσῃ τῷδε τῷ ψηφίσματι, ἔνοχος ἔστω τοῖς τῆς 38
προδοσίας ἐπιτιμίοις, ἐὰν μή τι ἀδύνατον ἐπιδεικνύῃ περὶ ἑαυτὸν ὄν·
περὶ δὲ τοῦ ἀδυνάτου ἐπικρινέτω ὁ ἐπὶ τῶν ὅπλων στρατηγὸς καὶ ὁ ἐπὶ
τῆς διοικήσεως καὶ ὁ γραμματεὺς τῆς βουλῆς. Κατακομίζειν δὲ καὶ τὰ
ἐκ τῶν ἀγρῶν πάντα τὴν ταχίστην, τὰ μὲν ἐντὸς σταδίων ἑκατὸν εἴκοσιν
εἰς ἄστυ καὶ Πειραιᾶ, τὰ δὲ ἐκτὸς σταδίων ἑκατὸν εἴκοσιν εἰς Ἐλευσῖνα
καὶ Φυλὴν καὶ Ἄφιδναν καὶ Ῥαμνοῦντα καὶ Σούνιον. Εἶπε Καλλισθένης Φαληρεύς.

Ἆρ᾽ ἐπὶ ταύταις ταῖς ἐλπίσι τὴν εἰρήνην ἐποιεῖσθε,
ἢ ταῦτ᾽ ἐπηγγέλλεθ᾽ ὑμῖν οὗτος ὁ μισθωτός;

39 Λέγε δὴ τὴν ἐπιστολὴν ἣν δεῦρ᾿ ἔπεμψε Φίλιππος μετὰ ταῦτα.

ΕΠΙΣΤΟΛΗ ΦΙΛΙΠΠΟΥ.

Βασιλεὺς Μακεδόνων Φίλιππος Ἀθηναίων τῇ βουλῇ καὶ τῷ δήμῳ χαίρειν. Ἴστε ἡμᾶς παρεληλυθότας εἴσω Πυλῶν καὶ τὰ κατὰ τὴν Φωκίδα ὑφ᾿ ἑαυτοὺς πεποιημένους, καὶ ὅσα μὲν ἑκουσίως προσετίθετο τῶν πολισμάτων, φρουρὰς εἰσαγηοχότας [εἰς αὐτά], τὰ δὲ μὴ ὑπα- 238
κούοντα κατὰ κράτος λαβόντες καὶ ἐξανδραποδισάμενοι κατεσκάψαμεν. Ἀκούων δὲ καὶ ὑμᾶς παρασκευάζεσθαι βοηθεῖν αὐτοῖς, γέγραφα ὑμῖν, ἵνα μὴ ἐπὶ πλεῖον ἐνοχλῆσθε περὶ τούτων. Τοῖς μὲν γὰρ ὅλοις οὐδὲν μέτριόν μοι δοκεῖτε ποιεῖν, τὴν εἰρήνην συνθέμενοι καὶ ὁμοίως ἀντιπαρεξάγοντες, καὶ ταῦτα οὐδὲ συμπεριειλημμένων τῶν Φωκέων ἐν ταῖς κοιναῖς ἡμῶν συνθήκαις. Ὥστε ἐὰν μὴ ἐμμένητε τοῖς ὡμολογημένοις, οὐδὲν προτερήσετε ἔξω τοῦ ἐφθακέναι ἀδικοῦντες.

40 Ἀκούετε ὡς σαφῶς δηλοῖ καὶ διορίζεται ἐν τῇ πρὸς ὑμᾶς ἐπιστολῇ πρὸς τοὺς ἑαυτοῦ συμμάχους, ὅτι ἐγὼ ταῦτα πεποίηκα ἀκόντων Ἀθηναίων καὶ λυπουμένων, ὥστ᾿ εἴπερ εὖ φρονεῖτε, ὦ Θηβαῖοι καὶ Θετταλοί, τούτους μὲν ἐχθροὺς ὑπολήψεσθε, ἐμοὶ δὲ πιστεύσετε, οὐ τούτοις τοῖς ῥήμασι γράψας, ταῦτα δὲ βουλόμενος δεικνύναι. Τοιγαροῦν ἐκ τούτων ᾤχετο ἐκείνους λαβὼν εἰς τὸ μηδ᾿ ὁτιοῦν προορᾶν τῶν μετὰ ταῦτα μηδ᾿ αἰσθάνεσθαι, ἀλλ᾿ ἐᾶσαι πάντα τὰ πράγματα ἐκεῖνον ὑφ᾿ ἑαυτῷ ποιήσασθαι· ἐξ ὧν ταῖς παρούσαις συμφοραῖς οἱ ταλαίπωροι Θη-
41 βαῖοι κέχρηνται. Ὁ δὲ ταύτης τῆς πίστεως αὐτῷ συνεργὸς καὶ συναγωνιστὴς καὶ ὁ δεῦρ᾿ ἀπαγγείλας τὰ ψευδῆ καὶ φενακίσας ὑμᾶς οὗτός ἐστιν, ὁ τὰ Θηβαίων ὀδυρόμενος νῦν πάθη καὶ διεξιὼν ὡς οἰκτρά, καὶ τούτων και τῶν ἐν Φωκεῦσι κακῶν καὶ ὅσ᾿ ἄλλα πεπόνθασιν

οἱ Ἕλληνες ἁπάντων αὐτὸς ὢν αἴτιος. Δῆλον γὰρ ὅτι
σὺ μὲν ἀλγεῖς ἐπὶ τοῖς συμβεβηκόσιν, Αἰσχίνη, καὶ
τοὺς Θηβαίους ἐλεεῖς, κτήματ' ἔχων ἐν τῇ Βοιωτίᾳ καὶ
γεωργῶν τὰ ἐκείνων, ἐγὼ δὲ χαίρω, ὃς εὐθὺς ἐξῃτούμην
ὑπὸ τοῦ ταῦτα πράξαντος.

Ἀλλὰ γὰρ ἐμπέπτωκα εἰς λόγους οὓς αὐτίκα μᾶλλον 42
ἴσως ἁρμόσει λέγειν. Ἐπάνειμι δὴ πάλιν ἐπὶ τὰς
ἀποδείξεις, ὡς τὰ τούτων ἀδικήματα τῶν νυνὶ παρόντων
πραγμάτων γέγονεν αἴτια.

Ἐπειδὴ γὰρ ἐξηπάτησθε μὲν ὑμεῖς ὑπὸ τοῦ Φιλίππου διὰ τούτων τῶν ἐν ταῖς πρεσβείαις μισθωσάντων
ἑαυτοὺς καὶ οὐδὲν ἀληθὲς ὑμῖν ἀπαγγειλάντων, ἐξηπά-
τηντο δὲ οἱ ταλαίπωροι Φωκεῖς καὶ ἀνῄρηντο αἱ πόλεις
αὐτῶν, τί ἐγένετο; Οἱ μὲν κατάπτυστοι Θετταλοὶ καὶ 43
ἀναίσθητοι Θηβαῖοι φίλον, εὐεργέτην, σωτῆρα τὸν
Φίλιππον ἡγοῦντο· πάντ' ἐκεῖνος ἦν αὐτοῖς· οὐδὲ φωνὴν ἤκουον, εἴ τις ἄλλο τι βούλοιτο λέγειν. Ὑμεῖς δὲ
ὑφορώμενοι τὰ πεπραγμένα καὶ δυσχεραίνοντες ἤγετε
τὴν εἰρήνην ὅμως· οὐ γὰρ ἦν ὅ τι ἂν ἐποιεῖτε μόνοι.
Καὶ οἱ ἄλλοι δὲ Ἕλληνες, ὁμοίως ὑμῖν πεφενακισμένοι
καὶ διημαρτηκότες ὧν ἤλπισαν, ἦγον τὴν εἰρήνην ἄσμε-
νοι, καὶ αὐτοὶ τρόπον τινὰ ἐκ πολλοῦ πολεμούμενοι.
Ὅτε γὰρ περιιὼν ὁ Φίλιππος Ἰλλυριοὺς καὶ Τριβαλ- 44
λούς, τινὰς δὲ καὶ τῶν Ἑλλήνων κατεστρέφετο, καὶ
δυνάμεις πολλὰς καὶ μεγάλας ἐποιεῖθ' ὑφ' ἑαυτῷ, καί
τινες τῶν ἐκ τῶν πόλεων ἐπὶ τῇ τῆς εἰρήνης ἐξουσίᾳ
βαδίζοντες ἐκεῖσε διεφθείροντο, ὧν εἷς οὗτος ἦν, τότε

πάντες, ἐφ' οὓς ταῦτα παρεσκευάζετ' ἐκεῖνος, ἐπολε-
15 μοῦντο. Εἰ δὲ μὴ ᾔσθάνοντο, ἕτερος λόγος οὗτος, οὐ πρὸς ἐμέ. Ἐγὼ μὲν γὰρ προὔλεγον καὶ διεμαρτυρόμην καὶ παρ' ὑμῖν ἀεὶ καὶ ὅποι πεμφθείην· αἱ δὲ πόλεις ἐνόσουν, τῶν μὲν ἐν τῷ πολιτεύεσθαι καὶ πράττειν δωροδοκούντων καὶ διαφθειρομένων ἐπὶ χρήμασι, τῶν δὲ ἰδιωτῶν καὶ πολλῶν τὰ μὲν οὐ προορωμένων, τὰ δὲ 241
τῇ καθ' ἡμέραν ῥᾳστώνῃ καὶ σχολῇ δελεαζομένων, καὶ τοιουτονί τι πάθος πεπονθότων ἁπάντων, πλὴν οὐκ ἐφ' ἑαυτοὺς ἑκάστων οἰομένων τὸ δεινὸν ἥξειν, ἀλλὰ διὰ τῶν ἑτέρων κινδύνων τὰ ἑαυτῶν ἀσφαλῶς σχήσειν ὅταν βούλωνται.

16 Εἶτ', οἶμαι, συμβέβηκε τοῖς μὲν πλήθεσιν, ἀντὶ τῆς πολλῆς καὶ ἀκαίρου ῥᾳθυμίας τὴν ἐλευθερίαν ἀπολωλεκέναι, τοῖς δὲ προεστηκόσι καὶ τἆλλα πλὴν ἑαυτοὺς οἰομένοις πωλεῖν, πρώτους ἑαυτοὺς πεπρακόσιν αἰσθέσθαι. Ἀντὶ γὰρ φίλων καὶ ξένων, ἃ τότε ὠνομάζοντο ἡνίκα ἐδωροδόκουν, νῦν κόλακες καὶ θεοῖς ἐχθροὶ
17 καὶ τἆλλ' ἃ προσήκει πάντ' ἀκούουσιν. Εἰκότως· οὐδεὶς γάρ, ὦ ἄνδρες Ἀθηναῖοι, τὸ τοῦ προδιδόντος συμφέρον ζητῶν χρήματ' ἀναλίσκει, οὐδ' ἐπειδὰν ὧν ἂν πρίηται κύριος γένηται, τῷ προδότῃ συμβούλῳ περὶ τῶν λοιπῶν ἔτι χρῆται· οὐδὲν γὰρ ἂν ἦν εὐδαιμονέστερον προδότου. Ἀλλ' οὐκ ἔστι ταῦτα, οὐκ ἔστιν· πόθεν; Πολλοῦ γε καὶ δεῖ. Ἀλλ' ἐπειδὰν τῶν πραγμάτων ἐγκρατὴς ὁ ζητῶν ἄρχειν καταστῇ, καὶ τῶν ταῦτα ἀποδομένων δεσπότης ἐστί, τὴν δὲ πονηρίαν εἰδώς, τότε δή,

τότε καὶ μισεῖ καὶ ἀπιστεῖ καὶ προπηλακίζει. Σκο- 48
πεῖτε δέ· καὶ γὰρ εἰ παρελήλυθεν ὁ τῶν πραγμάτων
καιρός, ὁ τοῦ γε εἰδέναι τὰ τοιαῦτα καιρὸς ἀεὶ πάρεστι
τοῖς εὖ φρονοῦσιν. Μέχρι τούτου Λασθένης φίλος
ὠνομάζετο Φιλίππου, ἕως προὔδωκεν Ὄλυνθον· μέχρι
τούτου Τιμόλαος, ἕως ἀπώλεσε Θήβας· μέχρι τούτου
Εὔδικος καὶ Σῖμος οἱ Λαρισαῖοι, ἕως Θετταλίαν ὑπὸ
Φιλίππῳ ἐποίησαν. Εἶτ' ἐλαυνομένων καὶ ὑβριζομέ-
242 νων καὶ τί κακὸν οὐχὶ πασχόντων πᾶσα ἡ οἰκουμένη
μεστὴ γέγονε προδοτῶν. Τί δ' Ἀρίστρατος ἐν Σι- 49
κυῶνι, καὶ τί Περίλαος ἐν Μεγάροις; Οὐκ ἀπερριμ-
μένοι; Ἐξ ὧν καὶ σαφέστατ' ἄν τις ἴδοι ὅτι ὁ μάλιστα φυλάττων τὴν ἑαυτοῦ πατρίδα καὶ πλεῖστα ἀντι-
λέγων τούτοις, οὗτος ὑμῖν, Αἰσχίνη, τοῖς προδιδοῦσι καὶ
μισθαρνοῦσι τὸ ἔχειν ἐφ' ὅτῳ δωροδοκήσετε περιποιεῖ,
καὶ διὰ τοὺς πολλοὺς τουτωνὶ καὶ τοὺς ἀνθισταμένους
τοῖς ὑμετέροις βουλήμασιν ὑμεῖς ἐστὲ σῷοι καὶ ἔμμι-
σθοι· ἐπεὶ διά γε ὑμᾶς αὐτοὺς πάλαι ἂν ἀπολώλειτε.

Καὶ περὶ μὲν τῶν τότε πραχθέντων ἔχων ἔτι πολλὰ 50
λέγειν, καὶ ταῦτα ἡγοῦμαι πλείω τῶν ἱκανῶν εἰρῆσθαι.
Αἴτιος δ' οὗτος, ὥσπερ ἑωλοκρασίαν τινά μου τῆς πο-
νηρίας τῆς ἑαυτοῦ καὶ τῶν ἀδικημάτων κατασκεδάσας,
ἣν ἀναγκαῖον ἦν πρὸς τοὺς νεωτέρους τῶν πεπραγμένων
ἀπολύσασθαι. Παρηνώχλησθε δὲ καὶ ὑμεῖς ἴσως, οἵ,
καὶ πρὶν ἐμὲ εἰπεῖν ὁτιοῦν, εἰδότες τὴν τούτου τότε
μισθαρνίαν. Καίτοι φιλίαν γε καὶ ξενίαν αὐτὴν ὀνο- 51
μάζει, καὶ νῦν εἶπέ που λέγων, ὁ τὴν Ἀλεξάνδρου

*ξενίαν ὀνειδίζων ἐμοί. Ἐγώ σοι ξενίαν Ἀλεξάν-
δρου; Πόθεν λαβόντι ἢ πῶς ἀξιωθέντι; Οὔτε Φιλίππου ξένον οὔτ' Ἀλεξάνδρου φίλον εἴποιμ' ἂν ἐγώ σε,
οὐχ οὕτω μαίνομαι, εἰ μὴ καὶ τοὺς θεριστὰς καὶ τοὺς
ἄλλο τι μισθοῦ πράττοντας φίλους καὶ ξένους δεῖ κα-
52 λεῖν τῶι μισθωσαμένων. Ἀλλ' οὐκ ἔστι ταῦτα· πόθεν; Πολλοῦ γε καὶ δεῖ. Ἀλλὰ μισθωτὸν ἐγώ σε
Φιλίππου πρότερον καὶ νῦν Ἀλεξάνδρου καλῶ καὶ οὗτοι
πάντες. Εἰ δ' ἀπιστεῖς, ἐρώτησον αὐτούς· μᾶλλον δ'
ἐγὼ τοῦθ' ὑπὲρ σοῦ ποιήσω. Πότερον ὑμῖν, ὦ ἄνδρες
Ἀθηναῖοι, δοκεῖ μισθωτὸς Αἰσχίνης ἢ ξένος εἶναι Ἀλεξάνδρου; — Ἀκούεις ἃ λέγουσιν.* 243

53 *Βούλομαι τοίνυν ἤδη καὶ περὶ τῆς γραφῆς αὐτῆς
ἀπολογήσασθαι καὶ διεξελθεῖν τὰ πεπραγμέν' ἐμαυτῷ,
ἵνα καίπερ εἰδὼς Αἰσχίνης ὅμως ἀκούσῃ, δι' ἅ φημι καὶ
τούτων τῶν προβεβουλευμένων καὶ πολλῷ μειζόνων ἔτι
τούτων δωρεῶν δίκαιος εἶναι τυγχάνειν. Καί μοι λέγε
τὴν γραφὴν αὐτὴν λαβών.*

ΓΡΑΦΗ.

54 Ἐπὶ Χαιρώνδου ἄρχοντος, Ἐλαφηβολιῶνος ἕκτῃ ἱσταμένου, Αἰσχίνης Ἀτρομήτου Κοθωκίδης ἀπήνεγκε πρὸς τὸν ἄρχοντα παρανόμων γραφὴν κατὰ Κτησιφῶντος τοῦ Λεωσθένους Ἀναφλυστίου, ὅτι ἔγραψε παράνομον ψήφισμα, ὡς ἄρα δεῖ στεφανῶσαι Δημοσθένην Δημοσθένους Παιανιέα χρυσῷ στεφάνῳ, καὶ ἀναγορεῦσαι ἐν τῷ θεάτρῳ Διονυσίοις τοῖς μεγάλοις, τραγῳδοῖς καινοῖς, ὅτι στεφανοῖ ὁ δῆμος Δημοσθένην Δημοσθένους Παιανιέα χρυσῷ στεφάνῳ ἀρετῆς ἕνεκα, καὶ εὐνοίας ἧς ἔχων διατελεῖ εἴς τε τοὺς Ἕλληνας ἅπαντας καὶ τὸν δῆμον τὸν Ἀθηναίων, καὶ ἀνδραγαθίας, καὶ ὅτι διατελεῖ πράττων καὶ λέγων τὰ βέλ-

γιστα τῷ δήμῳ καὶ πρόθυμός ἐστι ποιεῖν ὅ τι ἂν δύνηται ἀγαθόν, —πάντα ταῦτα ψευδῆ γράψας καὶ παράνομα, τῶν νό- 55
μων οὐκ ἐώντων πρῶτον μὲν ψευδεῖς γραφὰς εἰς τὰ δημόσια γράμματα
καταβάλλεσθαι, εἶτα τὸν ὑπεύθυνον στεφανοῦν· ἔστι δὲ Δημοσθένης
τειχοποιὸς καὶ ἐπὶ τῷ θεωρικῷ τεταγμένος· ἔτι δὲ μὴ ἀναγορεύειν τὸν
111 στέφανον ἐν τῷ θεάτρῳ Διονυσίοις τραγῳδῶν τῇ καινῇ, ἀλλ' ἐὰν μὲν
ἡ βουλὴ στεφανοῖ, ἐν τῷ βουλευτηρίῳ ἀνειπεῖν, ἐὰν δὲ ἡ πόλις, ἐν
Πυκνὶ ἐν τῇ ἐκκλησίᾳ. Τίμημα τάλαντα πεντήκοντα. Κλήτορες, Κηφισοφῶν Κηφισοφῶντος Ῥαμνούσιος, Κλέων Κλέωνος Κοθωκίδης.

Ἃ μὲν διώκει τοῦ ψηφίσματος, ὦ ἄνδρες Ἀθηναῖοι, 56
ταῦτ' ἐστίν. Ἐγὼ δ' ἀπ' αὐτῶν τούτων πρῶτον οἶμαι
δῆλον ὑμῖν ποιήσειν ὅτι πάντα δικαίως ἀπολογήσομαι·
τὴν γὰρ αὐτὴν τούτῳ ποιησάμενος τῶν γεγραμμένων
τάξιν, περὶ πάντων ἐρῶ καθ' ἕκαστον ἐφεξῆς καὶ οὐδὲν
ἑκὼν παραλείψω. Τοῦ μὲν οὖν γράψαι, πράττοντα 57
καὶ λέγοντα τὰ βέλτιστά με τῷ δήμῳ διατε-
λεῖν καὶ πρόθυμον εἶναι ποιεῖν ὅ τι ἂν δύνωμαι ἀγαθόν, καὶ ἐπαινεῖν ἐπὶ τούτοις, ἐν τοῖς
πεπολιτευμένοις τὴν κρίσιν εἶναι νομίζω· ἀπὸ γὰρ τούτων ἐξεταζομένων εὑρεθήσεται, εἴτε ἀληθῆ περὶ ἐμοῦ
γέγραφε Κτησιφῶν ταῦτα καὶ προσήκοντα εἴτε καὶ
ψευδῆ. Τὸ δὲ μὴ προσγράψαντα, ἐπειδὰν τὰς εὐ- 58
θύνας δῷ στεφανοῦν, καὶ ἀνειπεῖν ἐν τῷ θεάτρῳ τὸν
στέφανον κελεῦσαι, κοινωνεῖν μὲν ἡγοῦμαι καὶ τοῦτο
τοῖς πεπολιτευμένοις, εἴτε ἄξιός εἰμι τοῦ στεφάνου καὶ
τῆς ἀναρρήσεως τῆς ἐν τούτοις εἴτε καὶ μή· ἔτι μέντοι
καὶ τοὺς νόμους δεικτέον εἶναί μοι δοκεῖ καθ' οὓς ταῦτα
γράφειν ἐξῆν τούτῳ. Οὑτωσὶ μέν, ὦ ἄνδρες Ἀθηναῖοι,
δικαίως καὶ ἁπλῶς τὴν ἀπολογίαν ἔγνωκα ποιεῖσθαι·
βαδιοῦμαι δ' ἐπ' αὐτὰ ἃ πέπρακταί μοι. Καί με μη- 59

δεὶς ὑπολάβῃ ἀπαρτᾶν τὸν λόγον τῆς γραφῆς, ἐὰν εἰς
Ἑλληνικὰς πράξεις καὶ λόγους ἐμπέσω· ὁ γὰρ διώκων
τοῦ ψηφίσματος τὸ λέγειν καὶ πράττειν τὰ ἄριστά με, 21
καὶ γεγραμμένος ταῦτα ὡς οὐκ ἀληθῆ, οὗτός ἐστιν ὁ
τοὺς περὶ ἁπάντων τῶν ἐμοὶ πεπολιτευμένων λόγους
οἰκείους καὶ ἀναγκαίους τῇ γραφῇ πεποιηκώς. Εἶτα
καὶ πολλῶν προαιρέσεων οὐσῶν τῆς πολιτείας τὴν περὶ
τὰς Ἑλληνικὰς πράξεις εἱλόμην ἐγώ, ὥστε καὶ τὰς
ἀποδείξεις ἐκ τούτων δίκαιός εἰμι ποιεῖσθαι.

60 Ἃ μὲν οὖν πρὸ τοῦ πολιτεύεσθαι καὶ δημηγορεῖν ἐμὲ
προὔλαβε καὶ κατέσχε Φίλιππος, ἐάσω· οὐδὲν γὰρ
ἡγοῦμαι τούτων εἶναι πρὸς ἐμέ· ἃ δ' ἀφ' ἧς ἡμέρας
ἐπὶ ταῦτα ἐπέστην ἐγὼ διεκωλύθη, ταῦτα ἀναμνήσω
καὶ τούτων ὑφέξω λόγον, τοσοῦτον ὑπειπών. Πλεο-
νέκτημα, ὦ ἄνδρες Ἀθηναῖοι, μέγα ὑπῆρξε Φιλίππῳ.
61 Παρὰ γὰρ τοῖς Ἕλλησιν, οὐ τισὶν ἀλλ' ἅπασιν ὁμοίως,
φορὰν προδοτῶν καὶ δωροδόκων καὶ θεοῖς ἐχθρῶν ἀνθρώπων συνέβη γενέσθαι τοσαύτην ὅσην οὐδείς πω
πρότερον μέμνηται γεγονυῖαν· οὓς συναγωνιστὰς καὶ
συνεργοὺς λαβών, καὶ πρότερον κακῶς τοὺς Ἕλληνας
ἔχοντας πρὸς ἑαυτοὺς καὶ στασιαστικῶς ἔτι χεῖρον
διέθηκε, τοὺς μὲν ἐξαπατῶν, τοῖς δὲ διδούς, τοὺς δὲ
πάντα τρόπον διαφθείρων, καὶ διέστησεν εἰς μέρη
πολλά, ἑνὸς τοῦ συμφέροντος ἅπασιν ὄντος, κωλύειν
62 ἐκεῖνον μέγαν γίγνεσθαι. — Ἐν τοιαύτῃ δὲ καταστάσει
καὶ ἔτι ἀγνοίᾳ τοῦ συνισταμένου καὶ φυομένου κακοῦ
τῶν ἁπάντων Ἑλλήνων ὄντων, δεῖ σκοπεῖν ὑμᾶς, ὦ

ἄνδρες Ἀθηναῖοι, τί προσῆκον ἦν ἑλέσθαι πράττειν καὶ ποιεῖν τὴν πόλιν, καὶ τούτων λόγον παρ' ἐμοῦ λαβεῖν· ὁ γὰρ ἐνταῦθα ἑαυτὸν τάξας τῆς πολιτείας εἰμὶ ἐγώ.

246 Πότερον αὐτὴν ἐχρῆν, Αἰσχίνη, τὸ φρόνημα ἀφεῖσαν 63
καὶ τὴν ἀξίαν τὴν αὐτῆς, ἐν τῇ Θετταλῶν καὶ Δολόπων τάξει συγκατακτᾶσθαι Φιλίππῳ τὴν τῶν Ἑλλήνων ἀρχὴν καὶ τὰ τῶν προγόνων καλὰ καὶ δίκαια ἀναιρεῖν; Ἢ τοῦτο μὲν μὴ ποιεῖν (δεινὸν γὰρ ὡς ἀληθῶς), ἃ δ' ἑώρα συμβησόμενα, εἰ μηδεὶς κωλύσει, καὶ προῃσθάνεθ', ὡς ἔοικεν, ἐκ πολλοῦ, ταῦτα περιιδεῖν γιγνόμενα;
Ἀλλὰ νῦν ἔγωγε τὸν μάλιστα ἐπιτιμῶντα τοῖς πε- 64
πραγμένοις ἡδέως ἂν ἐροίμην, τῆς ποίας μερίδος γενέσθαι τὴν πόλιν ἐβούλετ' ἄν, πότερον τῆς συναιτίας τῶν συμβεβηκότων τοῖς Ἕλλησι κακῶν καὶ αἰσχρῶν, ἧς ἂν Θετταλοὺς καὶ τοὺς μετὰ τούτων εἴποι τις, ἢ τῆς περιεωρακυίας ταῦτα γιγνόμενα ἐπὶ τῇ τῆς ἰδίας πλεονεξίας ἐλπίδι, ἧς ἂν Ἀρκάδας καὶ Μεσσηνίους καὶ Ἀργείους θείημεν; Ἀλλὰ καὶ τούτων πολλοί, μᾶλλον 65
δὲ πάντες, χεῖρον ἡμῶν ἀπηλλάχασιν. Καὶ γὰρ εἰ μὲν ὡς ἐκράτησε Φίλιππος ᾤχετ' εὐθέως ἀπιὼν καὶ μετὰ ταῦτ' ἦγεν ἡσυχίαν, μήτε τῶν αὑτοῦ συμμάχων μήτε τῶν ἄλλων Ἑλλήνων μηδένα μηδὲν λυπήσας, ὅμως ἦν ἄν τις κατὰ τῶν οὐκ ἐναντιωθέντων οἷς ἔπραττεν ἐκεῖνος μέμψις καὶ κατηγορία· εἰ δὲ ὁμοίως ἁπάντων τὸ ἀξίωμα, τὴν ἡγεμονίαν, τὴν ἐλευθερίαν περιείλετο, μᾶλλον δὲ καὶ τὰς πολιτείας, ὅσων ἠδύνατο, πῶς οὐχ ἁπάντων ἐνδοξότατα ὑμεῖς ἐβουλεύσασθε ἐμοὶ πεισθέντες;

66 Ἀλλ' ἐκεῖσε ἐπανέρχομαι. Τί τὴν πόλιν, Αἰσχίνη,
προσῆκε ποιεῖν ἀρχὴν καὶ τυραννίδα τῶν Ἑλλήνων
ὁρῶσαν ἑαυτῷ κατασκευαζόμενον Φίλιππον; Ἢ τί 247
τὸν σύμβουλον ἔδει λέγειν ἢ γράφειν τὸν Ἀθήνῃσιν ἐμέ;
(καὶ γὰρ τοῦτο πλεῖστον διαφέρει,) ὃς συνῄδειν μὲν ἐκ
παντὸς τοῦ χρόνου μέχρι τῆς ἡμέρας ἀφ' ἧς αὐτὸς ἐπὶ
τὸ βῆμα ἀνέβην, ἀεὶ περὶ πρωτείων καὶ τιμῆς καὶ δόξης
ἀγωνιζομένην τὴν πατρίδα, καὶ πλείω καὶ χρήματα καὶ
σώματα ἀναλωκυῖαν ὑπὲρ φιλοτιμίας καὶ τῶν πᾶσι
συμφερόντων ἢ τῶν ἄλλων Ἑλλήνων ὑπὲρ αὑτῶν ἀνα-
67 λώκασιν ἕκαστοι· ἑώρων δ' αὐτὸν τὸν Φίλιππον, πρὸς
ὃν ἦν ἡμῖν ὁ ἀγών, ὑπὲρ ἀρχῆς καὶ δυναστείας τὸν
ὀφθαλμὸν ἐκκεκομμένον, τὴν κλεῖν κατεαγότα, τὴν
χεῖρα, τὸ σκέλος πεπηρωμένον, πᾶν ὅ τι βουληθείη
μέρος ἡ τύχη τοῦ σώματος παρελέσθαι, τοῦτο ῥᾳδίως
καὶ ἑτοίμως προϊέμενον, ὥστε τῷ λοιπῷ μετὰ τιμῆς καὶ
68 δόξης ζῆν. Καὶ μὴν οὐδὲ τοῦτό γε οὐδεὶς ἂν εἰπεῖν
τολμήσειεν, ὡς τῷ μὲν ἐν Πέλλῃ τραφέντι, χωρίῳ
ἀδόξῳ τότε γε ὄντι καὶ μικρῷ, τοσαύτην μεγαλοψυχίαν
προσῆκεν ἐγγενέσθαι, ὥστε τῆς τῶν Ἑλλήνων ἀρχῆς
ἐπιθυμῆσαι καὶ τοῦτ' εἰς τὸν νοῦν ἐμβαλέσθαι, ὑμῖν δ'
οὖσιν Ἀθηναίοις καὶ κατὰ τὴν ἡμέραν ἑκάστην ἐν πᾶσι
καὶ λόγοις καὶ θεωρήμασι τῆς τῶν προγόνων ἀρετῆς
ὑπομνήμαθ' ὁρῶσι τοσαύτην κακίαν ὑπάρξαι, ὥστε τῆς
τῶν Ἑλλήνων ἐλευθερίας αὐτεπαγγέλτους ἐθελοντὰς
παραχωρῆσαι Φιλίππῳ. Οὐδ' ἂν εἷς ταῦτα φήσειεν.
69 Λοιπὸν τοίνυν ἦν καὶ ἀναγκαῖον ἅμα, πᾶσιν οἷς ἐκεῖ

νος ἔπραττεν ἀδικῶν ὑμᾶς ἐναντιοῦσθαι δικαίως. Τοῦτ' ἐποιεῖτε μὲν ὑμεῖς ἐξ ἀρχῆς εἰκότως καὶ προσηκόντως, ἔγραφον δὲ καὶ συνεβούλευον καὶ ἐγὼ καθ' οὓς ἐπολι-
248 τευόμην χρόνους. Ὁμολογῶ. Ἀλλὰ τί ἐχρῆν με ποιεῖν; Ἤδη γάρ σ' ἐρωτῶ, πάντα τἆλλ' ἀφείς, Ἀμφίπολιν, Πύδναν, Ποτίδαιαν, Ἁλόννησον· οὐδενὸς τούτων μέμνημαι· Σέῤῥιον δὲ καὶ Δορίσκον καὶ τὴν 70
Πεπαρήθου πόρθησιν καὶ ὅσ' ἄλλα τοιαῦτα ἡ πόλις ἠδίκητο, οὐδ' εἰ γέγονεν οἶδα. Καίτοι σύ γ' ἔφησθά με ταῦτα λέγοντα εἰς ἔχθραν ἐμβαλεῖν τουτουσί, Εὐβούλου καὶ Ἀριστοφῶντος καὶ Διοπείθους τῶν περὶ τούτων ψηφισμάτων ὄντων, οὐκ ἐμῶν, ὦ λέγων εὐχερῶς ὅ τι ἂν βουληθῇς. Οὐδὲ νῦν περὶ τούτων ἐρῶ. Ἀλλ' 71
ὁ τὴν Εὔβοιαν ἐκεῖνος σφετεριζόμενος καὶ κατασκευάζων ἐπιτείχισμα ἐπὶ τὴν Ἀττικήν, καὶ Μεγάροις ἐπιχειρῶν, καὶ καταλαμβάνων Ὠρεόν, καὶ κατασκάπτων Πορθμόν, καὶ καθιστὰς ἐν μὲν Ὠρεῷ Φιλιστίδην τύραννον, ἐν δ' Ἐρετρίᾳ Κλείταρχον, καὶ τὸν Ἑλλήσποντον ὑφ' ἑαυτῷ ποιούμενος, καὶ Βυζάντιον πολιορκῶν, καὶ πόλεις Ἑλληνίδας τὰς μὲν ἀναιρῶν, εἰς τὰς δὲ τοὺς φυγάδας κατάγων, πότερον ταῦτα πάντα ποιῶν ἠδίκει καὶ παρεσπόνδει καὶ ἔλυε τὴν εἰρήνην ἢ οὔ; Καὶ πότερον φανῆναί τινα τῶν Ἑλλήνων τὸν ταῦτα κωλύσοντα ποιεῖν αὐτὸν ἐχρῆν ἢ μή; Εἰ μὲν γὰρ μὴ ἐχρῆν, ἀλλὰ 72
τὴν Μυσῶν λείαν καλουμένην τὴν Ἑλλάδα οὖσαν ὀφθῆναι ζώντων καὶ ὄντων Ἀθηναίων, περιείργασμαι μὲν ἐγὼ περὶ τούτων εἰπών, περιείργασται δ' ἡ πόλις ἡ

πεισθεῖσα ἐμοί, ἔστω δὲ ἀδικήματα πάντα ἃ πέπρακται
καὶ ἁμαρτήματα ἐμά. Εἰ δὲ ἔδει τινὰ τούτων κωλυτὴν
φανῆναι, τίνα ἄλλον ἢ τὸν Ἀθηναίων δῆμον προσῆκε 249
γενέσθαι; Ταῦτα τοίνυν ἐπολιτευόμην ἐγώ, καὶ ὁρῶν
καταδουλούμενον πάντας ἀνθρώπους ἐκεῖνον ἠναντιού-
μην, καὶ προλέγων καὶ διδάσκων μὴ προΐεσθαι ταῦτα
Φιλίππῳ διετέλουν.

73 Καὶ μὴν τὴν εἰρήνην γ' ἐκεῖνος ἔλυσε τὰ πλοῖα λαβών, οὐχ ἡ πόλις, Αἰσχίνη. Φέρε δὲ αὐτὰ τὰ ψηφίσματα καὶ τὴν ἐπιστολὴν τὴν τοῦ Φιλίππου, καὶ λέγε ἐφεξῆς· ἀπὸ γὰρ τούτων ἐξεταζομένων, τίς τίνος αἴτιός ἐστι γενήσεται φανερόν. Λέγε.

ΨΗΦΙΣΜΑ.

Ἐπὶ ἄρχοντος Νεοκλέους, μηνὸς Βοηδρομιῶνος, ἐκκλησίας συγκλήτου ὑπὸ στρατηγῶν, Εὔβουλος Μνησιθέου Κόπριος εἶπεν· Ἐπειδὴ
προσήγγειλαν οἱ στρατηγοὶ ἐν τῇ ἐκκλησίᾳ, ὡς ἄρα Λεωδάμαντα τὸν
ναύαρχον καὶ τὰ μετ' αὐτοῦ ἀποσταλέντα σκάφη εἴκοσιν ἐπὶ τὴν τοῦ
σίτου παραπομπὴν εἰς Ἑλλήσποντον ὁ παρὰ Φιλίππου στρατηγὸς
Ἀμύντας καταγήοχεν εἰς Μακεδονίαν καὶ ἐν φυλακῇ ἔχει, ἐπιμεληθῆναι τοὺς πρυτάνεις καὶ τοὺς στρατηγοὺς ὅπως ἡ βουλὴ συναχθῶσι
74 καὶ αἱρεθῶσι πρέσβεις πρὸς Φίλιππον, οἳ παραγενόμενοι διαλέξονται
πρὸς αὐτὸν περὶ τοῦ ἀφεθῆναι τὸν ναύαρχον καὶ τὰ πλοῖα καὶ τοὺς
στρατιώτας. Καὶ εἰ μὲν δι' ἄγνοιαν ταῦτα πεποίηκεν ὁ Ἀμύντας,
ὅτι οὐ μεμψιμοιρεῖ ὁ δῆμος οὐδὲν αὐτῷ· εἰ δέ τι πλημμελοῦντα παρὰ
τὰ ἐπεσταλμένα λαβών, ὅτι ἐπισκεψάμενοι Ἀθηναῖοι ἐπιτιμήσουσι
κατὰ τὴν τῆς ὀλιγωρίας ἀξίαν. Εἰ δὲ μηδέτερον τούτων ἐστίν, ἀλλ 250
ἰδίᾳ τι ἀγνωμονοῦσιν ἢ ὁ ἀποστείλας ἢ ὁ ἀπεσταλμένος, καὶ τοῦτο
γράψαι λέγειν, ἵνα αἰσθανόμενος ὁ δῆμος βουλεύσηται τί δεῖ ποιεῖν.

75 Τοῦτο μὲν τοίνυν τὸ ψήφισμα Εὔβουλος ἔγραψεν, οὐκ ἐγώ, τὸ δ' ἐφεξῆς Ἀριστοφῶν, εἶθ' Ἡγήσιππος, εἶτ' Ἀριστοφῶν πάλιν, εἶτα Φιλοκράτης, εἶτα Κηφισοφῶν, εἶτα πάντες οἱ ἄλλοι· ἐγὼ δ' οὐδὲν περὶ τούτων. Λέγε.

ΨΗΦΙΣΜΑ.

Ἐπὶ Νεοκλέους ἄρχοντος, Βοηδρομιῶνος ἕνῃ καὶ νέᾳ, βουλῆς γνώμῃ, πρυτάνεις καὶ στρατηγοὶ ἐχρημάτισαν τὰ ἐκ τῆς ἐκκλησίας ἀνενεγκόντες, ὅτι ἔδοξε τῷ δήμῳ πρέσβεις ἑλέσθαι πρὸς Φίλιππον περὶ τῆς τῶν πλοίων ἀνακομιδῆς καὶ ἐντολὰς δοῦναι καὶ τὰ ἐκ τῆς ἐκκλησίας ψηφίσματα. Καὶ εἵλοντο τούσδε, Κηφισοφῶντα Κλέωνος Ἀναφλύστιον, Δημόκριτον Δημοφῶντος Ἀναγυράσιον, Πολύκριτον Ἀπημάντου Κοθωκίδην. Πρυτανείᾳ φυλῆς Ἱπποθοωντίδος, Ἀριστοφῶν Κολυττεὺς πρόεδρος εἶπεν.

Ὥσπερ τοίνυν ἐγὼ ταῦτα δεικνύω τὰ ψηφίσματα, 76
οὕτω καὶ σὺ δεῖξον, Αἰσχίνη, ποῖον ἐγὼ γράψας ψήφισμα αἴτιός εἰμι τοῦ πολέμου. Ἀλλ' οὐκ ἂν ἔχοις· εἰ γὰρ εἶχες, οὐδὲν ἂν αὐτοῦ πρότερον νυνὶ παρέσχου. Καὶ μὴν οὐδ' ὁ Φίλιππος οὐδὲν αἰτιᾶται ἐμὲ ὑπὲρ τοῦ πολέμου, ἑτέροις ἐγκαλῶν. Λέγε δ' αὐτὴν τὴν ἐπιστολὴν τὴν τοῦ Φιλίππου.

ΕΠΙΣΤΟΛΗ ΦΙΛΙΠΠΟΥ.

Βασιλεὺς Μακεδόνων Φίλιππος Ἀθηναίων τῇ βουλῇ καὶ τῷ δήμῳ 77
250 χαίρειν. Παραγενόμενοι πρὸς ἐμὲ οἱ παρ' ὑμῶν πρεσβευταί, Κηφισοφῶν καὶ Δημόκριτος καὶ Πολύκριτος, διελέγοντο περὶ τῆς τῶν πλοίων ἀφέσεως ὧν ἐναυάρχει Λαομέδων. Καθ' ὅλου μὲν οὖν ἔμοιγε φαίνεσθε ἐν μεγάλῃ εὐηθείᾳ ἔσεσθαι, εἰ οἴεσθ' ἐμὲ λανθάνειν, ὅτι ἐξαπεστάλη ταῦτα τὰ πλοῖα πρόφασιν μὲν ὡς τὸν σῖτον παραπέμψοντα ἐκ τοῦ Ἑλλησπόντου εἰς Λῆμνον, βοηθήσοντα δὲ Σηλυμβριανοῖς τοῖς ὑπ' ἐμοῦ μὲν πολιορκουμένοις, οὐ συμπεριειλημμένοις δὲ ἐν ταῖς τῆς φιλίας κοινῇ κειμέναις ἡμῖν συνθήκαις. Καὶ ταῦτα συνετάχθη 78
τῷ ναυάρχῳ ἄνευ μὲν τοῦ δήμου τοῦ Ἀθηναίων, ὑπὸ δέ τινων ἀρχόντων καὶ ἑτέρων ἰδιωτῶν μὲν νῦν ὄντων, ἐκ παντὸς δὲ τρόπου βουλομένων τὸν δῆμον ἀντὶ τῆς νῦν ὑπαρχούσης πρὸς ἐμὲ φιλίας τὸν πόλεμον ἀναλαβεῖν, πολλῷ μᾶλλον φιλοτιμουμένων τοῦτο συντετελέσθαι ἢ τοῖς Σηλυμβριανοῖς βοηθῆσαι. Καὶ ὑπολαμβάνουσιν αὐτοῖς τὸ τοιοῦτο πρόσοδον ἔσεσθαι· οὐ μέντοι μοι δοκεῖ τοῦτο χρήσιμον ὑπάρχειν οὔθ' ὑμῖν οὔτ' ἐμοί. Διόπερ τά τε νῦν καταχθέντα πλοῖα πρὸς ἡμᾶς ἀφίημι ὑμῖν, καὶ τοῦ λοιποῦ, ἐὰν βούλησθε μὴ ἐπιτρέπειν τοῖς προεστηκόσιν ὑμῶν κακοήθως πολιτεύεσθαι, ἀλλ' ἐπιτιμᾶτε, πειράσομαι κἀγὼ διαφυλάττειν τὴν εἰρήνην. Εὐτυχεῖτε.

79 Ἐνταῦθ' οὐδαμοῦ Δημοσθένην γέγραφεν, οὐδ' αἰτίαν
οὐδεμίαν κατ' ἐμοῦ. Τί ποτ' οὖν τοῖς ἄλλοις ἐγκαλῶν
τῶν ἐμοὶ πεπραγμένων οὐχὶ μέμνηται; Ὅτι τῶν ἀδικημάτων ἂν ἐμέμνητο τῶν αὑτοῦ, εἴ τι περὶ ἐμοῦ γέ-
γραφε· τούτων γὰρ εἰχόμην ἐγὼ καὶ τούτοις ἠναντιού-
μην. Καὶ πρῶτον μὲν τὴν εἰς Πελοπόννησον πρεσβείαν 251
ἔγραψα, ὅτε πρῶτον ἐκεῖνος εἰς Πελοπόννησον παρε-
δύετο, εἶτα τὴν εἰς Εὔβοιαν, ἡνίκ' Εὐβοίας ἥπτετο, εἶτα
τὴν ἐπ' Ὠρεὸν ἔξοδον, οὐκέτι πρεσβείαν, καὶ τὴν εἰς
Ἐρέτριαν, ἐπειδὴ τυράννους ἐκεῖνος ἐν ταύταις ταῖς
80 πόλεσι κατέστησεν. Μετὰ ταῦτα δὲ τοὺς ἀποστόλους
ἅπαντας ἀπέστειλα, καθ' οὓς Χεῤῥόνησος ἐσώθη καὶ
Βυζάντιον καὶ πάντες οἱ σύμμαχοι. Ἐξ ὧν ὑμῖν μὲν
τὰ κάλλιστα, ἔπαινοι, δόξαι, τιμαί, στέφανοι, χάρι-
τες παρὰ τῶν εὖ πεπονθότων ὑπῆρχον· τῶν δ' ἀδι-
κουμένων τοῖς μὲν ὑμῖν τότε πεισθεῖσιν ἡ σωτηρία
περιεγένετο, τοῖς δ' ὀλιγωρήσασι τὸ πολλάκις ὧν ὑμεῖς
προείπατε μεμνῆσθαι, καὶ νομίζειν ὑμᾶς μὴ μόνον εὔνους
ἑαυτοῖς, ἀλλὰ καὶ φρονίμους ἀνθρώπους καὶ μάντεις
εἶναι· πάντα γὰρ ἐκβέβηκεν ἃ προείπατε.

81 Καὶ μὴν ὅτι πολλὰ μὲν ἂν χρήματα ἔδωκε Φιλιστί-
δης ὥστ' ἔχειν Ὠρεόν, πολλὰ δὲ Κλείταρχος ὥστ' ἔχειν
Ἐρέτριαν, πολλὰ δ' αὐτὸς ὁ Φίλιππος ὥστε ταῦθ'
ὑπάρχειν ἐφ' ὑμᾶς αὑτῷ καὶ περὶ τῶν ἄλλων μηδὲν
ἐξελέγχεσθαι μηδ' ἃ ποιῶν ἠδίκει μηδένα ἐξετάζειν
82 πανταχοῦ, οὐδεὶς ἀγνοεῖ, καὶ πάντων ἥκιστα σύ· οἱ γὰρ
παρὰ τοῦ Κλειτάρχου καὶ τοῦ Φιλιστίδου τότε πρέσβεις

δεῦρ' ἀφικνούμενοι παρὰ σοὶ κατέλυον, Αἰσχίνη, καὶ σὺ
προὐξένεις αὐτῶν· οὓς ἡ μὲν πόλις ὡς ἐχθροὺς καὶ οὔτε
δίκαια οὔτε συμφέροντα λέγοντας ἀπήλασε, σοὶ δ' ἦσαν
φίλοι. Οὐ τοίνυν ἐπράχθη τούτων οὐδέν, ὦ βλασφη-
μῶν περὶ ἐμοῦ καὶ λέγων ὡς σιωπῶ μὲν λαβών, βοῶ δ'
253 ἀναλώσας! Ἀλλ' οὐ σύ γε, ἀλλὰ βοᾷς μὲν ἔχων,
παύσει δὲ οὐδέποτ', ἐὰν μή σε οὗτοι παύσωσιν ἀτιμώ-
σαντες τήμερον.

Στεφανωσάντων τοίνυν ὑμῶν ἐμὲ ἐπὶ τούτοις τότε, καὶ 83
γράψαντος Ἀριστονίκου τὰς αὐτὰς συλλαβὰς ἅσπερ
οὑτοσὶ Κτησιφῶν νῦν γέγραφε, καὶ ἀναῤῥηθέντος ἐν τῷ
θεάτρῳ τοῦ στεφάνου, καὶ δευτέρου κηρύγματος ἤδη μοι
τούτου γιγνομένου, οὔτ' ἀντεῖπεν Αἰσχίνης παρὼν οὔτε
τὸν εἰπόντα ἐγράψατο. Καί μοι λέγε καὶ τοῦτο τὸ
ψήφισμα λαβών.

ΨΗΦΙΣΜΑ.

Ἐπὶ Χαιρώνδου Ἡγέμονος ἄρχοντος, Γαμηλιῶνος ἕκτῃ ἀπιόντος, 84
φυλῆς πρυτανευούσης Λεοντίδος, Ἀριστόνικος Φρεάῤῥιος εἶπεν·
Ἐπειδὴ Δημοσθένης Δημοσθένους Παιανιεὺς πολλὰς καὶ μεγάλας
χρείας παρέσχηται τῷ δήμῳ τῷ Ἀθηναίων, καὶ πολλοῖς τῶν συμμάχων καὶ πρότερον καὶ ἐν τῷ παρόντι καιρῷ βεβοήθηκε διὰ τῶν ψηφισμάτων καί τινας τῶν ἐν τῇ Εὐβοίᾳ πόλεων ἠλευθέρωκε, καὶ διατελεῖ εὔνους ὢν τῷ δήμῳ τῷ Ἀθηναίων, καὶ λέγει καὶ πράττει ὅ τι ἂν
δύνηται ἀγαθὸν ὑπέρ τε αὐτῶν Ἀθηναίων καὶ τῶν ἄλλων Ἑλλήνων,
δεδόχθαι τῇ βουλῇ καὶ τῷ δήμῳ τῷ Ἀθηναίων ἐπαινέσαι Δημοσθένην
Δημοσθένους Παιανιέα καὶ στεφανῶσαι χρυσῷ στεφάνῳ, καὶ ἀναγορεῦσαι τὸν στέφανον ἐν τῷ θεάτρῳ Διονυσίοις, τραγῳδοῖς καινοῖς· τῆς
δὲ ἀναγορεύσεως τοῦ στεφάνου ἐπιμεληθῆναι τὴν πρυτανεύουσαν φυ-
254 λὴν καὶ τὸν ἀγωνοθέτην. Εἶπεν Ἀριστόνικος Φρεάῤῥιος.

Ἔστιν οὖν ὅστις ὑμῶν οἶδέ τινα αἰσχύνην τῇ πόλει 85
συμβᾶσαν διὰ τοῦτο τὸ ψήφισμα ἢ χλευασμὸν ἢ γέλω-

τα, ἃ νῦν οὗτος ἔφη συμβήσεσθαι, ἐὰν ἐγὼ στεφανῶμαι; Καὶ μὴν ὅταν ᾖ νέα καὶ γνώριμα πᾶσι τὰ πράγματα, ἐάν τε καλῶς ἔχῃ, χάριτος τυγχάνει, ἐάν θ' ὡς ἑτέρως, τιμωρίας. Φαίνομαι τοίνυν ἐγὼ χάριτος τετυχηκὼς τότε, καὶ οὐ μέμψεως οὐδὲ τιμωρίας.

86 Οὐκοῦν μέχρι μὲν τῶν χρόνων ἐκείνων ἐν οἷς ταῦτ' ἐπράχθη, πάντας ἀνωμολόγημαι τοὺς χρόνους τὰ ἄριστα πράττειν τῇ πόλει, τῷ νικᾶν, ὅτ' ἐβουλεύεσθε, λέγων καὶ γράφων, τῷ καταπραχθῆναι τὰ γραφέντα καὶ στεφάνους ἐξ αὐτῶν τῇ πόλει καὶ ἐμοὶ καὶ πᾶσιν ὑμῖν γενέσθαι, τῷ θυσίας τοῖς θεοῖς καὶ προσόδους ὡς ἀγαθῶν τούτων ὄντων ὑμᾶς πεποιῆσθαι.

87 Ἐπειδὴ τοίνυν ἐκ τῆς Εὐβοίας ὁ Φίλιππος ἐξηλάθη,
τοῖς μὲν ὅπλοις ὑφ' ὑμῶν, τῇ δὲ πολιτείᾳ καὶ τοῖς ψηφίσμασι (κἂν διαῤῥαγῶσί τινες τούτων), ὑπ' ἐμοῦ,
ἕτερον κατὰ τῆς πόλεως ἐπιτειχισμὸν ἐζήτει. Ὁρῶν
δ' ὅτι σίτῳ πάντων ἀνθρώπων πλείστῳ χρώμεθ' ἐπει-
σάκτῳ, βουλόμενος τῆς σιτοπομπίας κύριος γενέσθαι,
παρελθὼν ἐπὶ Θρᾴκης Βυζαντίους συμμάχους ὄντας
αὐτῷ τὸ μὲν πρῶτον ἠξίου συμπολεμεῖν τὸν πρὸς ὑμᾶς
πόλεμον, ὡς δ' οὐκ ἤθελον οὐδ' ἐπὶ τούτοις ἔφασαν τὴν
συμμαχίαν πεποιῆσθαι, λέγοντες ἀληθῆ, χαράκωμα
βαλόμενος πρὸς τῇ πόλει καὶ μηχανήματ' ἐπιστήσας
88 ἐπολιόρκει. Τούτων δὲ γιγνομένων, ὅ τι μὲν προσῆκε
ποιεῖν ὑμᾶς οὐκέτ' ἐρωτήσω· δῆλον γάρ ἐστιν ἅπασιν. 255
Ἀλλὰ τίς ἦν ὁ βοηθήσας τοῖς Βυζαντίοις καὶ σώσας
αὐτούς; Τίς ὁ κωλύσας τὸν Ἑλλήσποντον ἀλλοτριω-

θῆναι κατ' ἐκείνους τοὺς χρόνους; Ὑμεῖς, ὦ ἄνδρες
Ἀθηναῖοι. Το δ' ὑμεῖς ὅταν λέγω, τὴν πόλιν λέγω.
Τίς δ' ὁ τῇ πόλει λέγων καὶ γράφων καὶ πράττων καὶ
ἁπλῶς ἑαυτὸν εἰς τὰ πράγματα ἀφειδῶς διδούς; Ἐγώ.

Ἀλλὰ μὴν ἡλίκα ταῦτα ὠφέλησεν ἅπαντας, οὐκέτ' 89
ἐκ τοῦ λόγου δεῖ μαθεῖν, ἀλλ' ἔργῳ πεπείρασθε· ὁ γὰρ
τότε ἐνστὰς πόλεμος, ἄνευ τοῦ καλὴν δόξαν ἐνεγκεῖν, ἐν
πᾶσι τοῖς κατὰ τὸν βίον ἀφθονωτέροις καὶ εὐωνοτέροις
διῆγεν ὑμᾶς τῆς νῦν εἰρήνης, ἣν οὗτοι κατὰ τῆς πατρίδος
τηροῦσιν οἱ χρηστοὶ ἐπὶ ταῖς μελλούσαις ἐλπίσιν, ὧν
διαμάρτοιεν, καὶ μὴ μετάσχοιεν ὧν ὑμεῖς οἱ τὰ βέλτιστα
τοὺς θεοὺς αἰτεῖτε, μηδὲ μεταδοῖεν ὑμῖν ὧν αὐτοὶ προῄ-
ρηνται! Λέγε δ' αὐτοῖς καὶ τοὺς τῶν Βυζαντίων στεφάνους καὶ τοὺς τῶν Περινθίων, οἷς ἐστεφάνουν ἐκ
τούτων τὴν πόλιν.

ΨΗΦΙΣΜΑ ΒΥΖΑΝΤΙΩΝ.

Ἐπὶ ἱερομνάμονος Βοσπορίχω Δαμάγητος ἐν τᾷ ἁλίᾳ ἔλεξεν, ἐκ 90
τᾶς βωλᾶς λαβὼν ῥήτραν· Ἐπειδὴ ὁ δᾶμος ὁ Ἀθηναίων, ἔν τε τοῖς
προγενομένοις καιροῖς εὐνοέων διατελεῖ Βυζαντίοις καὶ τοῖς συμμάχοις
καὶ συγγενέσι Περινθίοις καὶ πολλὰς καὶ μεγάλας χρείας παρέσχηται,
ἔν τε τῷ παρεστακότι καιρῷ Φιλίππω τῶ Μακεδόνος ἐπιστρατεύσαντος
ἐπὶ τὰν χώραν καὶ τὰν πόλιν ἐπ' ἀναστάσει Βυζαντίων καὶ Περινθίων
256 καὶ τὰν χώραν δαίοντος καὶ δενδροκοπέοντος, βοηθήσας πλοίοις ἑκατὸν
καὶ εἴκοσι καὶ σίτῳ καὶ βέλεσι καὶ ὁπλίταις ἐξείλετο ἄμμε ἐκ τῶν
μεγάλων κινδύνων καὶ ἀποκατέστασε τὰν πάτριον πολιτείαν καὶ τὼς
νόμως καὶ τὼς τάφως, δεδόχθαι τῷ δάμῳ τῷ Βυζαντίων καὶ Περινθίων 91
Ἀθηναίοις δόμεν ἐπιγαμίαν, πολιτείαν, ἔγκτασιν γᾶς καὶ οἰκιᾶν, προε-
δρίαν ἐν τοῖς ἀγῶσι, πόθοδον ποτὶ τὰν βωλὰν καὶ τὸν δᾶμον πράτοις
μετὰ τὰ ἱερά, καὶ τοῖς κατοικεῖν ἐθέλουσι τὰν πόλιν ἀλειτουργήτοις
ἦμεν πασᾶν τᾶν λειτουργιᾶν· στᾶσαι δὲ καὶ εἰκόνας τρεῖς ἑκκαιδεκα-
πήχεις ἐν τῷ Βοσπόρῳ, στεφανούμενον τὸν δᾶμον τὸν Ἀθηναίων ὑπὸ
τῶ δάμω τῶ Βυζαντίων καὶ Περινθίων· ἀποστεῖλαι δὲ καὶ θεωρίας ἐς
τὰς ἐν τᾷ Ἑλλάδι πανηγύριας, Ἴσθμια καὶ Νέμεα καὶ Ὀλύμπια καὶ

Πύθια, καὶ ἀνακαρῦξαι τὼς στεφάνως ὡς ἐστεφάνωται ὁ δᾶμος ὁ Ἀθηναίων ὑφ' ἡμῶν, ὅπως ἐπιστέωνται οἱ Ἕλλανες πάντες Ἀθηναίων ἀρετὰν καὶ τὰν Βυζαντίων καὶ Περινθίων εὐχαριστίαν.

92 *Λέγε καὶ τοὺς παρὰ τῶν ἐν Χεῤῥονήσῳ στεφάνους.*

ΨΗΦΙΣΜΑ ΧΕΡΡΟΝΗΣΙΤΩΝ.

Χεῤῥονησιτῶν οἱ κατοικοῦντες Σηστόν, Ἐλεοῦντα, Μάδυτον, Ἀλωπεκόννησον στεφανοῦσιν Ἀθηναίων τὴν βουλὴν καὶ τὸν δῆμον χρυσῷ στεφάνῳ ἀπὸ ταλάντων ἑξήκοντα, καὶ χάριτος βωμὸν ἱδρύονται καὶ δήμου Ἀθηναίων, ὅτι πάντων μεγίστου ἀγαθῶν παραίτιος γέγονε Χεῤῥονησίταις, ἐξελόμενος ἐκ τῆς Φιλίππου καὶ ἀποδοὺς τὰς πατρίδας, τοὺς νόμους, τὴν ἐλευθερίαν, τὰ ἱερά. Καὶ ἐν τῷ μετὰ ταῦτα αἰῶνι 257
παντὶ οὐκ ἐλλείψει εὐχαριστῶν καὶ ποιῶν ὅ τι ἂν δύνηται ἀγαθόν Ταῦτα ἐψηφίσαντο ἐν κοινῷ βουλευτηρίῳ.

93 *Οὐκοῦν οὐ μόνον τὸ Χεῤῥόνησον καὶ Βυζάντιον σῶσαι, οὐδὲ τὸ κωλῦσαι τὸν Ἑλλήσποντον ὑπὸ Φιλίππῳ γενέσθαι τότε, οὐδὲ τὸ τιμᾶσθαι τὴν πόλιν ἐκ τούτων, ἡ προαίρεσις ἡ ἐμὴ καὶ ἡ πολιτεία διεπράξατο, ἀλλὰ καὶ πᾶσιν ἔδειξεν ἀνθρώποις τήν τε τῆς πόλεως καλοκἀγαθίαν καὶ τὴν Φιλίππου κακίαν. Ὁ μὲν γὰρ σύμμαχος ὢν τοῖς Βυζαντίοις, πολιορκῶν αὐτοὺς ἑωρᾶτο ὑπὸ πάντων, οὗ τί γένοιτ' ἂν αἴσχιον ἢ μιαρώτερον;*
94 *Ὑμεῖς δ', οἱ καὶ μεμψάμενοι πολλὰ καὶ δίκαια ἂν ἐκείνοις εἰκότως περὶ ὧν ἠγνωμονήκεσαν εἰς ὑμᾶς ἐν τοῖς ἔμπροσθε χρόνοις, οὐ μόνον οὐ μνησικακοῦντες οὐδὲ προϊέμενοι τοὺς ἀδικουμένους, ἀλλὰ καὶ σώζοντες ἐφαίνεσθε· ἐξ ὧν δόξαν, εὔνοιαν, τιμὴν παρὰ πάντων ἐκτᾶσθε. Καὶ μὴν ὅτι μὲν πολλοὺς ἐστεφανώκατ' ἤδη τῶν πολιτευομένων ἅπαντες ἴσασι· δι' ὅντινα δ' ἄλλον ἡ πόλις ἐστεφάνωται, σύμβουλον λέγω καὶ ῥήτορα, πλὴν δι' ἐμέ, οὐδ' ἂν εἷς εἰπεῖν ἔχοι.*

Ἵνα τοίνυν καὶ τὰς βλασφημίας ἃς κατὰ τῶν Εὐ- 95
βοέων καὶ τῶν Βυζαντίων ἐποιήσατο, εἴ τι δυσχερὲς αὐτοῖς ἐπέπρακτο πρὸς ὑμᾶς ὑπομιμνήσκων, συκοφαντίας οὔσας ἐπιδείξω, μὴ μόνον τῷ ψευδεῖς εἶναι (τοῦτο μὲν γὰρ ὑπάρχειν ὑμᾶς εἰδότας ἡγοῦμαι), ἀλλὰ καὶ τῷ, εἰ τὰ μάλιστ' ἦσαν ἀληθεῖς, οὕτως ὡς ἐγὼ κέχρημαι τοῖς πράγμασι συμφέρειν χρήσασθαι, ἓν ἢ δύο βούλομαι τῶν καθ' ὑμᾶς πεπραγμένων καλῶν τῇ πόλει διεξελθεῖν, καὶ ταῦτ' ἐν βραχέσιν. Καὶ γὰρ ἄνδρα ἰδίᾳ καὶ πόλιν κοινῇ πρὸς τὰ κάλλιστα τῶν ὑπαρχόντων ἀεὶ δεῖ πειρᾶσθαι τὰ λοιπὰ πράττειν.

Ὑμεῖς τοίνυν, ὦ ἄνδρες Ἀθηναῖοι, Λακεδαιμονίων γῆς 96
καὶ θαλάττης ἀρχόντων καὶ τὰ κύκλῳ τῆς Ἀττικῆς κατεχόντων ἁρμοσταῖς καὶ φρουραῖς, Εὔβοιαν, Τάναγραν, τὴν Βοιωτίαν ἅπασαν, Μέγαρα, Αἴγιναν, Κλεωνάς, τὰς ἄλλας νήσους, οὐ ναῦς, οὐ τείχη τῆς πόλεως τότε κεκτημένης, ἐξήλθετε εἰς Ἁλίαρτον καὶ πάλιν οὐ πολλαῖς ἡμέραις ὕστερον εἰς Κόρινθον, τῶν τότε Ἀθηναίων πόλλ' ἂν ἐχόντων μνησικακῆσαι καὶ Κορινθίοις καὶ Θηβαίοις τῶν περὶ τὸν Δεκελεικὸν πόλεμον πραχθέντων· ἀλλ' οὐκ ἐποίουν τοῦτο, οὐδ' ἐγγύς. Καίτοι 9
τότε ταῦτα ἀμφότερα, Αἰσχίνη, οὔθ' ὑπὲρ εὐεργετῶν ἐποίουν οὔτ' ἀκίνδυνα ἑώρων. Ἀλλ' οὐ διὰ ταῦτα προεῖντο τοὺς καταφεύγοντας ἐφ' ἑαυτούς, ἀλλ' ὑπὲρ εὐδοξίας καὶ τιμῆς ἤθελον τοῖς δεινοῖς αὑτοὺς διδόναι, ὀρθῶς καὶ καλῶς βουλευόμενοι. Πέρας μὲν γὰρ ἅπασιν ἀνθρώποις ἐστὶ τοῦ βίου θάνατος, κἂν ἐν οἰκίσκῳ τις

αὐτὸν καθείρξας τηρῇ· δεῖ δὲ τοὺς ἀγαθοὺς ἄνδρας
ἐγχειρεῖν μὲν ἅπασιν ἀεὶ τοῖς καλοῖς, τὴν ἀγαθὴν προ-
βαλλομένους ἐλπίδα, φέρειν δ' ὅ τι ἂν ὁ θεὸς διδῷ
γενναίως.

98 Ταῦτ' ἐποίουν οἱ ὑμέτεροι πρόγονοι, ταῦθ' ὑμῶν οἱ
πρεσβύτεροι, οἵ, Λακεδαιμονίους οὐ φίλους ὄντας οὐδ'
εὐεργέτας, ἀλλὰ πολλὰ τὴν πόλιν ἡμῶν ἠδικηκότας καὶ
μεγάλα, ἐπειδὴ Θηβαῖοι κρατήσαντες ἐν Λεύκτροις ἀνελεῖν ἐπεχείρουν, διεκωλύσατε, οὐ φοβηθέντες τὴν τότε 259
Θηβαίοις ῥώμην καὶ δόξαν ὑπάρχουσαν, οὐδ' ὑπὲρ οἷα
πεποιηκότων ἀνθρώπων κινδυνεύσετε διαλογισάμενοι.
99 Καὶ γάρ τοι πᾶσι τοῖς Ἕλλησιν ἐδείξατε ἐκ τούτων
ὅτι, κἂν ὁτιοῦν τις εἰς ὑμᾶς ἐξαμάρτῃ, τούτων τὴν ὀργὴν
εἰς τἆλλα ἔχετε, ἂν δ' ὑπὲρ σωτηρίας ἢ ἐλευθερίας
κίνδυνός τις αὐτοὺς καταλαμβάνῃ, οὔτε μνησικακήσετε
οὔθ' ὑπολογιεῖσθε. Καὶ οὐκ ἐπὶ τούτων μόνον οὕτως
ἐσχήκατε, ἀλλὰ πάλιν σφετεριζομένων Θηβαίων τὴν
Εὔβοιαν οὐ περιείδετε, οὐδ' ὧν ὑπὸ Θεμίσωνος καὶ
Θεοδώρου περὶ Ὠρωπὸν ἠδίκησθε ἀνεμνήσθητε, ἀλλ'
ἐβοηθήσατε καὶ τούτοις, τῶν ἐθελοντῶν τότε τριηράρχων
πρώτον γενομένων τῇ πόλει, ὧν εἷς ἦν ἐγώ. Ἀλλ'
100 οὔπω περὶ τούτων. Καίτοι καλὸν μὲν ἐποιήσατε καὶ
τὸ σῶσαι τὴν νῆσον, πολλῷ δ' ἔτι τούτου κάλλιον τὸ
καταστάντες κύριοι καὶ τῶν σωμάτων καὶ τῶν πόλεων
ἀποδοῦναι ταῦτα δικαίως αὐτοῖς τοῖς ἐξημαρτηκόσιν εἰς
ὑμᾶς, μηδὲν ὧν ἠδίκησθε ἐν οἷς ἐπιστεύθητε ὑπολογι-
σάμενοι. Μυρία τοίνυν ἕτερα εἰπεῖν ἔχων παραλείπω,

ναυμαχίας, ἐξόδους πεζάς, στρατείας, καὶ πάλαι γεγονυίας καὶ νῦν ἐφ' ὑμῶν αὐτῶν, ἃς ἁπάσας ἡ πόλις τῆς τῶν ἄλλων ἕνεχ' Ἑλλήνων ἐλευθερίας καὶ σωτηρίας πεποίηται.

Εἶτ' ἐγὼ τεθεωρηκὼς ἐν τοσούτοις καὶ τοιούτοις τὴν 101
πόλιν ὑπὲρ τῶν τοῖς ἄλλοις συμφερόντων ἐθέλουσαν ἀγωνίζεσθαι, ὑπὲρ αὐτῆς τρόπον τινὰ τῆς βουλῆς οὔσης τί ἔμελλον κελεύσειν ἢ τί συμβουλεύσειν αὐτῇ ποιεῖν; Μνησικακεῖν νὴ Δία πρὸς τοὺς βουλομένους σώζεσθαι, καὶ προφάσεις ζητεῖν δι' ἃς ἅπαντα προησόμεθα. Καὶ τίς οὐκ ἂν ἀπέκτεινέ με δικαίως, εἴ τι τῶν ὑπαρχόντων τῇ πόλει καλῶν λόγῳ μόνον καταισχύνειν ἐπεχείρησ' ἄν; Ἐπεὶ τό γε ἔργον οὐκ ἂν ἐποιήσαθ' ὑμεῖς, ἀκριβῶς οἶδ' ἐγώ· εἰ γὰρ ἠβούλεσθε, τί ἦν ἐμποδών; Οὐκ ἐξῆν; Οὐχ ὑπῆρχον οἱ ταῦτ' ἐροῦντες οὗτοι;

Βούλομαι τοίνυν ἐπανελθεῖν ἐφ' ἃ τούτων ἑξῆς ἐπο- 102
λιτευόμην· καὶ σκοπεῖτε ἐν τούτοις πάλιν αὖ τί τὸ τῇ πόλει βέλτιστον ἦν. Ὁρῶν γάρ, ὦ ἄνδρες Ἀθηναῖοι, τὸ ναυτικὸν ὑμῶν καταλυόμενον, καὶ τοὺς μὲν πλουσίους ἀτελεῖς ἀπὸ μικρῶν ἀναλωμάτων γιγνομένους, τοὺς δὲ μέτρια ἢ μικρὰ κεκτημένους τῶν πολιτῶν τὰ ὄντα ἀπολλύντας, ἔτι δ' ὑστερίζουσαν ἐκ τούτων τὴν πόλιν τῶν καιρῶν, ἔθηκα νόμον καθ' ὃν τοὺς μὲν τὰ δίκαια ποιεῖν ἠνάγκασα, τοὺς πλουσίους, τοὺς δὲ πένητας ἔπαυσ' ἀδικουμένους, τῇ πόλει δ' ὅπερ ἦν χρησιμώτατον, ἐν καιρῷ γίγνεσθαι τὰς παρασκευὰς ἐποίησα. Καὶ 103
γραφεὶς τὸν ἀγῶνα τοῦτον εἰς ὑμᾶς εἰσῆλθον καὶ ἀπέ-

φυγον, καὶ τὸ μέρος τῶν ψήφων ὁ διώκων οὐκ ἔλαβεν.
Καίτοι πόσα χρήματα τοὺς ἡγεμόνας τῶν συμμοριῶν ἢ
τοὺς δευτέρους καὶ τρίτους οἴεσθέ μοι διδόναι, ὥστε
μάλιστα μὲν μὴ θεῖναι τὸν νόμον τοῦτον, εἰ δὲ μή,
.01 καταβαλόντα ἐᾶν ἐν ὑπωμοσίᾳ; Τοσαῦτ', ὦ ἄνδρες
Ἀθηναῖοι, ὅσα ὀκνήσαιμ' ἂν πρὸς ὑμᾶς εἰπεῖν. Καὶ
ταῦτ' εἰκότως ἔπραττον ἐκεῖνοι. Ἦν γὰρ αὐτοῖς ἐκ μὲν
τῶν προτέρων νόμων συνεκκαίδεκα λειτουργεῖν, αὐτοῖς
μὲν μικρὰ καὶ οὐδὲν ἀναλίσκουσι, τοὺς δ' ἀπόρους τῶν
πολιτῶν ἐπιτρίβουσιν· ἐκ δὲ τοῦ ἐμοῦ νόμου τὸ γιγνό- 28
μενον κατὰ τὴν οὐσίαν ἕκαστον τιθέναι, καὶ δυοῖν ἐφάνη
τριήραρχος ὁ τῆς μιᾶς ἕκτος καὶ δέκατος πρότερον
συντελής· οὐδὲ γὰρ τριηράρχους ἔτι ὠνόμαζον ἑαυτούς,
ἀλλὰ συντελεῖς. Ὥστε δὴ ταῦτα λυθῆναι καὶ μὴ τὰ
δίκαια ποιεῖν ἀναγκασθῆναι, οὐκ ἔσθ' ὅ τι οὐκ ἐδίδοσαν.
105 Καί μοι λέγε πρῶτον μὲν τὸ ψήφισμα καθ' ὃ εἰσῆλθον
τὴν γραφήν, εἶτα τοὺς καταλόγους, τόν τ' ἐκ τοῦ προτέρου νόμου καὶ τὸν κατὰ τὸν ἐμόν. Λέγε.

ΨΗΦΙΣΜΑ.

Ἐπὶ ἄρχοντος Πολυκλέους, μηνὸς Βοηδρομιῶνος ἕκτῃ ἐπὶ δέκα, φυλῆς πρυτανευούσης Ἱπποθοωντίδος, Δημοσθένης Δημοσθένους Παιανιεὺς εἰσήνεγκε νόμον τριηραρχικὸν ἀντὶ τοῦ προτέρου, καθ' ὃν αἱ συντέλειαι ἦσαν τῶν τριηράρχων· καὶ ἐπεχειροτόνησεν ἡ βουλὴ καὶ ὁ δῆμος· Καὶ ἀπήνεγκε παρανόμων Δημοσθένει Πατροκλῆς Φλυεύς, καὶ τὸ μέρος τῶν ψήφων οὐ λαβὼν ἀπέτισε τὰς πεντακοσίας δραχμάς

06 Φέρε δὴ καὶ τὸν καλὸν κατάλογον.

ΚΑΤΑΛΟΓΟΣ.

Τοὺς τριηράρχους καλεῖσθαι ἐπὶ τὴν τριήρη συνεκκαίδεκα ἐκ τῶν ἐν τοῖς λόχοις συντελειῶν, ἀπὸ εἴκοσι καὶ πέντε ἐτῶν εἰς τετταράκοντα, ἐπὶ ἴσον τῇ χορηγίᾳ χρωμένους.

Φέρε δὴ παρὰ τοῦτον τὸν ἐκ τοῦ ἐμοῦ νόμου κατάλογον.

ΚΑΤΑΛΟΓΟΣ.

Τοὺς τριηράρχους αἱρεῖσθαι ἐπὶ τὴν τριήρη ἀπὸ τῆς οὐσίας κατὰ τίμησιν, ἀπὸ ταλάντων δέκα· ἐὰν δὲ πλειόνων ἡ οὐσία ἀποτετιμημένη ᾖ χρημάτων, κατὰ τὸν ἀναλογισμὸν ἕως τριῶν πλοίων καὶ ὑπηρετικοῦ ἡ λειτουργία ἔστω. Κατὰ τὴν αὐτὴν δὲ ἀναλογίαν ἔστω καὶ οἷς ἐλάττων οὐσία ἐστὶ τῶν δέκα ταλάντων, εἰς συντέλειαν συναγομένοις εἰς τὰ δέκα τάλαντα.

Ἆρά γε μικρὰ βοηθῆσαι τοῖς πένησιν ὑμῶν δοκῶ, 107
ἢ μικρὰ ἀναλῶσαι ἂν τοῦ μὴ τὰ δίκαια ποιεῖν οἱ πλούσιοι; Οὐ τοίνυν μόνον τῷ μὴ καθυφεῖναι ταῦτα σεμνύνομαι, οὐδὲ τῷ γραφεὶς ἀποφυγεῖν, ἀλλὰ καὶ τῷ συμφέροντα θεῖναι τὸν νόμον καὶ τῷ πεῖραν ἔργῳ δεδωκέναι. Πάντα γὰρ τὸν πόλεμον τῶν ἀποστόλων γιγνομένων κατὰ τὸν νόμον τὸν ἐμόν, οὐχ ἱκετηρίαν ἔθηκε τριήραρχος οὐδεὶς πώποθ' ὡς ἀδικούμενος παρ' ὑμῖν, οὐκ ἐν Μουνυχίᾳ ἐκαθέζετο, οὐχ ὑπὸ τῶν ἀποστολέων ἐδέθη, οὐ τριήρης οὔτ' ἔξω καταληφθεῖσα ἀπώλετο τῇ πόλει, οὔτ' αὐτοῦ ἀπελείφθη οὐ δυναμένη ἀνάγεσθαι.
Καίτοι κατὰ τοὺς προτέρους νόμους ἅπαντα ταῦτα 108
ἐγίγνετο. Τὸ δ' αἴτιον, ἐν τοῖς πένησιν ἦν το λειτουργεῖν· πολλὰ δὴ τὰ ἀδύνατα συνέβαινεν. Ἐγὼ δ' ἐκ τῶν ἀπόρων εἰς τοὺς εὐπόρους μετήνεγκα τὰς τριηραρχίας· πάντ' οὖν τὰ δέοντα ἐγίγνετο. Καὶ μὴν καὶ κατ' αὐτὸ τοῦτο ἄξιός εἰμι ἐπαίνου τυχεῖν, ὅτι πάντα τὰ τοιαῦτα προῃρούμην πολιτεύματα ἀφ' ὧν ἅμα δόξαι

καὶ τιμαὶ καὶ δυνάμεις συνέβαινον τῇ πόλει· βάσκανον 283
δὲ καὶ πικρὸν καὶ κακόηθες οὐδέν ἐστι πολίτευμα ἐμόν,
109 οὐδὲ ταπεινόν, οὐδὲ τῆς πόλεως ἀνάξιον. Ταὐτὸ τοίνυν ἦθος ἔχων ἔν τε τοῖς κατὰ τὴν πολιν πολιτεύμασι καὶ ἐν τοῖς Ἑλληνικοῖς φανήσομαι· οὔτε γὰρ ἐν τῇ πόλει τὰς παρὰ τῶν πλουσίων χάριτας μᾶλλον ἢ τὰ τῶν πολλῶν δίκαια εἱλόμην, οὔτ᾽ ἐν τοῖς Ἑλληνικοῖς τὰ Φιλίππου δῶρα καὶ τὴν ξενίαν ἠγάπησα ἀντὶ τῶν κοινῇ πᾶσι τοῖς Ἕλλησι συμφερόντων.

110 Ἡγοῦμαι τοίνυν λοιπὸν εἶναί μοι περὶ τοῦ κηρύγματος εἰπεῖν καὶ τῶν εὐθυνῶν· τὸ γὰρ ὡς τὰ ἄριστά τε ἔπραττον καὶ διὰ παντὸς εὔνους εἰμὶ καὶ πρόθυμος εὖ ποιεῖν ὑμᾶς ἱκανῶς ἐκ τῶν εἰρημένων δεδηλῶσθαί μοι νομίζω. Καίτοι τὰ μέγιστά γε τῶν πεπολιτευμένων καὶ πεπραγμένων ἐμαυτῷ παραλείπω, ὑπολαμβάνων πρῶτον μὲν ἐφεξῆς τοὺς περὶ αὐτοῦ τοῦ παρανόμου λόγους ἀποδοῦναί με δεῖν, εἶτα, κἂν μηδὲν εἴπω περὶ τῶν λοιπῶν πολιτευμάτων, ὁμοίως παρ᾽ ὑμῶν ἑκάστῳ τὸ συνειδὸς ὑπάρχειν μοι.

111 Τῶν μὲν οὖν λόγων οὓς οὗτος ἄνω καὶ κάτω διακυκῶν ἔλεγε περὶ τῶν παραγεγραμμένων νόμων, οὔτε μὰ τοὺς θεοὺς οἶμαι ὑμᾶς μανθάνειν, οὔτ᾽ αὐτὸς ἠδυνάμην συνεῖναι τοὺς πολλούς· ἁπλῶς δὲ τὴν ὀρθὴν περὶ τῶν δικαίων διαλέξομαι. Τοσούτου γὰρ δέω λέγειν ὡς οὐκ εἰμὶ ὑπεύθυνος, ὃ νῦν οὗτος διέβαλλε καὶ διωρίζετο, ὥσθ᾽ ἅπαντα τὸν βίον ὑπεύθυνος εἶναι ὁμολογῶ ὧν ἢ διακεχείρικα ἢ πεπολίτευμαι παρ᾽ ὑμῖν. Ὧν μέντοι γε

ἐκ τῆς ἰδίας οὐσίας ἐπαγγειλάμενος δέδωκα τῷ δήμῳ, οὐδεμίαν ἡμέραν ὑπεύθυνος εἶναί φημι, (ἀκούεις Αἰσχίνη;) οὐδ' ἄλλον οὐδένα, οὐδ' ἂν τῶν ἐννέα ἀρχόντων τις ὢν τύχῃ. Τίς γάρ ἐστι νόμος τοσαύτης ἀδικίας καὶ μισανθρωπίας μεστός, ὥστε τὸν δόντα τι τῶν ἰδίων καὶ ποιήσαντα πρᾶγμα φιλάνθρωπον καὶ φιλόδωρον τῆς χάριτος μὲν ἀποστερεῖν, εἰς τοὺς συκοφάντας δ' ἄγειν, καὶ τούτους ἐπὶ τὰς εὐθύνας ὧν ἔδωκεν ἐφιστάναι; Οὐδὲ εἷς. Εἰ δέ φησιν οὗτος, δειξάτω, κἀγὼ στέρξω καὶ σιωπήσομαι.

'Αλλ' οὐκ ἔστιν, ὦ ἄνδρες 'Αθηναῖοι, ἀλλ' οὗτος 113
συκοφαντῶν, ὅτι ἐπὶ τῷ θεωρικῷ τότε ὢν ἐπέδωκα τὰ χρήματα, ἐπήνεσεν αὐτόν φησιν ἡ βουλὴ ὑπεύθυνον ὄντα. Οὐ περὶ τούτων γε οὐδενὸς ὧν ὑπεύθυνος ἦν, ἀλλ' ἐφ' οἷς ἐπέδωκα, ὦ συκοφάντα. 'Αλλὰ καὶ τειχοποιὸς ἦσθα, φησίν. Καὶ διά γε τοῦτο ὀρθῶς επῃνούμην, ὅτι τἀνηλωμένα ἐπέδωκα καὶ οὐκ ἐλογιζόμην. 'Ο μὲν γὰρ λογισμὸς εὐθυνῶν καὶ τῶν ἐξετασόντων προσδεῖται, ἡ δὲ δωρεὰ χάριτος καὶ ἐπαίνου δικαία ἐστὶ τυγχάνειν· διόπερ ταῦτ' ἔγραψεν ὁδὶ περὶ ἐμοῦ. "Οτι 114
δ' οὕτω ταῦτα οὐ μόνον ἐν τοῖς νόμοις, ἀλλὰ καὶ ἐν τοῖς ὑμετέροις ἤθεσιν ὥρισται, ἐγὼ ῥᾳδίως πολλαχόθεν δείξω. Πρῶτον μὲν γὰρ Ναυσικλῆς στρατηγῶν, ἐφ' οἷς ἀπὸ τῶν ἰδίων προεῖτο πολλάκις ἐστεφάνωται ὑφ' ὑμῶν· εἶθ' ὅτε τὰς ἀσπίδας Διότιμος ἔδωκε καὶ πάλιν Χαρίδημος, ἐστεφανοῦντο· εἶθ' οὑτοσὶ Νεοπτόλεμος, πολλῶν ἔργων ἐπιστάτης ὤν, ἐφ' οἷς ἐπέδωκε τετίμηται. Σχέ-

τλιον γὰρ ἂν εἴη τοῦτό γε, εἰ τῷ τινὰ ἀρχὴν ἄρχοντι ἢ διδόναι τῇ πόλει τὰ ἑαυτοῦ διὰ τὴν ἀρχὴν μὴ ἐξέσται, ἢ τῶν δοθέντων ἀντὶ τοῦ κομίσασθαι χάριν εὐθύνας
115 ὑφέξει. Ὅτι τοίνυν ταῦτ' ἀληθῆ λέγω, λέγε τὰ 266
ψηφίσματά μοι τὰ τούτοις γεγενημένα αὐτὰ λαβών. Λέγε.

ΨΗΦΙΣΜΑ.

Ἄρχων Δημόνικος Φλυεύς, Βοηδρομιῶνος ἕκτῃ μετ' εἰκάδα, γνώμῃ βουλῆς καὶ δήμου, Καλλίας Φρεάῤῥιος εἶπεν, ὅτι δοκεῖ τῇ βουλῇ καὶ τῷ δήμῳ στεφανῶσαι Ναυσικλέα τὸν ἐπὶ τῶν ὅπλων, ὅτι Ἀθηναίων ὁπλιτῶν δισχιλίων ὄντων ἐν Ἴμβρῳ καὶ βοηθούντων τοῖς κατοικοῦσιν Ἀθηναίων τὴν νῆσον, οὐ δυναμένου Φίλωνος τοῦ ἐπὶ τῆς διοικήσεως κεχειροτονημένου διὰ τοὺς χειμῶνας πλεῦσαι καὶ μισθοδοτῆσαι τοὺς ὁπλίτας, ἐκ τῆς ἰδίας οὐσίας ἔδωκε καὶ οὐκ εἰσέπραξε τὸν δῆμον, καὶ ἀναγορεῦσαι τὸν στέφανον Διονυσίοις τραγῳδοῖς καινοῖς.

ἝΤΕΡΟΝ ΨΗΦΙΣΜΑ.

116 Εἶπε Καλλίας Φρεάῤῥιος, πρυτάνεων λεγόντων βουλῆς γνωμῃ· Ἐπειδὴ Χαρίδημος ὁ ἐπὶ τῶν ὁπλιτῶν, ἀποσταλεὶς εἰς Σαλαμῖνα, καὶ Διότιμος ὁ ἐπὶ τῶν ἱππέων, ἐν τῇ ἐπὶ τοῦ ποταμοῦ μάχῃ τῶν στρατιωτῶν τινῶν ὑπὸ τῶν πολεμίων σκυλευθέντων, ἐκ τῶν ἰδίων ἀναλωμάτων καθώπλισαν τοὺς νεανίσκους ἀσπίσιν ὀκτακοσίαις, δεδόχθαι τῇ βουλῇ καὶ τῷ δήμῳ στεφανῶσαι Χαρίδημον καὶ Διότιμον χρυσῷ στεφάνῳ καὶ ἀναγορεῦσαι Παναθηναίοις τοῖς μεγάλοις ἐν τῷ γυμνικῷ ἀγῶνι κα. Διονυσίοις τραγῳδοῖς καινοῖς· τῆς δὲ ἀναγορεύσεως ἐπιμεληθῆναι θεσμοθέτας, πρυτάνεις, ἀγωνοθέτας.

117 Τούτων ἕκαστος, Αἰσχίνη, τῆς μὲν ἀρχῆς ἧς ἦρχεν ὑπεύθυνος ἦν, ἐφ' οἷς δ' ἐστεφανοῦτο οὐχ ὑπεύθυνος. Οὐκοῦν οὐδ' ἐγώ· ταὐτὰ γὰρ δίκαιά ἐστί μοι περὶ τῶν αὐτῶν τοῖς ἄλλοις δήπου. Ἐπέδωκα· ἐπαινοῦμαι διὰ ταῦτα, οὐκ ὢν ὧν ἐπέδωκα ὑπεύθυνος. Ἦρχον· καὶ δέδωκά γε εὐθύνας ἐκείνων, οὐχ ὧν ἐπέδωκα. Νὴ Δί',

ἀλλ' ἀδίκως ἦρξα· εἶτα παρών, ὅτε με εἰσῆγον οἱ λογισταί, οὐ κατηγόρεις;

Ἵνα τοίνυν εἰδῆτε ὅτι αὐτὸς οὗτός μοι μαρτυρεῖ ἐφ' 118
οἷς οὐχ ὑπεύθυνος ἦν ἐστεφανῶσθαι, λαβὼν ἀνάγνωθι τὸ ψήφισμα ὅλον τὸ γραφέν μοι. Οἷς γὰρ οὐκ ἐγράψατο τοῦ προβουλεύματος, τούτοις ἃ διώκει συκοφαντῶν φανήσεται. Λέγε.

ΨΗΦΙΣΜΑ.

Ἐπὶ ἄρχοντος Εὐθυκλέους, Πυανεψιῶνος ἐνάτῃ ἀπιόντος, φυλῆς 119
πρυτανευούσης Οἰνηΐδος, Κτησιφῶν Λεωσθένους Ἀναφλύστιος εἶπεν· Ἐπειδὴ Δημοσθένης Δημοσθένους Παιανιεὺς γενόμενος ἐπιμελητὴς τῆς τῶν τειχῶν ἐπισκευῆς καὶ προσαναλώσας εἰς τὰ ἔργα ἀπὸ τῆς ἰδίας οὐσίας τρία τάλαντα ἐπέδωκε ταῦτα τῷ δήμῳ, καὶ ἐπὶ τοῦ θεωρικοῦ κατασταθεὶς ἐπέδωκε τοῖς ἐκ πασῶν τῶν φυλῶν θεωρικοῖς ἑκατὸν μνᾶς εἰς θυσίας, δεδόχθαι τῇ βουλῇ καὶ τῷ δήμῳ τῷ Ἀθηναίων ἐπαινέσαι Δημοσθένην Δημοσθένους Παιανιᾶ, ἀρετῆς ἕνεκα καὶ καλοκαγαθίας ἧς ἔχων διατελεῖ ἐν παντὶ καιρῷ εἰς τὸν δῆμον τὸν Ἀθηναίων, καὶ στεφανῶσαι χρυσῷ στεφάνῳ, καὶ ἀναγορεῦσαι τὸν στέφανον ἐν τῷ θεάτρῳ Διονυσίοις τραγῳδοῖς καινοῖς· τῆς δὲ ἀναγορεύσεως ἐπιμεληθῆναι τὸν ἀγωνοθέτην.

Οὐκοῦν ἃ μὲν ἐπέδωκα, ταῦτ' ἐστίν, ὧν οὐδὲν σὺ γέγραψαι· ἃ δέ φησιν ἡ βουλὴ δεῖν ἀντὶ τούτων γενέσθαι μοι, ταῦτ' ἔσθ' ἃ διώκεις. Τὸ λαβεῖν οὖν τὰ διδόμενα ὁμολογῶν ἔννομον εἶναι, τὸ χάριν τούτων ἀποδοῦναι παρανόμων γράφῃ. Ὁ δὲ παμπόνηρος ἄνθρωπος καὶ θεοῖς ἐχθρὸς καὶ βάσκανος ὄντως ποῖός τις ἂν εἴη πρὸς θεῶν; Οὐχ ὁ τοιοῦτος;

Καὶ μὴν περὶ τοῦ γ' ἐν τῷ θεάτρῳ κηρύττεσθαι, τὸ 120
μὲν μυριάκις μυρίους κεκηρῦχθαι παραλείπω καὶ τὸ πολλάκις αὐτὸς ἐστεφανῶσθαι πρότερον. Ἀλλὰ πρὸς

θεῶν οὕτω σκαιὸς εἶ καὶ ἀναίσθητος, Αἰσχίνη, ὥστ᾽ οὐ δύνασαι λογίσασθαι ὅτι τῷ μὲν στεφανουμένῳ τὸν αὐτὸν ἔχει ζῆλον ὁ στέφανος, ὅπου ἂν ἀναῤῥηθῇ, τοῦ δὲ τῶν στεφανούντων ἕνεκα συμφέροντος ἐν τῷ θεάτρῳ γίγνεται τὸ κήρυγμα; οἱ γὰρ ἀκούσαντες ἅπαντες εἰς τὸ ποιεῖν εὖ τὴν πόλιν προτρέπονται, καὶ τοὺς ἀποδιδόντας τὴν χάριν μᾶλλον ἐπαινοῦσι τοῦ στεφανουμένου· διόπερ τὸν νόμον τοῦτον ἡ πόλις γέγραφεν. Λέγε δ᾽ αὐτόν μοι τὸν νόμον λαβών.

ΝΟΜΟΣ.

Ὅσους στεφανοῦσί τινες τῶν δήμων, τὰς ἀναγορεύσεις τῶν στεφάνων ποιεῖσθαι ἐν αὐτοῖς ἑκάστους τοῖς ἰδίοις δήμοις, ἐὰν μή τινας ὁ δῆμος ὁ τῶν Ἀθηναίων ἢ ἡ βουλὴ στεφανοῖ· τούτους δ᾽ ἐξεῖναι ἐν τῷ θεάτρῳ Διονυσίοις ἀναγορεύεσθαι.

121 *Ἀκούεις, Αἰσχίνη, τοῦ νόμου λέγοντος σαφῶς, πλὴν
ἐάν τινας ὁ δῆμος ἢ ἡ βουλὴ ψηφίσηται τού- 268
τους δὲ ἀναγορευέτω. Τί οὖν, ὦ ταλαίπωρε, συκοφαντεῖς; Τί λόγους πλάττεις; Τί σαυτὸν οὐχ ἐλλεβορίζεις ἐπὶ τούτοις; Ἀλλ᾽ οὐδ᾽ αἰσχύνῃ φθόνου δίκην εἰσάγων, οὐκ ἀδικήματος οὐδενός, καὶ νόμους μεταποιῶν, τῶν δ᾽ ἀφαιρῶν μέρη, οὓς ὅλους δίκαιον ἦν ἀναγιγνώσκεσθαι τοῖς γε ὀμωμοκόσι κατὰ τοὺς νόμους ψηφιεῖ-
122 σθαι. Ἔπειτα τοιαῦτα ποιῶν λέγεις ἃ δεῖ προσεῖναι τῷ δημοτικῷ, ὥσπερ ἀνδριάντα ἐκδεδωκὼς κατὰ συγγραφήν, εἶτ᾽ οὐκ ἔχοντα ἃ προσῆκεν ἐκ τῆς συγγραφῆς κομιζόμενος, ἢ λόγῳ τοὺς δημοτικοὺς ἀλλ᾽ οὐ τοῖς πράγμασι καὶ τοῖς πολιτεύμασι γιγνωσκομένους. Καὶ*

βοᾷς ῥητὰ καὶ ἄῤῥητα ὀνομάζων, ὥσπερ ἐξ ἁμάξης, ἃ
σοὶ καὶ τῷ σῷ γένει πρόσεστιν, οὐκ ἐμοί.

Καίτοι καὶ τοῦτο, ὦ ἄνδρες Ἀθηναῖοι. Ἐγὼ λοιδο- 123
ρίαν κατηγορίας τούτῳ διαφέρειν ἡγοῦμαι, τῷ τὴν μὲν
κατηγορίαν ἀδικήματ' ἔχειν, ὧν ἐν τοῖς νόμοις εἰσὶν αἱ
τιμωρίαι, τὴν δὲ λοιδορίαν βλασφημίας, ἃς κατὰ τὴν
αὐτῶν φύσιν τοῖς ἐχθροῖς περὶ ἀλλήλων συμβαίνει λέγειν. Οἰκοδομῆσαι δὲ τοὺς προγόνους ταυτὶ τὰ δικα-
στήρια ὑπείληφα, οὐχ ἵνα συλλέξαντες ὑμᾶς εἰς ταῦτα
ἀπὸ τῶν ἰδίων κακῶς τὰ ἀπόῤῥητα λέγωμεν ἀλλήλους,
ἀλλ' ἵνα ἐξελέγχωμεν, ἐάν τις ἠδικηκώς τι τυγχάνῃ τὴν
πόλιν. Ταῦτα τοίνυν εἰδὼς Αἰσχίνης οὐδὲν ἧττον ἐμοῦ 124
πομπεύειν ἀντὶ τοῦ κατηγορεῖν εἵλετο. Οὐ μὴν οὐδ'
ἐνταῦθα ἔλαττον ἔχων δίκαιός ἐστιν ἀπελθεῖν. Ἤδη
δ' ἐπὶ ταῦτα πορεύσομαι, τοσοῦτον αὐτὸν ἐρωτήσας·
πότερόν σέ τις, Αἰσχίνη, τῆς πόλεως ἐχθρὸν ἢ ἐμὸν
260 εἶναι φῇ; Ἐμὸν δῆλον ὅτι. Εἶτα οὗ μὲν ἦν παρ'
ἐμοῦ δίκην κατὰ τοὺς νόμους ὑπὲρ τούτων λαβεῖν, εἴπερ
ἠδίκουν, ἐξέλιπες, ἐν ταῖς εὐθύναις, ἐν ταῖς γραφαῖς, ἐν
ταῖς ἄλλαις κρίσεσιν· οὗ δ' ἐγὼ μὲν ἀθῷος ἅπασι, τοῖς 125
νόμοις, τῷ χρόνῳ, τῇ προθεσμίᾳ, τῷ κεκρίσθαι περὶ
πάντων πολλάκις πρότερον, τῷ μηδεπώποτε ἐξελεγχθῆ-
ναι μηδὲν ὑμᾶς ἀδικῶν, τῇ πόλει δ' ἢ πλέον ἢ ἔλαττον
ἀνάγκη τῶν γε δημοσίᾳ πεπραγμένων μετεῖναι τῆς
δόξης, ἐνταῦθα ἀπήντηκας; Ὅρα μὴ τούτων μὲν
ἐχθρὸς ᾖς, ἐμὸς δὲ προσποιῇ.

Ἐπειδὴ τοίνυν ἡ μὲν εὐσεβὴς καὶ δικαία ψῆφος 126

ἅπασι δέδεικται, δεῖ δέ με, ὡς ἔοικε, καίπερ οὐ φιλολοί-
δορον ὄντα φύσει, διὰ τὰς ὑπὸ τούτου βλασφημίας
εἰρημένας, ἀντὶ πολλῶν καὶ ψευδῶν αὐτὰ τἀναγκαιότατ'
εἰπεῖν περὶ αὐτοῦ, καὶ δεῖξαι τίς ὢν καὶ τίνων ῥᾳδίως
οὕτως ἄρχει τοῦ κακῶς λέγειν, καὶ λόγους τίνας διασύ-
ρει, αὐτὸς εἰρηκὼς ἃ τίς οὐκ ἂν ὤκνησε τῶν μετρίων
127 ἀνθρώπων φθέγξασθαι; — Εἰ γὰρ Αἰακὸς ἢ Ῥαδά-
μανθυς ἢ Μίνως ἦν ὁ κατηγορῶν, ἀλλὰ μὴ σπερμολό-
γος, περίτριμμα ἀγορᾶς, ὄλεθρος γραμματεύς, οὐκ ἂν
αὐτὸν οἶμαι τοιαῦτ' εἰπεῖν οὐδ' ἂν οὕτως ἐπαχθεῖς λόγους πορίσασθαι, ὥσπερ ἐν τραγῳδίᾳ βοῶντα ὦ γῆ
καὶ ἥλιε καὶ ἀρετὴ καὶ τὰ τοιαῦτα, καὶ πάλιν σύνεσιν καὶ παιδείαν ἐπικαλούμενον, ᾗ τὰ καλὰ καὶ
τὰ αἰσχρὰ διαγιγνώσκεται· ταῦτα γὰρ δήπουθεν
128 ἠκούετ' αὐτοῦ λέγοντος. Σοὶ δὲ ἀρετῆς, ὦ κάθαρμα, ἢ
τοῖς σοῖς τίς μετουσία; Ἢ καλῶν ἢ μὴ τοιούτων τίς
διάγνωσις; Πόθεν ἢ πῶς ἀξιωθέντι; Ποῦ δὲ παι-
δείας σοι θέμις μνησθῆναι, ἧς τῶν μὲν ὡς ἀληθῶς τετυ-
χηκότων οὐδ' ἂν εἷς εἴποι περὶ αὐτοῦ τοιοῦτον οὐδέν, 270
ἀλλὰ κἂν ἑτέρου λέγοντος ἐρυθριάσειεν, τοῖς δ' ἀπο-
λειφθεῖσι μέν, ὥσπερ σύ, προσποιουμένοις δ' ὑπ'
ἀναισθησίας, τὸ τοὺς ἀκούοντας ἀλγεῖν ποιεῖν, ὅταν
λέγωσιν, οὐ τὸ δοκεῖν τοιούτοις εἶναι περίεστιν.

129 Οὐκ ἀπορῶν δ' ὅ τι χρὴ περὶ σοῦ καὶ τῶν σῶν
εἰπεῖν, ἀπορῶ τοῦ πρώτου μνησθῶ, πότερ' ὡς ὁ πατήρ
σου Τρόμης ἐδούλευε παρ' Ἐλπίᾳ τῷ πρὸς τῷ Θησείῳ
διδάσκοντι γράμματα, χοίνικας παχείας ἔχων καὶ ξύλον,

ἢ ὡς ἡ μήτηρ τοῖς μεθημερινοῖς γάμοις ἐν τῷ κλισίῳ
τῷ πρὸς τῷ καλαμίτῃ Ἥρωϊ χρωμένη τὸν καλὸν ἀνδριάντα καὶ τριταγωνιστὴν ἄκρον ἐξέθρεψέ σε; Ἀλλὰ
πάντες ἴσασι ταῦτα, κἂν ἐγὼ μὴ λέγω. Ἀλλ' ὡς ὁ
τριηραυλης Φορμίων, ὁ Δίωνος τοῦ Φρεαῤῥίου δοῦλος,
ἀνέστησεν αὐτὴν ἀπὸ ταύτης τῆς καλῆς ἐργασίας;
Ἀλλὰ νὴ τὸν Δία καὶ τοὺς θεοὺς ὀκνῶ μὴ περὶ σοῦ τὰ
προσήκοντα λέγων αὐτὸς οὐ προσήκοντας ἐμαυτῷ δόξω
προῃρῆσθαι λόγους. Ταῦτα μὲν οὖν ἐάσω, ἀπ' αὐτῶν 130
δὲ ὧν αὐτὸς βεβίωκεν ἄρξομαι. Οὐδὲ γὰρ ὧν ἔτυχεν
ἦν, ἀλλ' οἷς ὁ δῆμος καταρᾶται. Ὀψὲ γάρ ποτε —,
ὀψὲ λέγω; Χθὲς μὲν οὖν καὶ πρῴην ἅμ' Ἀθηναῖος
καὶ ῥήτωρ γέγονε, καὶ δύο συλλαβὰς προσθεὶς τὸν μὲν
πατέρα ἀντὶ Τρόμητος ἐποίησεν Ἀτρόμητον, τὴν δὲ
μητέρα σεμνῶς πάνυ Γλαυκοθέαν, ἣν Ἔμπουσαν ἅπαντες ἴσασι καλουμένην, ἐκ τοῦ πάντα ποιεῖν καὶ πάσχειν
δηλονότι ταύτης τῆς ἐπωνυμίας τυχοῦσαν· πόθεν γὰρ
ἄλλοθεν; Ἀλλ' ὅμως οὕτως ἀχάριστος εἶ καὶ πονηρὸς 131
φύσει, ὥστ' ἐλεύθερος ἐκ δούλου καὶ πλούσιος ἐκ πτω-
χοῦ διὰ τουτουσὶ γεγονὼς οὐχ ὅπως χάριν αὐτοῖς ἔχεις,
ἀλλὰ μισθώσας σαυτὸν κατα τουτωνὶ πολιτεύῃ. Καὶ
περὶ ὧν μὲν ἐστί τις ἀμφισβήτησις, ὡς ἄρα ὑπὲρ τῆς
πόλεως εἴρηκεν, ἐάσω. ἃ δ' ὑπὲρ τῶν ἐχθρῶν φανερῶς
ἀπεδείχθη πράττων, ταῦτα ἀναμνήσω.

Τίς γὰρ ὑμῶν οὐκ οἶδε τὸν ἀποψηφισθέντα Ἀντι- 132
φῶντα, ὃς ἐπαγγειλάμενος Φιλίππῳ τὰ νεώρια ἐμπρή-
σειν εἰς τὴν πόλιν ἦλθεν; ὃν λαβόντος ἐμοῦ κεκρυμμέ-

νον ἐν Πειραιεῖ καὶ καταστήσαντος εἰς τὴν ἐκκλησίαν, βοῶν ὁ βάσκανος οὗτος καὶ κεκραγώς, ὡς ἐν δημοκρατίᾳ δεινὰ ποιῶ τοὺς ἠτυχηκότας τῶν πολιτῶν ὑβρίζων καὶ ἐπ' οἰκίας βαδίζων ἄνευ ψηφίσματος, ἀφεθῆναι ἐποίη-
33 σεν. Καὶ εἰ μὴ ἡ βουλὴ ἡ ἐξ Ἀρείου πάγου τὸ πρᾶγμα αἰσθομένη καὶ τὴν ὑμετέραν ἄγνοιαν ἐν οὐ δέοντι συμβεβηκυῖαν ἰδοῦσα ἐπεζήτησε τὸν ἄνθρωπον καὶ συλλαβοῦσα ἐπανήγαγεν ὡς ὑμᾶς, ἐξήρπαστ' ἂν ὁ τοιοῦτος καὶ τὸ δίκην δοῦναι διαδὺς ἐξεπέμπετ' ἂν ὑπὸ τοῦ σεμνολόγου τουτουί· νῦν δ' ὑμεῖς στρεβλώσαντες αὐτὸν
34 ἀπεκτείνατε, ὡς ἔδει γε καὶ τοῦτον. Τοιγαροῦν εἰδυῖα ταῦτα ἡ βουλὴ ἡ ἐξ Ἀρείου πάγου τότε τούτῳ πεπραγμένα, χειροτονησάντων αὐτὸν ὑμῶν σύνδικον ὑπὲρ τοῦ ἱεροῦ τοῦ ἐν Δήλῳ ἀπὸ τῆς αὐτῆς ἀγνοίας ἧσπερ πολλὰ προΐεσθε τῶν κοινῶν, ὡς προείλεσθε κἀκείνην καὶ τοῦ πράγματος κυρίαν ἐποιήσατε, τοῦτον μὲν εὐθὺς ἀπήλασεν ὡς προδότην, Ὑπερίδῃ δὲ λέγειν προσέταξεν· καὶ ταῦτα ἀπὸ τοῦ βωμοῦ φέρουσα τὴν ψῆφον ἔπραξε,
135 καὶ οὐδεμία ψῆφος ἠνέχθη τῷ μιαρῷ τούτῳ. Καὶ ὅτι ταῦτ' ἀληθῆ λέγω, κάλει τούτων τοὺς μάρτυρας.

ΜΑΡΤΥΡΕΣ.

Μαρτυροῦσι Δημοσθένει ὑπὲρ ἁπάντων οἵδε, Καλλίας Σουνιεύς, Ζήνων Φλυεύς, Κλέων Φαληρεύς, Δημόνικος Μαραθώνιος, ὅτι τοῦ δήμου ποτὲ χειροτονήσαντος Αἰσχίνην σύνδικον ὑπὲρ τοῦ ἱεροῦ τοῦ ἐν Δήλῳ εἰς τοὺς Ἀμφικτύονας συνεδρεύσαντες ἡμεῖς ἐκρίναμεν Ὑπερίδην ἄξιον εἶναι μᾶλλον ὑπὲρ τῆς πόλεως λέγειν, καὶ ἀπεστάλη Ὑπερίδης.

Οὐκοῦν ὅτε, τούτου μέλλοντος λέγειν, ἀπήλασεν ἡ

βουλὴ καὶ προσέταξεν ἑτέρῳ, τότε καὶ προδότην εἶναι καὶ κακόνουν ὑμῖν ἀπέφηνεν.

Ἓν μὲν τοίνυν τοῦτο τοιοῦτο πολίτευμα τοῦ νεανίου 136
τούτου, ὅμοιόν γε, (οὐ γάρ;) οἷς ἐμοῦ κατηγορεῖ· ἕτερον δὲ ἀναμιμνήσκεσθε. Ὅτε γὰρ Πύθωνα Φίλιππος
ἔπεμψε τὸν Βυζάντιον καὶ παρὰ τῶν αὐτοῦ συμμάχων
πάντων συνέπεμψε πρέσβεις, ὡς ἐν αἰσχύνῃ ποιήσων
τὴν πόλιν καὶ δείξων ἀδικοῦσαν, τότε ἐγὼ μὲν τῷ Πύ-
θωνι θρασυνομένῳ καὶ πολλῷ ῥέοντι καθ' ὑμῶν οὐκ εἶξα
οὐδ' ὑπεχώρησα, ἀλλ' ἀναστὰς ἀντεῖπον καὶ τὰ τῆς
πόλεως δίκαια οὐχὶ προὔδωκα, ἀλλ' ἀδικοῦντα Φίλιππον
ἐξήλεγξα φανερῶς οὕτως ὥστε τοὺς ἐκείνου συμμάχους
αὐτοὺς ἀνισταμένους ὁμολογεῖν· οὗτος δὲ συνηγωνίζετο
καὶ τἀναντία ἐμαρτύρει τῇ πατρίδι, καὶ ταῦτα ψευδῆ.

Καὶ οὐκ ἀπέχρη ταῦτα, ἀλλὰ πάλιν μετὰ ταῦθ' 137
ὕστερον Ἀναξίνῳ τῷ κατασκόπῳ συνιὼν εἰς τὴν Θρά-
273 σωνος οἰκίαν ἐλήφθη. Καίτοι ὅστις τῷ ὑπὸ τῶν πολεμίων πεμφθέντι μόνος μόνῳ συνῄει καὶ ἐκοινολογεῖτο,
οὗτος αὐτὸς ὑπῆρχε τῇ φύσει κατάσκοπος καὶ πολέμιος
τῇ πατρίδι. Καὶ ὅτι ταῦτ' ἀληθῆ λέγω, κάλει μοι τούτων τοὺς μάρτυρας.

ΜΑΡΤΥΡΕΣ.

Γελέδημος Κλέωνος, Ὑπερίδης Καλλαίσχρου, Νικόμαχος Διοφάντου μαρτυροῦσι Δημοσθένει καὶ ἐπωμόσαντο ἐπὶ τῶν στρατηγῶν, εἰδέναι Αἰσχίνην Ἀτρομήτου Κοθωκίδην συνερχόμενον νυκτὸς εἰς τὴν Θράσωνος οἰκίαν καὶ κοινολογούμενον Ἀναξίνῳ, ὃς ἐκρίθη εἶναι κατάσκοπος παρὰ Φιλίππου. Αὗται ἀπεδόθησαν αἱ μαρτυρίαι ἐπὶ Νικίου, Ἑκατομβαιῶνος τρίτῃ ἱσταμένου.

138 Μυρία τοίνυν ἕτερ' εἰπεῖν ἔχων περὶ αὐτοῦ παραλείπω. Καὶ γὰρ οὕτω πως ἔχει. Πολλὰ ἂν ἐγὼ ἔτι
τούτων ἔχοιμι δεῖξαι ὧν οὗτος κατ' ἐκείνους τοὺς χρόνους τοῖς μὲν ἐχθροῖς ὑπηρετῶν ἐμοὶ δ' ἐπηρεάζων
εὑρέθη· ἀλλ' οὐ τίθεται ταῦτα παρ' ὑμῖν εἰς ἀκριβῆ
μνήμην οὐδ' ἣν προσῆκεν ὀργήν, ἀλλὰ δεδώκατε ἔθει
τινὶ φαύλῳ πολλὴν ἐξουσίαν τῷ βουλομένῳ τὸν λέγοντά
τι τῶν ὑμῖν συμφερόντων ὑποσκελίζειν καὶ συκοφαντεῖν,
τῆς ἐπὶ ταῖς λοιδορίαις ἡδονῆς καὶ χάριτος τὸ τῆς πόλεως συμφέρον ἀνταλλαττόμενοι· διόπερ ῥᾷόν ἐστι καὶ
ἀσφαλέστερον ἀεὶ τοῖς ἐχθροῖς ὑπηρετοῦντα μισθαρνεῖν
ἢ τὴν ὑπὲρ ὑμῶν ἑλόμενον τάξιν πολιτεύεσθαι.

139 Καὶ τὸ μὲν δὴ πρὸ τοῦ πολεμεῖν φανερῶς συναγω-
νίζεσθαι Φιλίππῳ δεινὸν μέν, ὦ γῆ καὶ θεοί,—πῶς γὰρ 274
οὔ;—κατὰ τῆς πατρίδος· δότε δ' εἰ βούλεσθε, δότε
αὐτῷ τοῦτο. Ἀλλ' ἐπειδὴ φανερῶς ἤδη τὰ πλοῖα ἐσε-
σύλητο, Χεῤῥόνησος ἐπορθεῖτο, ἐπὶ τὴν Ἀττικὴν ἐπορεύεθ' ἄνθρωπος, οὐκέτ' ἐν ἀμφισβητησίμῳ τὰ πράγματα
ἦν ἀλλ' ἐνεστήκει πόλεμος, ὅ τι μὲν πώποτ' ἔπραξεν
ὑπὲρ ὑμῶν ὁ βάσκανος οὑτοσὶ ἰαμβειοφάγος οὐκ ἂν ἔχοι
δεῖξαι, οὐδ' ἔστιν οὔτε μεῖζον οὔτ' ἔλαττον ψήφισμα
οὐδὲν Αἰσχίνῃ ὑπὲρ τῶν συμφερόντων τῇ πόλει. Εἰ δέ
φησι, νῦν δειξάτω ἐπὶ τῷ ἐμῷ ὕδατι. Ἀλλ' οὐκ ἔστιν
οὐδέν. Καίτοι δυοῖν αὐτὸν ἀνάγκη θάτερον, ἢ μηδὲν
τοῖς πραττομένοις ὑπ' ἐμοῦ τότ' ἔχοντ' ἐγκαλεῖν μὴ
γράφειν παρὰ ταῦθ' ἕτερα, ἢ τὸ τῶν ἐχθρῶν συμφέρον
ζητοῦντα μὴ φέρειν εἰς μέσον τὰ τούτων ἀμείνω.

Ἀρ᾽ οὖν οὐδ᾽ ἔλεγεν, ὥσπερ οὐδ᾽ ἔγραφεν, ἡνίκα 140
ἐργάσασθαί τι δέοι κακόν; Οὐ μὲν οὖν ἦν εἰπεῖν
ἑτέρῳ. Καὶ τὰ μὲν ἄλλα καὶ φέρειν ἠδύναθ᾽, ὡς ἔοικεν, ἡ πόλις καὶ ποιῶν οὗτος λανθάνειν. ἓν δ᾽ ἐπε-
ξειργάσατο, ὦ ἄνδρες Ἀθηναῖοι, τοιοῦτον ὃ πᾶσι τοῖς
προτέροις ἐπέθηκε τέλος· περὶ οὗ τοὺς πολλοὺς ἀνά-
λωσε λόγους, τὰ τῶν Ἀμφισσέων τῶν Λοκρῶν διεξιὼν
δόγματα, ὡς διαστρέψων τἀληθές. Τὸ δ᾽ οὐ τοιοῦτόν
ἐστι· πόθεν; Οὐδέποτ᾽ ἐκνίψῃ σὺ τἀκεῖ πεπραγμένα
σαυτῷ· οὐχ οὕτω πολλὰ ἐρεῖς.

Καλῶ δ᾽ ἐναντίον ὑμῶν, ὦ ἄνδρες Ἀθηναῖοι, τοὺς 141
θεοὺς ἅπαντας καὶ πάσας, ὅσοι τὴν χώραν ἔχουσι τὴν
Ἀττικήν, καὶ τὸν Ἀπόλλω τὸν Πύθιον, ὃς πατρῷός
ἐστι τῇ πόλει, καὶ ἐπεύχομαι πᾶσι τούτοις, εἰ μὲν
ἀληθῆ πρὸς ὑμᾶς εἴποιμι καὶ εἶπον καὶ τότ᾽ εὐθὺς ἐν
τῷ δήμῳ, ὅτε πρῶτον εἶδον τουτονὶ τὸν μιαρὸν τούτου τοῦ πράγματος ἁπτόμενον (ἔγνων γάρ, εὐθέως
ἔγνων), εὐτυχίαν μοι δοῦναι καὶ σωτηρίαν, εἰ δὲ πρὸς
ἔχθραν ἢ φιλονεικίας ἰδίας ἕνεκ᾽ αἰτίαν ἐπάγω τούτῳ
ψευδῆ, πάντων τῶν ἀγαθῶν ἀνόνητόν με ποιῆσαι.

Τί οὖν ταῦτ᾽ ἐπήραμαι καὶ διετεινάμην οὑτωσὶ σφο- 142
δρῶς; Ὅτι γράμματ᾽ ἔχων ἐν τῷ δημοσίῳ κείμενα, ἐξ
ὧν ταῦτ᾽ ἐπιδείξω σαφῶς, καὶ ὑμᾶς εἰδὼς τὰ πεπραγμένα μνημονεύοντας, ἐκεῖνο φοβοῦμαι, μὴ τῶν εἰργασμέ-
νων αὐτῷ κακῶν ὑποληφθῇ οὗτος ἐλάττων, ὅπερ πρότερον συνέβη ὅτε τοὺς ταλαιπώρους Φωκέας ἐποίησεν
ἀπολέσθαι τὰ ψευδῆ δεῦρ᾽ ἀπαγγείλας. Τὸν γὰρ ἐν 143

Ἀμφίσσῃ πόλεμον, δι' ὃν εἰς Ἐλάτειαν ἦλθε Φίλιππος
καὶ δι' ὃν ᾑρέθη τῶν Ἀμφικτυόνων ἡγεμών, ὃς ἅπαντ'
ἀνέτρεψε τὰ τῶν Ἑλλήνων, οὗτός ἐστιν ὁ συγκατα-
σκευάσας καὶ πάντων εἷς ἀνὴρ τῶν μεγίστων αἴτιος
κακῶν. Καὶ τότ' εὐθὺς ἐμοῦ διαμαρτυρομένου καὶ
βοῶντος ἐν τῇ ἐκκλησίᾳ, πόλεμον εἰς τὴν Ἀττικὴν
εἰσάγεις, Αἰσχίνη, πόλεμον Ἀμφικτυονικον, οι
μὲν ἐκ παρακλήσεως συγκαθήμενοι οὐκ εἴων με λέγειν, οἱ δ' ἐθαύμαζον καὶ κενὴν αἰτίαν διὰ τὴν ἰδίαν
144 ἔχθραν ἐπάγειν με ὑπελάμβανον αὐτῷ. Ἥτις δ' ἡ
φύσις, ὦ ἄνδρες Ἀθηναῖοι, γέγονε τούτων τῶν πραγμάτων, καὶ τίνος ἕνεκα ταῦτα συνεσκευάσθη καὶ πῶς
ἐπράχθη, νῦν ἀκούσατε, ἐπειδὴ τότε ἐκωλύθητε· καὶ
γὰρ εὖ πρᾶγμα συντεθὲν ὄψεσθε, καὶ μεγάλα ὠφελή-
σεσθε πρὸς ἱστορίαν τῶν κοινῶν, καὶ ὅση δεινότης ἦν ἐν
τῷ Φιλίππῳ θεάσεσθε.

145 Οὐκ ἦν τοῦ πρὸς ὑμᾶς πολέμου πέρας οὐδ' ἀπαλλαγὴ
Φιλίππῳ, εἰ μὴ Θηβαίους καὶ Θετταλοὺς ἐχθροὺς ποιή- 278
σειε τῇ πόλει, ἀλλὰ καίπερ ἀθλίως καὶ κακῶς τῶν
στρατηγῶν τῶν ὑμετέρων πολεμούντων αὐτῷ ὅμως ὑπ'
αὐτοῦ τοῦ πολέμου καὶ τῶν λῃστῶν μυρία ἔπασχε κακά.
Οὔτε γὰρ ἐξήγετο τῶν ἐκ τῆς χώρας γιγνομένων οὐδέν,
146 οὔτ' εἰσήγετο ὧν ἐδεῖτ' αὐτῷ· ἦν δὲ οὔτ' ἐν τῇ θαλάττῃ
τότε κρείττων ὑμῶν, οὔτ' εἰς τὴν Ἀττικὴν ἐλθεῖν δυ-
νατὸς μήτε Θετταλῶν ἀκολουθούντων μήτε Θηβαίων
διιέντων· συνέβαινε δὲ αὐτῷ τῷ πολέμῳ κρατοῦντι τοὺς
ὁποιουσδήποθ' ὑμεῖς ἐξεπέμπετε στρατηγοὺς (ἐῶ γὰρ

τοῦτό γε) αὐτῇ τῇ φύσει τοῦ τόπου καὶ τῶν ὑπαρχόντων ἑκατέροις κακοπαθεῖν. Εἰ μὲν οὖν τῆς ἰδίας ἕνεκ' 147
ἔχθρας ἢ τοὺς Θετταλοὺς ἢ τοὺς Θηβαίους συμπείθοι
βαδίζειν ἐφ' ὑμᾶς, οὐδένα ἡγεῖτο προσέξειν αὐτῷ τὸν
νοῦν· ἂν δὲ τὰς ἐκείνων κοινὰς προφάσεις λαβὼν ἡγεμὼν αἱρεθῇ, ῥᾷον ἤλπιζε τὰ μὲν παρακρούσεσθαι, τὰ δὲ
πείσειν. Τί οὖν; Ἐπιχειρεῖ, θεάσασθ' ὡς εὖ, πόλεμον ποιῆσαι τοῖς Ἀμφικτύοσι καὶ περὶ τὴν πυλαίαν
ταραχήν· εἰς γὰρ ταῦτ' εὐθὺς αὐτοὺς υπελάμβανει
αὐτοῦ δεήσεσθαι. Εἰ μὲν τοίνυν τοῦτο ἢ τῶν παρ' 148
ἑαυτοῦ πεμπομένων ἱερομνημόνων ἢ τῶν ἐκείνου συμμάχων εἰσηγοῖτό τις, ὑπόψεσθαι τὸ πρᾶγμα ἐνόμιζε καὶ
τοὺς Θηβαίους καὶ τοὺς Θετταλοὺς καὶ πάντας φυλά-
ξεσθαι, ἂν δ' Ἀθηναῖος ᾖ καὶ παρ' ὑμῶν τῶν ὑπεναν-
τίων ὁ τοῦτο ποιῶν, εὐπόρως λήσειν· ὅπερ συνέβη. 149
Πῶς οὖν ταῦτ' ἐποίησεν; Μισθοῦται τουτονί. Οὐδενὸς δὲ προειδότος, οἶμαι, τὸ πρᾶγμα οὐδὲ φυλάττοντος,
ὥσπερ εἴωθε τὰ τοιαῦτα παρ' ὑμῖν γίγνεσθαι, προβλη-
θεὶς πυλαγόρας οὗτος καὶ τριῶν ἢ τεττάρων χειροτονησάντων αὐτὸν ἀνεῤῥήθη.

Ὡς δὲ τὸ τῆς πόλεως ἀξίωμα λαβὼν ἀφίκετο εἰς
τοὺς Ἀμφικτύονας, πάντα τἆλλ ἀφεὶς καὶ παριδὼν
ἐπέραινεν ἐφ' οἷς ἐμισθώθη, καὶ λόγους εὐπροσώπους
καὶ μύθους, ὅθεν ἡ Κιῤῥαία χώρα καθιερώθη, συνθεὶς
καὶ διεξελθών, ἀνθρώπους ἀπείρους λόγων καὶ τὸ μέλλον
οὐ προορωμένους, τοὺς ἱερομνήμονας, πείθει ψηφίσασθαι
περιελθεῖν τὴν χώραν, ἣν οἱ μὲν Ἀμφισσεῖς σφῶν 150

αὐτῶν οὖσαν γεωργεῖν ἔφασαν, οὗτος δὲ τῆς ἱερᾶς χώρας ᾐτιᾶτο εἶναι, οὐδεμίαν δίκην τῶν Λοκρῶν ἐπαγόντων ἡμῖν, οὐδ' ἃ νῦν οὗτος προφασίζεται, λέγων οὐκ ἀληθῆ. Γνώσεσθε δ' ἐκεῖθεν. Οὐκ ἐνῆν ἄνευ τοῦ προσκαλέσασθαι δήπου τοῖς Λοκροῖς δίκην κατὰ τῆς πόλεως τελέσασθαι. Τίς οὖν ἐκλήτευσεν ἡμᾶς; Ἐπὶ ποίας ἀρχῆς; Εἰπὲ τὸν εἰδότα, δεῖξον. Ἀλλ' οὐκ ἂν ἔχοις, ἀλλὰ κενῇ προφάσει ταύτῃ κατεχρῶ καὶ ψευδεῖ.

151 *Περιιόντων τοίνυν τὴν χώραν τῶν Ἀμφικτυόνων κατὰ τὴν ὑφήγησιν τὴν τούτου, προσπεσόντες οἱ Λοκροὶ μικροῦ κατηκόντισαν ἅπαντας, τινὰς δὲ καὶ συνήρπασαν τῶν ἱερομνημόνων. Ὡς δ' ἅπαξ ἐκ τούτων ἐγκλήματα καὶ πόλεμος πρὸς τοὺς Ἀμφισσεῖς ἐταράχθη, τὸ μὲν πρῶτον ὁ Κόττυφος αὐτῶν τῶν Ἀμφικτυόνων ἤγαγε στρατιάν· ὡς δ' οἱ μὲν οὐκ ἦλθον, οἱ δ' ἐλθόντες οὐδὲν ἐποίουν, εἰς τὴν ἐπιοῦσαν πυλαίαν ἐπὶ τὸν Φίλιππον εὐθέως ἡγεμόνα ἦγον οἱ κατεσκευασμένοι καὶ πάλαι πονηροὶ τῶν Θετταλῶν καὶ τῶν ἐν ταῖς ἄλλαις πόλεσιν.*
152 *Καὶ προφάσεις εὐλόγους εἰλήφεσαν· ἢ γὰρ αὐτοὺς εἰσφέρειν καὶ ξένους τρέφειν ἔφασαν δεῖν καὶ ζημιοῦν* 278
τοὺς μὴ ταῦτα ποιοῦντας, ἢ ἐκεῖνον αἱρεῖσθαι. Τί δεῖ τὰ πολλὰ λέγειν; Ἡιρέθη γὰρ ἐκ τούτων ἡγεμών. Καὶ μετὰ ταῦτ' εὐθὺς δύναμιν συλλέξας καὶ παρελθὼν ὡς ἐπὶ τὴν Κιῤῥαίαν, ἐῤῥῶσθαι φράσας πολλὰ Κιῤῥαίοις
153 *καὶ Λοκροῖς, τὴν Ἐλάτειαν καταλαμβάνει. Εἰ μὲν οὖν μὴ μετέγνωσαν εὐθέως ὡς τοῦτ' εἶδον οἱ Θηβαῖοι καὶ μεθ' ἡμῶν ἐγένοντο, ὥσπερ χειμάῤῥους ἂν ἅπαν τοῦτο*

τὸ πρᾶγμα εἰς τὴν πόλιν εἰσέπεσεν· νῦν δὲ τό γ'
ἐξαίφνης ἐπέσχον αὐτὸν ἐκεῖνοι, μάλιστα μέν, ὦ ἄνδρες
Ἀθηναῖοι, θεῶν τινὸς εὐνοίᾳ πρὸς ὑμᾶς, εἶτα μέντοι, καὶ
ὅσον καθ' ἕνα ἄνδρα, καὶ δι' ἐμέ. Δός δέ μοι τὰ
δογματα ταῦτα καὶ τοὺς χρόνους ἐν οἷς ἕκαστα πέπρακται, ἵν' εἰδῆτε ἡλίκα πράγματα ἡ μιαρὰ κεφαλὴ
ταράξασα αὕτη δίκην οὐκ ἔδωκεν. Λέγε μοι τὰ δόγ- 154
ματα.

ΔΟΓΜΑ ΑΜΦΙΚΤΥΟΝΩΝ.

Ἐπὶ ἱερέως Κλειναγόρου, ἐαρινῆς πυλαίας, ἔδοξε τοῖς Πυλαγόροις καὶ τοῖς συνέδροις τῶν Ἀμφικτυόνων καὶ τῷ κοινῷ τῶν Ἀμφικτυόνων, ἐπειδὴ Ἀμφισσεῖς ἐπιβαίνουσιν ἐπὶ τὴν ἱερὰν χώραν καὶ σπείρουσι καὶ βοσκήμασι κατανέμουσιν, ἐπελθεῖν τοὺς Πυλαγόρους καὶ τοὺς συνέδρους καὶ στήλαις διαλαβεῖν τοὺς ὅρους, καὶ ἀπειπεῖν τοῖς Ἀμφισσεῦσι τοῦ λοιποῦ μὴ ἐπιβαίνειν.

ἝΤΕΡΟΝ ΔΟΓΜΑ.

Ἐπὶ ἱερέως Κλειναγόρου, ἐαρινῆς πυλαίας, ἔδοξε τοῖς Πυλαγόροις 155
καὶ τοῖς συνέδροις τῶν Ἀμφικτυόνων καὶ τῷ κοινῷ τῶν Ἀμφικτυόνων, ἐπειδὴ οἱ ἐξ Ἀμφίσσης τὴν ἱερὰν χώραν κατανειμάμενοι γεωργοῦσι καὶ βοσκήματα νέμουσι, καὶ κωλυόμενοι τοῦτο ποιεῖν, ἐν τοῖς ὅπλοις παραγενόμενοι, τὸ κοινὸν τῶν Ἑλλήνων συνέδριον κεκωλύκασι μετὰ βίας, τινὰς δὲ καὶ τετραυματίκασι, τὸν στρατηγὸν τὸν ᾑρημένον τῶν Ἀμφικτυόνων Κόττυφον τὸν Ἀρκάδα πρεσβεῦσαι πρὸς Φίλιππον τὸν Μακεδόνα, καὶ ἀξιοῦν ἵνα βοηθήσῃ τῷ τε Ἀπόλλωνι καὶ τοῖς Ἀμφικτύοσιν, ὅπως μὴ περιίδῃ ὑπὸ τῶν ἀσεβῶν Ἀμφισσέων τὸν θεὸν πλημμελούμενον· καὶ διότι αὐτὸν στρατηγὸν αὐτοκράτορα αἱροῦνται οἱ Ἕλληνες οἱ μετέχοντες τοῦ συνεδρίου τῶν Ἀμφικτυόνων.

Λέγε δὴ καὶ τοὺς χρόνους ἐν οἷς ταῦτ' ἐγίγνετο· εἰσὶ γὰρ καθ' οὓς ἐπυλαγόρησεν οὗτος. Λέγε.

ΧΡΟΝΟΙ.

Ἄρχων Μνησιθείδης, μηνὸς Ἀνθεστηριῶνος ἕκτῃ ἐπὶ δεκάτῃ.

156 *Δὸς δή μοι τὴν ἐπιστολὴν ἥν, ὡς οὐχ ὑπήκουον οἱ Θηβαῖοι, πέμπει πρὸς τοὺς ἐν Πελοποννήσῳ συμμάχους ὁ Φίλιππος, ἵν' εἰδῆτε καὶ ἐκ ταύτης σαφῶς ὅτι τὴν μὲν ἀληθῆ πρόφασιν τῶν πραγμάτων, τὸ ταῦτ' ἐπὶ τὴν Ἑλλάδα καὶ τοὺς Θηβαίους καὶ ὑμᾶς πράττειν, ἀπεκρύπτετο, κοινὰ δὲ καὶ τοῖς Ἀμφικτύοσι δόξαντα ποιεῖν προσεποιεῖτο. Ὁ δὲ τὰς ἀφορμὰς ταύτας καὶ τὰς προφάσεις αὐτῷ παρασχὼν οὗτος ἦν. Λέγε.*

ΕΠΙΣΤΟΛΗ ΦΙΛΙΠΠΟΥ. 280

157 Βασιλεὺς Μακεδόνων Φίλιππος Πελοποννησίων τῶν ἐν τῇ συμμαχίᾳ τοῖς δημιουργοῖς καὶ τοῖς συνέδροις καὶ τοῖς ἄλλοις συμμάχοις πᾶσι χαίρειν. Ἐπειδὴ Λοκροὶ οἱ καλούμενοι Ὀζόλαι, κατοικοῦντες ἐν Ἀμφίσσῃ, πλημμελοῦσιν εἰς τὸ ἱερὸν τοῦ Ἀπόλλωνος τοῦ ἐν Δελφοῖς καὶ τὴν ἱερὰν χώραν ἐρχόμενοι μεθ' ὅπλων λεηλατοῦσι, βούλομαι τῷ θεῷ μεθ' ὑμῶν βοηθεῖν καὶ ἀμύνασθαι τοὺς παραβαίνοντάς τι τῶν ἐν ἀνθρώποις εὐσεβῶν. Ὥστε συναντᾶτε μετὰ τῶν ὅπλων εἰς τὴν Φωκίδα, ἔχοντες ἐπισιτισμὸν ἡμερῶν τεσσαράκοντα, τοῦ ἐνεστῶτος μηνὸς Λῴου, ὡς ἡμεῖς ἄγομεν, ὡς δὲ Ἀθηναῖοι, Βοηδρομιῶνος, ὡς δὲ Κορίνθιοι, Πανέμου. Τοῖς δὲ μὴ συναντήσασι πανδημεὶ χρησόμεθα, τοῖς δὲ συμβούλοις ἡμῖν κειμένοις ἐπιζημίοις. Εὐτυχεῖτε.

158 *Ὁρᾶθ' ὅτι φεύγει μὲν τὰς ἰδίας προφάσεις, εἰς δὲ τὰς Ἀμφικτυονικὰς καταφεύγει. Τίς οὖν ὁ ταῦτα συμπαρασκευάσας αὐτῷ; Τίς ὁ τὰς προφάσεις ταύτας ἐνδούς; Τίς ὁ τῶν κακῶν τῶν γεγενημένων μάλιστα αἴτιος; Οὐχ οὗτος; Μὴ τοίνυν λέγετε, ὦ ἄνδρες Ἀθηναῖοι, περιιόντες, ὡς ὑφ' ἑνὸς τοιαῦτα πέπονθεν ἡ Ἑλλὰς ἀνθρώπου. Οὐχ ὑφ' ἑνός, ἀλλ' ὑπὸ πολλῶν*
159 *καὶ πονηρῶν τῶν παρ' ἑκάστοις, ὦ γῆ καὶ θεοί, ὧν εἷς οὑτοσί, ὅν, εἰ μηδὲν εὐλαβηθέντα τἀληθὲς εἰπεῖν δέοι*

οὐκ ἂν ὀκνήσαιμι ἔγωγε κοινὸν ἀλιτήριον τῶν μετὰ
ταῦτα ἀπολωλότων ἁπάντων εἰπεῖν, ἀνθρώπων, τόπων,
πόλεων· ὁ γὰρ τὸ σπέρμα παρασχών, οὗτος τῶν φύν-
των αἴτιος. Ὃν ὅπως ποτὲ οὐκ εὐθὺς ἰδόντες ἀπεστρά-
φητε, θαυμάζω· πλὴν πολύ τι σκότος, ὡς ἔοικεν, ἐστὶ
παρ' ὑμῖν πρὸ τῆς ἀληθείας.

Συμβέβηκε τοίνυν μοι τῶν κατὰ τῆς πατρίδος τούτῳ 160
πεπραγμένων ἁψαμένῳ εἰς ἃ τούτοις ἐναντιούμενος
αὐτὸς πεπολίτευμαι ἀφῖχθαι· ἃ πολλῶν μὲν ἕνεκ' ἂν
εἰκότως ἀκούσαιτέ μου, μάλιστα δ' ὅτι αἰσχρόν ἐστιν,
ὦ ἄνδρες Ἀθηναῖοι, εἰ ἐγὼ μὲν τὰ ἔργα τῶν ὑπὲρ ὑμῶν
πόνων ὑπέμεινα, ὑμεῖς δὲ μηδὲ τοὺς λόγους αὐτῶν ἀνέ-
ξεσθε. Ὁρῶν γὰρ ἐγὼ Θηβαίους σχεδὸν δὲ καὶ ὑμᾶς, 161
ὑπὸ τῶν τὰ Φιλίππου φρονούντων καὶ διεφθαρμένων
παρ' ἑκατέροις, ὃ μὲν ἦν ἀμφοτέροις φοβερὸν καὶ φυλακῆς πολλῆς δεόμενον, τὸ τὸν Φίλιππον ἐᾶν αὐξάνεσθαι,
παρορῶντας καὶ οὐδὲ καθ' ἓν φυλαττομένους, εἰς ἔχθραν
δὲ καὶ τὸ προσκρούειν ἀλλήλοις ἑτοίμως ἔχοντας, ὅπως
τοῦτο μὴ γένοιτο παρατηρῶν διετέλουν· οὐκ ἀπὸ τῆς
ἐμαυτοῦ γνώμης μόνον ταῦτα συμφέρειν ὑπολαμβάνων, 162
ἀλλ' εἰδὼς Ἀριστοφῶντα καὶ πάλιν Εὔβουλον πάντα
τὸν χρόνον βουλομένους πρᾶξαι ταύτην τὴν φιλίαν, καὶ
περὶ τῶν ἄλλων πολλάκις ἀντιλέγοντας ἑαυτοῖς τοῦθ'
ὁμογνωμονοῦντας ἀεί. Οὓς σὺ ζῶντας μέν, ὦ κίναδος,
κολακεύων παρηκολούθεις, τεθνεώτων δ' οὐκ αἰσθάνει
κατηγορῶν· ἃ γὰρ περὶ Θηβαίων ἐπιτιμᾷς ἐμοί, ἐκεί

νων πολὺ μᾶλλον ἢ ἐμοῦ κατηγορεῖς, τῶν πρότερον ἢ ἐγὼ ταύτην τὴν συμμαχίαν δοκιμασάντων.

63 Ἀλλ' ἐκεῖσε ἐπάνειμι, ὅτι τὸν ἐν Ἀμφίσσῃ πόλεμον
τούτου μὲν ποιήσαντος, συμπεραναμένων δὲ τῶν ἄλλων
τῶν συνεργῶν αὐτῷ τὴν πρὸς Θηβαίους ἔχθραν, συνέβη
τὸν Φίλιππον ἐλθεῖν ἐφ' ἡμᾶς, οὗπερ ἕνεκα τὰς πόλεις 282
οὗτοι συνέκρουον· καὶ εἰ μὴ προεξανέστημεν μικρόν,
οὐδ' ἀναλαβεῖν ἂν ἠδυνήθημεν· οὕτω μέχρι πόῤῥω
προήγαγον οὗτοι τὸ πρᾶγμα. Ἐν οἷς δ' ἦτε ἤδη τὰ
πρὸς ἀλλήλους, τουτωνὶ τῶν ψηφισμάτων ἀκούσαντες
καὶ τῶν ἀποκρίσεων εἴσεσθε. Καί μοι λέγε ταῦτα
λαβών.

ΨΗΦΙΣΜΑ.

64 Ἐπὶ ἄρχοντος Ἡροπύθου, μηνὸς Ἐλαφηβολιῶνος ἕκτῃ φθίνοντος, φυλῆς πρυτανευούσης Ἐρεχθηΐδος, βουλῆς καὶ στρατηγῶν γνώμῃ· Ἐπειδὴ Φίλιππος ἃς μὲν κατείληφε πόλεις τῶν ἀστυγειτόνων, τινὰς δὲ πορθεῖ, κεφαλαίῳ δὲ ἐπὶ τὴν Ἀττικὴν παρασκευάζεται παραγίγνεσθαι, παρ' οὐδὲν ἡγούμενος τὰς ἡμετέρας συνθήκας, καὶ τοὺς ὅρκους λύειν ἐπιβάλλεται καὶ τὴν εἰρήνην, παραβαίνων τὰς κοινὰς πίστεις, δεδόχθαι τῇ βουλῇ καὶ τῷ δήμῳ πέμπειν πρὸς αὐτὸν πρέσβεις, οἵτινες αὐτῷ διαλέξονται καὶ παρακαλέσουσιν αὐτὸν μάλιστα μὲν τὴν πρὸς ἡμᾶς ὁμόνοιαν διατηρεῖν καὶ τὰς συνθήκας, εἰ δὲ μή, πρὸς τὸ βουλεύσασθαι δοῦναι χρόνον τῇ πόλει καὶ τὰς ἀνοχὰς ποιήσασθαι μέχρι τοῦ Θαργηλιῶνος μηνός. Ἡιρέθησαν ἐκ τῆς βουλῆς Σῖμος Ἀναγυράσιος Εὐθύδημος Φλυάσιος, Βουλαγόρας Ἀλωπεκῆθεν.

ἝΤΕΡΟΝ ΨΗΦΙΣΜΑ.

65 Ἐπὶ ἄρχοντος Ἡροπύθου, μηνὸς Μουνυχιῶνος ἕνῃ καὶ νέᾳ, πολε
μάρχου γνώμῃ, ἐπειδὴ Φίλιππος εἰς ἀλλοτριότητα Θηβαίους πρὸς
ἡμᾶς ἐπιβάλλεται καταστῆσαι, παρεσκεύασται δὲ καὶ παντὶ τῷ στρα-
τεύματι πρὸς τοὺς ἔγγιστα τῆς Ἀττικῆς παραγίγνεσθαι τόπους, παρα- 283
βαίνων τὰς πρὸς ἡμᾶς ὑπαρχούσας αὐτῷ συνθήκας, δεδόχθαι τῇ βουλῇ
καὶ τῷ δήμῳ πέμψαι πρὸς αὐτὸν κήρυκα καὶ πρέσβεις, οἵτινες ἀξιώ-
σουσι καὶ παρακαλέσουσιν αὐτὸν ποιήσασθαι τὰς ἀνοχάς, ὅπως ἐνδε-

χομένως ὁ δῆμος βουλεύσηται· καὶ γὰρ νῦν οὐ κέκρικε βοηθεῖν ἐν οὐδενὶ τῶν μετρίων. Ἡιρέθησαν ἐκ τῆς βουλῆς Νέαρχος Σωσινόμου, Πολυκράτης Ἐπίφρονος, καὶ κήρυξ Εὔνομος Ἀναφλύστιος ἐκ τοῦ δήμου.

Λέγε δὴ καὶ τὰς ἀποκρίσεις. 168

ΑΠΟΚΡΙΣΙΣ ΑΘΗΝΑΙΟΙΣ.

Βασιλεὺς Μακεδόνων Φίλιππος Ἀθηναίων τῇ βουλῇ καὶ τῷ δήμῳ χαίρειν. Ἣν μὲν ἀπ' ἀρχῆς εἴχετε πρὸς ἡμᾶς αἵρεσιν οὐκ ἀγνοῶ, καὶ τίνα σπουδὴν ποιεῖσθε προσκαλέσασθαι βουλόμενοι Θετταλοὺς καὶ Θηβαίους, ἔτι δὲ καὶ Βοιωτούς· βέλτιον δ' αὐτῶν φρονούντων καὶ μὴ βουλομένων ἐφ' ὑμῖν ποιήσασθαι τὴν ἑαυτῶν αἵρεσιν, ἀλλὰ κατὰ τὸ συμφέρον ἱσταμένων, νῦν ἐξ ὑποστροφῆς ἀποστείλαντες ὑμεῖς πρός με πρέσβεις καὶ κήρυκα συνθηκῶν μνημονεύετε καὶ τὰς ἀνοχὰς αἰτεῖσθε, κατ' οὐδὲν ὑφ' ἡμῶν πεπλημμελημένοι. Ἐγὼ μέντοι ἀκούσας τῶν πρεσβευτῶν συγκατατίθεμαι τοῖς παρακαλουμένοις καὶ ἕτοιμός εἰμι ποιεῖσθαι τὰς ἀνοχάς, ἄν περ τοὺς οὐκ ὀρθῶς συμβουλεύοντας ὑμῖν παραπέμψαντες τῆς προσηκούσης ἀτιμίας ἀξιώσητε. Ἔρρωσθε.

ΑΠΟΚΡΙΣΙΣ ΘΗΒΑΙΟΙΣ.

Βασιλεὺς Μακεδόνων Φίλιππος Θηβαίων τῇ βουλῇ καὶ τῷ δήμῳ 167
χαίρειν. Ἐκομισάμην τὴν παρ' ὑμῶν ἐπιστολήν, δι' ἧς μοι τὴν
284 ὁμόνοιαν καὶ τὴν εἰρήνην ἀνανεοῦσθε. Πυνθάνομαι μέντοι διότι πᾶσαν ὑμῖν Ἀθηναῖοι προσφέρονται φιλοτιμίαν βουλόμενοι ὑμᾶς συγκαταίνους γενέσθαι τοῖς ὑπ' αὐτῶν παρακαλουμένοις. Πρότερον μὲν οὖν ὑμῶν κατεγίγνωσκον ἐπὶ τῷ μέλλειν πείθεσθαι ταῖς ἐκείνων ἐλπίσι καὶ ἐπακολουθεῖν αὐτῶν τῇ προαιρέσει· νῦν δ' ἐπιγνοὺς ὑμᾶς τὰ πρὸς ἡμᾶς ἐζητηκότας ἔχειν εἰρήνην μᾶλλον ἢ ταῖς ἑτέρων ἐπακολουθεῖν γνώμαις, ἥσθην καὶ μᾶλλον ὑμᾶς ἐπαινῶ κατὰ πολλά, μάλιστα δ' ἐπὶ τῷ βουλεύσασθαι περὶ τούτων ἀσφαλέστερον καὶ τὰ πρὸς ἡμᾶς ἔχειν ἐν εὐνοίᾳ· ὅπερ οὐ μικρὰν ὑμῖν οἴσειν ἐλπίζω ῥοπήν, ἐάν περ ἐπὶ ταύτης μένητε τῆς προθέσεως. Ἔρρωσθε.

Οὕτω διαθεὶς ὁ Φίλιππος τὰς πόλεις πρὸς ἀλλήλας 168
διὰ τούτων, καὶ τούτοις ἐπαρθεὶς τοῖς ψηφίσμασι καὶ ταῖς ἀποκρίσεσιν, ἧκεν ἔχων τὴν δύναμιν καὶ τὴν Ἐλάτειαν κατέλαβεν, ὡς οὐδ' ἂν εἴ τι γένοιτο ἔτι συμπνευ-

σόντων ἂν ἡμῶν καὶ τῶν Θηβαίων. Ἀλλὰ μὴν τὸν τότε συμβάντα ἐν τῇ πόλει θόρυβον ἴστε μὲν ἅπαντες, μικρὰ δ' ἀκούσατε ὅμως, αὐτὰ τἀναγκαιότατα.

169 Ἑσπέρα μὲν γὰρ ἦν, ἧκε δ' ἀγγέλλων τις ὡς τοὺς πρυτάνεις ὡς Ἐλάτεια κατείληπται. Καὶ μετὰ ταῦτα οἱ μὲν εὐθὺς ἐξαναστάντες μεταξὺ δειπνοῦντες τούς τ' ἐκ τῶν σκηνῶν τῶν κατὰ τὴν ἀγορὰν ἐξεῖργον καὶ τὰ γέῤῥα ἐνεπίμπρασαν, οἱ δὲ τοὺς στρατηγοὺς μετεπέμποντο καὶ τὸν σαλπιγκτὴν ἐκάλουν, καὶ θορύβου πλήρης ἦν ἡ πόλις. Τῇ δ' ὑστεραίᾳ ἅμα τῇ ἡμέρᾳ οἱ μὲν πρυτάνεις τὴν βουλὴν ἐκάλουν εἰς τὸ βουλευτήριον, ὑμεῖς δ' εἰς 235
τὴν ἐκκλησίαν ἐπορεύεσθε, καὶ πρὶν ἐκείνην χρηματίσαι
170 καὶ προβουλεῦσαι πᾶς ὁ δῆμος ἄνω καθῆτο. Καὶ μετὰ ταῦτα ὡς εἰσῆλθεν ἡ βουλή, καὶ ἀπήγγειλαν οἱ πρυτάνεις τὰ προσηγγελμένα ἑαυτοῖς καὶ τὸν ἥκοντα παρήγαγον κἀκεῖνος εἶπεν, ἠρώτα μὲν ὁ κῆρυξ, τίς ἀγορεύειν βούλεται; Παρῄει δ' οὐδείς. Πολλάκις δὲ τοῦ κήρυκος ἐρωτῶντος οὐδὲν μᾶλλον ἀνίστατ' οὐδείς, ἁπάντων μὲν τῶν στρατηγῶν παρόντων, ἁπάντων δὲ τῶν ῥητόρων, καλούσης δὲ τῆς πατρίδος τῇ κοινῇ φωνῇ τὸν ἐροῦνθ' ὑπὲρ σωτηρίας· ἣν γὰρ ὁ κῆρυξ κατὰ τοὺς νόμους φωνὴν ἀφίησι, ταύτην κοινὴν τῆς πατρίδος δί-
171 καιόν ἐστιν ἡγεῖσθαι. Καίτοι εἰ μὲν τοὺς σωθῆναι τὴν πόλιν βουλομένους παρελθεῖν ἔδει, πάντες ἂν ὑμεῖς καὶ οἱ ἄλλοι Ἀθηναῖοι ἀναστάντες ἐπὶ τὸ βῆμα ἐβαδίζετε· πάντες γάρ, οἶδ' ὅτι, σωθῆναι αὐτὴν ἠβούλεσθε· εἰ δὲ τοὺς πλουσιωτάτους, οἱ τριακόσιοι· εἰ δὲ τοὺς ἀμφότερα

ταῦτα, καὶ εὔνους τῇ πόλει καὶ πλουσίους, οἱ μετὰ
ταῦτα τὰς μεγάλας ἐπιδόσεις ἐπιδόντες· καὶ γὰρ
εὐνοίᾳ καὶ πλούτῳ τοῦτ' ἐποίησαν. Ἀλλ', ὡς ἔοικεν, 172
ἐκεῖνος ὁ καιρὸς καὶ ἡ ἡμέρα ἐκείνη οὐ μόνον εὔνουν
καὶ πλούσιον ἄνδρα ἐκάλει, ἀλλὰ καὶ παρηκολου-
θηκότα τοῖς πράγμασιν ἐξ ἀρχῆς, καὶ συλλελογισμέ-
νον ὀρθῶς τίνος ἕνεκα ταῦτ' ἔπραττεν ὁ Φίλιππος καὶ
τί βουλόμενος· ὁ γὰρ μὴ ταῦτ' εἰδὼς μηδ' ἐξητακὼς
πόῤῥωθεν ἐπιμελῶς, οὔτ' εἰ εὔνους ἦν οὔτ' εἰ πλούσιος,
οὐδὲν μᾶλλον ἤμελλεν ὅ τι χρὴ ποιεῖν εἴσεσθαι οὐδ'
ὑμῖν ἕξειν συμβουλεύειν.

Ἐφάνην τοίνυν οὗτος ἐν ἐκείνῃ τῇ ἡμέρᾳ ἐγώ, καὶ 173
παρελθὼν εἶπον εἰς ὑμᾶς, ἅ μου δυοῖν ἕνεκ' ἀκούσατε
προσέχοντες τὸν νοῦν· ἑνὸς μέν, ἵν' εἰδῆτε ὅτι μόνος
τῶν λεγόντων καὶ πολιτευομένων ἐγὼ τὴν τῆς εὐνοίας
τάξιν ἐν τοῖς δεινοῖς οὐκ ἔλιπον, ἀλλὰ καὶ λέγων καὶ
γράφων ἐξηταζόμην τὰ δέονθ' ὑπὲρ ὑμῶν ἐν αὐτοῖς τοῖς
φοβεροῖς· ἑτέρου δέ, ὅτι μικρὸν ἀναλώσαντες χρόνον
πολλῷ πρὸς τὰ λοιπὰ τῆς πάσης πολιτείας ἔσεσθ'
ἐμπειρότεροι.

Εἶπον τοίνυν, ὅτι τοὺς μὲν ὡς ὑπαρχόντων Θη- 174
βαίων Φιλίππῳ λίαν θορυβουμένους ἀγνοεῖν
τὰ παρόντα πράγμαθ' ἡγοῦμαι. Εὖ γὰρ οἶδ'
ὅτι, εἰ τοῦθ' οὕτως ἐτύγχανεν ἔχον, οὐκ ἂν αὐτὸν ἠκούομεν ἐν Ἐλατείᾳ ὄντα, ἀλλ' ἐπὶ τοῖς
ἡμετέροις ὁρίοις. Ὅτι μέντοι ἵν' ἕτοιμα ποιή-
σηται τὰ ἐν Θήβαις ἥκει, σαφῶς ἐπίσταμαι.

175 Ὡς δ' ἔχει, ἔφην, ταῦτα ἀκούσατέ μου. Ἐκεῖνος ὅσους ἢ πεῖσαι χρήμασι Θηβαίων ἢ ἐξα-
πατῆσαι ἐνῆν, ἅπαντας ηὐτρέπισται, τοὺς δ'
ἀπ' ἀρχῆς ἀνθεστηκότας αὐτῷ καὶ νῦν ἐναντιουμένους οὐδαμῶς πεῖσαι δύναται. Τί οὖν
βούλεται καὶ τίνος ἕνεκα τὴν Ἐλάτειαν κατεί-
ληφεν; Πλησίον δύναμιν δείξας καὶ παρα-
στήσας τὰ ὅπλα τοὺς μὲν ἑαυτοῦ φίλους ἐπᾶραι
καὶ θρασεῖς ποιῆσαι, τοὺς δ' ἐναντιουμένους
καταπλῆξαι, ἵν' ἢ συγχωρήσωσι φοβηθέντες ἃ
176 νῦν οὐκ ἐθέλουσιν, ἢ βιασθῶσιν. Εἰ μὲν τοίνυν προαιρησόμεθ' ἡμεῖς, ἔφην, ἐν τῷ παρόντι,
εἴ τι δύσκολον πέπρακται Θηβαίοις πρὸς ἡμᾶς,
τούτου μεμνῆσθαι καὶ ἀπιστεῖν αὐτοῖς ὡς ἐν τῇ
τῶν ἐχθρῶν οὖσι μερίδι, πρῶτον μὲν ἃ ἂν εὔ-
ξαιτο Φίλιππος ποιήσομεν, εἶτα φοβοῦμαι μὴ
προσδεξαμένων τῶν νῦν ἀνθεστηκότων αὐτῷ καὶ 231
μιᾷ γνώμῃ πάντων φιλιππισάντων εἰς τὴν Ἀττικὴν ἔλθωσιν ἀμφότεροι. Ἢν μέντοι πεισθῆτ'
ἐμοὶ καὶ πρὸς τῷ σκοπεῖν ἀλλὰ μὴ φιλονεικεῖν
περὶ ὧν ἂν λέγω γένησθε, οἶμαι καὶ τὰ δέοντα
λέγειν δόξειν καὶ τὸν ἐφεστηκότα κίνδυνον τῇ
πόλει διαλύσειν.

77 Τί οὖν φημὶ δεῖν; Πρῶτον μὲν τὸν παρόντα
ἐπανεῖναι φόβον, εἶτα μεταθέσθαι καὶ φοβεῖ-
σθαι πάντας ὑπὲρ Θηβαίων· πολὺ γὰρ τῶν δεινῶν εἰσὶν ἡμῶν ἐγγυτέρω, καὶ προτέροις αὐτοῖς

ἐστὶν ὁ κίνδυνος· ἔπειτ' ἐξελθόντας Ἐλευσῖνάδε τοὺς ἐν ἡλικίᾳ καὶ τοὺς ἱππέας δεῖξαι πᾶσιν ὑμᾶς αὐτοὺς ἐν τοῖς ὅπλοις ὄντας, ἵνα τοῖς
ἐν Θήβαις φρονοῦσι τὰ ὑμέτερα ἐξ ἴσου γένηται τὸ παῤῥησιάζεσθαι περὶ τῶν δικαίων,
ἰδοῦσιν ὅτι, ὥσπερ τοῖς πωλοῦσι Φιλίππῳ τὴν
πατρίδα πάρεσθ' ἡ βοηθήσουσα δύναμις ἐν
Ἐλατείᾳ, οὕτω τοῖς ὑπὲρ τῆς ἐλευθερίας ἀγωνίζεσθαι βουλομένοις ὑπάρχεθ' ὑμεῖς ἕτοιμοι
καὶ βοηθήσετ', ἐάν τις ἐπ' αὐτοὺς ἴῃ. Μετὰ 173
ταῦτα χειροτονῆσαι κελεύω δέκα πρέσβεις,
καὶ ποιῆσαι τούτους κυρίους μετὰ τῶν στρατηγῶν καὶ τοῦ πότε δεῖ βαδίζειν ἐκεῖσε καὶ τῆς
ἐξόδου. Ἐπειδὰν δ' ἔλθωσιν οἱ πρέσβεις εἰς
Θήβας, πῶς χρήσασθαι τῷ πράγματι παραι-
νῶ; Τούτῳ πάνυ μοι προσέχετε τὸν νοῦν. Μὴ
δεῖσθαι Θηβαίων μηδὲν (αἰσχρὸς γὰρ ὁ καιρός), ἀλλ' ἐπαγγέλλεσθαι βοηθήσειν, ἐὰν κελεύωσιν, ὡς ἐκείνων ὄντων ἐν τοῖς ἐσχάτοις,
ἡμῶν δὲ ἄμεινον ἢ 'κεῖνοι τὸ μέλλον προορωμέ-
νων· ἵν' ἐὰν μὲν δέξωνται ταῦτα καὶ πεισθῶσιν
ἡμῖν, καὶ ἃ βουλόμεθα ὦμεν διῳκημένοι καὶ
μετὰ προσχήματος ἀξίου τῆς πόλεως ταῦτα
πράξωμεν, ἐὰν δ' ἄρα μὴ συμβῇ κατατυχεῖν,
ἐκεῖνοι μὲν ἑαυτοῖς ἐγκαλῶσιν, ἄν τι νῦν ἐξα-
μαρτάνωσιν, ἡμῖν δὲ μηδὲν αἰσχρὸν μηδὲ ταπει-
νὸν ᾖ πεπραγμένον.

179 Ταῦτα καὶ παραπλήσια τούτοις εἰπὼν κατέβην. Συνεπαινεσάντων δὲ πάντων καὶ οὐδενὸς εἰπόντος ἐναντίον οὐδέν, οὐκ εἶπον μὲν ταῦτα, οὐκ ἔγραψα δέ, οὐδ' ἔγραψα μέν, οὐκ ἐπρέσβευσα δέ, οὐδ' ἐπρέσβευσα μέν, οὐκ ἔπεισα δὲ Θηβαίους· ἀλλ' ἀπὸ τῆς ἀρχῆς διὰ πάντων ἄχρι τῆς τελευτῆς διεξῆλθον, καὶ ἔδωκ' ἐμαυτὸν ὑμῖν ἁπλῶς εἰς τοὺς περιεστηκότας τῇ πόλει κινδύνους. Καί μοι φέρε τὸ ψήφισμα τὸ τότε γενόμενον. —

180 Καίτοι τίνα βούλει σέ, Αἰσχίνη, καὶ τίνα ἐμαυτὸν ἐκείνην τὴν ἡμέραν εἶναι θῶ; Βούλει ἐμαυτὸν μέν, ὃν ἂν σὺ λοιδορούμενος καὶ διασύρων καλέσαις Βάταλον, σὲ δὲ μηδ' ἥρω τὸν τυχόντα, ἀλλὰ τούτων τινὰ τῶν ἀπὸ τῆς σκηνῆς, Κρεσφόντην ἢ Κρέοντα ἢ ὃν ἐν Κολυττῷ ποτὲ Οἰνόμαον κακὸς κακῶς ὑποκρινόμενος ἐπέτριψας; Τότε τοίνυν κατ' ἐκεῖνον τὸν καιρὸν ὁ Παιανιεὺς ἐγὼ Βάταλος Οἰνομάου τοῦ Κοθωκίδου σου πλείονος ἄξιος ὢν ἐφάνην τῇ πατρίδι. Σὺ μέν γε οὐδὲν οὐδαμοῦ χρήσιμος ἦσθα· ἐγὼ δὲ πάντα ὅσα προσῆκε τὸν ἀγαθὸν πολίτην ἔπραττον.

Λέγε τὸ ψήφισμα.

ΨΗΦΙΣΜΑ ΔΗΜΟΣΘΕΝΟΥΣ

181 Ἐπὶ ἄρχοντος Ναυσικλέους, φυλῆς πρυτανευούσης Αἰαντίδος, Σκιροφοριῶνος ἕκτῃ ἐπὶ δέκα, Δημοσθένης Δημοσθένους Παιανιεὺς εἶπεν· Ἐπειδὴ Φίλιππος ὁ Μακεδόνων βασιλεὺς ἔν τε τῷ παρεληλυθότι χρόνῳ 285 παραβαίνων φαίνεται τὰς γεγενημένας αὐτῷ συνθήκας πρὸς τὸν Ἀθηναίων δῆμον περὶ τῆς εἰρήνης, ὑπεριδὼν τοὺς ὅρκους καὶ τὰ παρὰ πᾶσι τοῖς Ἕλλησι νομιζόμενα εἶναι δίκαια, καὶ πόλεις παραιρεῖται οὐδὲν αὐτῷ προσηκούσας, τινὰς δὲ καὶ Ἀθηναίων οὔσας δοριαλώτους πεποίηκεν οὐδὲν προαδικηθεὶς ὑπὸ τοῦ δήμου τοῦ Ἀθηναίων, ἔν τε τῷ

παρόντι ἐπὶ πολὺ προάγει τῇ ὠμότητι· καὶ γὰρ Ἑλληνίδας πόλεις 182
ἃς μὲν ἐμφρούρους ποιεῖ καὶ τὰς πολιτείας καταλύει, τινὰς δὲ καὶ
ἐξανδραποδιζόμενος κατασκάπτει, εἰς ἐνίας δὲ καὶ ἀντὶ Ἑλλήνων βαρβάρους κατοικίζει ἐπὶ τὰ ἱερὰ καὶ τοὺς τάφους ἐπάγων, οὐδὲν ἀλλότριον ποιῶν οὔτε τῆς ἑαυτοῦ πατρίδος οὔτε τοῦ τρόπου, καὶ τῇ νῦν
αὐτῷ παρούσῃ τύχῃ κατακόρως χρώμενος, ἐπιλελησμένος ἑαυτοῦ ὅτι
ἐκ μικροῦ καὶ τοῦ τυχόντος γέγονεν ἀνελπίστως μέγας. — Καὶ ἕως 183
μὲν πόλεις ἑώρα παραιρούμενον αὐτὸν βαρβάρους καὶ ἰδίας, ὑπελάμ-
βανεν ἔλαττον εἶναι ὁ δῆμος ὁ Ἀθηναίων τὸ εἰς αὐτὸν πλημμελεῖσθαι·
νῦν δὲ ὁρῶν Ἑλληνίδας πόλεις τὰς μὲν ὑβριζομένας, τὰς δὲ ἀναστά-
τους γιγνομένας, δεινὸν ἡγεῖται εἶναι καὶ ἀνάξιον τῆς τῶν προγόνων
δόξης τὸ περιορᾶν τοὺς Ἕλληνας καταδουλουμένους. Διὸ δέδοκται 184
τῇ βουλῇ καὶ τῷ δήμῳ τῷ Ἀθηναίων, εὐξαμένους καὶ θύσαντας τοῖς
θεοῖς καὶ ἥρωσι τοῖς κατέχουσι τὴν πόλιν καὶ τὴν χώραν τὴν Ἀθηναίων, καὶ ἐνθυμηθέντας τῆς τῶν προγόνων ἀρετῆς (διότι περὶ πλείο-
290 νος ἐποιοῦντο τὴν τῶν Ἑλλήνων ἐλευθερίαν διατηρεῖν ἢ τὴν ἰδίαν
πατρίδα), διακοσίας ναῦς καθέλκειν εἰς τὴν θάλατταν καὶ τὸν ναύαρχον
ἀναπλεῖν ἐντὸς Πυλῶν, καὶ τὸν στρατηγὸν καὶ τὸν ἵππαρχον τὰς πεζὰς
καὶ τὰς ἱππικὰς δυνάμεις Ἐλευσῖνάδε ἐξάγειν· πέμψαι δὲ καὶ πρέσβεις πρὸς τοὺς ἄλλους Ἕλληνας, πρῶτον δὲ πάντων πρὸς Θηβαίους
διὰ τὸ ἐγγυτάτω εἶναι τὸν Φίλιππον τῆς ἐκείνων χώρας, παρακαλεῖν 185
δὲ αὐτοὺς μηδὲν καταπλαγέντας τὸν Φίλιππον ἀντέχεσθαι τῆς ἑαυτῶν
καὶ τῆς τῶν ἄλλων Ἑλλήνων ἐλευθερίας· καὶ ὅτι ὁ Ἀθηναίων δῆμος,
οὐδὲν μνησικακῶν εἴ τι πρότερον γέγονεν ἀλλότριον ταῖς πόλεσι πρὸς
ἀλλήλας, βοηθήσει καὶ δυνάμεσι καὶ χρήμασι καὶ βέλεσι καὶ ὅπλοις,
εἰδὼς ὅτι αὐτοῖς μὲν πρὸς ἀλλήλους διαμφισβητεῖν περὶ τῆς ἡγεμονίας οὖσιν Ἕλλησι καλόν, ὑπὸ δὲ ἀλλοφύλου ἀνθρώπου ἄρχεσθαι καὶ
τῆς ἡγεμονίας ἀποστερεῖσθαι ἀνάξιον εἶναι καὶ τῆς τῶν Ἑλλήνων
δόξης καὶ τῆς τῶν προγόνων ἀρετῆς. Ἔτι δὲ οὐδὲ ἀλλότριον ἡγεῖται 186
εἶναι ὁ Ἀθηναίων δῆμος τὸν Θηβαίων δῆμον οὔτε τῇ συγγενείᾳ οὔτε
τῷ ὁμοφύλῳ. Ἀναμιμνήσκεται δὲ καὶ τὰς τῶν προγόνων τῶν ἑαυτοῦ
εἰς τοὺς Θηβαίων προγόνους εὐεργεσίας· καὶ γὰρ τοὺς Ἡρακλέους
παῖδας ἀποστερουμένους ὑπὸ Πελοποννησίων τῆς πατρῴας ἀρχῆς
κατήγαγον, τοῖς ὅπλοις κρατήσαντες τοὺς ἀντιβαίνειν πειρωμένους τοῖς
Ἡρακλέους ἐγγόνοις, καὶ τὸν Οἰδίπουν καὶ τοὺς μετ' ἐκείνου ἐκπε-
σόντας ὑπεδεξάμεθα, καὶ ἕτερα πολλὰ ἡμῖν ὑπάρχει φιλάνθρωπα καὶ
291 ἔνδοξα πρὸς Θηβαίους. Διόπερ οὐδὲ νῦν ἀποστήσεται ὁ Ἀθηναίων 187
δῆμος τῶν Θηβαίοις τε καὶ τοῖς ἄλλοις Ἕλλησι συμφερόντων. Συν-
θέσθαι δὲ πρὸς αὐτοὺς καὶ συμμαχίαν καὶ ἐπιγαμίαν ποιήσασθαι καὶ
ὅρκους δοῦναι καὶ λαβεῖν. — Πρέσβεις Δημοσθένης Δημοσθένους
Παιανιεύς, Ὑπερίδης Κλεάνδρου Σφήττιος, Μνησιθείδης Ἀντιφάνους
Φρεάῤῥιος, Δημοκράτης Σωφίλου Φλυεύς, Κάλλαισχρος Διοτίμου
Κοθωκίδης.

188 Αὕτη τῶν περὶ Θήβας ἐγίγνετο πραγμάτων ἀρχὴ καὶ
κατάστασις πρώτη, τὰ πρὸ τούτων εἰς ἔχθραν καὶ μῖσος
καὶ ἀπιστίαν τῶν πόλεων ὑπηγμένων ὑπὸ τούτων.
Τοῦτο τὸ ψήφισμα τὸν τότε τῇ πόλει περιστάντα κίνδυνον παρελθεῖν ἐποίησεν ὥσπερ νέφος. Ἦν μὲν τοίνυν
τοῦ δικαίου πολίτου τότε δεῖξαι πᾶσιν, εἴ τι τούτων
189 εἶχεν ἄμεινον, μὴ νῦν ἐπιτιμᾶν. Ὁ γὰρ σύμβουλος
καὶ ὁ συκοφάντης, οὐδὲ τῶν ἄλλων οὐδὲν ἐοικότες, ἐν
τούτῳ πλεῖστον ἀλλήλων διαφέρουσιν· ὁ μέν γε πρὸ
τῶν πραγμάτων γνώμην ἀποφαίνεται, καὶ δίδωσιν αὑτὸν
ὑπεύθυνον τοῖς πεισθεῖσι, τῇ τύχῃ, τοῖς καιροῖς, τῷ
βουλομένῳ· ὁ δὲ σιγήσας ἡνίκ' ἔδει λέγειν, ἄν τι δύσκο-
190 λον συμβῇ, τοῦτο βασκαίνει. Ἦν μὲν οὖν, ὅπερ εἶπον,
ἐκεῖνος ὁ καιρὸς τοῦ γε φροντίζοντος ἀνδρὸς τῆς πόλεως
καὶ τῶν δικαίων λόγων· ἐγὼ δὲ τοσαύτην ὑπερβολὴν
ποιοῦμαι ὥστε ἂν νῦν ἔχῃ τις δεῖξαί τι βέλτιον, ἢ ὅλως
εἴ τι ἄλλο ἐνῆν πλὴν ὧν ἐγὼ προειλόμην, ἀδικεῖν ὁμολογῶ. Εἰ γὰρ ἔσθ' ὅ τι τις νῦν ἑώρακεν, ὃ συνήνεγκεν
ἂν τότε πραχθέν, τοῦτ' ἐγώ φημι δεῖν ἐμὲ μὴ λαθεῖν.
Εἰ δὲ μήτ' ἔστι μήτε ἦν μήτ' ἂν εἰπεῖν ἔχοι μηδεὶς
μηδέπω καὶ τήμερον, τί τὸν σύμβουλον ἐχρῆν ποιεῖν; 292
Οὐ τῶν φαινομένων καὶ ἐνόντων τὰ κράτιστα ἑλέσθαι;
191 Τοῦτο τοίνυν ἐποίησα ἐγώ, τοῦ κήρυκος ἐρωτῶντος,
Αἰσχίνη, τίς ἀγορεύειν βούλεται, οὐ, τίς αἰτιᾶ-
σθαι περὶ τῶν παρεληλυθότων, οὐδὲ τίς ἐγγυ-
ᾶσθαι τὰ μέλλοντ' ἔσεσθαι. Σοῦ δ' ἀφώνου κατ'
ἐκείνους τοὺς χρόνους ἐν ταῖς ἐκκλησίαις καθημένου,

ἐγὼ παριὼν ἔλεγον. Ἐπειδὴ δ' οὐ τότε, ἀλλὰ νῦν
δεῖξον, εἰπὲ τίς ἢ λόγος, ὅντιν' ἐχρῆν εὑρεῖν, ἢ καιρὸς
συμφέρων ὑπ' ἐμοῦ παρελείφθη τῇ πόλει; Τίς δὲ
συμμαχία, τίς πρᾶξις, ἐφ' ἣν μᾶλλον ἔδει με ἀγαγεῖν
τουτουσί;

Ἀλλὰ μὴν τὸ μὲν παρεληλυθὸς ἀεὶ παρὰ πᾶσιν 192
ἀφεῖται, καὶ οὐδεὶς περὶ τούτου προτίθησιν οὐδαμοῦ
βουλήν· τὸ δὲ μέλλον ἢ τὸ παρὸν τὴν τοῦ συμβούλου
τάξιν ἀπαιτεῖ. Τότε τοίνυν τὰ μὲν ἤμελλεν, ὡς ἐδόκει,
τῶν δεινῶν, τὰ δ' ἤδη παρῆν, ἐν οἷς τὴν προαίρεσίν μου
σκόπει τῆς πολιτείας, μὴ τὰ συμβάντα συκοφάντει.
Τὸ μὲν γὰρ πέρας ὡς ἂν ὁ δαίμων βουληθῇ πάντων
γίγνεται, ἡ δὲ προαίρεσις αὐτὴ τὴν τοῦ συμβούλου
διάνοιαν δηλοῖ. Μὴ δὴ τοῦτο ὡς ἀδίκημα ἐμὸν θῇς, εἰ 193
κρατῆσαι συνέβη Φιλίππῳ τῇ μάχῃ· ἐν γὰρ τῷ θεῷ τὸ
τούτου τέλος ἦν, οὐκ ἐν ἐμοί· ἀλλ' ὡς οὐχ ἅπαντα ὅσα
ἐνῆν κατ' ἀνθρώπινον λογισμὸν εἱλόμην, καὶ δικαίως
ταῦτα καὶ ἐπιμελῶς ἔπραξα καὶ φιλοπόνως ὑπὲρ δύναμιν, ἢ ὡς οὐ καλὰ καὶ τῆς πόλεως ἄξια πράγματα
ἐνεστησάμην καὶ ἀναγκαῖα, ταῦτά μοι δεῖξον, καὶ τότ'
ἤδη κατηγόρει μου. Εἰ δ' ὁ συμβὰς σκηπτὸς [ἢ χει- 194
μὼν] μὴ μόνον ἡμῶν, ἀλλὰ καὶ πάντων τῶν ἄλλων
Ἑλλήνων μείζων γέγονε, τί χρὴ ποιεῖν; Ὥσπερ ἂν
εἴ τις ναύκληρον πάντ' ἐπὶ σωτηρίᾳ πράξαντα καὶ πᾶσι
κατασκευάσαντα τὸ πλοῖον ἀφ' ὧν ὑπελάμβανε σωθή-
σεσθαι, εἶτα χειμῶνι χρησάμενον καὶ πονησάντων αὐτῷ
τῶν σκευῶν ἢ καὶ συντριβέντων ὅλως, τῆς ναυαγίας

*αἰτιῷτο. Ἀλλ' οὔτ' ἐκυβέρνων τὴν ναῦν, φήσειεν
ἂν (ὥσπερ οὐδ' ἐστρατήγουν ἐγώ), οὔτε τῆς τύχης
κύριος ἦν, ἀλλ' ἐκείνη τῶν πάντων.*

195 *Ἀλλ' ἐκεῖνο λογίζου καὶ ὅρα· εἰ μετὰ Θηβαίων
ἡμῖν ἀγωνιζομένοις οὕτως εἵμαρτο πρᾶξαι, τί χρῆν
προσδοκᾶν, εἰ μηδὲ τούτους ἔσχομεν συμμάχους, ἀλλὰ
Φιλίππῳ προσέθεντο, ὑπὲρ οὗ τότ' ἐκεῖνος πάσας
ἀφῆκε φωνάς; καὶ εἰ νῦν τριῶν ἡμερῶν ἀπὸ τῆς Ἀττικῆς ὁδὸν τῆς μάχης γενομένης τοσοῦτος κίνδυνος καὶ
φόβος περιέστη τὴν πόλιν, τί ἂν, εἴ που τῆς χώρας
ταὐτὸ τοῦτο πάθος συνέβη, προσδοκῆσαι χρῆν; Ἆρ'
οἶσθ' ὅτι νῦν μὲν στῆναι, συνελθεῖν, ἀναπνεῦσαι,
πολλὰ μία ἡμέρα καὶ δύο καὶ τρεῖς ἔδοσαν τῶν εἰς
σωτηρίαν τῇ πόλει· τότε δ' —, οὐκ ἄξιον εἰπεῖν ἅ γε
μηδὲ πεῖραν ἔδωκε θεῶν τινὸς εὔνοια καὶ τὸ προβαλέσθαι
τὴν πόλιν ταύτην τὴν συμμαχίαν, ἧς σὺ κατηγορεῖς.*

196 *Ἔστι δὲ ταυτὶ πάντα μοι τὰ πολλὰ πρὸς ὑμᾶς,
ἄνδρες δικασταί, καὶ τοὺς περιεστηκότας ἔξωθεν καὶ
ἀκροωμένους, ἐπεὶ πρός γε τοῦτον τὸν κατάπτυστον
βραχὺς καὶ σαφὴς ἐξήρκει λόγος. Εἰ μὲν γὰρ ἦν σοι
πρόδηλα τὰ μέλλοντα, Αἰσχίνη, μόνῳ τῶν ἄλλων, ὅτ'
ἐβουλεύεθ' ἡ πόλις περὶ τούτων, τότ' ἔδει προλέγειν.
Εἰ δὲ μὴ προῄδεις, τῆς αὐτῆς ἀγνοίας ὑπεύθυνος εἶ τοῖς
ἄλλοις· ὥστε τί μᾶλλον ἐμοῦ σὺ ταῦτα κατηγορεῖς ἢ* 294
197 *ἐγὼ σοῦ; Τοσοῦτον γὰρ ἀμείνων ἐγὼ σοῦ πολίτης
γέγονα εἰς αὐτὰ ταῦθ' ἃ λέγω (καὶ οὔπω περὶ τῶν
ἄλλων διαλέγομαι), ὅσον ἐγὼ μὲν ἔδωκα ἐμαυτὸν εἰς τὰ*

πᾶσι δοκοῦντα συμφέρειν, οὐδένα κίνδυνον ὀκνήσας ἴδιον οὐδ' ὑπολογισάμενος, σὺ δὲ οὔθ' ἕτερα εἶπες βελτίω τούτων (οὐ γὰρ ἂν τούτοις ἐχρῶντο), οὔτ' εἰς ταῦτα χρήσιμον οὐδὲν σαυτὸν παρέσχες, ὅπερ δ' ἂν ὁ φαυλότατος καὶ δυσμενέστατος ἄνθρωπος τῇ πόλει, τοῦτο πεποιηκὼς ἐπὶ τοῖς συμβᾶσιν ἐξήτασαι· καὶ ἅμα Ἀρίστρατος ἐν Νάξῳ καὶ Ἀριστόλεως ἐν Θάσῳ, οἱ καθάπαξ ἐχθροὶ τῆς πόλεως, τοὺς Ἀθηναίων κρίνουσι φίλους, καὶ Ἀθήνησιν Αἰσχίνης Δημοσθένους κατηγορεῖ. Καίτοι 198
ὅτῳ τὰ τῶν Ἑλλήνων ἀτυχήματα ἐνευδοκιμεῖν ἀπέκειτο, ἀπολωλέναι μᾶλλον οὗτός ἐστι δίκαιος ἢ κατηγορεῖν ἑτέρου· καὶ ὅτῳ συνενηνόχασιν οἱ αὐτοὶ καιροὶ καὶ τοῖς τῆς πόλεως ἐχθροῖς, οὐκ ἔνι τοῦτον εὔνουν εἶναι τῇ πατρίδι. Δηλοῖς δὲ καὶ ἐξ ὧν ζῇς καὶ ποιεῖς καὶ πολιτεύῃ καὶ πάλιν οὐ πολιτεύῃ. Πράττεταί τι τῶν ὑμῖν δοκούντων συμφέρειν· ἄφωνος Αἰσχίνης. Ἀντέκρουσέ τι καὶ γέγονεν οἷον οὐκ ἔδει· πάρεστιν Αἰσχίνης. Ὥσπερ τὰ ῥήγματα καὶ τὰ σπάσματα, ὅταν τι κακὸν τὸ σῶμα λάβῃ, τότε κινεῖται.

Ἐπειδὴ δὲ πολὺς τοῖς συμβεβηκόσιν ἔγκειται, βού- 199
λομαί τι καὶ παράδοξον εἰπεῖν. Καί μου, πρὸς Διὸς καὶ θεῶν, μηδεὶς τὴν ὑπερβολὴν θαυμάσῃ, ἀλλὰ μετ' εὐνοίας ὃ λέγω θεωρησάτω. Εἰ γὰρ ἦν ἅπασι πρόδηλα τὰ μέλλοντα γενήσεσθαι, καὶ προῄδεσαν πάντες, καὶ σὺ προὔλεγες, Αἰσχίνη, καὶ διεμαρτύρου βοῶν καὶ κεκραγώς, ὃς οὐδ' ἐφθέγξω, οὐδ' οὕτως ἀποστατέον τῇ πόλει τούτων ἦν, εἴπερ ἢ δόξης ἢ προγόνων ἢ τοῦ

200 μέλλοντος αἰῶνος εἶχε λόγον. Νῦν μέν γε ἀποτυχεῖν
δοκεῖ τῶν πραγμάτων, ὃ πᾶσι κοινόν ἐστιν ἀνθρώποις,
ὅταν τῷ θεῷ ταῦτα δοκῇ· τότε δ' ἀξιοῦσα προεστάναι
τῶν ἄλλων, εἶτ' ἀποστᾶσα τούτου, Φιλίππῳ προδεδω-
κέναι πάντας ἂν ἔσχεν αἰτίαν. Εἰ γὰρ ταῦτα προεῖτο
ἀκονιτί, περὶ ὧν οὐδένα κίνδυνον ὅντιν' οὐχ ὑπέμειναν
οἱ πρόγονοι, τίς οὐχὶ κατέπτυσεν ἂν σοῦ; Μὴ γὰρ
201 τῆς πόλεώς γε, μηδ' ἐμοῦ. Τίσι δ' ὀφθαλμοῖς πρὸς
Διὸς ἑωρῶμεν ἂν τοὺς εἰς τὴν πόλιν ἀνθρώπους ἀφι-
κνουμένους, εἰ τὰ μὲν πράγματ' εἰς ὅπερ νυνὶ περιέστη,
ἡγεμὼν δὲ καὶ κύριος ᾑρέθη Φίλιππος ἁπάντων, τὸν δ'
ὑπὲρ τοῦ μὴ γενέσθαι ταῦτ' ἀγῶνα ἕτεροι χωρὶς ἡμῶν
ἦσαν πεποιημένοι· καὶ ταῦτα μηδεπώποτε τῆς πόλεως
ἐν τοῖς ἔμπροσθε χρόνοις ἀσφάλειαν ἄδοξον μᾶλλον ἢ
202 τὸν ὑπὲρ τῶν καλῶν κίνδυνον ᾑρημένης. Τίς γὰρ οὐκ
οἶδεν Ἑλλήνων, τίς δὲ βαρβάρων, ὅτι καὶ παρὰ Θηβαίων καὶ παρὰ τῶν ἔτι τούτων πρότερον ἰσχυρῶν
γενομένων Λακεδαιμονίων καὶ παρὰ τοῦ Περσῶν βασι-
λέως μετὰ πολλῆς χάριτος τοῦτ' ἂν ἀσμένως ἐδόθη τῇ
πόλει, ὅ τι βούλεται λαβούσῃ καὶ τὰ ἑαυτῆς ἐχούσῃ τὸ
κελευόμενον ποιεῖν καὶ ἐᾶν ἕτερον τῶν Ἑλλήνων προε-
203 στάναι. Ἀλλ' οὐκ ἦν ταῦθ', ὡς ἔοικε, τοῖς τότ' Ἀθηναίοις πάτρια οὐδ' ἀνεκτὰ οὐδ' ἔμφυτα, οὐδ' ἠδυνήθη
πώποτε τὴν πόλιν οὐδεὶς ἐκ παντὸς τοῦ χρόνου πεῖσαι
τοῖς ἰσχύουσι μὲν μὴ δίκαια δὲ πράττουσι προσθεμένην
ἀσφαλῶς δουλεύειν, ἀλλ' ἀγωνιζομένη περὶ πρωτείων
καὶ τιμῆς καὶ δόξης κινδυνεύουσα πάντα τὸν αἰῶνα
διατετέλεκεν.

296 *Καὶ ταῦθ' οὕτω σεμνὰ καὶ προσήκοντα τοῖς ὑμετέ-* 204
ροις ἤθεσιν ὑμεῖς ὑπολαμβάνετ' εἶναι, ὥστε καὶ τῶν προγόνων τοὺς ταῦτα πράξαντας μάλιστ' ἐπαινεῖτε· εἰκότως. Τίς γὰρ οὐκ ἂν ἀγάσαιτο τῶν ἀνδρῶν ἐκείνων τῆς ἀρετῆς, οἳ καὶ τὴν χώραν καὶ τὴν πόλιν ἐκλιπεῖν ὑπέμειναν εἰς τὰς τριήρεις ἐμβάντες ὑπὲρ τοῦ μὴ τὸ κελευόμενον ποιῆσαι, τὸν μὲν ταῦτα συμβουλεύσαντα Θεμιστοκλέα στρατηγὸν ἑλόμενοι, τὸν δ' ὑπακούειν ἀποφηνάμενον τοῖς ἐπιταττομένοις Κυρσίλον καταλιθώσαντες, οὐ μόνον αὐτόν, ἀλλὰ καὶ αἱ γυναῖκες αἱ
ὑμέτεραι τὴν γυναῖκα αὐτοῦ. Οὐ γὰρ ἐζήτουν οἱ τότ' 205
Ἀθηναῖοι οὔτε ῥήτορα οὔτε στρατηγὸν δι' ὅτου δουλεύσουσιν εὐτυχῶς, ἀλλ' οὐδὲ ζῆν ἠξίουν εἰ μὴ μετ' ἐλευθερίας ἐξέσται τοῦτο ποιεῖν. Ἡγεῖτο γὰρ αὐτῶν ἕκαστος οὐχὶ τῷ πατρὶ καὶ τῇ μητρὶ μόνον γεγενῆσθαι, ἀλλὰ καὶ τῇ πατρίδι. Διαφέρει δὲ τί; Ὅτι ὁ μὲν τοῖς γονεῦσι μόνον γεγενῆσθαι νομίζων τὸν τῆς εἱμαρμένης καὶ τὸν αὐτόματον θάνατον περιμένει, ὁ δὲ καὶ τῇ πατρίδι ὑπὲρ τοῦ μὴ ταύτην ἐπιδεῖν δουλεύουσαν ἀποθνήσκειν ἐθελήσει, καὶ φοβερωτέρας ἡγήσεται τὰς ὕβρεις καὶ τὰς ἀτιμίας, ἃς ἐν δουλευούσῃ τῇ πόλει φέρειν ἀνάγκη, τοῦ θανάτου.

Εἰ μὲν τοίνυν τοῦτ' ἐπεχείρουν λέγειν, ὡς ἄρα ἐγὼ 206
προήγαγον ὑμᾶς ἄξια τῶν προγόνων φρονεῖν, οὐκ ἔσθ' ὅστις οὐκ ἂν εἰκότως ἐπιτιμήσειέ μοι. Νῦν δ' ἐγὼ μὲν ὑμετέρας τὰς τοιαύτας προαιρέσεις ἀποφαίνω, καὶ δείκνυμι ὅτι καὶ πρὸ ἐμοῦ τοῦτ' εἶχε τὸ φρόνημα ἡ πόλις,

τῆς μέντοι διακονίας τῆς ἐφ' ἑκάστοις τῶν πεπραγμένων
207 καὶ ἐμαυτῷ μετεῖναί φημι· οὗτος δὲ τῶν ὅλων κατηγο- 297
ρῶν, κελεύων ὑμᾶς ἐμοὶ πικρῶς ἔχειν ὡς φόβων καὶ κινδύνων αἰτίῳ τῇ πόλει, τῆς μὲν εἰς τὸ παρὸν τιμῆς ἐμὲ ἀποστερῆσαι γλίχεται, τὰ δ' εἰς ἅπαντα τὸν λοιπὸν χρόνον ἐγκώμια ὑμῶν ἀφαιρεῖται. Εἰ γὰρ ὡς οὐ τὰ βέλτιστα ἐμοῦ πολιτευσαμένου τουδὶ καταψηφιεῖσθε, ἡμαρτηκέναι δόξετε, οὐ τῇ τῆς τύχης ἀγνωμοσύνῃ τὰ
208 συμβάντα παθεῖν. Ἀλλ' οὐκ ἔστιν, οὐκ ἔστιν ὅπως ἡμάρτετε, ἄνδρες Ἀθηναῖοι, τὸν ὑπὲρ τῆς ἁπάντων ἐλευθερίας καὶ σωτηρίας κίνδυνον ἀράμενοι, μὰ τοὺς Μαραθῶνι προκινδυνεύσαντας τῶν προγόνων καὶ τοὺς ἐν Πλαταιαῖς παραταξαμένους καὶ τοὺς ἐν Σαλαμῖνι ναυμαχήσαντας καὶ τοὺς ἐπ' Ἀρτεμισίῳ καὶ πολλοὺς ἑτέρους τοὺς ἐν τοῖς δημοσίοις μνήμασι κειμένους ἀγαθοὺς ἄνδρας, οὓς ἅπαντας ὁμοίως ἡ πόλις τῆς αὐτῆς ἀξιώσασα τιμῆς ἔθαψεν, Αἰσχίνη, οὐχὶ τοὺς κατορθώσαντας αὐτῶν οὐδὲ τοὺς κρατήσαντας μόνους. Δικαίως· ὃ μὲν γὰρ ἦν ἀγαθῶν ἀνδρῶν ἔργον, ἅπασι πέπρακται, τῇ τύχῃ δ', ἣν ὁ δαίμων ἔνειμεν ἑκάστοις, ταύτῃ κέχρηνται.

209 Ἔπειτ', ὦ κατάρατε καὶ γραμματοκύφων, σὺ μὲν τῆς παρὰ τουτωνὶ τιμῆς καὶ φιλανθρωπίας ἔμ' ἀποστερῆσαι βουλόμενος, τρόπαια καὶ μάχας καὶ παλαιὰ ἔργα ἔλεγες, ὧν τίνος προσεδεῖτο ὁ παρὼν ἀγὼν ουτοσί; Ἐμὲ δέ, ὦ τριταγωνιστά, τὸν περὶ τῶν πρωτείων σύμβουλον τῇ πόλει παριόντα τὸ τίνος φρόνημα λαβόντ' ἀναβαίνειν

ἐπὶ τὸ βῆμ' ἔδει; Τὸ τοῦ τούτων ἀνάξια ἐροῦντος; Δικαίως μέντἂν ἀπέθανον. Ἐπεὶ οὐδ' ὑμᾶς, ἄνδρες 210 Ἀθηναῖοι, ἀπὸ τῆς αὐτῆς διανοίας δεῖ τάς τε ἰδίας δίκας καὶ τὰς δημοσίας κρίνειν, ἀλλὰ τὰ μὲν τοῦ καθ' ἡμέραν βίου συμβόλαια ἐπὶ τῶν ἰδίων νόμων καὶ ἔργων σκοποῦντας, τὰς δὲ κοινὰς προαιρέσεις εἰς τὰ τῶν προγόνων ἀξιώματα ἀποβλέποντας· καὶ παραλαμβάνειν γε ἅμα τῇ βακτηρίᾳ καὶ τῷ συμβόλῳ τὸ φρόνημα τὸ τῆς πόλεως νομίζειν ἕκαστον ὑμῶν δεῖ, ὅταν τὰ δημόσια εἰσίητε κρινοῦντες, εἴπερ ἄξια ἐκείνων πράττειν οἴεσθε χρῆναι.

Ἀλλὰ γὰρ ἐμπεσὼν εἰς τὰ πεπραγμένα τοῖς προγό- 211 νοις ὑμῶν, ἔστιν ἃ τῶν ψηφισμάτων παρέβην καὶ τῶν πραχθέντων. Ἐπανελθεῖν οὖν ὁπόθεν ἐνταῦθ' ἐξέβην βούλομαι. Ὡς γὰρ ἀφικόμεθ' εἰς τὰς Θήβας, κατελαμβάνομεν Φιλίππου καὶ Θετταλῶν καὶ τῶν ἄλλων συμμάχων παρόντας πρέσβεις, καὶ τοὺς μὲν ἡμετέρους φίλους ἐν φόβῳ, τοὺς δ' ἐκείνου θρασεῖς. Ὅτι δ' οὐ νῦν ταῦτα λέγω τοῦ συμφέροντος ἕνεκα ἐμαυτῷ, λέγε μοι τὴν ἐπιστολὴν ἣν τότ' ἐπέμψαμεν εὐθὺς οἱ πρέσβεις. Καίτοι τοσαύτῃ γ' ὑπερβολῇ συκοφαντίας 212 οὗτος κέχρηται, ὥστ' εἰ μέν τι τῶν δεόντων ἐπράχθη, τὸν καιρόν, οὐκ ἐμέ φησιν αἴτιον γεγενῆσθαι, τῶν δ' ὡς ἑτέρως συμβάντων ἁπάντων ἐμὲ καὶ τὴν ἐμὴν τύχην αἰτίαν εἶναι· καὶ ὡς ἔοικεν, ὁ σύμβουλος καὶ ῥήτωρ ἐγὼ τῶν μὲν ἐκ λόγου καὶ τοῦ βουλεύσασθαι πραχθέντων οὐδὲν αὐτῷ συναίτιος εἶναι δοκῶ, τῶν δ' ἐν τοῖς ὅπλοις καὶ κατὰ τὴν στρατηγίαν ἀτυχηθέντων μόνος αἴτιος εἶναι. Πῶς ἂν ὠμότερος συκοφάντης γένοιτ᾽ ἢ καταρατότερος; Λέγε τὴν ἐπιστολήν.

213 ## ΕΠΙΣΤΟΛΗ.

Ἐπειδὴ τοίνυν ἐποιήσαντο τὴν ἐκκλησίαν, προσῆγον 299
ἐκείνους προτέρους διὰ τὸ τὴν τῶν συμμάχων τάξιν ἐκείνους ἔχειν. Καὶ παρελθόντες ἐδημηγόρουν, πολλὰ μὲν Φίλιππον ἐγκωμιάζοντες, πολλὰ δ᾽ ὑμῶν κατηγοροῦντες, πάνθ᾽ ὅσα πώποτ᾽ ἐναντία ἐπράξατε Θηβαίοις ἀναμιμνήσκοντες. Τὸ δ᾽ οὖν κεφαλαῖον, ἠξίουν ὧν μὲν εὖ πεπόνθεσαν ὑπὸ Φιλίππου χάριν αὐτοὺς ἀποδοῦναι, ὧν δ᾽ ὑφ᾽ ὑμῶν ἠδίκηντο δίκην λαβεῖν, ὁποτέρως βούλονται, ἢ διέντας αὐτοὺς ἐφ᾽ ὑμᾶς ἢ συνεμβαλόντας εἰς τὴν Ἀττικήν. Καὶ ἐδείκνυσαν, ὡς ᾤοντο, ἐκ μὲν ὧν αὐτοὶ συνεβούλευον τὰ ἐκ τῆς Ἀττικῆς βοσκήματα καὶ ἀνδράποδα καὶ τἆλλ᾽ ἀγαθὰ εἰς τὴν Βοιωτίαν ἥξοντα, ἐκ δὲ ὧν ἡμᾶς ἐρεῖν ἔφασαν τὰ ἐν τῇ Βοιωτίᾳ διαρπασθησόμενα ὑπὸ τοῦ πολέμου. Καὶ ἄλλα πολλὰ πρὸς
214 τούτοις, εἰς ταὐτὰ δὲ πάντα συντείνοντ᾽ ἔλεγον. Ἃ δ᾽ ἡμεῖς πρὸς ταῦτα ἀντείπομεν, τὰ μὲν καθ᾽ ἕκαστα ἐγὼ μὲν ἀντὶ παντὸς ἂν τιμησαίμην εἰπεῖν τοῦ βίου, ὑμᾶς δὲ δέδοικα, μὴ παρεληλυθότων τῶν καιρῶν, ὥσπερ ἂν εἰ κατακλυσμὸν γεγενῆσθαι τῶν πραγμάτων ἡγούμενοι, μάταιον ὄχλον τοὺς περὶ τούτων λόγους νομίσητε· ὅ τι δ᾽ οὖν ἐπείσαμεν ἡμεῖς καὶ ἡμῖν ἀπεκρίναντο ἀκούσατε. Λέγε ταυτὶ λαβών.

Μετὰ ταῦτα τοίνυν ἐκάλουν ὑμᾶς καὶ μετεπέμποντο. Ἐξῆτε, ἐβοηθεῖτε, (ἵνα τἀν μέσῳ παραλείπω) οὕτως οἰκείως ὑμᾶς ἐδέχοντο, ὥστ', ἔξω τῶν ὁπλιτῶν καὶ τῶν ἱππέων ὄντων, εἰς τὰς οἰκίας καὶ τὸ ἄστυ δέχεσθαι τὴν στρατιὰν ἐπὶ παῖδας καὶ γυναῖκας καὶ τὰ τιμιώτατα. Καίτοι τρία ἐν ἐκείνῃ τῇ ἡμέρᾳ πᾶσιν ἀνθρώποις ἔδειξαν ἐγκώμια Θηβαῖοι καθ' ὑμῶν τὰ κάλλιστα, ἓν μὲν ἀνδρίας, ἕτερον δὲ δικαιοσύνης, τρίτον δὲ σωφροσύνης. Καὶ γὰρ τὸν ἀγῶνα μᾶλλον μεθ' ὑμῶν ἢ πρὸς ὑμᾶς ἑλόμενοι ποιήσασθαι, καὶ ἀμείνους εἶναι καὶ δικαιότερ' ἀξιοῦν ὑμᾶς ἔκριναν Φιλίππου· καὶ τὰ παρ' αὐτοῖς καὶ παρὰ πᾶσι δ' ἐν πλείστῃ φυλακῇ, παῖδας καὶ γυναῖκας, ἐφ' ὑμῖν ποιήσαντες, σωφροσύνης πίστιν περὶ ὑμῶν ἔχοντες ἔδειξαν. Ἐν οἷς πᾶσιν, ἄνδρες Ἀθηναῖοι, κατά 216
γ' υμᾶς ὀρθῶς ἐφάνησαν ἐγνωκότες. Οὔτε γὰρ εἰς τὴν πόλιν εἰσελθόντος τοῦ στρατοπέδου οὐδεὶς οὐδὲν οὐδὲ ἀδίκως ὑμῖν ἐνεκάλεσεν· οὕτω σώφρονας παρέσχετε ὑμᾶς αὐτούς· δίς τε συμπαραταξάμενοι τὰς πρώτας μάχας, τήν τ' ἐπὶ τοῦ ποταμοῦ καὶ τὴν χειμερινήν, οὐκ ἀμέμπτους μόνον ὑμᾶς αὐτούς, ἀλλὰ καὶ θαυμαστοὺς ἐδείξατε τῷ κόσμῳ, ταῖς παρασκευαῖς, τῇ προθυμίᾳ. Ἐφ' οἷς παρὰ μὲν τῶν ἄλλων ὑμῖν ἐγίγνοντο ἔπαινοι, παρὰ δ' ὑμῶν θυσίαι καὶ πομπαὶ τοῖς θεοῖς. Καὶ 217
ἔγωγε ἡδέως ἂν ἐροίμην Αἰσχίνην, ὅτε ταῦτ' ἐπράττετο καὶ ζήλου καὶ χαρᾶς καὶ ἐπαίνων ἡ πόλις ἦν μεστή,

πότερον συνέθυε καὶ συνευφραίνετο τοῖς πολλοῖς, ἢ λυπούμενος καὶ στένων καὶ δυσμεναίνων τοῖς κοινοῖς ἀγαθοῖς οἴκοι καθῆτο. Εἰ μὲν γὰρ παρῆν καὶ μετὰ τῶν ἄλλων ἐξητάζετο, πῶς οὐ δεινὰ ποιεῖ, μᾶλλον δ' οὐδ' ὅσια, εἰ ὧν ὡς ἀρίστων αὐτὸς τοὺς θεοὺς ἐποιήσατο μάρτυρας, ταῦθ' ὡς οὐκ ἄριστα νῦν ὑμᾶς ἀξιοῖ ψηφίσασθαι τοὺς ὀμωμοκότας τοὺς θεούς; Εἰ δὲ μὴ παρῆν, 30
πῶς οὐκ ἀπολωλέναι πολλάκις ἐστὶ δίκαιος, εἰ ἐφ' οἷς ἔχαιρον οἱ ἄλλοι, ταῦτα ἐλυπεῖτο ὁρῶν; Λέγε δὴ καὶ ταῦτα τὰ ψηφίσματά μοι.

ΨΗΦΙΣΜΑΤΑ ΘΥΣΙΩΝ.

218 Οὐκοῦν ἡμεῖς μὲν ἐν θυσίαις ἦμεν τότε, Θηβαῖοι δ' ἐν τῷ δι' ἡμᾶς σεσῶσθαι νομίζειν, καὶ περιειστήκει τοῖς βοηθείας δεήσεσθαι δοκοῦσιν ἀφ' ὧν ἔπραττον οὗτοι, αὐτοὺς βοηθεῖν ἑτέροις ἐξ ὧν ἐπείσθητ' ἐμοί. Ἀλλὰ μὴν οἵας τότ' ἠφίει φωνὰς ὁ Φίλιππος καὶ ἐν οἵαις ἦν ταραχαῖς ἐπὶ τούτοις, ἐκ τῶν ἐπιστολῶν τῶν ἐκείνου μαθήσεσθε, ὧν εἰς Πελοπόννησον ἔπεμπεν. Καί μοι λέγε ταύτας λαβών, ἵν' εἰδῆτε ἡ ἐμὴ συνέχεια καὶ πλάνοι καὶ ταλαιπωρίαι καὶ τὰ πολλὰ ψηφίσματα, ἃ νῦν οὗτος διέσυρε, τί ἀπειργάσατο. —

219 Καίτοι πολλοὶ παρ' ὑμῖν, ἄνδρες Ἀθηναῖοι, γεγόνασι ῥήτορες ἔνδοξοι καὶ μεγάλοι πρὸ ἐμοῦ, Καλλίστρατος ἐκεῖνος, Ἀριστοφῶν, Κέφαλος, Θρασύβουλος, ἕτεροι μυρίοι· ἀλλ' ὅμως οὐδεὶς πώποτε τούτων διὰ παντὸς ἔδωκεν ἑαυτὸν εἰς οὐδὲν τῇ πόλει, ἀλλ' ὁ μὲν γράφων

οὐκ ἂν ἐπρέσβευσεν, ὁ δὲ πρεσβεύων οὐκ ἂν ἔγραψεν.
Ὑπέλειπε γὰρ αὐτῶν ἕκαστος ἑαυτῷ ἅμα μὲν ῥᾳστώνην,
ἅμα δ' εἴ τι γένοιτ', ἀναφοράν. Τί οὖν;—εἴποι τις ἄν, 220
— σὺ τοσοῦτον ὑπερῆρας τοὺς ἄλλους ῥώμῃ καὶ τόλμῃ,
ὥστε πάντα ποιεῖν αὐτός; Οὐ ταῦτα λέγω, ἀλλ'
οὕτως ἐπεπείσμην μέγαν εἶναι τὸν κατειληφότα κίνδυνον τὴν πόλιν, ὥστ' οὐκ ἐδόκει μοι χώραν οὐδὲ πρόνοιαν
οὐδεμίαν τῆς ἰδίας ἀσφαλείας διδόναι, ἀλλ' ἀγαπητὸν
302 εἶναι, εἰ μηδὲν παραλείπων τις ἃ δεῖ πράξειεν. Ἐπε- 221
πείσμην δ' ὑπὲρ ἐμαυτοῦ, τυχὸν μὲν ἀναισθητῶν, ὅμως
δ' ἐπεπείσμην, μήτε γράφοντ' ἂν ἐμοῦ γράψαι βέλτιον
μηδένα, μήτε πράττοντα πρᾶξαι, μήτε πρεσβεύοντα
πρεσβεῦσαι προθυμότερον μηδὲ δικαιότερον. Διὰ ταῦτα
ἐν πᾶσιν ἐμαυτὸν ἔταττον. — Λέγε τὰς ἐπιστολὰς τὰς
τοῦ Φιλίππου.

ΕΠΙΣΤΟΛΑΙ.

Εἰς ταῦτα κατέστησε Φίλιππον ἡ ἐμὴ πολιτεία, 222
Αἰσχίνη· ταύτην τὴν φωνὴν ἐκεῖνος ἀφῆκε δι' ἐμέ, πολλοὺς καὶ θρασεῖς τὰ πρὸ τούτων τῇ πόλει ἐπαιρόμενος λόγους. Ἀνθ' ὧν δικαίως ἐστεφανούμην ὑπὸ τουτωνί, καὶ σὺ παρὼν οὐκ ἀντέλεγες, ὁ δὲ γραψάμενος Διώνδας τὸ μέρος τῶν ψήφων οὐκ ἔλαβεν. Καί μοι λέγε ταῦτα τὰ ψηφίσματα τὰ τότε μὲν ἀποπεφευγότα, ὑπὸ τούτου δ' οὐδὲ γραφέντα.

ΨΗΦΙΣΜΑΤΑ.

Ταυτὶ τὰ ψηφίσματ', ὦ ἄνδρες Ἀθηναῖοι, τὰς αὐτὰς 223

συλλαβὰς καὶ ταὐτὰ ῥήματ' ἔχει ἅπερ πρότερον μὲν Ἀριστόνικος, νῦν δὲ Κτησιφῶν γέγραφεν ουτοσί. Καὶ ταῦτ' Αἰσχίνης οὔτ' ἐδίωξεν αὐτὸς οὔτε τῷ γραψαμένῳ συγκατηγόρησεν. Καίτοι τότε τὸν Δημομέλη τὸν ταῦτα γράφοντα καὶ τὸν Ὑπερίδην, εἴπερ ἀληθῆ μου νῦν κατηγορεῖ, μᾶλλον ἂν εἰκότως ἢ τόνδ' ἐδίωκεν.
224 Διὰ τί; Ὅτι τῷ μὲν ἔστ' ἀνενεγκεῖν ἐπ' ἐκείνους καὶ τὰς τῶν δικαστηρίων γνώσεις καὶ τὸ τοῦτον αὐτὸν ἐκείνων μὴ κατηγορηκέναι ταὐτὰ γραψάντων ἅπερ οὗτος νῦν, καὶ τὸ τοὺς νόμους μηκέτ' ἐὰν περὶ τῶν οὕτω 303
πραχθέντων κατηγορεῖν, καὶ πολλὰ ἕτερα· τότε δ' αὐτὸ τὸ πρᾶγμ' ἂν ἐκρίνετο ἐφ' αὑτοῦ, πρίν τι τούτων προ-
225 λαβεῖν. Ἀλλ' οὐκ ἦν, οἶμαι, τότε, ὃ νυνὶ ποιεῖ, ἐκ παλαιῶν χρόνων καὶ ψηφισμάτων πολλῶν ἐκλέξαντα, ἃ μήτε προῄδει μηδεὶς μήτ' ἂν ᾠήθη τήμερον ῥηθῆναι, διαβάλλειν, καὶ μετενεγκόντα τοὺς χρόνους καὶ προφάσεις ἀντὶ τῶν ἀληθῶν ψευδεῖς μεταθέντα τοῖς πε-
226 πραγμένοις, δοκεῖν τι λέγειν. Οὐκ ἦν τότε ταῦτα, ἀλλ' ἐπὶ τῆς ἀληθείας, ἐγγὺς τῶν ἔργων, ἔτι μεμνημένων ὑμῶν καὶ μόνον οὐκ ἐν ταῖς χερσὶν ἕκαστα ἐχόντων, πάντες ἐγίγνοντ' ἂν οἱ λόγοι. Διόπερ τοὺς παρ' αὐτὰ τὰ πράγματ' ἐλέγχους φυγὼν νῦν ἥκει, ῥητόρων ἀγῶνα νομίζων, ὥς γ' ἐμοὶ δοκεῖ, καὶ οὐχὶ τῶν πεπολιτευμένων ἐξέτασιν ποιήσειν ὑμᾶς, καὶ λόγου κρίσιν, οὐ τοῦ τῇ πόλει συμφέροντος ἔσεσθαι.

227 Εἶτα σοφίζεται, καὶ φησὶ προσήκειν ἧς μὲν οἴκοθεν ἥκετ' ἔχοντες δόξης περὶ ἡμῶν ἀμελῆσαι· ὥσπερ δ',

ὅταν οἰόμενοι περιεῖναι χρήματά τῳ λογίζησθε, ἂν καθαραὶ ὦσιν αἱ ψῆφοι καὶ μηδὲν περιῇ, συγχωρεῖτε, οὕτω καὶ νῦν τοῖς ἐκ τοῦ λόγου φαινομένοις προσθέσθαι. Θεάσασθε τοίνυν ὡς σαθρὸν, ὡς ἔοικεν, ἐστὶ φύσει πᾶν ὅ τι ἂν μὴ δικαίως ᾖ πεπραγμένον. Ἐκ γὰρ αὐτοῦ 228
τοῦ σοφοῦ τούτου παραδείγματος ὡμολόγηκε νῦν γ' ὑμᾶς ὑπάρχειν ἐγνωσμένους ἐμὲ μὲν λέγειν ὑπὲρ τῆς
81 πατρίδος, αὐτὸν δ' ὑπὲρ Φιλίππου· οὐ γὰρ ἂν μεταπείθειν ὑμᾶς ἐζήτει μὴ τοιαύτης οὔσης τῆς ὑπαρχούσης ὑπολήψεως περὶ ἑκατέρου. Καὶ μὴν ὅτι γε οὐ δίκαια 229
λέγει μεταθέσθαι ταύτην τὴν δόξαν ἀξιῶν, ἐγὼ διδάξω ῥᾳδίως, οὐ τιθεὶς ψήφους (οὐ γάρ ἐστιν ὁ τῶν πραγμάτων οὗτος λογισμός), ἀλλ' ἀναμιμνήσκων ἕκαστα ἐν βραχέσι, λογισταῖς ἅμα καὶ μάρτυσι τοῖς ἀκούουσιν ὑμῖν χρώμενος.

Ἡ γὰρ ἐμὴ πολιτεία, ἧς οὗτος κατηγορεῖ, ἀντὶ μὲν τοῦ Θηβαίους μετὰ Φιλίππου συνεμβαλεῖν εἰς τὴν χώραν, ὃ πάντες ᾤοντο, μεθ' ἡμῶν παραταξαμένους ἐκεῖνον κωλύειν ἐποίησεν· ἀντὶ δὲ τοῦ ἐν τῇ Ἀττικῇ 230
τὸν πόλεμον εἶναι, ἑπτακόσια στάδια ἀπὸ τῆς πόλεως ἐπὶ τοῖς Βοιωτῶν ὁρίοις γενέσθαι· ἀντὶ δὲ τοῦ τοὺς λῃστὰς ἡμᾶς φέρειν καὶ ἄγειν ἐκ τῆς Εὐβοίας, ἐν εἰρήνῃ τὴν Ἀττικὴν ἐκ θαλάττης εἶναι πάντα τὸν πόλεμον· ἀντὶ δὲ τοῦ τὸν Ἑλλήσποντον ἔχειν Φίλιππον, λαβόντα Βυζάντιον, συμπολεμεῖν τοὺς Βυζαντίους μεθ' ἡμῶν πρὸς ἐκεῖνον. Ἆρά σοι ψήφοις ὅμοιος ὁ τῶν ἔργων 231
λογισμὸς φαίνεται; Ἢ δεῖν ἀντανελεῖν ταῦτα, ἀλλ' οὐχ ὅπως τὸν ἅπαντα χρόνον μνημονευθήσεται σκέψα-

σθαι; Καὶ οὐκέτι προστίθημι, ὅτι τῆς μὲν ὠμότητος, ἣν ἐν οἷς καθάπαξ τινῶν κύριος κατέστη Φίλιππος ἔστιν ἰδεῖν, ἑτέροις πειραθῆναι συνέβη, τῆς δὲ φιλανθρωπίας, ἣν τὰ λοιπὰ τῶν πραγμάτων ἐκεῖνος περιβαλλόμενος ἐπλάττετο, ὑμεῖς καλῶς ποιοῦντες τοὺς καρποὺς κεκόμισθε. Ἀλλ' ἐῶ ταῦτα.

232 Καὶ μὴν οὐδὲ τοῦτ' εἰπεῖν ὀκνήσω, ὅτι ὁ τὸν ῥήτορα βουλόμενος δικαίως ἐξετάζειν καὶ μὴ συκοφαντεῖν οὐκ ἄν, οἷα σὺ νῦν ἔλεγες, τοιαῦτα κατηγόρει, παραδείγματα 306
πλάττων καὶ ῥήματα καὶ σχήματα μιμούμενος (πάνυ γὰρ παρὰ τοῦτο, — οὐχ ὁρᾷς; — γέγονε τὰ τῶν Ἑλλήνων, εἰ τουτὶ τὸ ῥῆμα, ἀλλὰ μὴ τουτὶ διελέχθην ἐγώ, ἢ δευρὶ
233 τὴν χεῖρα, ἀλλὰ μὴ δευρὶ παρήνεγκα), ἀλλ' ἐπ' αὐτῶν τῶν ἔργων ἂν ἐσκόπει τίνας εἶχεν ἀφορμὰς ἡ πόλις καὶ τίνας δυνάμεις, ὅτ' εἰς τὰ πράγματ' εἰσῄειν, καὶ τίνας συνήγαγον αὐτῇ μετὰ ταῦτ' ἐπιστὰς ἐγώ, καὶ πῶς εἶχε τὰ τῶν ἐναντίων. Εἶτ' εἰ μὲν ἐλάττους ἐποίησα τὰς δυνάμεις, παρ' ἐμοὶ τἀδίκημ' ἂν ἐδείκνυεν ὄν, εἰ δὲ πολλῷ μείζους, οὐκ ἂν ἐσυκοφάντει. Ἐπειδὴ δὲ σὺ τοῦτο πέφευγας, ἐγὼ ποιήσω· καὶ σκοπεῖτε εἰ δικαίως χρήσομαι τῷ λόγῳ.

234 Δύναμιν μὲν τοίνυν εἶχεν ἡ πόλις τοὺς νησιώτας, οὐχ ἅπαντας, ἀλλὰ τοὺς ἀσθενεστάτους· οὔτε γὰρ Χίος οὔτε Ῥόδος οὔτε Κέρκυρα μεθ' ἡμῶν ἦν· χρημάτων δὲ σύνταξιν εἰς πέντε καὶ τετταράκοντα τάλαντα, καὶ ταῦτ' ἦν προεξειλεγμένα· ὁπλίτην δ' ἢ ἱππέα πλὴν τῶν οἰκείων οὐδένα. Ὃ δὲ πάντων καὶ φοβερώτατον

καὶ μάλισθ' ὑπὲρ τῶν ἐχθρῶν, οὗτοι παρεσκευάκεισαν
τοὺς περιχώρους πάντας ἔχθρας ἢ φιλίας ἐγγυτέρω,
Μεγαρεῖς, Θηβαίους, Εὐβοέας. Τὰ μὲν τῆς πόλεως 235
οὕτως ὑπῆρχεν ἔχοντα, καὶ οὐδεὶς ἂν ἔχοι παρὰ ταῦτ'
εἰπεῖν ἄλλο οὐδέν· τὰ δὲ τοῦ Φιλίππου, πρὸς ὃν ἦν
ἡμῖν ὁ ἀγών, σκέψασθε πῶς. Πρῶτον μὲν ἦρχε τῶν
ἀκολουθούντων αὐτὸς αὐτοκράτωρ ὤν, ὃ τῶν εἰς τὸν
πόλεμον μέγιστόν ἐστιν ἁπάντων· εἶθ' οὗτοι τὰ ὅπλα
εἶχον ἐν ταῖς χερσὶν ἀεί· ἔπειτα χρημάτων εὐπόρει,
καὶ ἔπραττεν ἃ δόξειεν αὐτῷ, οὐ προλέγων ἐν τοῖς
ψηφίσμασιν, οὐδ' ἐν τῷ φανερῷ βουλευόμενος, οὐδ' ὑπὸ
τῶν συκοφαντούντων κρινόμενος, οὐδὲ γραφὰς φεύγων
παρανόμων, οὐδ' ὑπεύθυνος ὢν οὐδενί, ἀλλ' ἁπλῶς αὐτὸς
δεσπότης, ἡγεμών, κύριος πάντων. Ἐγὼ δ' ὁ πρὸς 236
τοῦτον ἀντιτεταγμένος, καὶ γὰρ τοῦτ' ἐξετάσαι δίκαιον,
τίνος κύριος ἦν; Οὐδενός· Αὐτὸ γὰρ τὸ δημηγορεῖν
πρῶτον, οὗ μόνου μετεῖχον ἐγώ, ἐξ ἴσου προὐτίθεθ'
ὑμεῖς τοῖς παρ' ἐκείνου μισθαρνοῦσι καὶ ἐμοί, καὶ ὅσα
οὗτοι περιγένοιντο ἐμοῦ (πολλὰ δ' ἐγίγνετο ταῦτα, δι'
ἣν ἕκαστον τύχοι πρόφασιν), ταῦθ' ὑπὲρ τῶν ἐχθρῶν
ἀπῆτε βεβουλευμένοι. Ἀλλ' ὅμως ἐκ τοιούτων ἐλατ- 237
τωμάτων ἐγὼ συμμάχους μὲν ὑμῖν ἐποίησα Εὐβοέας,
Ἀχαιούς, Κορινθίους, Θηβαίους, Μεγαρέας, Λευκα-
δίους, Κερκυραίους, ἀφ' ὧν μύριοι μὲν καὶ πεντακισχί-
λιοι ξένοι, δισχίλιοι δ' ἱππεῖς ἄνευ τῶν πολιτικῶν
δυνάμεων συνήχθησαν· χρημάτων δὲ ὅσων ἠδυνήθην
ἐγὼ πλείστην συντέλειαν ἐποίησα.

238 Εἰ δὲ λέγεις ἢ τὰ πρὸς Θηβαίους δίκαια, Αἰσχίνη, ἢ τα πρὸς Βυζαντίους ἢ τὰ πρὸς Εὐβοέας, ἢ περὶ τῶν ἴσων νυνὶ διαλέγῃ, πρῶτον μὲν ἀγνοεῖς ὅτι καὶ πρότερον τῶν ὑπὲρ τῶν Ἑλλήνων ἐκείνων ἀγωνισαμένων τριήρων, τριακοσίων οὐσῶν τῶν πασῶν, τὰς διακοσίας ἡ πόλις παρέσχετο, καὶ οὐκ ἐλαττοῦσθαι νομίζουσα οὐδὲ κρίνουσα τοὺς ταῦτα συμβουλεύσαντας οὐδὲ ἀγανακτοῦσα ἐπὶ τούτοις ἑωρᾶτο, αἰσχρὸν γάρ, ἀλλὰ τοῖς θεοῖς ἔχουσα χάριν, εἰ κοινοῦ κινδύνου τοῖς Ἕλλησι περιστάντος αὐτὴ διπλάσια τῶν ἄλλων εἰς τὴν ἁπάντων
239 σωτηρίαν παρέσχετο. Εἶτα κενάς γε χαρίζῃ χάριτας τουτοισὶ συκοφαντῶν ἐμέ. Τί γὰρ νῦν λέγεις οἷα ἐχρῆν 305
πράττειν, ἀλλ' οὐ τότ' ὢν ἐν τῇ πόλει καὶ παρὼν ταῦτ' ἔγραφες, εἴπερ ἐνεδέχετο παρὰ τοὺς παρόντας καιρούς, ἐν οἷς οὐχ ὅσα ἠβουλόμεθα, ἀλλ' ὅσα δοίη τὰ πράγματ' ἔδει δεχεσθαι· ὁ γὰρ ἀντωνούμενος καὶ ταχὺ τοὺς παρ' ἡμῶν ἀπελαυνομένους προσδεξόμενος καὶ χρήματα προσθήσων ὑπῆρχεν ἕτοιμος.

240 Ἀλλ' εἰ νῦν ἐπὶ τοῖς πεπραγμένοις κατηγορίας ἔχω, τί ἂν οἴεσθε, εἰ τότ' ἐμοῦ περὶ τούτων ἀκριβολογουμένου ἀπῆλθον αἱ πόλεις καὶ προσέθεντο Φιλίππῳ, καὶ ἅμα Εὐβοίας καὶ Θηβῶν καὶ Βυζαντίου κύριος κατέστη — τί ποιεῖν ἂν ἢ τί λέγειν τοὺς ἀσεβεῖς ἀνθρώπους
241 τουτουσί; Οὐχ ὡς ἐξεδόθησαν; Οὐχ ὡς ἀπηλάθησαν βουλόμενοι μεθ' ἡμῶν εἶναι; Εἶτα τοῦ μὲν Ἑλλησπόντου διὰ Βυζαντίων ἐγκρατὴς καθέστηκε καὶ τῆς σιτοπομπίας τῆς τῶν Ἑλλήνων κύριος, πόλεμος δ'

ὅμορος καὶ βαρὺς εἰς τὴν Ἀττικὴν διὰ Θηβαίων κεκό-
μισται, ἄπλους δ' ἡ θάλαττα ὑπὸ τῶν ἐκ τῆς Εὐβοίας
ὁρμωμένων λῃστῶν γέγονεν; Οὐκ ἂν ταῦτ' ἔλεγον
καὶ πολλά γε πρὸς τούτοις ἕτερα; Πονηρόν, ὦ ἄνδρες 212
Ἀθηναῖοι, πονηρὸν ὁ συκοφάντης ἀεὶ καὶ πανταχόθεν
βάσκανον καὶ φιλαίτιον· τοῦτο δὲ καὶ φύσει κίναδος
τἀνθρώπιόν ἐστιν, οὐδὲν ἐξ ἀρχῆς ὑγιὲς πεποιηκὸς οὐδ'
ἐλεύθερον, αὐτοτραγικὸς πίθηκος, ἀρουραῖος Οἰνόμαος,
παράσημος ῥήτωρ. Τί γὰρ ἡ σὴ δεινότης εἰς ὄνησιν
ἥκει τῇ πατρίδι; Νῦν ἡμῖν λέγεις περὶ τῶν παρεληλυθότων; 213
Ὥσπερ ἂν εἴ τις ἰατρὸς ἀσθενοῦσι μὲν τοῖς
κάμνουσιν εἰσιὼν μὴ λέγοι μηδὲ δεικνύοι δι' ὧν ἀποφεύ-
304 ξονται τὴν νόσον, ἐπειδὴ δὲ τελευτήσειέ τις αὐτῶν καὶ
τὰ νομιζόμενα αὐτῷ φέροιτο, ἀκολουθῶν ἐπὶ τὸ μνῆμα
διεξίοι, εἰ τὸ καὶ τὸ ἐποίησεν ἄνθρωπος οὑτοσί, οὐκ ἂν ἀπέθανεν. Ἐμβρόντητε, εἶτα νῦν λέγεις;

Οὐ τοίνυν οὐδὲ τὴν ἧτταν (εἰ ταύτῃ γαυριᾷς ἐφ' ᾗ 214
στένειν σε ὦ κατάρατε προσῆκεν), ἐν οὐδενὶ τῶν παρ'
ἐμοῦ γεγονυῖαν εὑρήσετε τῇ πόλει. Οὑτωσὶ δὲ λογί-
ζεσθε. Οὐδαμοῦ πώποθ', ὅποι πρεσβευτὴς ἐπέμφθην
ὑφ' ὑμῶν ἐγώ, ἡττηθεὶς ἀπῆλθον τῶν παρὰ Φιλίππου
πρέσβεων, οὐκ ἐκ Θετταλίας, οὐκ ἐξ Ἀμβρακίας, οὐκ
ἐξ Ἰλλυριῶν, οὐ παρὰ τῶν Θρᾳκῶν βασιλέων, οὐκ ἐκ
Βυζαντίου, οὐκ ἄλλοθεν οὐδαμόθεν, οὐ τὰ τελευταῖα ἐκ
Θηβῶν, ἀλλ' ἐν οἷς κρατηθεῖεν οἱ πρέσβεις αὐτοῦ τῷ
λόγῳ, ταῦτα τοῖς ὅπλοις ἐπιὼν κατεστρέφετο. Ταῦτ' 215

οὖν ἀπαιτεῖς παρ' ἐμοῦ, καὶ οὐκ αἰσχύνει τὸν αὐτὸν εἴς τε μαλακίαν σκώπτων καὶ τῆς Φιλίππου δυνάμεως ἀξιῶν ἕνα ὄντα κρείττω γενέσθαι; Καὶ ταῦτα τοῖς λόγοις; Τίνος γὰρ ἄλλου κύριος ἦν ἐγώ; Οὐ γὰρ τῆς γε ἑκάστου ψυχῆς, οὐδὲ τῆς τύχης τῶν παραταξαμένων, οὐδὲ τῆς στρατηγίας, ἧς ἔμ' ἀπαιτεῖς εὐθύνας·
246 οὕτω σκαιὸς εἶ. Ἀλλὰ μὴν ὧν γ' ἂν ὁ ῥήτωρ ὑπεύθυνος εἴη πᾶσαν ἐξέτασιν λάμβανε· οὐ παραιτοῦμαι. Τίνα οὖν ἐστὶ ταῦτα; Ἰδεῖν τὰ πράγματα ἀρχόμενα καὶ προαισθέσθαι καὶ προειπεῖν τοῖς ἄλλοις. Ταῦτα πέπρακταί μοι. Καὶ ἔτι τὰς ἑκασταχοῦ βραδυτῆτας, ὄκνους, ἀγνοίας, φιλονεικίας, ἃ πολιτικὰ ταῖς πόλεσι 308
πρόσεστιν ἁπάσαις καὶ ἀναγκαῖα ἁμαρτήματα, ταῦθ' ὡς εἰς ἐλάχιστα συστεῖλαι, καὶ τοὐναντίον εἰς ὁμόνοιαν καὶ φιλίαν καὶ τοῦ τὰ δέοντα ποιεῖν ὁρμὴν προτρέψαι. Καὶ ταῦτά μοι πάντα πεποίηται, καὶ οὐδεὶς μήποθ' εὕρῃ τὸ κατ' ἐμὲ οὐδὲν ἐλλειφθέν.

247 Εἰ τοίνυν τις ἔροιτο ὁντινοῦν, τίσι τὰ πλεῖστα Φίλιππος ὧν κατέπραξε διῳκήσατο, πάντες ἂν εἴποιεν, τῷ στρατοπέδῳ καὶ τῷ διδόναι καὶ διαφθείρειν τοὺς ἐπὶ τῶν πραγμάτων. Οὐκοῦν τῶν μὲν δυνάμεων οὔτε κύριος οὔθ' ἡγεμὼν ἦν ἐγώ, ὥστε οὐδ' ὁ λόγος τῶν κατὰ ταῦτα πραχθέντων πρὸς ἐμέ. Καὶ μὴν τῷ γε μὴ διαφθαρῆναι χρήμασι κεκράτηκα Φιλίππου· ὥσπερ γὰρ ὁ ὠνούμενος νενίκηκε τὸν λαβόντα, ἐὰν πρίηται, οὕτως ὁ μὴ λαβὼν μηδὲ διαφθαρεὶς νενίκηκε τὸν ὠνούμενον. Ὥστε ἀήττητος ἡ πόλις τὸ κατ' ἐμέ.

Ἃ μὲν τοίνυν ἐγὼ παρεσχόμην εἰς τὸ δικαίως τοιαῦτα 248
γράφειν τουτονὶ περὶ ἐμοῦ, πρὸς πολλοῖς ἑτέροις ταῦτα καὶ παραπλήσια τούτοις ἐστίν· ἃ δ' οἱ πάντες ὑμεῖς, ταῦτ' ἤδη λέξω. Μετὰ γὰρ τὴν μάχην εὐθὺς ὁ δῆμος, εἰδὼς καὶ ἑωρακὼς πάντα ὅσα ἔπραττον ἐγώ, ἐν αὐτοῖς τοῖς δεινοῖς καὶ φοβεροῖς ἐμβεβηκώς, ἡνίκ' οὐδ' ἀγνωμονῆσαί τι θαυμαστὸν ἦν τοὺς πολλοὺς πρὸς ἐμέ, πρῶτον μὲν περὶ σωτηρίας τῆς πόλεως τὰς ἐμὰς γνώμας ἐχειροτόνει, καὶ πάνθ' ὅσα τῆς φυλακῆς ἕνεκα ἐπράτ-
310 τετο, ἡ διάταξις τῶν φυλάκων, αἱ τάφροι, τὰ εἰς τὰ τείχη χρήματα, διὰ τῶν ἐμῶν ψηφισμάτων ἐγίγνετο· ἔπειθ' αἱρούμενος σιτώνην ἐκ πάντων ἐμὲ ἐχειροτόνησεν
ὁ δῆμος. Καὶ μετὰ ταῦτα συστάντων οἷς ἦν ἐπιμελὲς 249
κακῶς ἐμὲ ποιεῖν, καὶ γραφάς, εὐθύνας, εἰσαγγελίας, πάντα ταῦτ' ἐπαγόντων μοι, οὐ δι' ἑαυτῶν τό γε πρῶτον, ἀλλὰ δι' ὧν μάλισθ' ὑπελάμβανον ἀγνοήσεσθαι, (ἴστε γὰρ δήπου καὶ μέμνησθε ὅτι τοὺς πρώτους χρόνους κατὰ τὴν ἡμέραν ἑκάστην ἐκρινόμην ἐγώ, καὶ οὔτ' ἀπόνοια Σωσικλέους οὔτε συκοφαντία Φιλοκράτους οὔτε Διώνδου καὶ Μελάντου μανία οὔτ' ἄλλ' οὐδὲν ἀπείρατον ἦν τούτοις κατ' ἐμοῦ), ἐν τοίνυν τούτοις πᾶσι μάλιστα μὲν διὰ τοὺς θεούς, δεύτερον δὲ δι' ὑμᾶς καὶ τοὺς ἄλλους Ἀθηναίους ἐσωζόμην. Δικαίως· τοῦτο γὰρ καὶ ἀληθές ἐστι καὶ ὑπὲρ τῶν ὀμωμοκότων καὶ γνόντων τὰ εὔορκα δικαστῶν.

Οὐκοῦν ἐν μὲν οἷς εἰσηγγελλόμην, ὅτ' ἀπεψηφίζεσθέ 250
μου καὶ τὸ μέρος τῶν ψήφων τοῖς διώκουσιν οὐ μετε-

δίδοτε, τότ' ἐψηφίζεσθε τὰ ἄριστά με πράττειν· ἐν οἷς δὲ τὰς γραφὰς ἀπέφευγον, ἔννομα καὶ γράφειν καὶ λέγειν ἀπεδεικνύμην· ἐν οἷς δὲ τὰς εὐθύνας ἐπεσημαίνεσθε, δικαίως καὶ ἀδωροδοκήτως πάντα πεπρᾶχθαί μοι προσωμολογεῖτε. Τούτων οὖν οὕτως ἐχόντων, τί προσῆκεν ἢ τί δίκαιον ἦν τοῖς ὑπ' ἐμοῦ πεπραγμένοις θέσθαι τὸν Κτησιφῶντα ὄνομα; Οὐχ ὃ τὸν δῆμον ἑώρα τιθέμενον, οὐχ ὃ τοὺς ὀμωμοκότας δικαστάς, οὐχ ὃ τὴν ἀλήθειαν παρὰ πᾶσι βεβαιοῦσαν;

251 Ναί, φησιν, ἀλλὰ τὸ τοῦ Κεφάλου καλόν, τὸ μηδεμίαν γραφὴν φυγεῖν. Καὶ νὴ Δί' εὔδαιμόν γε. Ἀλλὰ 31
τί μᾶλλον ὁ πολλάκις μὲν φυγών, μηδεπώποτε δ' ἐξελεγχθεὶς ἀδικῶν ἐν ἐγκλήματι γίγνοιτ' ἂν διὰ τοῦτο δικαίως; Καίτοι πρός γε τοῦτον, ἄνδρες Ἀθηναῖοι, καὶ τὸ τοῦ Κεφάλου καλὸν εἰπεῖν ἔστι μοι· οὐδεμίαν γὰρ πώποτ' ἐγράψατό με οὐδ' ἐδίωξε γραφήν, ὥστε ὑπὸ σοῦ γε ὡμολόγημαι μηδὲν εἶναι τοῦ Κεφάλου χείρων πολίτης.

252 Πολλαχόθεν μὲν τοίνυν ἄν τις ἴδοι τὴν ἀγνωμοσύνην αὐτοῦ καὶ τὴν βασκανίαν, οὐχ ἥκιστα δ' ἀφ' ὧν περὶ τῆς τύχης διελέχθη. Ἐγὼ δ' ὅλως μέν, ὅστις ἄνθρωπος ὢν ἀνθρώπῳ τύχην προφέρει, ἀνόητον ἡγοῦμαι· ἣν γὰρ ὁ βέλτιστα πράττειν νομίζων καὶ ἀρίστην ἔχειν οἰόμενος, οὐκ οἶδεν εἰ μενεῖ τοιαύτη μέχρι τῆς ἑσπέρας, πῶς χρὴ περὶ ταύτης λέγειν ἢ πῶς ὀνειδίζειν ἑτέρῳ; Ἐπειδὴ δ' οὗτος πρὸς πολλοῖς ἄλλοις καὶ περὶ τούτων ὑπερηφάνως χρῆται τῷ λόγῳ, σκέψασθ', ὦ ἄνδρες

Ἀθηναῖοι, καὶ θεωρήσατε ὅσῳ καὶ ἀληθέστερον καὶ
ἀνθρωπινώτερον ἐγὼ περὶ τῆς τύχης τούτου διαλεχθή-
σομαι. Ἐγὼ τὴν μὲν τῆς πόλεως τύχην ἀγαθὴν ἡγοῦ- 253
μαι, καὶ ταῦθ᾽ ὁρῶ καὶ τὸν Δία τὸν Δωδωναῖον ἡμῖν
καὶ τὸν Ἀπόλλω τὸν Πύθιον μαντευόμενον· τὴν μέντοι
τῶν πάντων ἀνθρώπων, ἣ νῦν ἐπέχει, χαλεπὴν καὶ
δεινήν· τίς γὰρ Ἑλλήνων ἢ τίς βαρβάρων οὐ πολλῶν
κακῶν ἐν τῷ παρόντι πεπείραται; Τὸ μὲν τοίνυν 254
προελέσθαι τὰ κάλλιστα καὶ τὸ τῶν οἰηθέντων Ἑλλήνων, εἰ προεῖντο ἡμᾶς, ἐν εὐδαιμονίᾳ διάξειν, τούτων
αὐτῶν ἄμεινον πράττειν τῆς ἀγαθῆς τύχης τῆς πόλεως
εἶναι τίθημι· τὸ δὲ προσκροῦσαι καὶ μὴ πάνθ᾽ ὡς
312 ἠβουλόμεθ᾽ ἡμῖν συμβῆναι, τῆς τῶν ἄλλων ἀνθρώπων
τύχης τὸ ἐπιβάλλον ἐφ᾽ ἡμᾶς μέρος μετειληφέναι νομίζω τὴν πόλιν. Τὴν δ᾽ ἰδίαν τύχην τὴν ἐμὴν καὶ τὴν 255
ἑνὸς ἡμῶν ἑκάστου ἐν τοῖς ἰδίοις ἐξετάζειν δίκαιον εἶναι
νομίζω. Ἐγὼ μὲν οὑτωσὶ περὶ τῆς τύχης ἀξιῶ, ὀρθῶς
καὶ δικαίως, ὡς ἐμαυτῷ δοκῶ, νομίζω δὲ καὶ ὑμῖν· ὁ δὲ
τὴν ἰδίαν τύχην τὴν ἐμὴν τῆς κοινῆς τῆς πόλεως κυριωτέραν εἶναί φησι, τὴν μικρὰν καὶ φαύλην τῆς ἀγαθῆς
καὶ μεγάλης. Καὶ πῶς ἔνι τοῦτο γενέσθαι;

Καὶ μὴν εἴ γε τὴν ἐμὴν τύχην πάντως ἐξετάζειν, 256
Αἰσχίνη, προαιρεῖ, πρὸς τὴν σαυτοῦ σκόπει, κἂν εὕρῃς
τὴν ἐμὴν βελτίω τῆς σῆς, παῦσαι λοιδορούμενος αὐτῇ.
Σκόπει τοίνυν εὐθὺς ἐξ ἀρχῆς. Καί μου πρὸς Διὸς
μηδεμίαν ψυχρότητα καταγνῷ μηδείς. Ἐγὼ γὰρ οὔτ᾽
εἴ τις πενίαν προπηλακίζει, νοῦν ἔχειν ἡγοῦμαι, οὔτ᾽ εἰ

τις ἐν ἀφθόνοις τραφεὶς ἐπὶ τούτῳ σεμνύνεται· ἀλλ' ὑπὸ τῆς τουτουὶ τοῦ χαλεποῦ βλασφημίας καὶ συκοφαντίας εἰς τοιούτους λόγους ἐμπίπτειν ἀναγκάζομαι, οἷς ἐκ τῶν ἐνόντων ὡς ἂν δύνωμαι μετριώτατα χρήσομαι.

257 Ἐμοὶ μὲν τοίνυν ὑπῆρξεν, Αἰσχίνη, παιδὶ μὲν ὄντι φοιτᾶν εἰς τὰ προσήκοντα διδασκαλεῖα, καὶ ἔχειν ὅσα χρὴ τὸν μηδὲν αἰσχρὸν ποιήσοντα δι' ἔνδειαν· ἐξελθόντι δὲ ἐκ παίδων ἀκόλουθα τούτοις πράττειν, χορηγεῖν, τριηραρχεῖν, εἰσφέρειν, μηδεμιᾶς φιλοτιμίας μήτε ἰδίας μήτε δημοσίας ἀπολείπεσθαι, ἀλλὰ καὶ τῇ πόλει καὶ τοῖς φίλοις χρήσιμον εἶναι· ἐπειδὴ δὲ πρὸς τὰ κοινὰ προσελθεῖν ἔδοξέ μοι, τοιαῦτα πολιτεύματα ἑλέσθαι ὥστε καὶ ὑπὸ τῆς πατρίδος καὶ ὑπ' ἄλλων Ἑλλήνων 313
πολλῶν πολλάκις ἐστεφανῶσθαι, καὶ μηδὲ τοὺς ἐχθροὺς ὑμᾶς ὡς οὐ καλά γ' ἦν ἃ προειλόμην ἐπιχειρεῖν λέγειν.
258 Ἐγὼ μὲν δὴ τοιαύτῃ συμβεβίωκα τύχῃ, καὶ πόλλ' ἂν ἔχων ἕτερ' εἰπεῖν περὶ αὐτῆς παραλείπω, φυλαττόμενος τὸ λυπῆσαί τινα ἐν οἷς σεμνύνομαι.

Σὺ δ', ὁ σεμνὸς ἀνὴρ καὶ διαπτύων τοὺς ἄλλους, σκόπει πρὸς ταύτην ποίᾳ τινὶ κέχρησαι τύχῃ· δι' ἣν παῖς μὲν ὢν μετὰ πολλῆς ἐνδείας ἐτράφης, ἅμα τῷ πατρὶ πρὸς τῷ διδασκαλείῳ προσεδρεύων, τὸ μέλαν τρίβων καὶ τὰ βάθρα σπογγίζων καὶ τὸ παιδαγωγεῖον κορῶν, οἰκέτου τάξιν, οὐκ ἐλευθέρου παιδὸς ἔχων· ἀνὴρ
259 δὲ γενόμενος τῇ μητρὶ τελούσῃ τὰς βίβλους ἀνεγίγνωσκες καὶ τἆλλα συνεσκευωροῦ, τὴν μὲν νύκτα νεβρίζων

καὶ κρατηρίζων καὶ καθαίρων τοὺς τελουμένους καὶ
ἀπομάττων τῷ πηλῷ καὶ τοῖς πιτύροις, καὶ ἀνιστὰς ἀπὸ
τοῦ καθαρμοῦ κελεύων λέγειν ἔφυγον κακόν, εὗρον
ἄμεινον, ἐπὶ τῷ μηδένα πώποτε τηλικοῦτ' ὀλολύξαι
σεμνυνόμενος, (καὶ ἔγωγε νομίζω· μὴ γὰρ οἴεσθ' αὐτὸν
φθέγγεσθαι μὲν οὕτω μέγα, ὀλολύζειν δ' οὐχ ὑπέρ-
λαμπρον,) ἐν δὲ ταῖς ἡμέραις τοὺς καλοὺς θιάσους ἄγων 260
διὰ τῶν ὁδῶν, τοὺς ἐστεφανωμένους τῷ μαράθῳ καὶ τῇ
λεύκῃ, τοὺς ὄφεις τοὺς παρείας θλίβων καὶ ὑπὲρ τῆς
κεφαλῆς αἰωρῶν, καὶ βοῶν εὐοῖ σαβοῖ, καὶ ἐπορχού-
μενος ὕης ἄττης ἄττης ὕης, ἔξαρχος καὶ προηγε-
314 μὼν καὶ κιστοφόρος καὶ λικνοφόρος καὶ τοιαῦτα ὑπὸ
τῶν γρᾳδίων προσαγορευόμενος, μισθὸν λαμβάνων τούτων ἔνθρυπτα καὶ στρεπτοὺς καὶ νεήλατα· ἐφ' οἷς τίς
οὐκ ἂν ὡς ἀληθῶς αὑτὸν εὐδαιμονίσειε καὶ τὴν αὑτοῦ
τύχην;

Ἐπειδὴ δ' εἰς τοὺς δημότας ἐνεγράφης ὁπωσδήποτε 261
(ἐῶ γὰρ τοῦτο), ἐπειδὴ δ' οὖν ἐνεγράφης, εὐθέως τὸ
κάλλιστον ἐξελέξω τῶν ἔργων, γραμματεύειν καὶ ὑπη-
ρετεῖν τοῖς ἀρχιδίοις. Ὡς δ' ἀπηλλάγης ποτὲ καὶ
τούτου, πάνθ' ἃ τῶν ἄλλων κατηγορεῖς αὐτὸς ποιήσας,
οὐ κατῄσχυνας μὰ Δί' οὐδὲν τῶν προϋπηργμένων τῷ 262
μετὰ ταῦτα βίῳ, ἀλλὰ μισθώσας αὑτὸν τοῖς βαρυστό-
νοις ἐπικαλουμένοις ἐκείνοις ὑποκριταῖς, Σιμύλῳ καὶ
Σωκράτει, ἐτριταγωνίστεις, σῦκα καὶ βότρυς καὶ ἐλάας
συλλέγων ὥσπερ ὀπωρώνης ἐκ τῶν ἀλλοτρίων χωρίων,
πλείω λαμβάνων ἀπὸ τούτων ἢ τῶν ἀγώνων, οὓς ὑμεῖς

περὶ τῆς ψυχῆς ἠγωνίζεσθε· ἦν γὰρ ἄσπονδος καὶ
ἀκήρυκτος ὑμῖν πρὸς τοὺς θεατὰς πόλεμος, ὑφ' ὧν
πολλὰ τραύματ' εἰληφὼς εἰκότως τοὺς ἀπείρους τῶν
263 τοιούτων ὡς δειλοὺς σκώπτεις. Ἀλλὰ γὰρ παρεὶς ὧν
τὴν πενίαν αἰτιάσαιτ' ἄν τις, πρὸς αὐτὰ τὰ τοῦ τρόπου
σου βαδιοῦμαι κατηγορήματα. Τοιαύτην γὰρ εἵλου
πολιτείαν, ἐπειδή ποτε καὶ τοῦτ' ἐπῆλθέ σοι ποιῆσαι,
δι' ἣν εὐτυχούσης μὲν τῆς πατρίδος λαγὼ βίον ἔζης,
δεδιὼς καὶ τρέμων καὶ ἀεὶ πληγήσεσθαι προσδοκῶν ἐφ'
οἷς σαυτῷ συνῄδεις ἀδικοῦντι, ἐν οἷς δ' ἠτύχησαν οἱ
264 ἄλλοι, θρασὺς ὢν ὑφ' ἁπάντων ὦψαι. Καίτοι ὅστις
χιλίων πολιτῶν ἀποθανόντων ἐθάῤῥησε, τί οὗτος παθεῖν
ὑπὸ τῶν ζώντων δίκαιός ἐστιν; Πολλὰ τοίνυν ἕτερ' 315
εἰπεῖν ἔχων περὶ αὐτοῦ παραλείψω· οὐ γὰρ ὅσ' ἂν
δείξαιμι προσόντ' αἰσχρὰ τούτῳ καὶ ὀνείδη, πάντ' οἶμαι
δεῖν εὐχερῶς λέγειν, ἀλλ' ὅσα μηδὲν αἰσχρόν ἐστιν
εἰπεῖν ἐμοί.

265 Ἐξέτασον τοίνυν παρ' ἄλληλα τὰ σοὶ κἀμοὶ βεβιω-
μένα, πρᾴως καὶ μὴ πικρῶς, Αἰσχίνη· εἶτ' ἐρώτησον
τουτουσί, τὴν ποτέρου τύχην ἂν ἕλοιθ' ἕκαστος αὐτῶν.
Ἐδίδασκες γράμματα, ἐγὼ δ' ἐφοίτων. Ἐτέλεις, ἐγὼ
δ' ἐτελούμην. Ἐχόρευες, ἐγὼ δ' ἐχορήγουν. Ἐγραμ-
μάτευες, ἐγὼ δ' ἠκκλησίαζον. Ἐτριταγωνίστεις, ἐγὼ
δ' ἐθεώρουν. Ἐξέπιπτες, ἐγὼ δ' ἐσύριττον. Ὑπὲρ
τῶν ἐχθρῶν πεπολίτευσαι πάντα, ἐγὼ δ' ὑπὲρ τῆς
266 πατρίδος. Ἐῶ τἆλλα, ἀλλὰ νυνὶ τήμερον ἐγὼ μὲν
ὑπὲρ τοῦ στεφανωθῆναι δοκιμάζομαι, τὸ δὲ μηδ' ὁτιοῦν

ἀδικεῖν ἀνωμολόγημαι, σοὶ δὲ συκοφάντῃ μὲν εἶναι δοκεῖν ὑπάρχει, κινδυνεύεις δὲ εἴτε δεῖ σ' ἔτι τοῦτο ποιεῖν, εἴτ' ἤδη πεπαῦσθαι μὴ μεταλαβόντα τὸ [πέμπτον] μέρος τῶν ψήφων. Ἀγαθῇ γε (οὐχ ὁρᾷς ;) τύχῃ συμβεβιωκὼς τῆς ἐμῆς [ὡς φαύλης] κατηγορεῖς.

Φέρε δὴ καὶ τὰς τῶν λειτουργιῶν μαρτυρίας ὧν λε- 267
λειτούργηκα ὑμῖν ἀναγνῶ· παρ' ἃς παρανάγνωθι καὶ
σύ μοι τὰς ῥήσεις ἃς ἐλυμήνω,

Ἥκω λιπὼν κευθμῶνα καὶ σκότου πύλας

καὶ

Κακαγγελεῖν μὲν ἴσθι μὴ θέλοντά με,

καὶ κακὸν κακῶς σε μάλιστα μὲν οἱ θεοί, ἔπειτα οὗτοι πάντες ἀπολέσειαν πονηρὸν ὄντα καὶ πολίτην καὶ τριταγωνιστήν.

Λέγε τὰς μαρτυρίας.

ΜΑΡΤΥΡΙΑΙ.

Ἐν μὲν τοίνυν τοῖς πρὸς τὴν πόλιν τοιοῦτος· ἐν δὲ 268
316 τοῖς ἰδίοις εἰ μὴ πάντες ἴστε ὅτι κοινὸς καὶ φιλάνθρω-
πος καὶ τοῖς δεομένοις ἐπαρκῶν, σιωπῶ καὶ οὐδὲν ἂν
εἴποιμι οὐδὲ παρασχοίμην περὶ τούτων οὐδεμίαν μαρτυ-
ρίαν, οὔτ' εἴ τινας ἐκ τῶν πολεμίων ἐλυσάμην, οὔτ' εἴ
τισι θυγατέρας συνεξέδωκα, οὔτε τῶν τοιούτων οὐδέν.
Καὶ γὰρ οὕτω πως ὑπείληφα. Ἐγὼ νομίζω τὸν μὲν 269
εὖ παθόντα δεῖν μεμνῆσθαι τὸν πάντα χρόνον, τὸν δὲ
ποιήσαντα εὐθὺς ἐπιλελῆσθαι, εἰ δεῖ τὸν μὲν χρηστοῦ
τὸν δὲ μὴ μικροψύχου ποιεῖν ἔργον ἀνθρώπου. Τὸ δὲ

τὰς ἰδίας εὐεργεσίας ὑπομιμνήσκειν καὶ λέγειν μικροῦ δεῖν ὅμοιόν ἐστι τῷ ὀνειδίζειν. Οὐ δὴ ποιήσω τοιοῦτον οὐδέν, οὐδὲ προαχθήσομαι, ἀλλ' ὅπως ποθ' ὑπείλημμαι περὶ τούτων, ἀρκεῖ μοι.

270 Βούλομαι δὲ τῶν ἰδίων ἀπαλλαγεὶς ἔτι μικρὰ πρὸς
ὑμᾶς εἰπεῖν περὶ τῶν κοινῶν. Εἰ μὲν γὰρ ἔχεις,
Αἰσχίνη, τῶν ὑπὸ τοῦτον τὸν ἥλιον εἰπεῖν ἀνθρώπων
ὅστις ἀθῷος τῆς Φιλίππου πρότερον καὶ νῦν τῆς Ἀλεξάνδρου δυναστείας γέγονεν, ἢ τῶν Ἑλλήνων ἢ τῶν
βαρβάρων, ἔστω, συγχωρῶ σοι τὴν ἐμήν, εἴτε τύχην
εἴτε δυστυχίαν ὀνομάζειν βούλει, πάντων αἰτίαν γεγε-
271 νῆσθαι. Εἰ δὲ καὶ τῶν μηδεπώποτ' ἰδόντων ἐμὲ μηδὲ
φωνὴν ἀκηκοότων ἐμοῦ πολλοὶ πολλὰ καὶ δεινὰ πεπόν-
θασι, μὴ μόνον κατ' ἄνδρα ἀλλὰ καὶ πόλεις ὅλαι καὶ
ἔθνη, πόσῳ δικαιότερον καὶ ἀληθέστερον τὴν ἁπάντων,
ὡς ἔοικεν, ἀνθρώπων τύχην κοινὴν καὶ φοράν τινα
πραγμάτων χαλεπὴν καὶ οὐχ οἵαν ἔδει τούτων αἰτίαν
272 ἡγεῖσθαι. Σὺ τοίνυν ταῦτ' ἀφεὶς ἐμὲ τὸν παρὰ τουτοισὶ πεπολιτευμένον αἰτιᾷ, καὶ ταῦτ' εἰδὼς ὅτι, καὶ εἰ
μὴ τὸ ὅλον, μέρος γ' ἐπιβάλλει τῆς βλασφημίας ἅπασι, 31:
καὶ μάλιστα σοί. Εἰ μὲν γὰρ ἐγὼ κατ' ἐμαυτὸν αὐτοκράτωρ ὢν περὶ τῶν πραγμάτων ἐβουλευόμην, ἦν ἂν
273 τοῖς ἄλλοις ῥήτορσιν ὑμῖν ἐμὲ αἰτιᾶσθαι· εἰ δὲ παρῆτε
μὲν ἐν ταῖς ἐκκλησίαις ἁπάσαις ἀεί, ἐν κοινῷ δὲ τὸ
συμφέρον ἡ πόλις προὐτίθει σκοπεῖν, πᾶσι δὲ ταῦτ'
ἐδόκει τότ' ἄριστ' εἶναι, καὶ μάλιστα σοί, (οὐ γὰρ ἐπ'
εὐνοίᾳ γ' ἐμοὶ παρεχώρεις ἐλπίδων καὶ ζήλου καὶ τιμῶν,

ἃ πάντα προσῆν τοῖς τότε πραττομένοις ὑπ' ἐμοῦ, ἀλλὰ
τῆς ἀληθείας ἡττώμενος δηλονότι καὶ τῷ μηδὲν ἔχειν
εἰπεῖν βέλτιον,) πῶς οὐκ ἀδικεῖς καὶ δεινὰ ποιεῖς τούτοις
νῦν ἐγκαλῶν ὧν τότ' οὐκ εἶχες λέγειν βελτίω;

Παρὰ μὲν τοίνυν τοῖς ἄλλοις ἔγωγ' ὁρῶ πᾶσιν 274
ἀνθρώποις διωρισμένα καὶ τεταγμένα πως τὰ τοιαῦτα.
Ἀδικεῖ τις ἑκών· ὀργὴν καὶ τιμωρίαν κατὰ τούτου.
Ἐξήμαρτέ τις ἄκων· συγγνώμην ἀντὶ τῆς τιμωρίας
τούτῳ. Οὔτ' ἀδικῶν τις οὔτ' ἐξαμαρτάνων εἰς τὰ πᾶσι
δοκοῦντα συμφέρειν ἑαυτὸν δοὺς οὐ κατώρθωσε μεθ'
ἁπάντων· οὐκ ὀνειδίζειν οὐδὲ λοιδορεῖσθαι τῷ τοιούτῳ
δίκαιον, ἀλλὰ συνάχθεσθαι. Φανήσεται ταῦτα πάντα 275
οὕτως οὐ μόνον ἐν τοῖς νομίμοις, ἀλλὰ καὶ ἡ φύσις
αὐτὴ τοῖς ἀγράφοις νόμοις καὶ τοῖς ἀνθρωπίνοις ἤθεσι
διώρικεν. Αἰσχίνης τοίνυν τοσοῦτον ὑπερβέβληκεν
ἅπαντας ἀνθρώπους ὠμότητι καὶ συκοφαντίᾳ, ὥστε
καὶ ὧν αὐτὸς ὡς ἀτυχημάτων ἐμέμνητο, καὶ ταῦτ' ἐμοῦ
κατηγορεῖ.

Καὶ πρὸς τοῖς ἄλλοις, ὥσπερ αὐτὸς ἁπλῶς καὶ μετ' 276
εὐνοίας πάντας εἰρηκὼς τοὺς λόγους, φυλάττειν ἐμὲ καὶ
τηρεῖν ἐκέλευεν, ὅπως μὴ παρακρούσομαι μηδ' ἐξαπα-
τήσω, δεινὸν καὶ γόητα καὶ σοφιστὴν καὶ τὰ τοιαῦτ'
ὀνομάζων, ὡς, ἐὰν πρότερός τις εἴπῃ τὰ προσόνθ' ἑαυτῷ
περὶ ἄλλου, καὶ δὴ ταῦθ' οὕτως ἔχοντα, καὶ οὐκέτι τοὺς
ἀκούοντας σκεψομένους τίς ποτ' αὐτός ἐστιν ὁ ταῦτα
λέγων. Ἐγὼ δ' οἶδ' ὅτι γιγνώσκετε τοῦτον ἅπαντες,
καὶ πολὺ τούτῳ μᾶλλον ἢ ἐμοὶ νομίζετε ταῦτα προσεῖ-

277 ναι. Κἀκεῖνο δ' εὖ οἶδ', ὅτι τὴν ἐμὴν δεινότητα —
ἔστω γάρ· (καίτοι ἔγωγ' ὁρῶ τῆς τῶν λεγόντων δυνάμεως τοὺς ἀκούοντας τὸ πλεῖστον κυρίους· ὡς γὰρ ἂν
ὑμεῖς ἀποδέξησθε καὶ προς ἕκαστον ἔχητ' εὐνοίας, οὕτως
ὁ λέγων ἔδοξε φρονεῖν). Εἰ δ' οὖν ἐστὶ καὶ παρ' ἐμοί
τις ἐμπειρία τοιαύτη, ταύτην μὲν εὑρήσετε πάντες ἐν
τοῖς κοινοῖς ἐξεταζομένην ὑπὲρ ὑμῶν ἀεὶ καὶ οὐδαμοῦ
καθ' ὑμῶν οὐδ' ἰδίᾳ· τὴν δὲ τούτου τοὐναντίον, οὐ
μόνον τῷ λέγειν ὑπὲρ τῶν ἐχθρῶν, ἀλλὰ καὶ εἴ τις
ἐλύπησέ τι τοῦτον ἢ προσέκρουσέ που, κατὰ τούτων.
Οὐ γὰρ αὐτῇ δικαίως, οὐδ' ἐφ' ἃ συμφέρει τῇ πόλει,
278 χρῆται. Οὔτε γὰρ τὴν ὀργὴν οὔτε τὴν ἔχθραν οὔτ'
ἄλλο οὐδὲν τῶν τοιούτων τὸν καλὸν κἀγαθὸν πολίτην
δεῖ τοὺς ὑπὲρ τῶν κοινῶν εἰσεληλυθότας δικαστὰς ἀξιοῦν
αὑτῷ βεβαιοῦν, οὐδ' ὑπὲρ τούτων εἰς ὑμᾶς εἰσιέναι,
ἀλλὰ μάλιστα μὲν μὴ ἔχειν ταῦτ' ἐν τῇ φύσει, εἰ δ'
ἄρ' ἀνάγκη, πράως καὶ μετρίως διακείμεν' ἔχειν.

Ἐν τίσιν οὖν σφοδρὸν εἶναι τὸν πολιτευόμενον και
τὸν ῥήτορα δεῖ; Ἐν οἷς τῶν ὅλων τι κινδυνεύεται τῇ
πόλει, καὶ ἐν οἷς πρὸς τοὺς ἐναντίους ἐστὶ τῷ δήμῳ, ἐν
τούτοις· ταῦτα γὰρ γενναίου καὶ ἀγαθοῦ πολίτου.
279 Μηδενὸς δὲ ἀδικήματος πώποτε δημοσίου, προσθήσω δὲ 31
μηδ' ἰδίου, δίκην ἀξιώσαντα λαβεῖν παρ' ἐμοῦ μήθ'
ὑπὲρ τῆς πόλεως μήθ' ὑπὲρ αὑτοῦ, στεφάνου καὶ ἐπαίνου κατηγορίαν ἥκειν συνεσκευασμένον, καὶ τοσουτουσὶ
λόγους ἀνηλωκέναι ἰδίας ἔχθρας καὶ φθόνου καὶ μικρο-
ψυχίας ἐστὶ σημεῖον, οὐδενὸς χρηστοῦ. Τὸ δὲ δὴ και

τους πρὸς ἐμὲ αὐτὸν ἀγῶνας ἐάσαντα νῦν ἐπὶ τόνδ'
ἥκειν πᾶσαν ἔχει κακίαν. Καί μοι δοκεῖς ἐκ τούτων, 230
Αἰσχίνη, λόγων ἐπίδειξίν τινα καὶ φωνασκίας βουλόμενος ποιήσασθαι τοῦτον προελέσθαι τὸν ἀγῶνα, οὐκ
ἀδικήματος οὐδενὸς λαβεῖν τιμωρίαν. Ἔστι δ' οὐχ ὁ
λόγος τοῦ ῥήτορος, Αἰσχίνη, τίμιον, οὐδ' ὁ τόνος τῆς
φωνῆς, ἀλλὰ τὸ ταὐτὰ προαιρεῖσθαι τοῖς πολλοῖς καὶ
τὸ τοὺς αὐτοὺς μισεῖν καὶ φιλεῖν οὕσπερ ἂν ἡ πατρίς.
Ὁ γὰρ οὕτως ἔχων τὴν ψυχήν, οὗτος ἐπ' εὐνοίᾳ πάντ' 231
ἐρεῖ· ὁ δ' ἀφ' ὧν ἡ πόλις προορᾶταί τινα κίνδυνον
ἑαυτῇ, τούτους θεραπεύων οὐκ ἐπὶ τῆς αὐτῆς ὁρμεῖ τοῖς
πολλοῖς, οὔκουν οὐδὲ τῆς ἀσφαλείας τὴν αὐτὴν ἔχει
προσδοκίαν. Ἀλλ', ὁρᾷς; Ἐγώ· ταὐτὰ γὰρ συμ-
φέρονθ' εἱλόμην τουτοισί, καὶ οὐδὲν ἐξαίρετον οὐδ' ἴδιον
πεποίημαι. Ἆρ' οὖν οὐδὲ σύ; Καὶ πῶς; Ὃς εὐ- 232
θέως μετὰ τὴν μάχην πρεσβευτὴς ἐπορεύου πρὸς Φίλιππον, ὃς ἦν τῶν ἐν ἐκείνοις τοῖς χρόνοις συμφορῶν
αἴτιος τῇ πατρίδι, καὶ ταῦτ', ἀρνούμενος πάντα τὸν
ἔμπροσθε χρόνον ταύτην τὴν χρείαν, ὡς πάντες ἴσα-
σιν.

Καίτοι τίς ὁ τὴν πόλιν ἐξαπατῶν; Οὐχ ὁ μὴ
λέγων ἃ φρονεῖ; Τῷ δ' ὁ κῆρυξ καταρᾶται δικαίως;
Οὐ τῷ τοιούτῳ; Τί δὲ μεῖζον ἔχοι τις ἂν εἰπεῖν ἀδίκημα κατ' ἀνδρὸς ῥήτορος ἢ εἰ μὴ ταὐτὰ φρονεῖ καὶ
λέγει; Σὺ τοίνυν οὗτος εὑρέθης. Εἶτα σὺ φθέγγῃ 233
καὶ βλέπειν εἰς τὰ τούτων πρόσωπα τολμᾷς; Πότερ'
οὐχ ἡγεῖ γιγνώσκειν αὐτοὺς ὅστις εἶ; Ἢ τοσοῦτον

ὕπνον καὶ λήθην ἅπαντας ἔχειν ὥστ' οὐ μεμνῆσθαι
τοὺς λόγους οὓς ἐδημηγόρεις ἐν τῷ δήμῳ, καταρώμενος
καὶ διομνύμενος μηδὲν εἶναι σοὶ καὶ Φιλίππῳ πρᾶγμα,
ἀλλ' ἐμὲ τὴν αἰτίαν σοι ταύτην ἐπάγειν τῆς ἰδίας ἕνεκ'
254 ἔχθρας, οὐκ οὖσαν ἀληθῆ; Ὡς δ' ἀπηγγέλθη τάχισθ'
ἡ μάχη, οὐδὲν τούτων φροντίσας εὐθέως ὡμολόγεις καὶ
προσεποιοῦ φιλίαν καὶ ξενίαν εἶναί σοι πρὸς αὐτόν, τῇ
μισθαρνίᾳ ταῦτα μετατιθέμενος τὰ ὀνόματα· ἐκ ποίας
γὰρ ἴσης ἢ δικαίας προφάσεως Αἰσχίνῃ τῷ Γλαυκοθέας
τῆς τυμπανιστρίας ξένος ἢ φίλος ἢ γνώριμος ἦν Φίλιππος; Ἐγὼ μὲν οὐχ ὁρῶ, ἀλλ' ἐμισθώθης ἐπὶ τῷ
τὰ τουτωνὶ συμφέροντα διαφθείρειν. Ἀλλ' ὅμως οὕτω
φανερῶς αὐτὸς εἰλημμένος προδότης καὶ κατὰ σαυτοῦ
μηνυτὴς ἐπὶ τοῖς συμβᾶσι γεγονὼς ἐμοὶ λοιδορεῖ καὶ
ὀνειδίζεις ταῦτα, ὧν πάντας μᾶλλον αἰτίους εὑρήσεις.

255 Πολλὰ καὶ καλὰ καὶ μεγάλα ἡ πόλις, Αἰσχίνη, καὶ
προείλετο καὶ κατώρθωσε δι' ἐμοῦ, ὧν οὐκ ἠμνημόνησεν.
Σημεῖον δέ· χειροτονῶν γὰρ ὁ δημος τὸν ἐροῦντ' ἐπὶ
τοῖς τετελευτηκόσι παρ' αὐτὰ τὰ συμβάντα οὐ σὲ ἐχει-
ροτόνησε προβληθέντα, καίπερ εὔφωνον ὄντα, οὐδὲ Δη-
μάδην, ἄρτι πεποιηκότα τὴν εἰρήνην, οὐδ' Ἡγήμονα,
οὐδ' ἄλλον ὑμῶν οὐδένα, ἀλλ' ἐμέ. Καὶ παρελθόντος
σοῦ καὶ Πυθοκλέους ὠμῶς καὶ ἀναιδῶς, ὦ Ζεῦ καὶ θεοί, 321
καὶ κατηγορούντων ἐμοῦ ταὐτὰ ἃ καὶ σὺ νυνί, καὶ λοι-
256 δορουμένων, ἔτ' ἄμεινον ἐχειροτόνησεν ἐμέ. Το δ'
αἴτιον οὐκ ἀγνοεῖς μέν, ὅμως δὲ φράσω σοι κἀγώ.
Ἀμφότερ' ᾔδεσαν αὐτοί, τήν τ' ἐμὴν εὔνοιαν καὶ προ-

θυμίαν, μεθ' ἧς τὰ πράγματ' ἔπραττον, καὶ τὴν ὑμετέραν ἀδικίαν· ἃ γὰρ εὐθενούντων τῶν πραγμάτων ἠρνεῖ-
σθε διομνύμενοι, ταῦτ' ἐν οἷς ἔπταισεν ἡ πόλις ὡμολο-
γήσατε. Τοὺς οὖν ἐπὶ τοῖς κοινοῖς ἀτυχήμασιν ὧν
ἐφρόνουν λαβόντας ἄδειαν ἐχθροὺς μὲν πάλαι, φανεροὺς
δὲ τόθ' ἡγήσαντο αὑτοῖς γεγενῆσθαι. Εἶτα καὶ προσή- 287
κειν ὑπολαμβάνοντες τὸν ἐροῦντ' ἐπὶ τοῖς τετελευτηκόσι
καὶ τὴν ἐκείνων ἀρετὴν κοσμήσοντα μήθ' ὁμωρόφιον
μήθ' ὁμόσπονδον γεγενημένον εἶναι τοῖς πρὸς ἐκείνους
παραταξαμένοις, μηδ' ἐκεῖ μὲν κωμάζειν καὶ παιωνίζειν
ἐπὶ ταῖς τῶν Ἑλλήνων συμφοραῖς μετὰ τῶν αὐτοχείρων
τοῦ φόνου, δεῦρο δ' ἐλθόντα τιμᾶσθαι, μηδὲ τῇ φωνῇ
δακρύειν ὑποκρινόμενον τὴν ἐκείνων τύχην, ἀλλὰ τῇ
ψυχῇ συναλγεῖν. Τοῦτο δ' ἑώρων παρ' ἑαυτοῖς καὶ
παρ' ἐμοί, παρὰ δ' ὑμῖν οὔ. Διὰ ταῦτ' ἐμὲ ἐχειροτό-
νησαν καὶ οὐχ ὑμᾶς.

Καὶ οὐχ ὁ μὲν δῆμος οὕτως, οἱ δὲ τῶν τετελευτηκό- 288
των πατέρες καὶ ἀδελφοὶ οἱ ὑπὸ τοῦ δήμου τόθ' αἱρε-
θέντες ἐπὶ τὰς ταφὰς ἄλλως πως, ἀλλὰ δέον ποιεῖν
αὐτοὺς τὸ περίδειπνον ὡς παρ' οἰκειοτάτῳ τῶν τετελευ-
τηκότων, ὥσπερ τἆλλ' εἴωθε γίγνεσθαι, τοῦτ' ἐποίησαν παρ' ἐμοί. Εἰκότως· γένει μὲν γὰρ ἕκαστος
ἑκάστῳ μᾶλλον οἰκεῖος ἦν ἐμοῦ, κοινῇ δὲ πᾶσιν οὐδεὶς
ἐγγυτέρω· ᾧ γὰρ ἐκείνους σωθῆναι καὶ κατορθῶσαι
μάλιστα διέφερεν, οὗτος καὶ παθόντων, ἃ μη ποτ'
ὤφελον, τῆς ὑπὲρ ἁπάντων λύπης πλεῖστον μετεῖχεν.
Λέγε δ' αὐτῷ τουτὶ τὸ ἐπίγραμμα, ὃ δημοσίᾳ προεί- 289

λετο ἡ πόλις αὐτοῖς ἐπιγράψαι, ἵν' εἰδῇς, Αἰσχίνη, καὶ ἐν αὐτῷ τούτῳ σαυτὸν ἀγνώμονα καὶ συκοφάντην ὄντα καὶ μιαρόν. Λέγε.

ΕΠΙΓΡΑΜΜΑ.

Οἵδε πάτρας ἕνεκα σφετέρας εἰς δῆριν ἔθεντο
"Οπλα, καὶ ἀντιπάλων ὕβριν ἀπεσκέδασαν.
Μαρνάμενοι δ' ἀρετῆς καὶ δείματος οὐκ ἐσάωσαν
Ψυχάς, ἀλλ' Ἀΐδην κοινὸν ἔθεντο βράβην,
Οὕνεκεν Ἑλλήνων, ὡς μὴ ζυγὸν αὐχένι θέντες
Δουλοσύνης στυγερὰν ἀμφὶς ἔχωσιν ὕβριν.
Γαῖα δὲ πατρὶς ἔχει κόλποις τῶν πλεῖστα καμόντων
Σώματ', ἐπεὶ θνητοῖς ἐκ Διὸς ἥδε κρίσις.
Μηδὲν ἁμαρτεῖν ἐστὶ θεῶν καὶ πάντα κατορθοῦν
Ἐν βιοτῇ, μοῖραν δ' οὔ τι φυγεῖν ἔπορεν.

290 Ἀκούεις, Αἰσχίνη, καὶ ἐν αὐτῷ τούτῳ ὡς τὸ μηδὲν ἁμαρτεῖν ἐστὶ θεῶν καὶ πάντα κατορθοῦν; οὐ τῷ συμβούλῳ τὴν τοῦ κατορθοῦν τοὺς ἀγωνιζομένους ἀνέθηκε δύναμιν, ἀλλὰ τοῖς θεοῖς. Τί οὖν, ὦ κατάρατ', ἐμοὶ περὶ τούτων λοιδορεῖ, καὶ λέγεις ἃ σοὶ καὶ τοῖς σοῖς οἱ θεοὶ τρέψειαν εἰς κεφαλήν;

291 Πολλὰ τοίνυν, ὦ ἄνδρες Ἀθηναῖοι, καὶ ἄλλα κατηγορηκότος αὐτοῦ καὶ κατεψευσμένου, μάλιστ' ἐθαύμασα πάντων, ὅτι τῶν συμβεβηκότων τότε τῇ πόλει μνησθεὶς οὐχ ὡς ἂν εὔνους καὶ δίκαιος πολίτης ἔσχε τὴν γνώμην, οὐδ' ἐδάκρυσεν, οὐδ' ἔπαθε τοιοῦτον οὐδὲν τῇ ψυχῇ,

323 ἀλλ᾽ ἐπάρας τὴν φωνὴν καὶ γεγηθὼς καὶ λαρυγγίζων ᾤετο μὲν ἐμοῦ κατηγορεῖν δηλονότι, δεῖγμα δ᾽ ἐξέφερε καθ᾽ ἑαυτοῦ ὅτι τοῖς γεγενημένοις ἀνιαροῖς οὐδὲν ὁμοίως ἔσχε τοῖς ἄλλοις. Καίτοι τὸν τῶν νόμων καὶ τῆς πο- 292
λιτείας φάσκοντα φροντίζειν, ὥσπερ οὗτος νυνί, καὶ εἰ μηδὲν ἄλλο, τοῦτό γ᾽ ἔχειν δεῖ, ταὐτὰ λυπεῖσθαι καὶ ταὐτὰ χαίρειν τοῖς πολλοῖς, καὶ μὴ τῇ προαιρέσει τῶν κοινῶν ἐν τῷ τῶν ἐναντίων μέρει τετάχθαι. Ὃ σὺ νυνὶ πεποιηκὼς εἶ φανερός, ἐμὲ πάντων αἴτιον καὶ δι᾽ ἐμὲ εἰς πράγματα φάσκων ἐμπεσεῖν τὴν πόλιν, οὐκ ἀπὸ τῆς ἐμῆς πολιτείας οὐδὲ προαιρέσεως ἀρξαμένων ὑμῶν τοῖς Ἕλλησι βοηθεῖν. Ἐπεὶ ἔμοιγ᾽ εἰ τοῦτο δοθείη 293
παρ᾽ ὑμῶν, δι᾽ ἐμὲ ὑμᾶς ἠναντιῶσθαι τῇ κατὰ τῶν Ἑλλήνων ἀρχῇ πραττομένῃ, μείζων ἂν δοθείη δωρεὰ συμπασῶν ὧν τοῖς ἄλλοις δεδώκατε. Ἀλλ᾽ οὔτ᾽ ἂν ἐγὼ ταῦτα φήσαιμι, ἀδικοίην γὰρ ἂν ὑμᾶς, οὔτ᾽ ἂν ὑμεῖς εὖ οἶδ᾽ ὅτι συγχωρήσαιτε· οὗτός τ᾽ εἰ δίκαια ἐποίει, οὐκ ἂν ἕνεκα τῆς πρὸς ἐμὲ ἔχθρας τὰ μέγιστα τῶν ὑμετέρων καλῶν ἔβλαπτε καὶ διέβαλλεν.

Ἀλλὰ τί ταῦτ᾽ ἐπιτιμῶ, πολλῷ σχετλιώτερα ἄλλα 294
κατηγορηκότος αὐτοῦ καὶ κατεψευσμένου; Ὃς γὰρ ἐμοῦ φιλιππισμόν, ὦ γῆ καὶ θεοί, κατηγορεῖ, τί οὗτος οὐκ ἂν εἴποι; Καίτοι, νὴ τὸν Ἡρακλέα καὶ πάντας θεούς, εἴ γ᾽ ἐπ᾽ ἀληθείας δέοι σκοπεῖσθαι, τὸ καταψεύδεσθαι καὶ δι᾽ ἔχθραν τι λέγειν ἀνελόντας ἐκ μέσου, τίνες ὡς ἀληθῶς εἰσὶν οἷς ἂν εἰκότως καὶ δικαίως τὴν τῶν γεγενημένων αἰτίαν ἐπὶ τὴν κεφαλὴν ἀναθεῖεν

ἅπαντες, τοὺς ὁμοίους τούτῳ παρ' ἑκάστῃ τῶν πόλεων
295 εὕροι τις ἄν, οὐ τοὺς ἐμοί· οἳ ὅτ' ἦν ἀσθενῆ τὰ Φιλίππου πράγματα καὶ κομιδῇ μικρά, πολλάκις προλεγόν-
των ἡμῶν καὶ παρακαλούντων καὶ διδασκόντων τὰ
βέλτιστα, τῆς ἰδίας ἕνεκ' αἰσχροκερδείας τὰ κοινῇ
συμφέροντα προΐεντο, τοὺς ὑπάρχοντας ἕκαστοι πολίτας
ἐξαπατῶντες καὶ διαφθείροντες, ἕως δούλους ἐποίησαν,
Θετταλοὺς Δάοχος, Κινέας, Θρασύλαος· Ἀρκάδας
Κερκιδᾶς, Ἱερώνυμος, Εὐκαμπίδας· Ἀργείους Μύρτις,
Τελέδαμος, Μνασέας· Ἠλείους Εὐξίθεος, Κλεότιμος,
Ἀρίσταιχμος· Μεσσηνίους οἱ Φιλιάδου τοῦ θεοῖς
ἐχθροῦ παῖδες, Νέων καὶ Θρασύλοχος· Σικυωνίους
Ἀρίστρατος, Ἐπιχάρης· Κορινθίους Δείναρχος, Δη-
μάρατος· Μεγαρέας Πτοιόδωρος, Ἕλιξος, Περίλαος·
Θηβαίους Τιμόλας, Θεογείτων, Ἀνεμοίτας· Εὐβοέας
296 Ἵππαρχος, Κλείταρχος, Σωσίστρατος· ἐπιλείψει με
λέγοντα ἡ ἡμέρα τὰ τῶν προδοτῶν ὀνόματα. Οὗτοι
πάντες εἰσίν, ἄνδρες Ἀθηναῖοι, τῶν αὐτῶν βουλευμάτων
ἐν ταῖς αὑτῶν πατρίσιν ὧνπερ οὗτοι παρ' ὑμῖν, ἄνθρω-
ποι μιαροὶ καὶ κόλακες καὶ ἀλάστορες, ἠκρωτηριασμένοι
τὰς ἑαυτῶν ἕκαστοι πατρίδας, τὴν ἐλευθερίαν προπε-
πωκότες πρότερον μὲν Φιλίππῳ, νῦν δὲ Ἀλεξάνδρῳ, τῇ
γαστρὶ μετροῦντες καὶ τοῖς αἰσχίστοις τὴν εὐδαιμονίαν,
τὴν δ' ἐλευθερίαν καὶ τὸ μηδένα ἔχειν δεσπότην αὑτῶν,
ἃ τοῖς προτέροις Ἕλλησιν ὅροι τῶν ἀγαθῶν ἦσαν καὶ
κανόνες, ἀνατετραφότες.

297 Ταύτης τοίνυν τῆς οὕτως αἰσχρᾶς καὶ περιβοήτου

295 *συστάσεως καὶ κακίας, μᾶλλον δ', ὦ ἄνδρες Ἀθηναῖοι, προδοσίας, εἰ δεῖ μὴ ληρεῖν, τῆς τῶν Ἑλλήνων ἐλευθερίας, ἥ τε πόλις παρὰ πᾶσιν ἀνθρώποις ἀναίτιος γέγονεν ἐκ τῶν ἐμῶν πολιτευμάτων καὶ ἐγὼ παρ' ὑμῖν. Εἶτά μ' ἐρωτᾷς ἀντὶ ποίας ἀρετῆς ἀξιῶ τιμᾶσθαι; Ἐγὼ δή σοι λέγω, ὅτι τῶν πολιτευομένων παρὰ τοῖς Ἕλλησι διαφθαρέντων ἁπάντων, ἀρξαμένων ἀπὸ σοῦ, πρότερον μὲν ὑπὸ Φιλίππου, νῦν δ' ὑπ' Ἀλεξάνδρου,*
ἐμὲ οὔτε καιρὸς οὔτε φιλανθρωπία λόγων οὔτ' ἐπαγγε- 298
λιῶν μέγεθος οὔτ' ἐλπὶς οὔτε φόβος οὔτ' ἄλλο οὐδὲν ἐπῆρεν οὐδὲ προηγάγετο ὧν ἔκρινα δικαίων καὶ συμφερόντων τῇ πατρίδι οὐδὲν προδοῦναι· οὐδ' ὅσα συμβεβούλευκα πώποτε τουτοισί, ὁμοίως ὑμῖν, ὥσπερ ἐν τρυτάνῃ ῥέπων ἐπὶ τὸ λῆμμα συμβεβούλευκα, ἀλλ' ἀπ' ὀρθῆς καὶ δικαίας καὶ ἀδιαφθόρου τῆς ψυχῆς τὰ πάντα μοι πέπρακται, καὶ μεγίστων δὴ πραγμάτων τῶν κατ' ἐμαυτὸν ἀνθρώπων προστὰς πάντα ταῦτα ὑγιῶς καὶ δικαίως πεπολίτευμαι. Διὰ ταῦτ' ἀξιῶ τιμᾶσθαι.

Τὸν δὲ τειχισμὸν τοῦτον, ὃν σύ μου διέσυρες, καὶ τὴν 299
ταφρείαν ἄξια μὲν χάριτος καὶ ἐπαίνου κρίνω (πῶς γὰρ οὔ;) πόρρω μέντοι που τῶν ἐμαυτῷ πεπολιτευμένων τίθεμαι. Οὐ λίθοις ἐτείχισα τὴν πόλιν οὐδὲ πλίνθοις ἐγώ, οὐδ' ἐπὶ τούτοις μέγιστον τῶν ἐμαυτοῦ φρονῶ· ἀλλ' ἐὰν τὸν ἐμὸν τειχισμὸν βούλῃ δικαίως σκοπεῖν, εὑρήσεις ὅπλα καὶ πόλεις καὶ τόπους καὶ λιμένας καὶ ναῦς καὶ [πολλοὺς] ἵππους καὶ τοὺς ὑπὲρ τούτων ἀμυνουμένους. Ταῦτα προὐβαλόμην ἐγὼ πρὸ τῆς Ἀττικῆς, 300

ὅσον ἦν ἀνθρωπίνῳ λογισμῷ δυνατόν, καὶ τούτοις ἐτείχισα τὴν χώραν, οὐχὶ τὸν κύκλον τοῦ Πειραιῶς οὐδὲ 324
τοῦ ἄστεος. Οὐδέ γ' ἡττήθην ἐγὼ τοῖς λογισμοῖς Φιλίππου, πολλοῦ γε καὶ δεῖ, οὐδὲ ταῖς παρασκευαῖς, ἀλλ' οἱ τῶν συμμάχων στρατηγοὶ καὶ αἱ δυνάμεις τῇ τύχῃ. Τίνες αἱ τούτων ἀποδείξεις; Ἐναργεῖς καὶ φανεραί. Σκοπεῖτε δέ.

301 Τί χρῆν τὸν εὔνουν πολίτην ποιεῖν, τί τὸν μετὰ
πάσης προνοίας καὶ προθυμίας καὶ δικαιοσύνης ὑπὲρ τῆς πατρίδος πολιτευόμενον; Οὐκ ἐκ μὲν θαλάττης τὴν Εὔβοιαν προβαλέσθαι πρὸ τῆς Ἀττικῆς, ἐκ δὲ τῆς μεσογείας τὴν Βοιωτίαν, ἐκ δὲ τῶν πρὸς Πελοπόννησον τόπων τοὺς ὁμόρους ταύτῃ; Οὐ τὴν σιτοπομπίαν, ὅπως παρὰ πᾶσαι φιλίαν ἄχρι τοῦ Πειραιῶς κομισθήσεται,
302 προϊδέσθαι; Καὶ τὰ μὲν σῶσαι τῶν ὑπαρχόντων
ἐκπέμποντα βοηθείας καὶ λέγοντα καὶ γράφοντα τοιαῦτα, τὴν Προκόννησον, τὴν Χερρόνησον, τὴν Τένεδον, τὰ δ' ὅπως οἰκεῖα καὶ σύμμαχ' ὑπάρξει πρᾶξαι, τὸ Βυζάντιον, τὴν Ἄβυδον, τὴν Εὔβοιαν; Καὶ τῶν μὲν τοῖς ἐχθροῖς ὑπαρχουσῶν δυνάμεων τὰς μεγίστας ἀφελεῖν, ὧν δ' ἐνέλειπε τῇ πόλει, ταῦτα προσθεῖναι;

303 Ταῦτα τοίνυν ἅπαντα πέπρακται τοῖς ἐμοῖς ψη-
φίσμασι καὶ τοῖς ἐμοῖς πολιτεύμασιν, ἃ καὶ βεβουλευμένα, ὦ ἄνδρες Ἀθηναῖοι, ἐὰν ἄνευ φθόνου τις βούληται σκοπεῖν, ὀρθῶς εὑρήσει καὶ πεπραγμένα πάσῃ δικαιοσύνῃ, καὶ τὸν ἑκάστου καιρὸν οὐ παρεθέντα οὐδ' ἀγνοηθέντα οὐδὲ προεθέντα ὑπ' ἐμοῦ, καὶ ὅσα εἰς ἑνὸς ἀνδρὸς

δύναμιν καὶ λογισμὸν ἧκεν, οὐδὲν ἐλλειφθέν. Εἰ δὲ ἡ δαίμονός τινος ἢ τύχης ἰσχὺς ἢ στρατηγῶν φαυλότης ἢ τῶν προδιδόντων τὰς πόλεις ὑμῶν κακία ἢ πάντα
327 ταῦτα ἅμα ἐλυμαίνετο τοῖς ὅλοις, ἕως ἀνέτρεψε, τί Δημοσθένης ἀδικεῖ; Εἰ δ' οἷος ἐγὼ παρ' ὑμῖν κατὰ 304
τὴν ἐμαυτοῦ τάξιν, εἷς ἐν ἑκάστῃ τῶν Ἑλληνίδων πόλεων ἀνὴρ ἐγένετο, μᾶλλον δ' εἰ ἕνα ἄνδρα μόνον Θετταλία καὶ ἕνα ἄνδρα Ἀρκαδία ταὐτὰ φρονοῦντα ἔσχεν ἐμοί, οὐδεὶς οὔτε τῶν ἔξω Πυλῶν Ἑλλήνων οὔτε τῶν εἴσω τοῖς παροῦσι κακοῖς ἐκέχρητ' ἄν, ἀλλὰ πάντες 305
ἂν ὄντες ἐλεύθεροι καὶ αὐτόνομοι μετὰ πάσης ἀδείας ἀσφαλῶς ἐν εὐδαιμονίᾳ τὰς ἑαυτῶν ᾤκουν πατρίδας, τῶν τοσούτων καὶ τοιούτων ἀγαθῶν ὑμῖν καὶ τοῖς ἄλλοις Ἀθηναίοις ἔχοντες χάριν δι' ἐμέ. Ἵνα δ' εἰδῆτε ὅτι πολλῷ τοῖς λόγοις ἐλάττοσι χρῶμαι τῶν ἔργων, εὐλαβούμενος τὸν φθόνον, λέγε μοι ταυτὶ καὶ ἀνάγνωθι λαβὼν [τὸν ἀριθμὸν τῶν βοηθειῶν κατὰ τὰ ἐμὰ ψηφίσματα].

ΑΡΙΘΜΟΣ ΒΟΗΘΕΙΩΝ.

Ταῦτα καὶ τοιαῦτα πράττειν, Αἰσχίνη, τὸν καλὸν 306
κἀγαθὸν πολίτην δεῖ, ὧν κατορθουμένων μὲν [ὦ γῆ καὶ θεοὶ] μεγίστοις ἀναμφισβητήτως ὑπῆρχεν εἶναι καὶ το δικαίως προσῆν, ὡς ἑτέρως δὲ συμβάντων τὸ γοῦν εὐδοκιμεῖν περίεστι καὶ τὸ μηδένα μέμφεσθαι τὴν πόλιν μηδὲ τὴν προαίρεσιν αὐτῆς, ἀλλὰ τὴν τύχην κακίζειν
τὴν οὕτω τὰ πράγματα κρίνασαν· οὐ μὰ Δί' οὐκ 307

ἀποστάντα τῶν συμφερόντων τῇ πόλει, μισθώσαντα δ' αὑτὸν τοῖς ἐναντίοις, τοὺς ὑπὲρ τῶν ἐχθρῶν καιροὺς ἀντὶ τῶν τῆς πατρίδος θεραπεύειν· οὐδὲ τὸν μὲν πράγματα ἄξια τῆς πόλεως ὑποστάντα λέγειν καὶ γράφειν καὶ μένειν ἐπὶ τούτων προελόμενον βασκαίνειν, ἐὰν δέ τις ἰδίᾳ τι λυπήσῃ, τοῦτο μεμνῆσθαι καὶ τηρεῖν· οὐδέ γ' ἡσυχίαν ἄγειν ἄδικον καὶ ὕπουλον, ὃ σὺ ποιεῖς
308 πολλάκις. Ἔστι γάρ, ἔστιν ἡσυχία δικαία καὶ συμφέ- 328
ρουσα τῇ πόλει ἣν οἱ πολλοὶ τῶν πολιτῶν ὑμεῖς ἁπλῶς ἄγετε. Ἀλλ' οὐ ταύτην οὗτος ἄγει τὴν ἡσυχίαν, πολλοῦ γε καὶ δεῖ, ἀλλ' ἀποστὰς ὅταν αὐτῷ δόξῃ τῆς πολιτείας (πολλάκις δὲ δοκεῖ) φυλάττει πηνίκ' ἐστὲ μεστοὶ τοῦ συνεχῶς λέγοντος, ἢ παρὰ τῆς τύχης τι συμβέβηκεν ἐναντίωμα, ἢ ἄλλο τι δύσκολον γέγονε (πολλὰ δὲ τἀνθρώπινα)· εἶτ' ἐπὶ τούτῳ τῷ καιρῷ ῥήτωρ ἐξαίφνης ἐκ τῆς ἡσυχίας ὥσπερ πνεῦμ' ἐφάνη, καὶ πεφωνασκηκὼς καὶ συνειλοχὼς ῥήματα καὶ λόγους συνείρει τούτους σαφῶς καὶ ἀπνευστί, ὄνησιν μὲν οὐδεμίαν φέροντας οὐδ' ἀγαθοῦ κτῆσιν οὐδενός, συμφορὰν δὲ τῷ τυχόντι τῶν πολιτῶν καὶ κοινὴν αἰσχύνην. Καίτοι
309 ταύτης τῆς μελέτης καὶ τῆς ἐπιμελείας, Αἰσχίνη, εἴπερ ἐκ ψυχῆς δικαίας ἐγίγνετο καὶ τὰ τῆς πατρίδος συμφέροντα προῃρημένης, τοὺς καρποὺς ἔδει γενναίους καὶ καλοὺς καὶ πᾶσιν ὠφελίμους εἶναι, συμμαχίας πόλεων, πόρους χρημάτων, ἐμπορίου κατασκευήν, νόμων συμφερόντων θέσεις, τοῖς ἀποδειχθεῖσιν ἐχθροῖς ἐναντιώματα.

Τούτων γὰρ ἁπάντων ἦν ἐν τοῖς ἄνω χρόνοις ἐξέ- 310
τασις, καὶ ἔδωκεν ὁ παρελθὼν χρόνος πολλὰς ἀποδείξεις
ἀνδρὶ καλῷ τε κἀγαθῷ, ἐν οἷς οὐδαμοῦ σὺ φανήσει
γεγονώς, οὐ πρῶτος, οὐ δεύτερος, οὐ τρίτος, οὐ τέταρτος,
οὐ πέμπτος, οὐχ ἕκτος, οὐχ ὁποστοσοῦν, οὔκουν ἐπί
γε οἷς ἡ πατρὶς ηὐξάνετο. Τίς γὰρ συμμαχία σοῦ 311
πράξαντος γέγονε τῇ πόλει; Τίς δὲ βοήθεια ἢ κτῆσις
330 εὐνοίας ἢ δόξης; Τίς δὲ πρεσβεία; Τίς διακονία δι'
ἣν ἡ πόλις ἐντιμοτέρα γέγονεν; Τί τῶν οἰκείων ἢ
τῶν Ἑλληνικῶν καὶ ξενικῶν, οἷς ἐπέστης, ἐπηνώρθωται
διὰ σέ; Ποῖαι τριήρεις; Ποῖα βέλη; Ποῖοι νε-
ώσοικοι; Τίς ἐπισκευὴ τειχῶν; Ποῖον ἱππικόν; Τί
τῶν ἁπάντων σὺ χρήσιμος εἶ; Τίς ἢ τοῖς εὐπόροις
ἢ τοῖς ἀπόροις πολιτικὴ καὶ κοινὴ βοήθεια χρημάτων
παρὰ σοῦ; Οὐδεμία. Ἀλλ', ὦ τᾶν, εἰ μηδὲν τούτων, 312
εὔνοιά γε καὶ προθυμία; Ποῦ; Πότε; Ὅστις, ὦ
πάντων ἀδικώτατε, οὐδ' ὅτε ἅπαντες ὅσοι πώποτ'
ἐφθέγξαντο ἐπὶ τοῦ βήματος εἰς σωτηρίαν ἐπεδίδοσαν,
καὶ τὸ τελευταῖον Ἀριστόνικος τὸ συνειλεγμένον εἰς τὴν
ἐπιτιμίαν ἀργύριον, οὐδὲ τότε οὔτε παρῆλθες οὔτ' ἐπέδωκας οὐδέν, οὐκ ἀπορῶν, — πῶς γάρ; — ὅς γε κεκληρονόμηκας μὲν τῶν Φίλωνος τοῦ κηδεστοῦ χρημάτων
πλειόνων ἢ πεντεταλάντων, διτάλαντον δ' εἶχες ἔρανον
δωρεὰν παρὰ τῶν ἡγεμόνων τῶν συμμοριῶν ἐφ' οἷς ἐλυμήνω τὸν τριηραρχικὸν νόμον. Ἀλλ' ἵνα μὴ λόγον ἐκ 313
λόγου λέγων τοῦ παρόντος ἐμαυτὸν ἐκκρούσω, παραλείψω ταῦτα. Ἀλλ' ὅτι γ' οὐχὶ δι' ἔνδειαν οὐκ ἐπέδωκας,

9*

ἐκ τούτων δῆλον, ἀλλὰ φυλάττων τὸ μηδὲν ἐναντίον
γενέσθαι παρὰ σοῦ τούτοις οἷς ἅπαντα πολιτεύῃ. Ἐν
τίσιν οὖν σὺ νεανίας καὶ πηνίκα λαμπρός; Ἡνίκ' ἂν
εἰπεῖν κατὰ τούτων τι δέῃ, ἐν τούτοις λαμπροφωνότα-
τος, μνημονικώτατος, ὑποκριτὴς ἄριστος, τραγικὸς Θε-
οκρίνης.

314 Εἶτα τῶν πρότερον γεγενημένων ἀγαθῶν ἀνδρῶν
μέμνησαι. Καὶ καλῶς ποιεῖς. Οὐ μέντοι δίκαιόν
ἐστιν, ἄνδρες Ἀθηναῖοι, τὴν πρὸς τοὺς τετελευτηκότας
εὔνοιαν ὑπάρχουσαν προλαβόντα παρ' ὑμῶν, πρὸς ἐκεί- 330
νους ἐξετάζειν καὶ παραβάλλειν ἐμὲ τὸν νῦν ζῶντα μεθ'
315 ὑμῶν. Τίς γὰρ οὐκ οἶδε τῶν πάντων ὅτι τοῖς μὲν ζῶσι
πᾶσιν ὕπεστί τις ἢ πλείων ἢ ἐλάττων φθόνος, τοὺς
τεθνεῶτας δὲ οὐδὲ τῶν ἐχθρῶν οὐδεὶς ἔτι μισεῖ; Οὕτως
οὖν ἐχόντων τούτων τῇ φύσει, πρὸς τοὺς πρὸ ἐμαυτοῦ
νῦν ἐγὼ κρίνωμαι καὶ θεωρῶμαι; Μηδαμῶς· οὔτε γὰρ
δίκαιον οὔτ' ἴσον, Αἰσχίνη, ἀλλὰ πρὸς σὲ καὶ ἄλλον
εἴ τινα βούλει τῶν ταὐτά σοι προῃρημένων καὶ ζώντων.
316 Κἀκεῖνο σκόπει· πότερον κάλλιον καὶ ἄμεινον τῇ πόλει
διὰ τὰς τῶν πρότερον εὐεργεσίας, οὔσας ὑπερμεγέθεις,
οὐ μὲν οὖν εἴποι τις ἂν ἡλίκας, τὰς ἐπὶ τὸν παρόντα
βίον γιγνομένας εἰς ἀχαριστίαν καὶ προπηλακισμὸν
ἄγειν, ἢ πᾶσιν ὅσοι τι μετ' εὐνοίας πράττουσι, τῆς
παρὰ τούτων τιμῆς καὶ φιλανθρωπίας μετεῖναι.

317 Καὶ μὴν εἰ καὶ τοῦτ' ἄρα δεῖ με εἰπεῖν, ἡ μὲν ἐμὴ
πολιτεία καὶ προαίρεσις, ἄν τις ὀρθῶς σκοπῇ, ταῖς τῶν
τότ' ἐπαινουμένων ἀνδρῶν ὁμοία καὶ ταὐτὰ βουλομένη

φανήσεται, ἡ δὲ σὴ ταῖς τῶν τοὺς τοιούτους τότε συκοφαντούντων· δῆλον γὰρ ὅτι καὶ κατ᾽ ἐκείνους ἦσάν τινες, οἳ διασύροντες τοὺς ὄντας τότε, τοὺς δὲ πρότερον γεγενημένους ἐπῄνουν, βάσκανον πρᾶγμα καὶ ταὐτὸ
ποιοῦντες σοί. Εἶτα λέγεις ὡς οὐδὲν ὅμοιός εἰμι ἐκεί- 318
νοις ἐγώ; Σὺ δ᾽ ὅμοιος, Αἰσχίνη; Ὁ δ᾽ ἀδελφὸς ὁ σός; Ἄλλος δέ τις τῶν νῦν ῥητόρων; Ἐγὼ μὲν γὰρ οὐδένα φημί. Ἀλλὰ πρὸς τοὺς ζῶντας, ὦ χρηστέ, ἵνα μηδὲν ἄλλ᾽ εἴπω, τὸν ζῶντα ἐξέταζε καὶ τοὺς καθ᾽
331 αὑτόν, ὥσπερ τἆλλα πάντα, τοὺς ποιητάς, τοὺς χορούς,
τοὺς ἀγωνιστάς· ὁ Φιλάμμων οὐχ ὅτι Γλαύκου τοῦ 319
Καρυστίου καί τινων ἑτέρων πρότερον γεγενημένων ἀθλητῶν ἀσθενέστερος ἦν, ἀστεφάνωτος ἐκ τῆς Ὀλυμπίας ἀπῄει, ἀλλ᾽ ὅτι τῶν εἰσελθόντων πρὸς αὑτὸν ἄριστα ἐμάχετο, ἐστεφανοῦτο καὶ νικῶν ἀνηγορεύετο. Καὶ σὺ πρὸς τοὺς νῦν ὅρα με ῥήτορας, πρὸς σαυτόν,
πρὸς ὅντινα βούλει τῶν ἁπάντων· οὐδένα ἐξίσταμαι. 320
Ὧν, ὅτε μὲν τῇ πόλει τὰ βέλτιστα ἑλέσθαι παρῆν, ἐφαμίλλου τῆς εἰς τὴν πατρίδα εὐνοίας ἐν κοινῷ πᾶσι κειμένης, ἐγὼ κράτιστα λέγων ἐφαινόμην, καὶ τοῖς ἐμοῖς ψηφίσμασι καὶ νόμοις καὶ πρεσβείαις ἅπαντα διῳκεῖτο, ὑμῶν δὲ οὐδεὶς ἦν οὐδαμοῦ, πλὴν εἰ τούτοις ἐπηρεάσαι τι δέοι· ἐπειδὴ δὲ ἃ μή ποτ᾽ ὤφελε συνέβη, καὶ οὐκέτι συμβούλων, ἀλλὰ τῶν τοῖς ἐπιταττομένοις ὑπηρετούντων καὶ τῶν κατὰ τῆς πατρίδος μισθαρνεῖν ἑτοίμων καὶ τῶν κολακεύειν ἑτέρους βουλομένων ἐξέτασις ἦν, τηνικαῦτα σὺ καὶ τούτων ἕκαστος ἐν τάξει καὶ μέγας καὶ

λαμπρὸς ἱπποτρόφος, ἐγὼ δ' ἀσθενής, ὁμολογῶ, ἀλλ'
εὔνους μᾶλλον ὑμῶν τουτοισί.

321 Δύο δ', ἄνδρες Ἀθηναῖοι, τὸν φύσει μέτριον πολίτην
ἔχειν δεῖ (οὕτω γάρ μοι περὶ ἐμαυτοῦ λέγοντι ἀνε-
πιφθονώτατον εἰπεῖν), ἐν μὲν ταῖς ἐξουσίαις τὴν τοῦ
γενναίου καὶ τοῦ πρωτείου τῇ πόλει προαίρεσιν διαφυλάττειν, ἐν παντὶ δὲ καιρῷ καὶ πράξει τὴν εὔνοιαν·
τούτου γὰρ ἡ φύσις κυρία, τοῦ δύνασθαι δὲ καὶ ἰσχύειν
ἕτερα. Ταύτην τοίνυν παρ' ἐμοὶ μεμενηκυῖαν εὑρήσετε
322 ἁπλῶς. Ὁρᾶτε δέ. Οὐκ ἐξαιτούμενος, οὐκ Ἀμφικτυονικὰς δίκας ἐπαγόντων, οὐκ ἀπειλούντων, οὐκ ἐπαγ- 332
γελλομένων, οὐχὶ τοὺς καταράτους τούτους ὥσπερ
θηρία μοι προσβαλλόντων, οὐδαμῶς ἐγὼ προδέδωκα
τὴν εἰς ὑμᾶς εὔνοιαν. Τὸ γὰρ ἐξ ἀρχῆς εὐθὺς ὀρθὴν
καὶ δικαίαν τὴν ὁδὸν τῆς πολιτείας εἱλόμην, τὰς τιμάς,
τὰς δυναστείας, τὰς εὐδοξίας τὰς τῆς πατρίδος θερα-
323 πεύειν, ταύτας αὔξειν, μετὰ τούτων εἶναι. Οὐκ ἐπὶ
μὲν τοῖς ἑτέρων εὐτυχήμασι φαιδρὸς ἐγὼ καὶ γεγηθὼς
κατὰ τὴν ἀγορὰν περιέρχομαι, τὴν δεξιὰν προτείνων
καὶ εὐαγγελιζόμενος τούτοις οὓς ἂν ἐκεῖσε ἀπαγγέλλειν
οἴωμαι, τῶν δὲ τῆς πόλεως ἀγαθῶν πεφρικὼς ἀκούω καὶ
στένων καὶ κύπτων εἰς τὴν γῆν, ὥσπερ οἱ δυσσεβεῖς
οὗτοι, οἳ τὴν μὲν πόλιν διασύρουσιν, ὥσπερ οὐχ αὑτοὺς
διασύροντες, ὅταν τοῦτο ποιῶσιν, ἔξω δὲ βλέπουσι, καὶ
ἐν οἷς ἀτυχησάντων τῶν Ἑλλήνων εὐτύχησεν ἕτερος,
ταῦτ' ἐπαινοῦσι καὶ ὅπως τὸν ἅπαντα χρόνον μενεῖ
φασὶ δεῖν τηρεῖν.

Μὴ δῆτ᾽, ὦ πάντες θεοί, μηδεὶς ταῦθ᾽ ὑμῶν ἐπι- 324
νεύσειεν, ἀλλὰ μάλιστα μὲν καὶ τούτοις βελτίω τινὰ
νοῦν καὶ φρένας ἐνθείητε· εἰ δ᾽ ἄρ᾽ ἔχουσιν ἀνιάτως,
τούτους μὲν αὐτοὺς καθ᾽ ἑαυτοὺς ἐξώλεις καὶ προώλεις
ἐν γῇ καὶ θαλάττῃ ποιήσατε, ἡμῖν δὲ τοῖς λοιποῖς τὴν
ταχίστην ἀπαλλαγὴν τῶν ἐπηρτημένων φόβων δότε καὶ
σωτηρίαν ἀσφαλῆ.

NOTES.

NOTES.

THIS speech of Demosthenes is a defence of himself against the attacks of Æschines, a personal and political enemy, made in his prosecution of Ctesiphon for proposing to bestow an honorary crown upon Demosthenes. It was delivered by the orator, as associate advocate with Ctesiphon, about six years after the indictment was moved by Æschines, — B. C. 330. The following may be taken as an outline of the course of thought: —

I. PLAN OF THE ORATION.

Exordium, §§ 1 – 8.
Refutation of charges foreign from the indictment, 9 – 52.
  a. Of a private nature, 10, 11.
  b. Of a public nature, 12 – 52.
Reply to the charges contained in the indictment, 53 – 125.
Strictures upon the character and course of his antagonist, compared with his own, 126 – 323.
Peroration, 324.

II. TOPICS IN SUCCESSION.

1. The orator calls upon the gods to dispose his judges to exercise as much kind feeling towards him as he continually has towards the city and all its inhabitants, and, as

pecially, to hear him impartially, as the laws and their oath of office require, §§ 1, 2.

2. He reminds his judges of two disadvantages which he labored under in replying to Æschines ; — (1.) The vastly greater interest which he had at stake than his antagonist ; (2.) The unwelcome task which was imposed upon him, of speaking in defence of his own character and conduct, 3, 4.

3. That he evidently was equally interested in this trial with Ctesiphon, 5.

4. He again reminds his judges of their obligations to hear him impartially, 6, 7.

5. He again calls upon the gods to enable them to do so, 8.

6. That it was necessary for him, before entering upon a refutation of the charges in the indictment, to reply briefly to certain charges foreign from the indictment, which Æschines had brought against him, relating both to his private and public life, 9.

7. That he would not attempt to refute the charges brought against his private life, but would leave his judges to decide whether they were true or not, from the acquaintance which they had with him, 10, 11.

8. That it was obvious at the outset, from the very course which his antagonist had taken to bring him to trial, that the charges against his public character and course were suggested by enmity, and were therefore without foundation, 12 – 16.

9. That he would show them to be so on one point which had been much insisted upon by his opponent, — the peace with Philip, 17.

10. That the divided state of Greece, not he, led to the peace referred to, 18 – 20.

11. That, in point of fact, he did not propose the peace first, but certain friends of Æschines. Much less did he prevent a general combination of the tribes of Greece to treat with Philip, as both facts and the nature of the case showed, 21 – 24.

12. That the part which he acted in making the peace was highly useful, by urging its completion with all despatch, 25 – 29.

13. That Æschines and his accomplices gave Philip an opportunity of gaining great advantages over Athens, by loitering an unreasonable length of time on their embassy, before they made an application to him to ratify the treaty on his part, 30.

14. That, besides this, they were bribed by Philip to delay their return from Macedonia, till he had got in readiness his expedition against Phocis, and had actually passed the straits of Thermopylæ, 31, 32.

15. And to crown the whole, that Æschines, apart from his associates, was bribed to make, on his return, a very favorable report of the designs and disposition of Philip towards the Athenians, by which they were blinded to his true character, and led to abandon to him Phocis, their ally without a struggle, 33 – 39.

16. That Philip, by the destruction of Phocis, gained credit with Thebes, her rival, and was thus enabled to acquire an ascendency in that city, 40, 41.

17. That from this he went on increasing his power, by subduing one place after another, among which were many Grecian cities, and employing traitors in every state to accomplish his purposes, which he then cast aside, as they deserved to be, 42 – 49.

18. That more might be said upon this point, but that, undoubtedly, more than enough had already been said; which, if it was the case, should be charged to the account of Æschines, who had compelled him to enter upon these extraneous matters in self-defence, 50 – 52.

19. That he would now enter upon a refutation of the charges in the indictment, which he proceeds to have read before the court, 53 – 55.

20. That he would reply to the charges contained in it, in the order in which they there stood; and should do this

by first reviewing his public life and measures, to which, in fact, they all alike pertained, and then by producing laws in their refutation, 56 – 59.

21. Passing over their relations with Philip previous to his devoting himself to the foreign policy of the city, he states, in defence of his policy in renewing the war with him; — First, that Philip was obviously taking advantage of the corrupt and divided state of the different tribes of Greece, to establish himself upon their ruins, 60, 61.

22. Second, that Athens could not, consistently with the character and position which she had always maintained, have taken any other course than to resist him, 62 – 68.

23. Third, that Philip first violated the peace, by seizing certain allied cities of Athens, 69 – 72.

24. Fourth, that he had violated it, also, by seizing certain vessels belonging to Athens, 73 – 75.

25. Fifth, that Philip himself had virtually acquitted him of any blame in the matter by a letter which he addressed to the Athenians at that time, 76 – 78.

26. Sixth, that his first measures of hostility towards Philip were in resisting his unjust encroachments; especially, in dispossessing him of Eubœa, for which he was crowned under precisely the same circumstances under which the decree of Ctesiphon proposed to crown him, 79 – 86.

27. Seventh, that the same might be said of the succor which he sent to the Byzantians and Perinthians, 87 – 94.

28. Eighth, that it was no valid objection to these measures, that they were devised for the relief of those who had sometimes injured Athens, as is shown from other instances in her history, 95 – 101.

29. That the modification which he introduced during this struggle into the system of equipping vessels was of great service to his country, and required great moral courage and integrity in himself to push it through, against the opposition and bribes of the rich, whom the change most affected, 102 – 109.

30. That it remained for him now to speak concerning the lawfulness of the proposed mode of proclaiming the crowning, and the obligation which he was under to render up an account of his public offices before it was lawful for him to be crowned, 110.

31. That he was under no obligation to give in an account of the money which he had contributed from his private fortune, and that it was for this for which it was proposed to crown him, 111–113.

32. He produces several decrees to show that others had been crowned under similar circumstances, 114–117.

33. That Æschines himself had virtually acknowledged that he was to be crowned for what he had given from his own purse, and was not therefore accountable for, by not objecting to the preamble of the decree of Ctesiphon, which expressly recommended the crowning upon this ground, 118, 119.

34. That while it was a matter of indifference to the one crowned where it was proclaimed, it was greatly for the interest of the state to have it proclaimed in the most public manner; which, in fact, was expressly provided for by law, 120–122.

35. That, as he conceived, courts were not constituted to furnish an arena for personal invective and abuse; but yet that he was compelled, in self-defence, to return some of the invective which had been thrown out so freely against him, which he should proceed to do, having first asked his opponent one question, 123–125.

36. That it was a matter of some interest to know who this was that had taken it upon himself to ridicule his language, and at the same time had himself used such language as no respectable man would have ventured to use, 126–128.

37. The origin of Æschines, and his late appearance in public life, 129–131.

38. That, even before the breaking out of the war, he

had given proof of a treasonable connection with Philip, — First, by the attention and favor which he showed to Antiphon, one of his emissaries, 132 – 135.

39. Second, by his coöperation with Python, another agent of Philip, 136.

40. Third, by his connection with Anaxinus, also engaged in the service of Philip, 137.

41. That numerous other instances of his treasonable practices in those times might be mentioned, were it necessary, 138.

42. That he still continued in the service of Philip after his designs were plainly manifested, and he had virtually made war upon Attica, 139.

43. That especially deserving of attention and reprobation was the aid which he had given Philip, in getting up the Amphictyonic War against Amphissa, and securing to him the conduct of it, 140 – 144.

44. That Philip, prevented from bringing his contest with Athens to a close by intervening Grecian tribes, sought some pretext of common interest, which should open a way for him into the heart of Greece; and, thinking that he discovered such a pretext in the desecration of the sacred region of Cirrha by the Amphissians, hired Æschines to procure a vote of the Amphictyons to make war upon them on that account, 145 – 150.

45. That the Amphictyons, undertaking the war, soon felt their need of the aid of Philip, as he anticipated they would, and applied to him to take the lead of the forces. But that he, being thus intrusted with carrying on the war, instead of proceeding against the Amphissians, turned aside and took Elatea, as a most favorable position from which to operate in his designs upon Greece, and especially upon Athens, 151 – 157.

46. That Æschines had furnished him with the opportunity for doing all this, and thus was the guilty cause of all the evils which had befallen his country, 158, 159.

47. That, while his opponent was thus engaged in the service of Philip, he was steadily resisting him; and, especially, watched to prevent a rupture between Athens and Thebes, and a union of the latter with Philip, 160 – 162.

48. That, by the intrigues of Philip and his accomplices, these cities were very near an open rupture, as is shown from various documents, 163 – 168.

49. That, amidst the trepidation and confusion occasioned by the arrival of the news of the capture of Elatea, he alone appeared as counsellor, and proposed such a course as was calculated to secure the confidence and alliance of Thebes, 169 – 173.

50. The course which he advised to be taken, 174 – 178.

51. That he not only proposed an embassy to Thebes, but afterwards went upon it himself, and succeeded in securing the object proposed to be effected by it, 179 – 187.

52. That, although the time when these measures were proposed was the proper time for making objections to them, still, as Æschines did not do it then, he would call upon him to do it now, if he could, but not to blame him for the issue, since this, in all cases, was in the hands of the Deity 188 – 194.

53. But that, even if the issue should be taken into the account, it ought to be considered how much lighter the stroke was rendered by his policy than it otherwise would have been, though it did not succeed in averting it, 195.

54. Furthermore, that if Æschines foresaw the result, it was his duty to have pointed it out at the time of the deliberations; but if he did not foresee it, he was as much accountable for this as himself, or any other one. That, in truth, Æschines had never given any timely and useful advice on any question, but only appeared in times of trouble, to augment the evil, like fractures and sprains when the body is weak, 196 – 198.

55. Besides, that, even if the issue had been distinctly foreseen, the city could not, consistently with the position

which she had always occupied among the powers of Greece, and the example of their ancestors, have taken any other course than the one which he advised, 199 - 205.

56. That, if Ctesiphon should be condemned according to the demand of Æschines, it would be saying, in effect, that they had done wrong in following his advice, and not that they had been frowned upon by fortune ; and, at the same time, would be showing a spirit unworthy of their ancestors, 206 – 210.

57. A resumption of the account of his proceedings at Thebes while on his embassy at that place, 211, 212.

58. The opposition which he encountered there, but his success against it all, 213, 214.

59. The cordiality and confidence with which the Athenian troops were received at Thebes, when at length they marched thither to unite with her against Philip, and the success which they met with in two different battles, 215 – 217.

60. The change which is produced in the tone and bearing of Philip, 218 – 221.

61. That he himself was crowned on the occasion, in consequence of the success of his measures, by a decree of precisely the same nature as that for which Ctesiphon was now arraigned ; and that Æschines might with more justice have prosecuted the proposers of this decree, than he now prosecutes Ctesiphon, 222 – 226.

62. That the reasoning of Æschines, in which he contends that these services are more than offset by his own and ought to leave no impression in his favor, is sophistical, 227 – 231.

63. That the proper view to take of the matter was to consider the resources which he had at his command, compared with the difficulties to be overcome, which he proceeds to do, 232 – 237.

64. That it was no objection to his policy, that he had made the burden light upon some of the allies, in order to

secure their alliance; since their ancestors had done so in a memorable instance, and since the circumstances of the case rendered it necessary, and he and his friends would have been sure to assail him for it, if he had let the opportunity of securing their alliance pass, 238-243.

65. That, in fact, the city had not been defeated in any thing coming under his charge, 244-247.

66. That the people and courts of justice had, by their conduct towards him since the unhappy issue of the struggle, warranted such a decree as that of Ctesiphon, 248-251.

67. That, as he was aware, it was no way to judge of a man by his fortune, especially with such unworthy views of fortune as his opponent had expressed; but yet, that, in self-defence, he was compelled to draw a comparison between his own fortune and that of Æschines, 252-256.

68. A comparison of their respective fortunes at the different periods of life, 257-264.

69. A recapitulation of the points of contrast in their fortunes, with some additional particulars, 265-267.

70. That, in disproving the charge of being attended by an ill-fortune, he did not consider it proper to speak of his private good deeds, 268, 269.

71. But of his public course it should be further observed, that, if any one had been freed from the power of Philip, it ought to be ascribed to him; but that their misfortunes, since they had been shared by all Greece, should be considered as a consequence of the evil fortune of all, or, at least, could not be charged to him, any more than to his countrymen generally, and especially to his adversary, 270-275.

72. That the caution given the judges by his adversary, to be on their guard against the influence of his artful oratory, was unnecessary; since whatever of that he possessed had always been employed for the good of his country, and on proper occasions, which was more than could be said of his antagonist, 276-284.

73. That the people had manifested their confidence in him, and their distrust of his adversary, by choosing him, in preference to all others, to deliver the funeral oration over the dead bodies of those who fell at Chæronea, 285 – 290.

74. That it was a very suspicious circumstance in Æschines, that he was not at all affected at the mention of the calamities which had befallen his country, but could recount them, for the purpose of charging them upon him, with perfect indifference, 291 – 293.

75. That nothing could be more malicious than the charge which his adversary had attempted to fix upon him, of acting for Philip, when it was notorious that he himself, and a band of others like him in every state, had been the busy promoters of his interest in Greece, 294 – 296.

76. That if then it be asked, why he deserved to be honored with a crown, he would reply, — First, because that, of all the public men of his time, he alone had shown himself proof against bribes, 297, 298.

77. Second, because of the protection which he had secured to Attica, not merely by repairing her fortifications, but, more especially, by the alliances and defence which he had gained for her by his measures, 299 – 305.

78. That these were the proper works of a statesman, and very different from those of his adversary, 306 – 313.

79. That the comparison which his antagonist had made between him and some of their predecessors was unjust, for various reasons; but, if he pleased, that he would stand a comparison with him, or any of his contemporaries, 314 – 320.

80. That at least it must be acknowledged that he had uniformly pursued a patriotic course, 321 – 323.

81. The peroration, containing a simple prayer to the gods to dispose these enemies of their country to better things, or, if they were incurable, to pursue them with destruction over sea and land, 324.

§ 1 – 9. EXORDIUM. This exordium has been justly admired. The style is flowing and graceful, and the spirit solemn and earnest. We are introduced immediately to the scene of the trial, and find ourselves in the presence, not only of the eager multitude of Athens, but of the gazing divinities of Olympus. We feel the fervor of the speaker, the first sentence he pronounces, and anticipate the solemn interests which he has at stake. As the circumstances of the case were sufficiently well known to his hearers, from the speech of his opponent and from general notoriety, the orator very properly employs his introductory remarks in preparing the way for a favorable hearing with his judges. This kind of introduction was called by the Greeks ἔφοδος, while those employed in explaining the cause, etc. were called προοίμια. As to its substance, it expresses a desire that his judges may hear him impartially, the reasons for that desire, and then a repetition of the desire; or, as Dissen has expressed it, *a wish, the grounds of the wish, and a return to the wish.*

1. ἄνδρες Ἀθηναῖοι] "men of Athens, Athenians." ἀνήρ was generally joined by the Greeks to the names of nations; also to titles, professions, etc. This is not uncommon in English; as, English*man*, police*man*, etc. By this title he addresses his hearers generally, but especially the judges. The cause was tried before one of the tribunals of the Heliasts. These were the popular courts, and took cognizance of the greater part of the causes which were tried at Athens. The Heliasts were six thousand in all, and were divided into sections, varying at different periods and on different occasions from two hundred to one thousand or fifteen hundred. Besides, these courts were open to and thronged by the people (see as evidence of this, among other passages, § 196, init.), and hence differed but little from the popular assemblies. — τοῖς θεοῖς εὔχομαι, κ. τ. λ.] This was the most solemn form of invocation used by the Greeks, it being substantially the same as that uttered by

the crier at the opening of the meetings of the assembly. See Schöm. Assembl. of Athenians, § 92. The importance of the cause justifies the earnestness of the appeal, and perhaps prompted it; though many have supposed that it was resorted to by the orator in order to remove from the minds of his hearers the suspicion of his impiety, which the speech of Æschines was calculated to leave upon them. — ὅσην εὔνοιαν . . . . τοσαύτην.] Perhaps a mere oratorical inversion of the members of the sentence for the sake of emphasis; but more probably, as Dissen suggests, for the purpose of stating the reason for the request he was about to make before the request itself. If he had always been well disposed to them, he certainly might ask that they should be kindly disposed to him on this occasion. — ὑπάρξαι] Not simply "to be," but "to begin to be," "to spring up," "to be ready at hand," "to be afforded." The aor. is used like the aorists below, παραστῆσαι, ποιήσασθαι, etc., because the act referred to is independent of circumstances and momentary in its nature. The request is simply for the present trial. K.* § 257, 1; C. § 63, 1. Both the meaning of the word and its tense contribute to bring out the opposition designed to be expressed to ἔχων ἐγὼ διατελῶ, "I continually have." — τουτονὶ] The ί adds to the demonstrative power of the pronoun, same as the adverb *here* does in English · hence, "this *here*," = "this present." C. § 28, 2. — ἔπειθ'] This marks the succession indicated by πρῶτον μέν in the first line, and hence is equivalent to δεύτερον δέ. The δέ, which regularly follows μέν in the adversative clause, is generally omitted with ἔπειτα, since this particle expresses the contrast sufficiently of itself. K. § 322, R. 4. This second reason, he says, has reference to them instead of himself, bearing alike upon their obligation to the gods to preserve their oath of office, and upon their reputation

---

* K. stands for *Kühner's Greek School Grammar* (1st American ed.) and C. for *Champlin's Greek Grammar*

among men. Observe the connectives, καὶ . . . . τε καὶ. τε καὶ refer, one to εὐσεβείας and the other to δόξης, while καὶ connects both of these with ὑμῶν ("for you, and indeed both for your piety and honor.") — σύμβουλον] "counsellor," "adviser." Æschines, in his oration (§§ 205, 206), had urged the judges to confine Demosthenes, in his reply, to the same order which he himself had pursued. This is further alluded to in § 2. — τοῦ πῶς ἀκούειν, κ. τ. λ.] This is an infinitive clause used as a noun. Such clauses are found in all Greek authors, but abound in Demosthenes more, perhaps, than in any other. The infinitive used as a noun expresses action divested of all its accidents and circumstances, — the very soul and essence of action, therefore. It possesses great energy and vivacity, and is favorable to condensation. It is natural, therefore, that it should be a favorite construction with a mind of such force and vehemence as that of Demosthenes.

2. τῇ τάξει καὶ τῇ ἀπολογίᾳ] "the order and the defence." Alluding to the restriction in this respect which Æschines (§§ 203–205) had urged the judges to lay upon him. These words are governed by χρήσασθαι, and form a part of the infinitive clause introduced by τό. The article which precedes each of them has a kind of possessive sense, = "*the* order and *the* defence *which each party is properly entitled to.*" Comp. τὸ μέρος τῶν ψήφων, "the *required* or *legal* part of the votes," § 222, et alias. It is also to be observed, with Dissen, that logical strictness would require a word of more general meaning than ἀπολογίᾳ in this place, as ἀποδείξει, for instance, which would apply to both parties in a suit; since ἀπολογία properly refers only to the defendant. But a special term was very naturally adopted in making a general remark with reference to a particular case. — ὡς βεβούληται καὶ προῄρηται] The relative clause here being placed before the demonstrative clause, makes the arrangement emphatic, as was observed in a similar case above, § 1. Of the two verbs, the former properly

means "has desired," and the latter "has preferred" or 'fixed upon." They are not synonymous, but cumulative, in their meaning.

3. *οὐ περὶ . . . . ἀγωνίζομαι*] "I do not contend concerning things of equal value," or "I have more at stake." All that Æschines had at stake was the fine of a thousand drachmas imposed upon the accuser in such causes, if he failed to obtain a fifth part of the votes of the judges in his favor, and the inability to institute similar prosecutions afterwards. Comp. Herm. Polit. Antiq. § 144. Demosthenes, on the contrary, had been charged with so weighty accusations by Æschines, that, had the cause been decided against Ctesiphon, he must have fallen with him, and lost all character with his fellow-citizens, both for wisdom and virtue. As he states at the commencement of § 8, his whole public and private life was involved in the cause. And this is what makes this, of all the orations of Demosthenes, the most valuable. It is a profound and statesmanlike discussion of his long course of public and private labors in the service of his country, — a discussion which involved every thing which he held dear, and to which he brought the experience and reflection of his ripest years. — *ἑλεῖν τὴν γραφήν*] A technical expression, meaning "to gain the cause." — *ἀλλ' ἐμοὶ μὲν, κ. τ. λ.*] A case of *aposiopesis*. The thought suppressed after *ἐμοὶ μὲν* may be best supplied, I think, as follows: "but while to me *every thing is at stake*." To this clause, the clause after the parenthesis corresponds. The only difficulty here is in *ἐκ περιουσίας*. *περιουσία* properly means "superfluity," "excess," and hence may mean "advantage," as it evidently does in Orat. de F. L., p. 366, init.: *τίς οὖν ἡ ταύτης περιουσία . . . . ;* "what then is the *advantage* of this?" *ἐκ περιουσίας*, then, would mean "from a vantage ground," or "with the advantage," which is the meaning given in the first edition. Upon more reflection, however, I am now inclined to the more common meaning of the phrase, "superfluously," "wantonly."

We may translate, therefore: "but while to me *every thing is at stake* (but I am unwilling to express any unpleasant forebodings at the commencement of my speech), he accuses me from mere wantonness," i. e. without any just cause, evidently without any apprehension of serious consequences to himself. — Ἕτερον δ'] He here states the second point of the disadvantage he labors under in comparison with his adversary, viz. the natural love in man for slander and crimination, and his disgust at self-commendation.

4. ὡς ἔπος εἰπεῖν] "so to speak." Denoting a limitation. K. § 341, R. 3; C. § 70, 15. — ἔχειν] "to have," "have wherewith," "be able." It governs ἀπολύσασθαι and δεικνύναι, — the first in the aor., because the charges to be refuted were a definite thing, and the refuting of them was conceived of as a single act; the second in the pres., because designed to describe a continued attempt to set forth his merits, extending through the whole oration, and bearing upon an indefinite number of particulars. — πεποίηκα καὶ πεπολίτευμαι] The difference in meaning between these words, as here applied, is not obvious, and perhaps none exists, but they are to be regarded as substantially synonymous, and joined together for the purpose of oratorical fulness and emphasis. We find each of them, in different places, joined with the verb πράττω; as, § 45, ἐν τῷ πολιτεύεσθαι καὶ πράττειν, and, § 62, πράττειν καὶ ποιεῖν; also, F. L., p. 373, fin., ὅτι πράξει ταῦτα καὶ ποιήσει. πολιτεύεσθαι properly means "to act as a citizen of a free state," i. e. "to take part in the public deliberations of the government," "to suggest measures of government," and hence, "to act the part of a statesman," "to effect as a statesman," "to manage," very like the Latin *gerere*. But πράττειν, as applied to public affairs, seems to refer to acting as a regularly appointed public officer, or as a regular business and for a livelihood, and hence with selfish and ambitious views, like the Latin *agere*. See § 45. ποιεῖν properly means "to make," like *facere* in Latin. But it often has a meaning

rery similar to πράττειν, "to do," "perform." Probably, nowever, ποιεῖν in all its meanings retains some allusion to its primitive meaning of producing a *result*, *creating* or *bringing about* something. It may be rendered, therefore, in these cases, "to carry through," "bring about," "make good." — ὡς μετριώτατα] "as moderately *or* briefly as possible." K. § 239, R. 2, (d); C. § 50, R. 5. — τὸ πρᾶγμα αὐτὸ] "the cause *itself*," i. e. without any seeking of his own. — ἐστὶ δίκαιος] Instead of ἐστὶ δίκαιον, — the personal instead of the impersonal construction, which is very common with δίκαιος, ἄξιος, etc. K. § 307, R. 6, (d).

5. καὶ οὐδὲν . . . . ἐμοί] This seems to be said in allusion to the assertion of Æschines (§ 210), that all his interest in the case had reference merely to the crown and the proclamation. We have seen, § 3, how Demosthenes was equally interested in the cause with Ctesiphon, who, as the one formally prosecuted, had first replied to Æschines, and now Demosthenes replies as equally implicated. — ἄλλως τε κἂν . . . . συμβαίνῃ] "especially if this happens to one by an enemy." κἄν, it will be perceived, is a crasis for καὶ ἄν; hence ἄλλως τε κἄν means, literally, "as in other cases, so particularly if" (καί being stronger than τέ, and making the last member prominent = *and especially*. K. 321, 1, c). Observe that the intransitive verb συμβαίνῃ takes the agent or author after it in the gen., with ὑπό, like the passive verb. K. 299, II. 2, (a). — εὐνοίας καὶ φιλανθρωπίας] "favorable regard and kindness." Which of course he would lose if the cause was decided in favor of Æschines, who had occupied nearly his whole speech in decrying Demosthenes. A decision in his adversary's favor, therefore, would be allowing the charges against himself. This high appreciation of their kindness and humanity must have been very grateful to his judges, since the Athenians prided themselves upon this virtue. See Orat. adv. Leptin., p. 490 · μεῖζον, ὦ ἄνδρες Ἀθηναῖοι, Θηβαῖοι φρονοῦσι ἐπ' ὠμότητι κα. ,,ονηρίᾳ ἢ ὑμεῖς ἐπὶ φιλανθρωπίᾳ καὶ τῷ τὰ δίκαια βούλεσθαι.

6. This and the following section, as Dissen observes, with his usual insight into the oratorical structure of sentences, are distinguishable into three parts, of which each succeeding part confirms and more fully explains the preceding. The first ends with *δικαίως*, the second with *ὀμωμοκέναι*, and the third concludes the period. — *οὓς ὁ τιθεὶς . . . . ὀμωμοκέναι*] "which Solon, their original framer, being kindly disposed to you and a friend of the people, thought should be controlling (supreme), not only by proposing them for enactment, but also by the fact, that you who sit in judgment have taken an oath to make them so." Solon, the framer of the democratic constitution of Athens, was regarded by the Athenians as eminently a friend of the people, and is often described as such by writers of all classes. He is alluded to in this character here, because the orator is about to assert the supremacy of the laws which he made; — he was highly democratic, it is confessed, but nevertheless he designed his law to be superior in authority to every thing else. The laws brought before the assembly of the people for enactment were always to be written down, and hence *γράφειν* in such case means "to propose." Logical strictness seems to require that *ὀμωμοκέναι* should mean "to place under oath," but the act. never has this meaning. The causative verb "to swear" is *ὁρκοῦν* or *ὁρκίζειν*. See § 30. The word was probably used as having a softer meaning; since it implied less control of the lawgiver over the judges.

7. *τὰς αἰτίας καὶ τὰς διαβολάς*] These two words are often found joined in Demosthenes, and instead of the last we frequently find *λοιδορία*. See § 15. *αἰτία*, as defined by Demosthenes, Orat. adv. Androt., p. 600, means "charges," i. e. mere accusations where no proof is given; *διαβολή* means "a false accusation," "slander." — *ὁ διώκων ἰσχύει*] "the prosecutor is strong, *or* has the advantage." *ὁ διώκων* properly means "one who pursues *or* follows up," just as *prosecutor* does with us; but the Greeks had a correspond-

ing term for defendant, ὁ φεύγων (see τῷ φεύγοντι in the next clause), which we have not. — παρελθεῖν] "to pass by," "to escape." A word adopted, evidently, to keep up the figure contained in διώκων and φεύγοντι. — ὑστέρου] I retain this in preference to ὕστερον, the other reading, since it corresponds better to πρότερος above. See Hom. Il. V. 15–17: Φηγεὺς ῥα πρότερος . . . . ὁ δ' ὕστερος ὤρνυτο χαλκῷ Τυδείδης. And if it be said that πρότερον is also found instead of πρότερος in some MSS., it may be replied, that this reading is undoubtedly wrong, as πρότερον means "formerly." See §§ 10, 142, 223, 238, 316. — καὶ . . . . καὶ] "both" . . . . "and," connect not only their respective verbs, but also the participial clauses standing in connection with them. — οὕτω τὴν διάγνωσιν, κ. τ. λ.] "shall thus make the decision concerning every particular" (i. e. in view of all the circumstances of the case).

8. ὡς ἔοικε] This is thrown in by way of limitation or abatement of the comprehensiveness of the assertion implied in παντός. Such limitations are common in Demosthenes, as in every cautious and accurate thinker. — ἔπειθ', κ. τ. λ.] "then, whatever is destined to contribute to the public honor and your individual piety, that this the gods may grant to you all to decide concerning the present indictment." μέλλει συνοίσειν forms a periphrastic future of very much the same nature as the Latin periphrastic future, consisting of the fut. part. and the verb *sum*; it does not indicate an action as simply future, but as *incomplete*, — what is on the point of taking place, or is destined to take place. κοινῇ properly means "in common," "collectively," "as a body": but as these introductory remarks were addressed not exclusively to the judges, but to the citizens generally, who thronged the court, and with whom equally with the judges he wished to gain an acquittal, it may very properly here be taken in the sense of "publicly," as above. The decision of this cause would bear upon their public honor, inasmuch as the measures of Demosthenes had been adopted and acted upon

so extensively by the city, that a condemnation of him would be a condemnation of the public policy. This idea he more fully develops in subsequent parts of the speech. It would bear upon the individual piety of those who sat in judgment upon him, since they were religiously bound as judges to give just decisions according to the laws.

9. The orator, having completed his exordium, now proceeds to reply to the speech of his opponent. And, first, to certain charges foreign to the indictment, relating both to his public and private life. — Εἰ μὲν οὖν, κ. τ. λ.] "If, therefore, Æschines had accused me only for those things on account of which he brought the prosecution," etc. The points for which the prosecution was brought are those contained in the indictment (γραφή), §§ 54 and 55. It will be apparent from examining this, that all charges brought against his private life were foreign to the cause. Certain public measures, also, especially the peace with Philip, he considers foreign to the cause; since he then acted only a secondary part, — the peace having been proposed and brought about by others, while he merely proposed a decree for obtaining the ratification of it on the part of Philip as soon as possible. — προβουλεύματος] "preliminary decree." Referring to the decree of Ctesiphon to crown Demosthenes, which Æschines, in his indictment of its author for proposing it, had represented as illegal on several grounds, and which, therefore, it was the business of Demosthenes to defend. This oration, therefore, may be, and indeed is, by its author, considered, at different times, as a defence of himself, as a defence of Ctesiphon, or of the decree which Ctesiphon had proposed; since they were all, in fact, arraigned by the indictment. This will be seen, if it be stated under what circumstances the prosecution arose. It was what was called, in Athenian law, γραφὴ παρανόμων, or *an indictment for proposing illegal decrees*, or such as were supposed to violate any law still in force. Any one on proposing such a decree was liable to be impeached for its

illegality, before the popular tribunals, by any of his fellow citizens. Now, in the present case, Ctesiphon, a friend of Demosthenes, had proposed a decree in the Senate to crown him on account of his eminent public services, which Æschines asserted was illegal, and commenced a public prosecution of its author for proposing it, and indirectly of Demosthenes, as unworthy of the praise bestowed upon him by it. It is called a *preliminary decree*, because it had never been ratified by the assembly of the people, and consequently was but a partial decree, expressing only the opinion of the Senate. Had it been sanctioned by the people, it would have become a ψήφισμα; but this was prevented by the indictment of its author, lodged by Æschines with the archon before it was acted upon by the assembly. — διεξιὼν] "rehearsing," "setting forth in detail." For the acc. of the thing, and the gen. of the author or cause, with κατεψεύσατο, see K. § 292, R; C. § 53, R. 11. — ἵνα μηδεὶς, κ. τ. λ.] "that no one of you, influenced by words foreign from the cause, may hear with more estrangement (aversion) my just remarks upon the indictment" ὑπέρ, which, like the Latin *super*, properly means "over," "above," comes to mean, when transferred to the relations of thought, "upon," "concerning," very much like περί; since, for instance, a dispute *over* a thing is substantially the same as a dispute *about* a thing; but the first implies a closer and more *essential* relation.

10. βεβλασφήμηκε] For the construction of this verb, see § 11, n. — ἀνάσχησθε.] The aor. subj. used as imperat., as is generally the case in prohibitive expressions with μή, K. § 259, 5. — ὑπέρευ] "over well," "ever so well." — καὶ μηδενὸς . . . . χείρονα] "and (that I may say nothing offensive) inferior to none of the middling *or* respectable sort of people." — ἧν] When placed thus in the same clause with its noun, it has the force of an adjective pronoun, as *what* often has in English ("*what* favor"). K. § 332, 8. — ἐνδέδειχθε] "you have shown forth," "exhibited," like the Latin *præ*

se ferre. The middle voice, but not used in the strictest sense of the middle. K. § 250, 1, (b).

11. Κακοήθης δ' ὢν .... τρέψεσθαι] "But, Æschines, being evil-*minded*, you altogether weak-*mindedly minded* (thought) this, that I, having passed by the account of my public acts [see § 4, note], should turn (i. e. to reply) to the slanders uttered by you" (as a malicious man like himself naturally would). There is a play upon the words κακοήθης, εὐηθες, ᾠήθης, which I have attempted to imitate in the translation. — τετύφωμαι] lit. "have become stupefied," "am a dunce." For the perf. here, as often, expresses rather the *result* of the action than the act itself, K. § 255, R. 5. — ὑπὲρ] = περί nearly; see § 9, note, and K. § 293, I. (2), (e). — ἃ κατεψεύδου καὶ διέβαλλες] "which you invented and slanderously stated," = *made out by falsehood and slander.* The acc. here denotes the *effect* or *result*, and the verbs are to be taken in the pregnant meaning. C. § 57, R. 1. The same is the case with ὅσα .... βεβλασφήμηκε (§ 10), "which reviling he has stated slanderously concerning me," = *made out by slander.* In the sense "falsely charge upon," καταψεύδεσθαι governs the gen. of person and acc. of thing. See §§ 9 and 24. But διαβάλλειν, in the simple sense "to slander," governs the acc. of the person. See § 24 (πόλιν being viewed as a person). These two usages being kept in view, these verbs will give the student no further difficulty. — τῆς δὲ πομπείας, κ. τ. λ.] "but this invective, so freely indulged in, I will afterwards call up, if there remain in these (i. e. his judges, etc.) a disposition to hear." πομπεία properly means "a procession," but as in the Dionysiac processions ribaldry and abuse were indulged in, it came to have the meaning here given to it. See § 122, note. Observe the Greek idiom with verbs of *willing*, *desiring*, and the contrary, in the phrase ἂν βουλομένοις ἀκούειν ᾖ τουτοισί, lit. "if it may be to these willing to hear." C. § 59, R. 3. — It will be observed from this and the preceding paragraphs, that the orator proposes to arrange

what he has to say under three general heads: 1st, to reply to the charges brought against him foreign to the indictment; 2d, to those contained in the indictment; and, 3d, to return some of the invective which his adversary had heaped upon him.

12. περὶ ὧν ἐνίων] "concerning which, some of them, at least." That ὧν does not depend upon ἐνίων is evident from the similar case in Dem. Aphob. II., § 23, where both words are in the acc. — διδόασι τιμωρίας] "give punishments." τιμωρία, then, was the regular punishment ordained by the laws in specific cases; but τίμημα was the arbitrary damage or penalty awarded by the judge. See τιμωρίαι, § 14, and τίμημα, § 55. In defence of the reading διδόασι, instead of the other reading τάττουσι, I refer, with Dissen, to Orat. adv. Leptin., p. 504: οἵ (νόμοι) τε τοῖς ἀγαθόν τι ποιοῦσι τὰς τιμὰς διδόντες καὶ οἱ τοῖς τἀναντία πράττουσι τὰς τιμωρίας. — τοῦ δὲ παρόντος ἀγῶνος . . . . τοιαῦτα] "but the very aim of the present trial has in view, at the same time, abuse, and insult, and reviling, and contumely, and all such things of an enemy." That is to say, it had in view the venting of his enmity upon Demosthenes, and not the vindication of justice to the city; it was, as he calls it in a subsequent part of the oration (§ 121), φθόνου δίκην, "a cause instituted from enmity." This he proceeds to substantiate. — οὐκ ἔνι τῇ πόλει] "it is not possible to the city." The city could not inflict punishment for such crimes, according to Dissen, because committed so long before, and not presented individually, but in a mass.

13. Οὐ γὰρ . . . . ἐστιν] "For it is not proper to take away from me the privilege of appearing before the people and addressing them; nor from abusiveness and envy to do this, — by the gods, — is it either right, or lawful, or just." That is to say, it was not proper thus to attack him in the the name of another (instead of bringing him to trial separately), with the hope of depriving him of the privilege of replying (see Æsch. adv. Ctes., p. 82), and especially when

done from malice and envy. The negatives οὔτε . . . . οὔτε . . . . οὔτε are merely an emphatic repetition, in the several clauses, of the general negation contained in οὐδ' (see § 186, n.). πολιτικὸν, "consistent with the laws of the state," = *lawful*. According to this view (which is substantially that of Dissen), γὰρ, of course, does not refer to the clause immediately preceding, but, as is often the case, to the leading subject of the whole preceding sentence, viz. the personal character and injustice of the cause. — ἐτραγῴδει] "set forth pompously." Alluding, as also by ὑποκρίνεται below, to the former profession of Æschines as an actor -- παρ' αὐτὰ τἀδικήματα] "immediately upon the commission of the crimes themselves." The infinitive immediately following these words depends on ἔδει, to be supplied from the previous sentence. The orator is here stating what course his opponent ought to have pursued. — εἰσαγγελίας] A term in Athenian law, descriptive of a kind of impeachment or information against any one deemed dangerous to the state, in cases not expressly provided for by the laws. Comp. Herm. Polit. Antiq. § 133. — εἰσαγγέλλοντα] A participle belonging to the subject of χρῆσθαι, and expressing the manner in which Æschines should have availed himself of the various processes for bringing him to justice, — a usage entirely parallel to that of the English in similar cases. K. § 312, 4, (e). — γράφοντα . . . . γραφόμενον] Observe the difference between the act. and mid. of this verb; the act. part. means "proposing," the mid. "indicting." The latter, like other verbs of accusing, governs the gen. of the crime or charge (παρανόμων, "illegal measures"), K. § 274, 2; C. § 53, 12. — οὐ γὰρ δήπου . . . . ἐγράψατο] "for surely it cannot be that he prosecutes Ctesiphon on my account, and that he would not have indicted me myself (ἐμὲ . . . . αὐτὸν), had he supposed that he should convict me." This is said to show that there must have been sufficient hostility to him on the part of Æschines to prompt a prosecution of him, had he seen any chance of success. The relation between the protasis and apodosis here is such as to deny the reality both of the condition and the thing conditioned. K. § 339, I. (b); C. § 74, 2. For ἐμέ . . . . αὐτόν, see § 279.

14. Καὶ μὴν] "and indeed," "furthermore." Often employed to introduce a new thought by way of confirmation. K. § 316, 1, (c). — εἰσὶ νόμοι . . . . χρῆσθαι] "there are laws concerning all cases, and punishments, and actions, and trials, having severe and heavy damages, and it was lawful to avail himself of all these." "τὰ ἐπιτίμια sunt omnino quæ quis luere debet, sive debeat παθεῖν sive ἀποτίσαι." *Dissen.* This is the definition which Demosthenes gives of τίμημα, Orat. adv. Mid., p. 523. The two words are substantially the same in meaning as they are in derivation. On this and also τιμωρίαι, see note on § 12. — καὶ ὁπηνίκα ἐφαίνετο, κ. τ. λ.] "and when he had appeared," etc.; i. e. in case he had. It will be observed that this is the protasis to the clause beginning with ὡμολογεῖτο, and hence should regularly be introduced by εἰ. K. § 339, I. (b). I do not recollect another case of this kind, though there may be others. — τοῖς πρὸς ἐμέ] "those suited to my case." πρὸς ἐμέ acquires a kind of substantive idea by having the article prefixed, like τοῖς ἐμοῖς, "mine," and hence the omission of the noun to which τοῖς refers. K. §§ 244, 10, and 263, d. See, also, τὸ κατ' ἐμέ, §§ 246, 247.

15. τοσούτοις ὕστερον χρόνοις] Not "after so long a time," but "in times so long after." Hence it is time definite, and therefore in the dat. K. § 283, 3; C. § 60, 7. — ὑποκρίνεται, "acts a part," "exaggerates the case," "makes sweeping charges," after the extravagant style of actors. The length of time which had elapsed since the pretended crimes, of course, was favorable to this. — Εἶτα . . . . φαίνεται] "Then he brings his charges against me, while he puts this man (i. e. Ctesiphon) on trial, and evinces as the cause (προΐσταται) of the whole trial the enmity he has against me, while never having directly met me for this

(i. e. on this ground), he ostensibly seeks to take away the political privileges of another." It may be observed, in illustration of this passage, that almost the entire speech of Æschines is taken up in severe remarks and strictures upon the character and course of Demosthenes, while next to nothing is said of Ctesiphon, and that in a comparatively mild tone. The way in which this suit would take away the political privileges of Ctesiphon was, by fixing a heavy penalty, which he could not pay, in case he lost his cause, and thus rendering him a public debtor, which would deprive him of all political rights until the debt was discharged. Herm. Polit. Antiq. § 124.

16. ἂν λέγειν] "might say." ἄν is used with the infinitive in all cases where it would be used in the construction with the finite verb, and hence gives the infin. something of the force of the moods. K. § 260, 2, (5), (a); C. § 73, 4. — ὅτι τῆς ἡμετέρας ἔχθρας .... ζητεῖν] "that it was just for us to fight out the battle of our enmity by ourselves, not to neglect a personal contest while we seek some other person upon whom to inflict an injury." ἐξετασμός does not seem to differ from ἐξέτασις, except it be, as Dissen suggests, a word of somewhat lower application, to disputes and wrangling. ἐξέτασιν ποιεῖν, § 226, means "to make an examination," and ἐξετασμὸν ποιεῖσθαι here might be rendered "to make a review," "measure the strength of," — the verb being in the mid. in the latter case on account of the action referring to themselves. ἑτέρῳ δ' ὅτῳ presents a case of inverted attraction, the antecedent being attracted into the case of the relative, instead of the reverse of this. K. § 332, R. 11; C. § 52, R. 7.

17. ἄν τις ἴδοι] "any one might see," i. e. if he would but consider the case. ἄν always refers to a condition either expressed or implied. K. § 260, 1. — ἐπ'] "in conformity with." K. § 296, (3), (c). — ὅσα ὑπὲρ .... μου] "what he falsely charged upon me concerning the peace and the embassy." See Æsch. contr. Ctesiph. § 62 seq. The peace

here referred to was the peace which the Athenians made with Philip, king of Macedonia, called the peace of Philocrates; and the embassy, that sent by the Athenians for the purpose of obtaining the ratification of the peace, on the part of Philip, which had been voted on their part just before (19th of Elaphebolion, B. C. 346, Dem. F. L., p. 359, § 64). A previous embassy had been sent a few months before. Demosthenes and Æschines were both placed upon each of these embassies. On the first embassy they were harmonious and on very intimate terms, but during the deliberations concerning the peace which took place on their return, they fell into some difference with regard to the conditions upon which the peace should be concluded, and from this point separated more and more widely, till they became most violent enemies. This enmity first vented itself publicly in the prosecution which Demosthenes brought against Æschines, after their return from the second embassy, for malversation. The speeches of both on this trial are extant, and contain a full account of the proceedings with regard to the peace and the embassy here alluded to. The last exhibition of this enmity was made in the prosecution which Æschines brought against Ctesiphon, for proposing to crown Demosthenes for his eminent public services, which gave rise to this oration and that of Æschines on the same subject. As to the peace itself, it had reference to certain difficulties which Athens had had with Philip in regard to Amphipolis, a city of Thrace, and other northern possessions. Philip, taking advantage of the Social War in which Athens was involved (B. C. 358), had taken Amphipolis, and also certain other places in Macedonia, Thessaly, and Thrace, which belonged to Athens. Athens attempted in return to gain these back, but, after contending for this with but little success for eleven years, and despairing of any assistance from the other Grecian states, who were taken up with their own petty variances (§§ 18–21), she finally consented to make peace with him. For a fuller account of this whole subject, see Thirlw., Vol. II. pp. 66 – 128. — Ἔστι δ' ἀναγκαῖον, κ. τ. λ.] "But it is necessary, O Athenians, and proper perhaps, to remind you how things were in those times, that you may contemplate each one of them in reference to the juncture in question," i. e. the making of the peace with Philip. ὑπάρχων is used both of the past and the present, according as the discourse is of the past or present. We also find τότε and νῦν with it sometimes, especially when the thing referred to had changed since some former period. See § 98: οὐ φοβηθέντες τὴν τότε Θηβαίοις ῥώμην καὶ δόξαν ὑπάρχουσαν, "the *then* existing" (though not now). Other participles are also used to designate the existence of things contemporaneous with the time of the speaker; as, ὤν, παρών, ὑπών, etc.; but they all have a different shade of meaning from ὑπαρχών. See § 1, note.

18. Τοῦ γὰρ Φωκικοῦ συστάντος πολέμου] The war here alluded to is better known under the name of the Second Sacred War. The Phocians had taken possession of, and subjected to cultivation, a portion of land in the vicinity of Delphi, consecrated to Apollo, and doomed by a decree of the Amphictyons to lie for ever waste. For this, at the instigation of the Thebans, they were threatened by the Amphictyons with the confiscation of their territory to the god whom they had robbed. Being rendered desperate by such a threat, they seized upon the temple of Apollo, and robbed it of its treasures, in order to obtain the means of defending themselves. At first the principal enemy they had to contend with was the Thebans, but afterwards these were joined by some Thessalian tribes, and finally by Philip. This war broke out in the year 355 B. C., and continued about ten years. See Thirlw., Ch. 43. — οὐ γὰρ δὴ ἔγωγε ἐπολιτευόμην πω τότε] "for not then as yet, as is well known (δή), was I engaged in proposing public measures." His first speech before the people, De Symmoriis, was made, according to Dissen, the year following the commencement

of the war. — πρῶτον μὲν ὑμεῖς οὕτω διέκεισθε] The orator here uses the mildest terms possible, on account of the popular feeling towards the Phocians for robbing the temple of Delphi. The fact is, however, that the Athenians, from their hatred to Philip, who, they saw, was fomenting the war against the Phocians for selfish purposes, early entered into an alliance with them, though they seem not to have taken any very active part in the war, other than to prevent the interference of Philip. — ἐν Λεύκτροις] "at Leuctra." A small town in Bœotia, where the Thebans, under their general, Epaminondas, gained a great victory over the Spartans (B. C. 371), which gave them the ascendency among the states of Greece, and made them very haughty and overbearing. This ascendency had been enjoyed successively by Sparta, by Athens, and now by Thebes. — ἔπειθ' . . . . ταραχή] "Besides, all Peloponnesus had become divided, and neither were those hating the Lacedemonians strong enough to subdue them, nor were those formerly supported in power by them (lit. ruling by means of them) masters of the cities; but there was both among these and all the other states a certain interminable strife and commotion." The state of things here described is that which existed in Greece some fifty years after the Peloponnesian war; when Sparta had been humbled by Thebes, and was but just able to maintain her ascendency in the Peloponnesus without extending her ambition to other parts of Greece, and Thebes was looked upon with distrust both by Sparta and Athens. By the enemies of Sparta in the Peloponnesus here alluded to were meant, more especially, the Messenians, the Arcadians, and the Argives; the three principal states in that peninsula besides Sparta, with which she was engaged in a constant struggle in order to keep them in proper subordination. When at the height of her power, at the close of the Peloponnesian war, her general, Lysander, had established in these and all other cities which fell into his hands her favorite form of oligarchical government, called δεκαδαρχία or δεκαρχία, by promoting to power, in each place, ten citizens the most devoted to her interests. For the character and working of these unnatural governments, see Isoc. Panegyr., pp. 63, 64. Compare also Herm. Polit. Antiq., § 39, 7 and 8. These, however, now, during her humiliation, they had succeeded in expelling, though they were not as yet able to gain any absolute ascendency over their former tyrannical mistress. This statement will sufficiently explain the passage under consideration.

19. τοῖς παρ' ἑκάστοις . . . . ἐφύετο] "lavishing treasures upon the traitors in each state, he set them all by the ears, and stirred them up against each other; then, while the others (i. e. the other Greeks besides the Athenians) were remiss in their duty (i. e. to come to the aid of Athens, in bringing her contest with Philip to a successful close, and thus preventing his encroachments upon Grecian interests), and were quarrelling among themselves, he was preparing himself and increasing in power against all." αὑτοὺς is the reflexive for the reciprocal pronoun (K. § 302, 7). The treasures here spoken of, by which Philip purchased adherents and advocates in every state, were obtained from the mining district of Pangæus, in Thrace, which he had obtained possession of by his northern conquests. In that corrupt age, in which almost every man could be bought, they were of great service to him in prosecuting his designs against Greece. — οἱ τότε . . . . Θηβαῖοι] "the then overbearing, but now unfortunate Thebans." The change in the condition of the Thebans here mentioned was occasioned by the destruction of Thebes by Alexander, the son and successor of Philip; who, on account of their attempt to throw off the Macedonian yoke, had (335 B. C.) razed the city to the ground, and sold the inhabitants as slaves. The times here contrasted were that of the Phocian war, and that of the delivery of this oration. At the former period, the Thebans were at the height of their power, it being not long after the battle of Leuctra. But since that

event some twenty-five years or more had passed, during which Thebes had been gradually losing power, till she finally met with this overthrow from Alexander. In order to make out this interval between the two periods, I place the time of the delivery of this oration, with most critics, about six years after the prosecution which called it forth was first instituted. It was thus deferred by the prosecutor, as is supposed, in order to obtain a more favorable opportunity for succeeding in his cause; which at length was thought to offer itself, when the Macedonian arms had completely triumphed in Greece under Alexander. It was at this juncture, therefore, that it was brought on for a final decision, though first moved soon after the battle of Chæronea. — *αἱ πόλεις*] Athens and Thebes. The Thebans, being hard pressed by the Phocians, would very naturally look to the Athenians for aid, since they were near at hand, and, though not particularly friendly, still were apparently no further interested in the war than to prevent the interference of Philip, with whom they were in a state of hostility. The wily king, therefore, threw them a sop, by offering them peace, and turned and joined himself to the Thebans against the Phocians.

20. *Τί οὖν . . . . εἰπεῖν*] "What then coöperated with him for taking you almost his willing dupes? (What contributed to his finding you so ready to listen to his proposals?) *The* of the other Greeks — (I hardly know whether it is proper to call it cowardice or ignorance, or both these together)." *ὀλίγου δεῖν* expresses a limitation, and properly depends upon *ὡς* understood. K. § 341, R. 3; C. § 70, 16. — *ὡς ἔργῳ φανερὸν γέγονεν*] "as has become evident from the issue." By the issue her. alluded to, as showing that the struggle against Philip, so long maintained by Athens, was for the common interest of Greece, is meant the subsequent course of Philip, who, having quieted the Athenians by offering them peace, proceeded to subjugate the Phocians, and then, n turn, the other tribes of Greece. — *συγχωρηθεῖσα*] "agreed

upon." — διέβαλλεν] See Æsch. §§ 60 – 63. — τὰ δὲ τούτων . . . . αὐτῇ] "but the wrong-doings and corruptions of these in making it." τούτων refers to Æschines and his party, who might not have all been present, but were spoken of thus as a well-known clique opposed to Demosthenes.

21. Καὶ ταυτὶ πάνθ' . . . . διεξέρχομαι] "And all these, for the sake of the truth, I am going accurately to examine and set forth." For this fut. use of the pres., see K. § 255, R. 4. We have here another instance of oratorical pleonasm for the purpose of fulness or emphasis. Such expressions are far from being mere tautology. When used with skill and moderation, as is generally the case with Demosthenes, and not to excess and merely for the sake of rhythm, as is often done by Cicero, the different words always present the idea under different aspects; the one being more general and the other more special, the one stronger and the other weaker, the one simple and the other figurative, or with some such difference. Dissen has collected the following instances from this oration, which it may be worth while to copy here: ἀξιῶ καὶ δέομαι, § 6; ἐτραγῴδει καὶ διεξῄει, § 13; κατεψεύδου καὶ διέβαλλες, § 11; βοᾶν καὶ διαμαρτύρεσθαι, § 23; δηλοῦν καὶ διορίζεσθαι, § 40; προὔλεγον καὶ διεμαρτυρόμην, § 45; οὐκ ὀνειδίζειν οὐδὲ λοιδορεῖσθαι, § 276; λοιδορούμενος καὶ διασύρων, § 180; πολεμεῖν καὶ διαφέρεσθαι, § 31; προορώμενος καὶ λογιζόμενος, § 27; μηδ' ὁτιοῦν προορᾶν μηδ' αἰσθάνεσθαι, § 40; εἰδὼς καὶ ἑωρακώς, § 248; βοῶν καὶ κεκραγώς, § 132; εἰπεῖν καὶ ἀπαγγεῖλαι, § 33; ζώντων Ἀθηναίων καὶ ὄντων, § 72; ἐδίδαξας καὶ διεξῆλθες, § 22; διέβαλλε καὶ διεξῄει, § 14. — Εἰ γὰρ . . . . πρὸς ἐμέ] "For if any wrong-doing, however great (τὰ μάλιστα), should appear in these transactions, surely it pertains in no respect to me." τὰ μάλιστα here is used as in Xen. Apol. § 18: ὅτε τὰ μάλιστα ἡ πόλις εὐδαιμονεῖ; also Orat. adv. Leptin. § 2; i. e. it is an adverbial acc. expressing quantity. K. § 279, R. 8; C. § 57, R. 6. See also § 95. How any wrong-doing in making the peace could have nothing to do

with him the orator proceeds to show, by stating, first, who suggested it, then who took up the suggestion and formally proposed the measure (ἐκδεξάμενος καὶ γράψας), and then those who helped these carry the measure through (οἱ δὲ συνειπόντες). — οὐδ' ἂν σὺ διαῤῥαγῇς ψευδόμενος] "not even if you split lying." Referring to the earnestness with which he had endeavored to prove an intimacy and concert of action in this matter between Demosthenes and Philocrates. See Æsch. contr. Ctes. § 62; F. L. § 13. — ὅτου δήποτε ἕνεκα,] "for whatever reason," i. e. for some reasons which he could not stop or did not care to state. For the force of δήποτε in such cases, see K. § 95, (b). — ἐγὼ δ' οὐδὲν οὐδαμοῦ] "but I nothing nowhere." Not to be taken in its most absolute sense. That Demosthenes desired and promoted the peace is certain, though his name does not appear among its original movers. — With regard to the individuals mentioned in different parts of this paragraph, not much is known of most of them; only that they were public men at that time of some prominence at Athens, and belonged to the party devoted to the interests of Philip. Eubulus was the most prominent of the number, and exerted an influence in favor of Philip but little inferior to that exerted by Æschines. Comp. Herm. Polit. Antiq. § 173, 11. One of them, it will be observed, was an actor, which shows that this class of men were held in more estimation then than they are now; perhaps on account of the greater respectability of the profession at that time, but principally, without doubt, on account of the greater demand there was for a popular mode of address in those who were engaged in the management of public affairs.

22. ἐπ' αὐτῆς τῆς ἀληθείας] "in accordance with the truth itself.' The charge alluded to in what follows was connected with the general charge, brought against him by Æschines, of being the author of the peace. It was, that he was so anxious to conclude a peace with Philip, and urged it forward so precipitately, that there was not time

for the delegates who had been sent for from the other states of Greece, to form a common alliance against him, to arrive before it was concluded. See Æsch. § 58. — ὡς ἄρα] "that forsooth, *if any one will believe it.*" It usually implies contempt or disbelief of the statement it introduces. See § 13; also Pop. Orat. of Dem., VIII. § 4, note. — Εἶτ ὦ . . . . διεξῆλθες;] "Then, O — (what uttering could any one address you appropriately?) is there anywhere that you, being present, seeing me depriving the city of so important a transaction and alliance as you just now described, manifested your indignation, or, coming forward, stated and explained these things which you now charge me with?" The first line of this passage presents an instance of a species of *aposiopesis*, of which there are several other examples in this oration. The figure here consists in stopping short when about to designate Æschines, and, instead of applying any epithet to him, signifying his inability to find one sufficiently opprobrious fitly to describe his character And this seems a suitable place to remark, that Demosthenes abounds much more in *figures* than in *tropes*; more in those turns of thought which affect the structure of the sentence, called by the Greeks σχήματα, than in those which concern the application of words. This, indeed, is true to some extent of all the ancient orators, and may be considered as one of the characteristic distinctions between ancient and modern oratory. Oratory was much more cultivated as an art by the ancients than by the moderns, which gave a peculiar cast to their oratorical style, making it almost as unlike their historical or familiar style as poetry to prose. They paid great attention to the rhythm of their sentences, i. e. to such a distribution of the emphatic and the unemphatic words as to produce a regular rising and falling in their sentences, or an harmonious flow. It follows from this, that striking modes of address, and artificial turns of sentences, would be much more likely to find a place in ancient than in modern oratory. However, even these do not very much abound in Demosthenes; — more than any other orator, probably, whether ancient or modern, he depended for success upon a thorough discussion, and a forcible and vivid presentation of the whole subject to his hearers.

23. Καὶ μὴν . . . . λοιπὸν ἦν] "And truly, if I had sold to Philip the preventing of the union of the Greeks, it remained to you not to be silent." The refutation here given of the charge is drawn from the fact that Æschines did not accuse him of it at the time. This argument is frequently made to tell against Æschines throughout the oration. Æschines anticipated it (§§ 215–229), and endeavored in vain to break its force. — τουτοισί] "to these," i. e. the Athenians. — οὔτε γὰρ . . . . ἐξεληλεγμένοι] "for neither was an embassy sent at that time to any of the Greeks, but, long before, all had been proved indifferent." Hence there was no motive for sending to them. The discrepancy between the statements of the rival orators on this point is rendered still more difficult of reconciliation by an expression of Demosthenes (F. L., p. 345), which recognizes the presence of certain ambassadors from other states on the occasion of making the peace. But this difficulty is obviated, by supposing that the ambassadors there referred to were merely the deputies of the *allies* of Athens, while Æschines pretended that deputies were expected also from the states not in alliance, so as to form a general alliance. See Thirlw., Vol. II. p. 120.

24. He now proceeds to a direct refutation of the charge by an argument drawn from the nature of the case. After stating in plain language the inconsistency implied in the charge, he finally shows its absurdity by an oratorical syllogism or *enthymem*, which, at the same time, he contrives to enliven, by throwing it into the interrogative form. — καὶ βουλόμενοι] "even wishing." — αὐτοὶ δὲ] "but yourselves." Opposed to τοὺς μὲν Ἕλληνας. — Εὐρυβάτου πρᾶγμα] "the deed of a Eurybatus." A proverbial expression, denoting shameless treachery, having its origin in the treacherous

conduct of a certain Ephesian by the name of Eurybatus or Eurynates, as some have it. — Οὔκουν οὔτε, κ. τ. λ.] "Therefore, I neither appear to be the original mover nor the cause of the peace, nor, of the other things which he falsely charged upon me, is any thing shown to be true." For the various usages of οὔκουν or οὐκοῦν, see K. § 324, R. 7. The negative contained in this particle extends to the whole sentence, while that of οὔτε . . . . οὔτε extends only to their respective clauses. For the participles with the verbs φαίνομαι and δείκνυται, see K. § 310, 4, (b), and for the difference between their construction with participles and infinitives, see K. § 311, 8 and 11.

25. βουλεύων] "being a senator," i. e. a member of the Senate of Five Hundred, with which all decrees originated. — πυνθάνωνται] This is preferable to the optat., since the precise words of the decree are quoted. — τοὺς ὅρκους] "the oaths," i. e. the ratification, on his part, of the treaty of peace. — οὐδὲ γράψαντος ἐμοῦ ταῦτα] "not even after I had proposed these things." K. § 312, 4, (a); C. § 71, III. — Τί δὲ τοῦτ' ἠδύνατο] "But what could this effect?"

26. ὁ δὲ . . . . ἐπραγματεύετο] "but he all the time was specially intent upon this," i. e. that the Athenians should give up all preparations for war. — ὅσα τῆς πόλεως] "whatever of what belonged to the city," i. e. Athens, which, by the Athenians, like Rome by the Romans, was called, by way of eminence, *the* city. — ἕξειν] "should hold." The fut. is often thus used in dependent clauses. K. § 255, 3.

27. The Thracians, here spoken of as the allies of Athens, were those occupying the southern part of Thrace, the subjects of Cersobleptes, to whom the Athenians were under obligation on account of his having ceded to them the Cherronesus. The places named as having been ridiculed (διέσυρε) by Æschines belonged to his kingdom, and were situated near the mouth of the river Hebrus, and in the vicinity of the Sacred Mountain, as it was called, one of the most important military posts in all that region. Being seaports,

they were accessible to the Athenian ships, which it was of great importance to Philip to exclude from the coast. Æschines in his speech (§ 82) had jumbled up these with several other similar names, in such a manner as to produce a ludicrous effect, and asserted that they were known, even in name, to Demosthenes alone. — οὕτω] "thus," "under these circumstances," i. e. while the Thracians were in possession of the strongholds alluded to. — τοὺς ἐπικαίρους τῶν τόπων] "the favorably situated of the places." The noun here, instead of agreeing in case with the adjective, is put in the gen. after it, as is often the case in Greek. K. § 264, R. 5, (a). — μηδὲ πολλῶν μὲν χρημάτων, κ. τ. λ.] "nor that having become possessed of much money and many men, by means of these might easily enter upon the other undertakings," i. e. the conquest of Greece.

28. We have here an instance of the skill of Demosthenes in mingling the weak arguments with the strong. Having made out a very strong case in his favor relative to the embassy, he seizes the opportunity of bringing up in contrast with this the petty charge of his adversary (Adv. Ctesiph. § 76), founded upon the attentions which he had bestowed upon the ambassadors of Philip, who had recently visited Athens to negotiate concerning the peace, in order to show his want of generosity in taunting him with the latter, while he gave him no credit for the former. There being no special minister of foreign affairs at Athens, the duty of receiving ambassadors devolved upon members of the Senate, and it was in this capacity, he says, that he entertained, and introduced to the assembly and the theatre, the ambassadors of Philip. — θέαν] "sight," "place to see," "seat in the theatre." — τὸν ἀρχιτέκτονα] "architect." So called because he kept the theatre in repair. He was properly the *lessee of the theatre*, who, upon condition of receiving the entrance-money, agreed to keep it in repair and pay to the state a certain sum. See Boeckh, Pub. Econ. Ath., Bk. II., 294. — ἐν τοῖν δυοῖν ὀβολοῖν,] "in the sum of

two oboli," "by means of two oboli." See Soph. Antig., v. 764: ἐν ὀφθαλμοῖς ὁρῶν, "seeing *with* the eyes." Or, perhaps, "in the two obols," i. e. the common seats. Two obols was the regular price for admission to the theatre, which, however, were given from a public fund, called the Theoricon, to all who applied for it. See Boeckh, as above. — τὰ δ' ὅλα] "the whole," "the highest interests of the state." — Λέγε] Addressed to the clerk. For the genuineness of this and the other documents found in this Oration, see Appendix.

29. Ἐπὶ ἄρχοντος Μνησιφίλου] In the time of Demosthenes, the chief magistracy at Athens was filled by Archons. There were nine of these chosen annually, one of whom was called *the* Archon by way of eminence, and also Eponymus, because the year was named from him: all writings receiving for their date, as the decree now under consideration, the day and month of the archonship of such and such a one, instead of such and such a year. The month Hecatombæon, here mentioned, was the first in the Attic year; so called from its being the season of offering hecatombs. It corresponded to the last part of our July and the first part of August. As the different Athenian months are often mentioned in the course of the Oration, and as the order of their succession and their relation to our months is a matter of some dispute among the learned, I subjoin here a list of them as arranged by the German chronologist, Ideler, taken from the supplement of Passow's Greek Lexicon. It should be observed, however, that, as their months were lunar, they were obliged every other year to introduce an intercalary month, which followed Poseideon and was called Poseideon II.

Hecatombæon	30	days	—	latter part of	July	and first of	Aug.
Metageitnion	29	"	—	"	Aug.	"	Sept.
Boedromion	30	"	—	"	Sept.	"	Oct.
Pyanepsion	29	"	—	"	Oct.	"	Nov.
Mæmacterion	30	"	—	"	Nov.	"	Dec.

Poseideon	29 days	— latter part of	Dec.	and first of	Jan.
Gamelion	30 "	— "	Jan.	"	Feb.
Anthesterion	29 "	— "	Feb.	"	Mar.
Elaphebolion	30 "	— "	Mar.	"	April.
Munychion	29 "	— "	April	"	May.
Thargelion	30 "	— "	May	"	June.
Scirophorion	29 "	— "	June	"	July.

The phrase ἕνῃ καὶ νέᾳ means, literally, *old and new.* This was a common designation for the last day of every month; probably from the months being lunar, and hence consisting of 29½ days each, while in the calendar they were reckoned, for the sake of convenience, as having alternately 29 and 30 days, giving to those of 30 days a half of a day more than properly belonged to them. Hence, the last day strictly belonged partly to the old and partly to the new month, which was indicated by the expression here quoted. And being once employed as a designation for the last day of the longer months, it would very naturally be applied, also, to the last day of the others. For the rest, it may be observed, that the first day of each month was called νουμηνία, and the second δευτέρα ἱσταμένου or ἀρχομένου μηνός; and so up to ten, repeating after each ordinal number ἱσταμένου or ἀρχομένου μηνός (*of the commencing month*). From ten to twenty, the same ordinal numbers, πρώτη, δευτέρα, etc., were placed before μεσοῦντος μηνός (*the middle of the month*), or before ἐπὶ δεκάδι or δέκα (*in addition to a decade*, or *ten*). From twenty to the end of the month, either the same ordinal numbers were prefixed to ἐπὶ εἰκάδι or εἴκοσι (*in addition to twenty*); or the ordinals were inverted, beginning for twenty-one with δεκάτη, if the month had 30 days, and ἐνάτη, if it had but 29, and proceeding in an inverted order down to δευτέρα, affixing to each the words φθίνοντος, παυομένου, or ἀπιόντος μηνός (*from the ceasing* or *close of the month*). — φυλῆς πρυτανευούσης] "the presiding tribe." The people of Attica were divided into ten tribes, and these again into a hundred, and afterwards into a hundred and seventy-four *demi* or boroughs. Each tribe had a name derived from some hero or mythic character connected with the nation, and in the time of Demosthenes were each represented in the Senate of Five Hundred by fifty senators. The delegation from each tribe undertook, in a regular order of succession, which they determined by lot, the presidency of the body, each for the space of 35 or 36 (in intercalary years 38 or 39) days. For this purpose each of the delegations elected from their own number, by lot, a president, called ἐπιστάτης, who was intrusted with the keys of the treasury and archive office, and with the state seal. His duty was to act as presiding officer in the Senate during the presidency of his tribe, and as the organ of the Senate in general, and of the presiding tribe in particular, in all matters of business. He originally, also, presided at the assemblies of the people, till the presidency of this body was assigned to nine πρόεδροι, appointed by himself, one out of each of the other nine tribes. This is Hermann's view; but, according to another view of the subject, which may be found in Smith's Dict. Antiq. (Art. Βουλή), the presiding tribe was divided into five sections of ten each (called πρόεδροι), which exercised the presidency in turn for seven days, and chose an ἐπιστάτης daily, while the *proëdri non contribules*, as they are called, exercised a very different function. The presiding tribe, besides presiding in the Senate and calling the assemblies of the people, acted as a committee of the Senate, to transact the various kinds of business which devolved upon that body as a supreme court, while not in session. For this purpose this tribe was maintained at the public expense at the Prytaneum, where they spent nearly the whole time, so as to be ready to act with authority in the occurrences of the day which required their intervention. Comp. Herm. Polit. Antiq. § 127. — ὁμολογουμένας] "acknowledged," "formally proposed." — δεδόχθαι] "that it be decreed." An infinitive depending upon εἰπεῖν above. — ἐν τῇ πρώτῃ ἐκκλησίᾳ] i. e. the first of the four regular assemblies held during each prytany. — ἐκ πάντων Ἀθηναίων] i. e. as a body, without regard to tribes. The patrial adjective belonging to each of the names of the ambassadors was to define the demus or borough to which each of them belonged, and where their names were originally registered as citizens. The list of ambassadors is defective and incorrect. See Appendix.

30. οἱ χρηστοὶ πρέσβεις οὗτοι] "these excellent ambassadors." χρηστός is often used thus, ironically. See § 89: ἣν οὗτοι κατὰ τῆς πατρίδος τηροῦσιν οἱ χρηστοὶ ἐπὶ ταῖς μελλούσαις ἐλπίσιν. — τρεῖς ὅλους μῆνας] This does not seem to be strictly true. It was nearly three months from the time the peace was *voted* to the time of the return of the ambassadors, but appears to have been but a little more than *two*, from the time of their actual departure from Athens to their return, — from Munychion 3d (B. C. 346) to Scirophorion 13th. See Æsch. F. L., p. 40, and Dem. F. L., p. 359. — ἦλθε] "returned." He was absent on an expedition to Thrace when they arrived, and they waited there till his return. — ἐξόν] "it being possible." An accusative absolute, concerning which see K. § 312, 5; C. § 71, III. 2. — τὸν Ἑλλήσποντον] The Thracian Cherronesus lying on the Hellespont, where Philip was engaged in reducing the places referred to above.

31. τοιοῦτον] That is, such as described above; — it refers both to κλέμμα and δωροδόκημα.

32. αὐτῶν . . . . ἀπίωμεν] I retain this reading, in preference either to putting the pronoun in the first person or the verb in the third, since Demosthenes means evidently to deny that he, though on the embassy, had any thing to do with the transaction in question. This is perfectly in keeping with all that he says on the subject in his Oration on the False Legation. He there represents himself as having been extremely impatient of the delay, and even, on one occasion, as having hired a ship to return alone, but as being prevented by his colleagues. See especially p. 405, init.,

and p. 445, init. — Πύλας] *Thermopylæ.* A narrow pass through the mountainous ridge separating Thessaly from Greece, presenting by far the most eligible route, and indeed almost the only one, from the northern regions to the south. Hence, if this was shut up against an enemy north of the mountains, his progress was effectually arrested. The occasion here alluded to, on which the Athenians closed this passage against Philip, was several years previous to the time of the peace here under discussion, in the early part of the Phocian war (B. C. 353). Since that time he had occupied himself mostly in reducing Olynthus, a powerful and independent city in the southern part of Macedonia, and at that time an ally of Athens.

33. Οὕτω . . . . τουτονί] "But Philip was in so much fear and anxiety, lest, even although he had taken these preliminary steps, you, having obtained information before the Phocians were destroyed, should vote to assist them, and his projects should fail of success, that he hires this despicable fellow here." οὕτω is often thus separated from its word. See §§ 163, 220. So also πολύς often stands with the second of two nouns to which it refers. See § 299. I have restored the common reading here (instead of Bekker's, which inserts εἰ before πρὸ and leaves out ἀκούσαντες, αὐτοῖς, and also καὶ before ἐκφύγοι) for what I consider sufficient reasons. In the first place, εἰ would require an ἄν in the corresponding clause (K. § 339, II. a.), which no MS. gives. Again, μή, expressing an end (*that* or *lest*), is generally used with the subjunctive and optative without ἄν, after verbs of *fear*, *anxiety*, etc. (Jelf's Kühner, § 814.) As to αὐτοῖς, though suspected by some, it seems to be required both by the connection and the laws of the language. See §§ 39, 292.

34. Ἀξιῶ, κ. τ. λ.] The reader will observe the tact with which the orator, on this and several other occasions, throws upon his opponent the blame of leading him into any discussions foreign to the subject.

35. ἔσται . . . . Θηβαίων] "for all things will turn out as you wish, if you remain quiet, and within two or three days you will hear that he has become the friend of those against whom he comes an enemy, and, on the contrary, the enemy of those to whom he comes a friend. For not words, he said, confirm friendships, uttering it with all gravity, but community of interests; and that it is alike for the interest of Philip and the Phocians, and you all, to be freed from the stupidity and oppressiveness of the Thebans." But perhaps ἀναλγησίας means "savageness," as this character is often ascribed to the Thebans. See Adv. Lept. § 109. The change of feeling in Philip, which Æschines is here represented as persuading the Athenians to believe was about to take place, had reference to the Athenians and Thebans. He had excited his countrymen to hope, that, from what he knew of Philip's character and intentions they had nothing to fear from him; but that he would very naturally become their friend, and the enemy of Thebes, as soon as he became acquainted with the true character and relations of the two nations. It will be seen from this, as well as the following passage, that the Thebans were very much disliked at Athens. This arose, in part, as has already been stated, from the tyrannical manner in which they exercised the superiority they gained at Leuctra; and in part, from their betraying the liberties of Greece in the Persian war, which was always remembered against them, and in part, on account of their stupidity and want of genius.

36. οὐκ εἰς μακράν] The news of the destruction of Phocis reached Athens fourteen days after the return of the embassy. — καὶ ἔτι . . . . Φιλίππῳ] "and even besides these things, that the hatred (formerly felt) towards the Thebans and Thessalians fell to the city, and the gratitude felt on account of what had been done fell to Philip." The destruction of the Phocians was a popular thing among many of the tribes of Greece, on account of the horror with

which they were looked upon for violating the temple of Apollo, and appropriating to themselves so unscrupulously the common offerings of the Greeks deposited there. Philip, therefore, gained favor with many by subduing them, and the Athenians incurred odium with the same by opposing him; since it could easily be said, that in opposing him they were sustaining the Phocians in their impiety.

37. συγκλήτου . . . . γνώμῃ] "at an assembly called by the generals, with the approbation both of the prytanes and the Senate." During each prytany, or the term for which each tribe presided, there were either three or four regular assemblies; any others which it was necessary to have during this time were extraordinary, and might be called either by the generals or by the prytanes, according as their object was to consult on military or civil affairs. This was naturally called by the generals, as it was in order to take precautionary measures against an invasion of Attica by Philip. "This measure," says Thirlwall (Vol. II. p. 126), "was no doubt less an effect of a real panic, than a burst of ill-humor, which it would have been wiser to suppress."

38. περὶ δὲ . . . . βουλῆς] "but concerning the impossibility, let the general of the infantry, and the commissary, and the clerk of the Senate, judge." They were appointed in the present emergency, as a kind of court, to judge of the validity of the excuses of those who refused to obey the directions given in the decree. For the meaning of ὅπλων in the sense of ὁπλιτῶν, see note, § 115. — Εἶπε Καλλισθένης Φαληρεύς] This statement is to be regarded as made by the proposer himself; but that at the first part of the decree as made by the clerk of the assembly in recording the decree.

39. This letter was written soon after the passing of the above decree, for the purpose of warning the Athenians against taking any measures to assist the Phocians, in which light he seems to have regarded the military movements above referred to. It has a calm and confident air about it

which shows that he felt his superiority. — τὰ κατὰ τὴν Φωκίδα] "what pertains to Phocis," "the cities of Phocis." — εἰσαγηοχότας] One form of the perf. act. part. of εἰσάγω. K. § 124, 2, (a). Observe that these introductory clauses employ participles like infinitives to complete the verbal idea of Ἴστε, but the concluding clause of the sentence takes the finite verb. Schäffer shows that this is not uncommon in Greek authors, from Homer downwards. See, also, Jelf's Kühner, §§ 759, Obs. 4, and 765, 2. — Τοῖς μὲν γὰρ ὅλοις] "for on the whole." A phrase very similar in meaning to καθ' ὅλου, found in another letter of Philip, § 77. — μέτριον] "moderate," "reasonable." — Ὥστε ἐὰν, κ. τ. λ.] "So that, if you do not abide by your stipulations, you will get the start of me in nothing except in being the first transgressors."

40. Τοιγαροῦν ἐκ τούτων ᾤχετο ἐκείνους λαβὼν] "Accordingly by these means he went on bearing them away," i. e. deceived them, blinded them. See F. L. § 22; also K. § 310, 4, (1). I have restored Θηβαῖοι to the text after ταλαίπωροι, since without it this word would naturally be referred to the Thessalians as well as Thebans.

41. συνεργὸς καὶ συναγωνιστὴς] "fellow-procurer and promoter." These nouns, besides the gen., take also the dat. by the force of σύν. This is a favorite construction with Demosthenes, since it promotes condensation. — καὶ γεωργῶν τὰ ἐκείνων] "and cultivating their soil." — ὃς εὐθὺς, κ. τ. λ.] "who was immediately demanded by him who did these things," i. e. by Alexander, who, on the destruction of Thebes, sent to Athens, demanding, as a condition of her own safety, nine of the leading anti-Macedonian orators, of whom Demosthenes was one. Æschines, in his speech (§§ 133, 156), had made a great show of sympathy for the Thebans, and rehearsed their calamities in a very touching manner, as being caused, according to his view of the case, by Demosthenes. On the contrary, Demosthenes, in this passage, by placing in contrast the manner in which their

downfall affected him and his antagonist respectively, endeavors to make it appear that his sympathy was wholly feigned, and that he himself has vastly more reason for regretting that event than his adversary. Æschines, for his services in the cause of Philip and his successor, Alexander, which eventually led to the destruction of the Thebans, had been presented with possessions in their country, by the masters whom he served; but he, by resisting them, had exposed himself to their indignation, and had actually been demanded for execution.

42. Ἀλλὰ γὰρ] These particles, coming together thus, always denote a correction or checking of one's self or another. Sometimes the verb expressing the correction is expressed, and sometimes it is understood, as here. An illustration of both usages may be found in Soph. Antig., within a few lines of each other, vv. 148 and 155. — δή] used thus often in resuming the subject. See Dem. Pop. Orat. IV. § 21.

43. Ὑμεῖς δὲ . . . . ὅμως] "But you, looking with suspicion upon what had been done, and being indignant, nevertheless kept the peace"; i. e. the peace before referred to, which was concluded with Philip just before the destruction of Phocis. — Καὶ οἱ ἄλλοι . . . . πολεμούμενοι] "And the other Greeks, also, having been deceived equally with you, and having failed of what they hoped for, gladly kept the peace, although, in a certain sense, being themselves made war upon for a long time." For καί . . . . δέ, "and also," see K. § 322, R. 7; and for the acc. τρόπον τινὰ, § 279, R. 3. The Athenians, and many other Grecian states, seem to have been led, by the representations of Æschines on returning from the second embassy, to expect that Philip, after chastising Phocis for her impiety, was about to humble Thebes. This the Athenians in particular expected he would do, by restoring to their freedom the Bœotian towns, which the Thebans, during their recent prosperous career, had reduced under their power. When, therefore, he proceeded

to unite his arms with those of Thebes, not simply for the chastisement, but for the total destruction of Phocis, her enemy and rival; and besides, to confirm Thebes in her possession of the Bœotian towns, and even to put her in possession of a part of the territory of Phocis; they discovered that they had been imposed upon, and were disappointed in their expectations. But notwithstanding this, and his continued course of unjust encroachments upon Grecian interests, as Demosthenes here states, they preserved peace with him: the Athenians, because they could effect nothing alone by an open rupture, and the other states from indifference, being contented with peace themselves, however much the interests of Greece at large might suffer. This selfish indifference, this want of an enlarged patriotism embracing every thing that was Grecian, is what Demosthenes complains of in this and the following passages, as well as in other parts of the Oration.

44. Ὅτε γὰρ περιιὼν ὁ Φίλιππος] "For when Philip going around," i. e. extending his conquests in different directions. Of the two tribes here mentioned, the first was situated on the north of Macedonia, and the last belonged to Thrace. — ἐπὶ τῇ τῆς εἰρήνης ἐξουσίᾳ βαδίζοντες] "going thither (i. e. where Philip was) under license of the peace."

45. ἕτερος λόγος οὗτος] "this is another's account." — αἱ δὲ πόλεις . . . . αἰσθέσθαι] "But the cities were diseased, those employed in the political and administrative departments being bribed and corrupted by gold, while the private citizens and the multitude in part did not foresee, and in part were caught with the bait of the present ease and quiet, and all had some such delusion as this, viz. each thought that the calamity would not fall upon themselves, but that, by means of the dangers of others, they should hold securely their own interests, whenever they wished." The genitives absolute in the latter part of this sentence depend upon the verb ἐνόσουν, they being introduced to describe the state of things implied in that verb. πολλῶν, being employed

here in the sense of "the many," would regularly have the article, but, as it stands in close connection with ἰδιωτῶν which has the article, it is omitted. K. § 245, 2; C. § 49, 9. In πλὴν οὐκ (lit. "except not"), οὐκ is used idiomatically, same as it often is after the comparative particle ἤ. K. § 318, R. 7. σχήσειν, a rare form for ἕξειν; but both forms are used indiscriminately by Demosthenes, as will be seen by referring to the following pages in different orations of his, viz. pp. 13, 45, 61, 209, and 234. But ἕξω usually has more strictly the meaning "to have."

46. Εἶτ' αἰσθέσθαι] "Then, I think, it has happened to the masses, instead of the much and unseasonable ease, to perceive that they have lost their liberty, but to the public men and those thinking to sell all else except themselves, that they have bartered away themselves first." πεπρακόσι is in the dat. from the influence of the object of συμβέβηκε, which is also the subject of αἰσθέσθαι. K. § 310, 2; C. § 70, 10. — ἀκούουσιν] "hear themselves called," "are esteemed." K. § 240, 2, (e).

47. οὐδ' ἐπειδὰν . . . . προδότου] "nor when he may have become master of what he has purchased does he any longer employ the traitor as counsellor concerning the remainder; for (were this the case) nothing would be more fortunate than a traitor." An analysis of this sentence will furnish an illustration of several important laws of the language. First, we have two subordinate clauses, one adverbial and the other adjective, each with ἄν and the subj., to represent the statement in each case as something conditioned and indefinite; K. §§ 337, 5, and 333, 3; and then the principal clause, which is followed by the principal clause of a conditional adverbial sentence (having, however, a coördinate connection with the preceding sentences) of which the condition is suppressed. K. § 340, 1. Observe, too, the use of οὐδέν instead of οὐδείς, in order to make the assertion more comprehensive. — πόθεν;] "how can it be so?" Implying very strongly that it could not be so. — Πολλοῦ γε

καὶ δεῖ] "It even wants much of it, indeed." "Very far from it, indeed." — *Ἀλλ' ἐπειδὰν . . . . καταστῇ*] "But when he who aspires to the supremacy may have established himself master of affairs." *τῶν πραγμάτων ἐγκρατὴς* means very much the same as *potitus rerum.*

48. *καὶ γὰρ . . . . εὖ φρονοῦσιν*] "for if the time of these events has passed, at least the time of understanding such things is always present to the wise." Observe the use of *καιρός*, of the "proper time," "a particular point of time," distinct from *χρόνος*, of "time in its duration." Also, of *εἰδέναι*, "to know by reflection," "to understand," distinct from *γιγνώσκειν*, "to perceive," "mark." *εὖ φρονοῦσιν* followed by a dat. would mean "to be well disposed." The individuals named in the following sentences were traitors, whom Philip had employed in the different states, and, when he had accomplished his purposes, cast off as useless. — *Εἶτ' ἐλαυνομένων, κ. τ. λ.*] "Then the whole habitable world was full of traitors rejected and insulted and suffering what not of evil." The use of *πᾶσα ἡ οἰκουμένη* here throws some light upon the use of this phrase, Luke ii. 1. For *τί κακὸν οὐχὶ*, see K. § 344, R. 6.

49. *Ἐξ ὧν, κ. τ. λ.*] "From which facts any one might see even most plainly, that he who guards his country most, and opposes these (traitors) most, this one, Æschines, procures for you traitors and hirelings, the having the means whereby you shall receive bribes; and that through the great mass of these (i. e. the Athenian citizens) and those opposing your designs, you are safe and paid, since, if left to yourselves, you would have perished long ago," i. e. by betraying the state to Philip, as they desired to, and then, like other traitors, being rejected and rendered outcasts. But they had been kept from this end by the patriotism of those who prevented the success of their treachery, and thus prevented them from completing their work and being discharged and cast aside as useless tools by their master.

50. *Καὶ*] "although." Often found thus in conjunction

with a participle expressing a concession. K. § 312, R. 8. The καὶ in the following line means "even," and εἰρῆσθαι is governed by ἱκανῶν. K. § 306, 1, (c). — Αἴτιος δ' . . . . μισθαρνίαν] "But this man is chargeable (i. e. for the speaker's having said so much), having bespattered me with a kind of stale mixture, as it were, of his own depravity and evil-doings, which, to those younger than the events referred to, it was necessary to clear myself of. But you, perhaps, have been wearied, who, even before I said any thing whatsoever, knew of his serving for hire at that time." I have rendered ἑωλοκρασίαν "a stale mixture," it being compounded of ἕωλος, "pertaining to yesterday," hence "old," "stale," and κρᾶσις, "mixture." The reference seems to have been to the remoteness of the events alluded to, and the triteness of the charges founded upon them, as they related to the earliest part of his political course, and had been oft repeated by his opponent. This accusative (ἑωλοκρασίαν), together with μοῦ, is governed by κατασκεδάσας, in the sense "to cast upon" (= *charge upon*), which it has in this place.

52. δοκεῖ μισθωτὸς] In some editions this noun is found with the accent on the antepenult, instead of the ultimate, where it properly belongs, in order to conform to the statement of Ulpian, that the orator purposely put the accent on the wrong syllable, with the design of eliciting a repetition of the word from his hearers, who, on account of the extreme delicacy of their ear to the harmony of language, were accustomed to correct such mistakes in pronunciation. But this story is not adopted by the most judicious critics, as the artifice seems too trivial to be ascribed to Demosthenes, and, indeed, could have availed nothing, as it would have been apparent for what purpose the cry of *hireling* was raised by the multitude. This call upon his hearers, however, to respond to his charge of corruption against his adversary, does manifest great confidence in the agreement of their views of his character with his own; and the per-

ception that he had, by the clear evidence and lively description which he had given of his corruption, made a favorable impression upon their minds, which he wished to render permanent, by inducing them, in the enthusiasm of the moment, to express it in words. The whole of this last paragraph is as fine a specimen of keen and lively raillery as can be found, perhaps, in any language, and forms a suitable close to the first general division of the speech. Having completed the examination of the charges foreign from the indictment, he commences, in the next paragraph, an examination of those contained in the indictment.

53. *ἵνα καίπερ . . . . τυγχάνειν*] "that Æschines, although knowing, nevertheless may hear, on account of what I say, that I am worthy to receive both these rewards decreed by the Senate (i. e. in the decree of Ctesiphon), and even by far greater rewards than these."

54. *ἀπήνεγκε . . . . γραφὴν*] "laid before the archon an indictment for illegal measures." By the archon here alluded to is meant, probably, the first archon. See § 29. The principal business of the archons was to receive complaints concerning crimes, and bring them before the courts for trial; and, indeed, in many cases, to conduct, themselves, the trial on the part of the state. Comp. Herm. Polit. Antiq. § 138. Such cases as this were commonly laid before the Thesmothetæ, but occasionally, as it appears, before the chief archon. — *ὡς ἄρα*] "that indeed, *or* to the effect that." For this usage of *ὡς ἄρα*, see § 73. It is different from that noticed in § 22. — *καὶ ἀναγορεῦσαι . . . . ὁ δῆμος*] "and to proclaim in the theatre at the great Dionysiac festival, at the contest of the new actors, that the people crown." In explanation of this passage, it may be stated that there were at least three different festivals of Dionysus or Bacchus in Attica; the Greater, the Lesser, or country Dionysia, and the Lenæa. The first of these was the most splendid and the best attended, it being open to all the allies of Athens, and even to foreigners. At this only new pieces were

represented, in the representation of which, consequently, the actors appeared in new characters, and were hence called new actors; while at the second, only old ones were represented; and at the last, both new and old, as might happen. Comp. Müller's Greek Literature, Vol. I. p. 296, note.

55. εἶτα τὸν ὑπεύθυνον στεφανοῦν] "in the second place (not permitting) to crown one undischarged of his accounts of office." The infinitive in this passage depends upon ἐώντων above, and so does the infinitive ἀναγορεύειν below. — ἔστι δὲ . . . . τεταγμένος] "but Demosthenes is repairer of the walls, and superintendent of the theoric fund." He was appointed to superintend the repairing of the walls of Athens immediately after the battle of Chæronea, or at least was one of the committee for repairing the walls for that year, and had not been discharged from this office by passing his accounts before the Logistæ when this prosecution was first instituted. He also was superintendent or treasurer of the theoric fund, designed to pay the fees of such as wished to attend the theatre, but had not the means of paying for their admission. It was a large fund, and therefore involved no inconsiderable pecuniary responsibility. — Πυκνὶ] The dative of πνύξ, "Pnyx," the ν being transposed in the nominative for the sake of euphony. It was the place where the assembly of the people met, and took its name from πυκνός, "thick," the people being crowded together there. — Τίμημα τάλαντα πεντήκοντα] "Penalty fifty talents." An immense sum, if we consider that the Attic talent of silver amounted to more than a thousand dollars, and the gold talent to about ten times that sum. The reason of fixing the penalty so high was to render it impossible for him to pay it, if convicted; and thus, according to a standing law, to deprive him of all his political privileges, or to fix upon him what was called the ἀτιμία or *public disgrace*, which had this effect. Comp. Herm. Polit. Antiq. § 124, 9. — Κλήτορες] "witnesses"; i. e. of his having summoned the defendant

to appear and answer to the charge. This indictment, it will be perceived, contains three charges. (1.) That the statements relative to the character and services of Demosthenes were false. (2.) That he was legally disqualified for receiving the honor proposed to be bestowed upon him, by the holding of certain offices. (3.) That the proposed mode of conferring the honor was illegal. These points Demosthenes now proceeds to deduce, and then replies to them in the order in which they here stand.

56. Ἐγὼ δ' . . . . ἀπολογήσομαι] "But from these very charges, I think I shall make it evident to you at the outset that I shall defend myself justly in all things." πρῶτον, when it means "in the first place," "the first in a series," takes μέν with it; see § 1; but without this particle it means simply "first of all," "at the outset"; since the absence of μέν shows that a succession of particulars is not intended. See § 141.—τὴν γὰρ αὐτὴν . . . . τάξιν] i. e. the same which Æschines had followed in his indictment, but not the same which he had followed in his speech. By this inadvertency of Æschines, Demosthenes gains the advantage of such an arrangement of topics as he desires, while he conforms to all that the rules of fair discussion require.

57. Τοῦ μὲν . . . . νομίζω] "Therefore, of the proposing (i. e. by Ctesiphon in his decree) that I continually do and say the best things for the people, and am zealous to do whatever good I can, and to praise me for these things, I think the test lies in my public life." All the first part of the sentence, it will be perceived, is used as a noun in the genitive, and is governed by κρίσιν.

58. Τὸ δὲ μὴ . . . . πεπολιτευμένοις] "But as to his not adding, to crown, 'when he shall have rendered up his accounts,' and his directing to proclaim the crown in the theatre, I think that this also has to do with my public life. Æschines had represented it as a special piece of impudence in Ctesiphon that he had not even added to his proposition to crown Demosthenes, *when he shall have rendered*

up his accounts. See Æsch. § 11. — ἐν τούτοις] "among these," i. e. the people of Athens, who were assembled in large numbers at the great Dionysiac festival. The καὶ after εἴτε was added to this member, according to Dissen, in order to show that the speaker viewed it as the least probable of the two suppositions. See Hom. Il. II. 349. — δεικτέον εἶναί μοι] "I must show." K. §§ 241, 3, and 284, 3, (12); C. § 59, 11.

59. Ἑλληνικὰς πράξεις καὶ λόγους] "Grecian doings and sayings," i. e. those which pertained to Greece at large, and not simply to Athens. All his measures in opposing Philip he considers of this nature, i. e. all enumerated to § 102. — ὁ γάρ, κ. τ. λ.] "for he who prosecutes (the statement) of the decree, that I do and say the best things, and has indicted these things as not true," etc. Strictly speaking, the whole phrase, τὸ λέγειν . . . . με, is a noun governing ψηφίσματος. — Εἶτα καὶ . . . . ἐγώ] "Then, there being many departments of the constitution *or* administration, I chose that which had reference to Grecian doings," i. e. the foreign department of the government. Amidst the general dissensions and jealousies of the different tribes, he chose to devote himself to the foreign relations of the state · in order, if possible, by a high-minded and generous policy towards the other states, to promote a spirit of union, and thus prevent a universal overthrow of the liberties of Greece. And such a line of policy, he contends, was in perfect keeping with, and, indeed, absolutely demanded by, the past history of Athens.

60. Ἃ μὲν οὖν] Demosthenes commences here, at the point where he considers himself responsible for the foreign policy of the city, inasmuch as from this time he gave the direction to this department of the policy. The point to which he refers is the renewal of hostilities with Philip, after the peace before alluded to, his speeches upon which subject were among his earliest political efforts. To this course he aroused the people, and is willing to meet the

responsibility of it; but for previous measures and disasters which his antagonist had charged upon him, he holds that he is not accountable. He thus passes over, with the remarks which have preceded, the first two periods during which Æschines had examined his career, as being irrelevant to the present cause, and commences with the third. See Æsch. §§ 54, 55. — ταῦτα ἀναμνήσω .... ὑπειπὼν] "these I will recall, and of these I will subjoin an account, having premised thus much," i. e. what follows as far as § 62. τοσοῦτος, though generally referring to what precedes, often refers to what follows. So § 124, τοσοῦτον αὐτὸν ἐρωτήσας; also, Xen. Anab. I. 3, 14, μετὰ δὲ τοῦτον Κλέαρχος εἶπε τοσοῦτον. K. § 303, R. 1.

61. φορὰν] "harvest," "rush," "multitude." See § 271, where it means "*force* of circumstances"; also Plato, Gorg. 451, C, where it refers to the *motion* of the heavenly bodies. — οὓς συναγωνιστὰς, κ. τ. λ] "whom having taken as coadjutors and fellow-laborers, he rendered yet more disaffected the Greeks, even before ill-disposed towards each other and divided into factions, by deceiving some, giving to others, and corrupting others in every way, and divided them into many parties, to all of whom there was one interest, to prevent him (Philip) from becoming powerful." χεῖρον is found in the neuter here, and not in agreement with Ἕλληνας, because it expresses an adverbial idea, or refers to its noun in a very general way. K. § 241, 2. For an account of this artful policy of Philip, see Dem. Olynth. II. §§ 6, 7.

62. πράττειν καὶ ποιεῖν] Schäfer says, "Pleonasmus est oratorius, ne putes discrimen significationis inter hæc verba intercedere." But see § 4, n. — ὁ γὰρ .... εἰμὶ ἐγώ] "for I am he who placed himself at this point of the administration," i. e. in the foreign department of the state. See § 59, n. πολιτείας is a partitive gen. depending upon ἐνταῦθα.

63. Πότερον .... γιγνόμενα;] "Whether, O Æschines,

was it fitting for her, relinquishing her own proper spirit and dignity, in the rank of Thessalians and Dolopians, to assist Philip in obtaining the supremacy of the Greeks, and to annul the honors and rights of our ancestors? or if not to do this (for this truly were horrible), yet to allow to take place what it perceived and foresaw, we must suppose, for a long time, was about to take place, if no one should prevent?" The rank formerly held by Athens among the tribes of Greece, especially during the Persian war, was that of leader and guide to the rest; so that she stood as the acknowledged head of them all, both in civilization and refinement. Demosthenes contends, therefore, that she could not, consistently with her past history, have descended from this lofty position in the contest with Philip, and put herself on a level with the rudest and meanest tribes, who had submitted to become his mere tools, by joining with them in helping him subjugate Greece. ὡς ἔοικεν has an ironical meaning here, something like οἶμαι, § 46.

64. ἐβούλετ'] This is also found with the augment ἠ in Demosthenes. See § 101; also Pop. Orat. II. § 15. — συναιτίας] This is an adjective agreeing with μερίδος, to be supplied from the preceding line, and, taken with the words in connection, may be rendered, "whether of that party which shared in causing the evils and disgraces which have befallen the Greeks," etc. Like αἴτιος, its primitive, it governs the genitive, and takes also the dative of the person or thing participated with, by virtue of the σύν with which it is compounded. In the present instance, the dative to be supplied is Φιλίππῳ. — πλεονεξίας] "advantage." The advantage which the states here alluded to hoped to gain from presenting no opposition to Philip was, that he would protect them against Sparta, and perhaps enable them to subdue this tyrannical state. For these were the hopes which he held out to them, and they were effectual in securing their acquiescence in his measures.

65. χεῖρον ἡμῶν ἀπηλλάχασιν] "have come off worse than

we." — Καὶ γὰρ] "and for," the γὰρ referring to a clause understood, which καὶ is designed to introduce, meaning "for this reason," or something of that sort. When these two particles stand together, strictly there is always something understood, which the first is designed to introduce, and the other to confirm; i. e. they are always employed where the case is a strong one and the reason obvious, and hence may be translated "for indeed," "for surely," like the Latin *et enim*. See § 42. The reason which the orator proceeds to give for considering those who acquiesced in the measures of Philip, or assisted him in accomplishing them, "worse off" than those who (like themselves) had opposed him, is in substance this: "that while such would have clearly shown themselves unworthy of the Grecian name, and been justly censurable for not resisting the efforts of Philip to obtain the sovereignty of Greece, however justly and mildly he might have exerted that sovereignty, how much better was their own case, now that he had exerted that power in destroying, as far as he was able, the dignity, supremacy, independence, and even the political institutions of all alike, both his allies and those who had opposed him." I have restored ὅμως and οὐκ to the text, since they seem to be obviously required by the sense. For an account of the treatment of the Thessalians by Philip, who are here especially alluded to, see Thirlw., Vol. II. pp. 132 and 133.

66. Ἢ τί τὸν σύμβουλον . . . . διαφέρει] "Or what was it necessary for the counsellor to advise or propose, the counsellor at Athens, myself? (for this makes the greatest difference)." Athens is the emphatic word in this sentence, and the parenthetical clause refers to it, or rather to the fact of his being counsellor in such a city, which, he says, was a circumstance all-important to be considered in deciding whether the policy which he advised was suitable or not. — A city, he goes on to say, which he well knew had, in all previous time, hazarded every thing for its own elevation and renown, and for the common interests of Greece. This

was especially true in the great contest with Persia, when Athens displayed an energy and patriotism far surpassing those of any other state. He asks then of his adversary, what other course he could have advised, under such circumstances and in such a city.

67. τὸν ὀφθαλμὸν, κ. τ. λ.] This, and the other nouns in this connection, are in the accusative, as denoting the *part affected.* See K. § 279, 7; C. § 57, R. 7. In the course of his numerous campaigns, Philip had been wounded in the various ways here described. — πᾶν ὅ τι . . . . ζῆν] "every, whatever part of his body fortune might wish to take away, readily and cheerfully yielding this up, so as to live with the remainder in honor and glory." πᾶν properly agrees with μέρος, but is separated from it by a part of the relative clause, which has the force of an attributive, in order to increase the intensity of its meaning. I have restored to the text the words ῥᾳδίως καὶ ἑτοίμως, as they seem perfectly consistent with the connection.

68. Πέλλῃ] The capital of Macedonia, where Philip was born and brought up; before his time a very inconsiderable and rude place, but afterwards adorned and rendered illustrious by him and his son Alexander. — μεγαλοψυχίαν] "magnanimity," "elevated views," "lofty ambition." — καὶ τοῦτ', κ. τ. λ.] "and to conceive this in his mind, while to you, being citizens of Athens, and witnessing every day, in all that is said and seen, the memorials of the valor of your ancestors, there should be such a want of spirit, as of your own choice freely to yield up to Philip the liberties of Greece." The Athenians were proud of their history, and were in the habit of dwelling upon it much in their speeches, as we see Demosthenes is, and of exhibiting their achievements in the theatre. In these, therefore, as well as other ways, they were reminded of the valor of their ancestors by what they heard and saw. The word αὐτεπαγγέλτους, "self-proposed," adds something to ἐθελοντὰς, and they are to be taken together as expressing a voluntary wil

.ingness originating with themselves, without being compelled to it.

69. Λοιπὸν . . . . δικαίως] "It remained, therefore, and at the same time was necessary, to resist rightfully all that he was doing wrongfully to you."—πάντα τἄλλ', κ. τ. λ.] "passing by every thing else, Amphipolis," etc. Of the three lists of places given in this and the succeeding sentences, the first presented instances of daring aggression by Philip upon the interests of Athens, before the peace which has been spoken of; the second, during the negotiations concerning the peace; and the third, after its ratification. Hence he says, that, in justification of his course in renewing hostilities with Philip, he will say nothing of the first two lists, but will speak only of the third.

70. οὐδ' εἰ γέγονεν οἶδα] "I do not even know if they have happened," i. e. he would know nothing about them in this connection, would make no account whatever of them. —Καίτοι σύ, κ. τ. λ.] "And yet you at least said, that I, speaking of these things (i. e. at the time of their occurrence), excited these (the Athenians) to hatred (against Philip), although the decrees proposed concerning these events (i. e. censuring the conduct of Philip) were those of Eubulus and Aristophon and Diopithes, not mine, O thou saying recklessly whatever thou pleasest." The charge of Æschines here referred to may be found §§ 82, 83 of his speech.

71. 'Αλλ' ὁ τὴν Εὔβοιαν . . . . τὴν 'Αττικήν] "But when he proceeds to appropriate to himself Eubœa, and prepare a fortification against Attica." Eubœa lay along the eastern coast of Attica, and of course, if possessed by an enemy, would afford an advantageous point from which to annoy the inhabitants. For the advantages of its position see Isoc. Panegyr. p. 63. The position of ἐκεῖνος here is somewhat peculiar, since it usually either precedes or follows both the noun and the article. Occasionally, however, we find it inserted between them, after a word which is to be made

emphatic; as Dem. Orat. de F. L. p. 407: τῆς προτέρας ἐκείνης πρεσβείας. — πόλεις 'Ελληνίδας] For the construction see § 18, note. — τοὺς φυγάδας] "the exiles," i. e. those who had been banished by the dominant or democratic party. These acts, therefore, were an interference with Grecian institutions, and especially insulting to Athens, on account of her highly democratic principles. — φανῆναι] Followed by a participle, as here, it means "to appear," "come forward"; but followed by an infinitive, "to seem." K. § 311, 8.

72. τὴν Μυσῶν λείαν καλουμένην] "the so-called prey of the Mysians." To be called the prey of the Mysians was equivalent to being called the prey of the weakest and most spiritless people; the Mysians, a people of Asia Minor, being proverbial for this character. — καὶ προλέγων, κ. τ. λ.] "and continued forewarning and admonishing you not to give up these things to Philip," i. e. the possessions, rights, interests, etc., spoken of before.

73. τίς τίνος αἴτιός ἐστι] "who is to blame, and of what." A double interrogative. For an explanation of the construction, see K. § 344, R. 7. — Κόπριος] This, and not Κύπριος, has been shown to be the correct reading by Boeckh. *Seewesen*, p. 384. — ἐπὶ τὴν τοῦ σίτου παραπομπὴν] "for the convoying of corn." The corn, as it appears from the letter of Philip, § 77, was brought from the Hellespont to the island of Lemnos. These vessels, being designed as an escort to those which brought the corn, were, of course, armed, and hence were seized by Philip, under the pretext that they were designed to aid the Selymbrians against him. See § 77. — συναχθῶσι] In the plural because βουλή is a noun of multitude.

74. ὅτι οὐ, κ. τ. λ.] λέγειν is to be understood with this clause, which is implied in διαλέξονται above, and is expressed below. — εἰ δέ . . . . λαβών] "but if Amyntas has done this (i. e. taken the vessels), having found the captain doing any thing contrary to his instructions." — καὶ τοῦτο γράψαι

λέγειν] "that they (the ambassadors) direct him (Philip) to write this also." I see no objection to interpreting this difficult passage thus, which leaves the text unmutilated. This meaning of γράφειν is not uncommon even in this Oration; see especially § 41, where it is used in speaking of the contents of Philip's letter.

75. εἶτα πάντες οἱ ἄλλοι] "then all others rather than I." Dissen. — βουλῆς γνώμῃ, κ. τ. λ.] "with the approbation of the Senate, the prytanes and generals, having reported the proceedings of the assembly, stated for their deliberation (ἐχρημάτισαν) that it was the will of the people that they (i. e. the Senate) should choose ambassadors," etc. The approbation of the Senate here, as Dissen supposes, refers to their adopting the measure proposed, = ἔδοξε τῇ βουλῇ. — Ἀριστοφῶν .... εἶπεν] "Aristophon of Colyttus, a proedrus, proposed it," i. e. the decree to elect the ambassadors here named. What we have here seems to be rather the record of the substance of a decree than the decree itself. By πρόεδρος must be meant one of the *proedri non contribules;* as Colyttus, the place to which he is said to have belonged, did not come within the limits of the tribe Hippothoontis, which is spoken of as the presiding tribe.

76. δεικνύω] The forms in ύω are used interchangeably with those in υμι. See Dem. Pop. Orat. II. § 12. — Ἀλλ' οὐκ .... παρέσχου] "But you could not; for if you had been able, you would just now (i. e. in his speech) have produced nothing sooner than this." The design here being to deny both the protasis and apodosis (K. § 339, I. b), we must use, in translation, the tenses employed for this purpose in English, which, it will be perceived, differ from the Greek. See Dem. Pop. Orat. IV. 1.

77. Λαομέδων] As this name differs from that given him in the decree, § 73, and as we know that to have been a Grecian name from Æsch. adv. Timarch., p. 15, fin., we must suppose Philip to have misunderstood it, and written a somewhat similar word in its stead. — Καθ' ὅλον .... ἔσε

σθαι] "In short, therefore, you appear to me to be about to be very silly," = "It appears to me that you will be in great folly." The peculiarity of the construction arises from the use of the personal instead of the impersonal form, which is quite common in Greek. See § 4, n.

78. ἄνευ μὲν τοῦ δήμου] "without the sanction of the people." — Καὶ . . . . ἔσεσθαι] "And they suppose that such a thing will be a revenue to themselves"; i. e. that it would, by creating troublous times, open prospects of gain and distinction to such desperate characters. — καὶ τοῦ λοιποῦ, ... εἰρήνην] "and for the future, if you are willing not to allow your leaders to act with bad faith (i. e. towards himself), but will punish them, I also will endeavor to keep the peace." Instead of τοῦ λοιποῦ, we find more frequently, except in the earlier authors, τὸ λοιπόν, sometimes τὰ λοιπά. Of these different forms, the gen. represents the time as a *cause*, i. e. an indispensable condition of the action, while the acc. represents it as the *measure*, in the sing. as a *unit*, but in the plur. as *composed of parts*. Demosthenes denies that he was one of those censured in this letter, because he had nothing to do with the measures referred to.

79. τούτων . . . . ἠναντιούμην] "for these I took my stand against, and these I opposed." Demosthenes had watched the course of Philip from the beginning, and made it his principal business to resist his encroachments, after he engaged in public affairs. — ἔγραψα] "I proposed." The occasions on which this and the subsequent embassies, etc. were proposed, arose out of the proceedings of Philip during the existence of the peace, and may be considered as some of the preliminary steps towards a rupture. He was found to be gaining influence, by his machinations with the enemies of Sparta in the Peloponnesus, when Demosthenes (B. C. 343) proposed, and even went upon, the embassy here referred to, in order to open their eyes to his true character and designs. The embassy to Eubœa was pro posed in the same year, soon after the destruction of Porth

mus by Philip, alluded to § 71, when he was seizing upon (ἥπτετο) the island, by taking that important port; and the expeditions not long after (B. C. 341), when he had established his partisans, Philistides and Clitarchus, as rulers in the two principal cities, Oreus and Eretria. The expedition against Clitarchus was under the command of Phocion (B. C. 341), as also were the naval armaments (ἀποστόλους) to the Cherronesus, Byzantium, and the other allies here mentioned. They were highly successful, and won much honor, both for the captain who conducted them, and the minister who despatched them.

80. τῶν εὖ πεπονθότων] "those befriended."—τῶν δ' .... εἶναι] "but to those of the injured (i. e. by Philip), who then confided in you, safety resulted, while to those standing aloof there resulted the frequent recollection of what you predicted, and the thinking that you were not only well disposed towards them, but shrewd men and prophets"; i. e. the arms of Athens were so successful at this time, that she was able to protect all who joined her as allies, while those who did not join her became the prey of Philip.

81. ὑπάρχειν .... αὐτῷ] "might remain to himself against you." On account of the favorableness of their position for annoying them.—καὶ περὶ .... πανταχοῦ] "and that nothing concerning the rest might be exposed, nor any one examine everywhere (as he did) his acts of injustice." Demosthenes alludes to these facts, in order to show how favorable an opportunity he had for receiving bribes in these cases, if he had been as easily bought as Æschines had represented him as being.

82. Οὐ τοίνυν .... τήμερον] "Therefore no one of these results was effected, O thou speaking slanderously concerning me, and saying that I am silent, having received, but clamor having spent. Not so you; but you clamor while you have, and never will cease, unless these (the judges), having disgraced you to-day, shall stop you." The results referred to as not having been effected were those men-

tioned above, viz. the permitting the tyrants Clitarchus and Philistides to remain in possession of their power, and the unjust acts of Philip to pass unexposed, on account of any bribes which they might offer him. Having thus presented the most convincing evidence of his being proof against corruption in these cases, the orator turns it to the best account, after his usual manner, by placing it in strong contrast with the charge of his adversary (§ 218), that he spoke only from the hope of pay, and, without this quickener of his eloquence, took no part in public affairs. Not so, he says, with his adversary, who was always clamoring for more, though always under pay.

83. *καὶ δευτέρου . . . . γιγνομένου*] "and this being to me already a second proclamation." I do not see how it is possible (unless perhaps *γενομένου* may have been the original reading) to avoid referring this to the proclamation of the crown proposed by Ctesiphon. I would suggest, therefore, in order to obviate the difficulty arising from his expressly referring to two crownings before this, §§ 222 and 223, that perhaps that of Demomeles and Hyperides was not proclaimed, or, if it was, not in the theatre. It may be considered as something in favor of this suggestion, that the orator makes special mention here of the *proclamation* of the crown of Aristonicus, and in § 120, although speaking of the subject of proclamations, and of the great number of them which had been made, is careful to say of himself, merely, that he has been often *crowned.*

84. *Ἡγέμονος*] The name of his father is added, perhaps, to distinguish him from the Chærondas referred to in § 54. — *τὸν ἀγωνοθέτην*] "the superintendent of the games.'

85. *ἃ . . . . ἔφη*] See § 231 of the speech of Æschines. — *Καὶ μὴν . . . . τιμωρίας*] "And surely, when deeds are recent and familiar to all, as, in case they seem good, they receive favor, so, if very otherwise, punishment." This clause is designed to show, that the time at which the approbation of his conduct here referred to was expressed,

was the most favorable time for obtaining a true expression of feeling. For ὡς ἑτέρως, see K. § 343, R. 2.

86. τῷ νικᾶν, κ. τ. λ.] "by prevailing in counselling and proposing decrees, when you were deliberating; by the measures proposed being carried into effect, and crowns following from them to the city, to me, and to you all; by your making sacrifices and processions to the gods as if these things were good." This is a summing up of the various indications which had been given, that his measures, up to the time here referred to, had been considered most useful to the city, as Ctesiphon had asserted them to be.

87. τοῖς μὲν ὅπλοις .... ὑπ' ἐμοῦ] "as far as arms were concerned, by you, but as far as policy and decrees were concerned (even though some of these burst with envy), by me." For this sense of πολιτεία, see § 93.—ἕτερον] "alius generis." Schäf.; K. § 246, 8, (b).—Ὁρῶν δ' .... ἐπεισάκτῳ] The soil of Attica was not very productive, and hence large quantities of grain were annually imported, principally from Pontus or the region near the Black Sea. See Boeckh, Pub. Econ. of Ath., Bk. II., chap. 15.—παρελθὼν ἐπὶ Θρᾴκης] "passing along by Thrace," i. e. to Byzantium, occupying the site now occupied by Constantinople. It was at this time, as appears, in alliance with Philip, though, as they are here represented as saying to him, for no such purpose as joining with him in a war against Athens. Indeed, it had formerly, during the palmy days of Athens, been in alliance with that city, and most probably even now was secretly looking to it, as the avowed enemy and opposer of Philip, for protection against his encroachments.—τὸ μὲν πρῶτον] "in the first place." Often used so with the article, §§ 151, 236.—χαράκωμα .... ἐπολιόρκει] "having pitched his camp before the city, and placed his engines near, he commenced the siege." ἐπιστήσας has this meaning, Orat. adv. Philip. III., p. 115, referred to by Dissen. These were rather the preliminary steps to a siege than an actual siege. The events here referred to were in B. C. 341 and 340.

88. οὐκέτ' ἐρωτήσω] "I will no longer ask," "I will not ask again," having already asked the question in a similar case. — ἁπλῶς] "simply," "absolutely."

89. ὁ γὰρ . . . . προῄρηνται] "for the war which then arose (i. e. in defence of Byzantium, etc.), besides having gained for you honorable renown, caused you to live (διῆγεν) with all things necessary for life more abundant and cheaper than the present peace, which these good citizens preserve, against the interests of their country, on account of future hopes; which may they fail of, and may they neither participate in those things which you, who ask the best things of the gods, have preferred, nor impart to you those which they have preferred." The peace here referred to was not that with Philip, which has been so often spoken of, but that made with Alexander, after the battle of Chæronea, which differed, indeed, but little from servitude. The two parties alluded to were the Macedonian party, to which Æschines belonged, and the Athenian party, at the head of which Demosthenes was. The former party were hoping for the complete triumph of the Macedonian arms and principles, and their own elevation in consequence; the latter, for the complete emancipation of their country from Macedonian influence, and the reëstablishment of the democracy in all its purity. The wish that Demosthenes here expresses concerning the former party is, that they may utterly fail of their hopes, and thus be excluded both from enjoying the benefit of the institutions which his party were contending for, and from imposing the evils of theirs upon them. For this plainly would have been a consequence of the failure of their hopes; since, if the Macedonian influence had not prevailed, it would have left them at the mercy of the party opposed to them, who would have destroyed or driven them from the city.

90. 'Επὶ ἱερομνάμονος Βοσποριχω] "Under the Hieromnemon Bosporichus." At Byzantium the year seems to have taken its name from the Hieromnemon, as it did at Athens

from the chief archon. This was the appellation of one class of the Amphictyonic deputies. It came into use at Byzantium, probably, from her connection with this council. The Byzantians were of Doric origin, and hence this decree is in the Doric dialect. Two of the prominent peculiarities of this dialect appear in the words here quoted, viz. the use of α for η, and ω for ου, in certain cases. — ἐκ τᾶς . . . . ῥήτραν] "obtaining permission to speak from the Senate." The provision in this respect, also, seems to have been the same as at Athens; where, as we have seen, it was necessary for every measure to be approved by the Senate before it came before the people. Indeed, it is probable that these forms were borrowed from Athens; as her constitution and laws were very renowned among the ancients, and would naturally be extensively adopted, especially by those who were at any time her allies. — καὶ τοῖς . . . . Περινθίοις] "and their allies and kinsmen, the Perinthians." Perinthus, afterwards called Heraclea, was a flourishing city, situated to the west of Byzantium, at no great distance, and connected with it by common interests, and, as it would seem from this passage, by a common origin.

91. Ἀθηναίοις . . . . λειτουργιᾶν] "to give to the Athenians the right of intermarriage, the right of citizenship, the right of possessing among us land and houses, an honorable seat at the games, admission to the Senate and Assembly first after the sacred rites, and to those wishing to dwell in the city, to be free from all public burdens." πράτοις is the Doric form for πρώτοις. The last word, λειτουργιᾶν, is the genitive plural Doric, and is governed by ἀλειτουργήτους. The sacred rites alluded to were those by which the session was opened, in the same manner as at Athens; and the privilege of being admitted at that time consisted in the fact, that, being thus admitted, their business would be attended to first. — στεφανούμενον τὸν δᾶμον] "the people crowned." This is what the statues represented, and hence

δᾶμον may be considered as in apposition with εἰκονας, in the preceding line. They were to be of gigantic proportions, and placed in a conspicuous place upon the banks of the Bosphorus, where all nations might see them as they passed that great commercial thoroughfare. — ὧς] This is the Doric for οὕς, and stands by attraction in the accusative, instead of the dative.

92. ἀπὸ . . . . Ἀθηναίων] " of sixty talents' value, and consecrate an altar of gratitude, and of the people of Athens," i e. commemorative of their own gratitude and of the benevolent character of the Athenians. — Καὶ ἐν, κ. τ. λ.] " And in all coming time they (the people of Cherronesus) will not fail to be thankful, and to do them (the Athenians) whatever good they can."

93. ἡ προαίρεσις . . . . πολιτεία] " my course and policy," " my course of policy." An instance of hendiadys, = ἡ προαίρεσίς μου τῆς πολιτείας, as in § 192, or perhaps a mere oratorical pleonasm. See §§ 192, 292, 317. — καλοκἀγαθίαν] The καλοκἀγαθὸς ἀνήρ was the perfect man of the Greeks. Consequently, καλοκἀγαθία must mean " the character or conduct suited to such a man," i. e. " honorableness," " nobleness."

94. Ὑμεῖς δ', ... ἐφαίνεσθε] " But you, who might with reason have brought both many and just charges against them, on account of their ungrateful conduct towards you in former times, were seen not only not resenting injuries, nor deserting them when wronged, but even protecting them." ἂν gives a conditional meaning to the preceding participle. K. § 260, 2, (5), (b). The ingratitude of the Byzantians here referred to was manifested in the Social War. — σύμβουλον . . . . ῥήτορα] " a counsellor and orator I mean." This was said to make an exception in favor of generals and military men, some of whom had procured this honor for the city.

95. Ἵνα . . . . πράττειν] " Therefore, in order that I may show also the reproaches which he (Æschines) uttered

against the Eubœans and Byzantians, calling up whatever of injury they may have done you, to be mere slanders, not only by their being false (for this I think you already know), but also by this, that, were they ever so true, it has been profitable to manage matters as I have managed them, I wish to relate one or two of the things honorable to the city done in your times, and these in few words; for it is always proper for a man privately, and a state publicly, to endeavor to perform what remains to be done, according to the most honorable of the deeds which have gone before." Æschines had made great complaints in his speech (§ 85 seq.) of the policy of Demosthenes in defending and entering into alliance with the Eubœans, on account of the injuries which they had formerly done to Athens, and the character which they sustained, all of which he had greatly exaggerated and misrepresented. Now it is these reproaches which he was thus led to utter against them that Demosthenes says he wishes to show to be mere slanders, or objections deserving to have no weight, not simply because they were false, but also because much good had resulted from the alliance.

96. *καὶ τὰ . . . . φρουραῖς*] "and occupying the places in the circle of (around) Attica, by Harmosts and garrisons." The time here alluded to was subsequent to the Peloponnesian war, when Sparta had wrested from Athens nearly all her foreign possessions and allies, and established in all the places thus won those odious military governments called *decadarchies* (see § 18, n.). Harmosts were the military governors sent out by Sparta, who exercised an arbitrary power over those committed to their care. See Smith's Dict. Antiq., Art. *Harmostæ*. — *ἐξῄλθετε εἰς Ἁλίαρτον*] "you made an expedition to Haliartus," i. e. during the Corinthian war (B. C. 395) to assist the Thebans in relieving that place from a siege by the Lacedæmonians. — *τῶν τότε . . . . μνησικακῆσαι*] "although the Athenians of that day might have indulged in resentment for many things against." For

the influence of ἄν here, see § 16, n., and for the force of the gen. absolute, see K. § 312, 4, (d); C. § 71, III. — περὶ . . . . πόλεμον] "relative to the Decelean war," i. e. the latter part of the Peloponnesian war, so called from Decelea, a place in the northern part of Attica, which the Lacedæmonians got possession of and fortified, greatly to the annoyance of Athens. This part of the war is alluded to, because it was at this time that the states here spoken of, and most of their allies, forsook the Athenians and joined themselves to Sparta. Of course, then, they had reason to complain of them principally with reference to this part of the war. Comp. Herm. Polit. Antiq. § 166, 6, 7.

97. οἰκίσκῳ] "chamber," "cage." — δεῖ . . . . γενναίως] "but it becomes brave men, while they always embark in every honorable undertaking, placing before them as a shield the hope of success, to bear manfully whatever the Deity may allot them." This is one of those elegant and lofty sentiments in which Demosthenes abounds above all the other Attic orators, and for which he is thought to have been somewhat indebted to the instruction of Plato; though the Stoics, from the nature of these sentiments, particularly from his so often distinguishing what is politic or expedient from what is right, and recommending virtue for its own sake, claimed him as belonging to their sect. Cicero, however, says (Brut. 31, 121), what undoubtedly is true: — "Lectitavisse Platonem studiose, audivisse etiam Demosthenes dicitur; idque apparet ex genere et granditate verborum."

98. ὑμῶν οἱ πρεσβύτεροι] "the older portion of you," i. e of the Athenians then living and present, as distinguished from πρόγονοι, a few words before this. — οἵ, Λακεδαιμονίους] The first of these words is nominative to διεκωλύσατε, and the other is governed by ἀνελεῖν. The arrangement of the words is highly emphatic and oratorical. — οὐδ' ὑπὲρ . . . . διαλογισάμενοι] "nor considering for men having done what, you would expose yourselves to danger," i. e. for what sort

of men, how injurious men. The future is employed because the speaker transports himself to the time referred to. See § 26, n.

99. ὅτι, κἂν . . . . ὑπολογεῖσθε] "that, even if any one of them (i. e. the Greeks) may have injured you in any thing whatever, you retain indignation for these in other things, but if any danger overtakes them relative to their safety and freedom, you will neither hold the grudge nor make any account of it." τούτων is the objective gen. after ὀργὴν, and refers to the collective pronoun ὁτιοῦν. Observe the difference between ὑπολογίζεσθαι, "to take into the account," "to make account of," and διαλογίζεσθαι, "to balance, as in settling an account." — οὕτως ἐσχήκατε] lit. "have you held yourselves thus," i. e. conducted thus. It was, for a reason already stated, of great importance to the Athenians to retain the Eubœans in their interest, and hence it was that they undertook the expedition here referred to, in order to counteract the influence of Thebes among them. Neither this nor the preceding instances given by Demosthenes, of assistance rendered to those who had injured them, were dictated, as is probable, by so pure a regard for their independence as is represented here, but by views of policy; as, for instance, for the purpose of maintaining the balance of power between Sparta and Thebes, or checking the progress of a rival. However, they served his purpose very well, in justifying the point in his policy for which they were adduced. The injuries alluded to as being received by the Athenians from Themison and Theodorus consisted in their establishing themselves in Oropus to the exclusion of the Athenians (B. C. 366). — τῶν ἐθελοντῶν . . . . πόλει] "there being then for the first time voluntary trierarchs to the city." Allusion is here made to the system adopted at Athens, after B. C. 357, for equipping galleys for the public service. According to this system, the twelve hundred richest citizens were divided into twenty *symmoriæ*, as they were called, and these again were subdivided into *synteliæ*

(comprising at the most but sixteen individuals), each of which was bound to equip a galley and keep it in repair for a year. Comp. Herm. Polit. Antiq. § 161. On the present occasion, however, it was ascertained that so many of these *syntelia* had already discharged their duty according to the requirements of the law, that there were not a sufficient number left, who were liable to be called upon, to meet the emergency. Such, however, was the public enthusiasm, that enough came forward at once of their own accord, and undertook the service, of whom Demosthenes says he was one. See Dem. in Mid. § 161. A trierarch, therefore, though originally the captain of a galley, was not generally at this period, but a man who equipped one.

100. Καίτοι . . . . ὑπολογισάμενοι] "But although you did a noble deed, even the saving of the island, nevertheless you did by far a more noble one than this, in that, being masters both of their persons and cities, you justly restored these to them, though they had injured you, having made no account of the injuries which you had received, in what you had been confided in." Observe the use of μέν and δέ in marking the correspondence of the clauses. K. § 322, 3.

101. τοσούτοις καὶ τοιούτοις] "in so great and such matters." — ὑπὲρ . . . . ποιεῖν ;] "what was I about to (what could I) urge and advise it to do, the question (βουλῆς) being in a manner concerning itself?" i. e. the city having so immediate and deep an interest in the matter. See § 71, n. — Μνησικακεῖν νὴ Δία] "Harbor ill-will, I dare say." A common use of νὴ Δία in answering for, or anticipating in an ironical way the objection of, another. See § 117; also, F. L., p. 390, § 174. — Ἐπεὶ τό, κ. τ. λ.] "Since you would not have performed the act (i. e. of leaving the Eubœans to become the prey of the Thebans), I well know; for if you wished to, what was in the way? Was it not in your power to do it? Were not these (i. e. Æschines and his associates) present, ready to advocate this course?" ἐροῦντες is in the future, and consequently conveys the idea of being about or ready to speak.

102. *καὶ τοὺς μὲν . . . . καιρῶν*] "and the rich discharged at a trifling expense, but those of the citizens who had acquired but moderate or small possessions expending all they had (*τὰ ὄντα*), and besides, the city by these means missing opportunities." Allusion is here made to a very natural abuse which grew out of the system for equipping galleys described above. As the different classes, or *symmoriæ*, of those upon whom it devolved by law to bear this burden were allowed to unite in companies, or *synteliæ*, for the purpose of equipping a galley, those who had capital, or the richer members, would undertake to equip the vessel for a certain sum. And as the other members had not capital sufficient to undertake it, they would not of course underbid them, and hence they obtained the job pretty much at their own price. Then, by hiring it done in an indifferent way, and for a small sum, and exacting of the other members their full quota of the price for which they contracted with them, they often contrived to save the whole of their own quota, which, besides, was no greater than that of the poorer members. This system, therefore, was unjust in two ways; (1) in imposing the same burden upon the poorer members of the companies as upon the richer; and, (2) in furnishing the richer members an opportunity of saving the comparatively small expense which fell upon them according to law. It resulted, further, from this system, that the vessels were poorly equipped, as all such job-work must be done poorly. Now the change which Demosthenes introduced by the law here spoken of, and which he goes on further to describe, was, to require one galley to be maintained by every ten talents of taxable capital; so that only individuals possessing less than this were allowed to club together for this purpose, till their property amounted to it, while those who were worth more than this sum furnished more than one galley. No single individual, however, could be compelled to equip more than three galleys and one transport. He might, therefore, justly pride him-

self on the superiority of his system to that which he found in operation. For a fuller account of this whole matter, the reader may consult the section in Hermann, referred to in § 99.

103. Καὶ γραφεὶς . . . . ἔλαβεν] "And being indicted, I entered upon this trial before you, and escaped conviction (was acquitted), and the prosecutor did not receive the required proportion of the votes." The preposition in εἰσῆλθον governs the acc. here, as when it stands alone. C. § 82, 5. See, also, below, § 105. He was prosecuted in this case for proposing a law contrary to an existing law which had not been annulled; but, as it seems, was acquitted by the judges so triumphantly, that the accuser did not receive even a fifth part of the votes, which it was necessary he should in order to save him from incurring a fine and the inability to institute such a prosecution in future. For the force of the article with μέρος, see K. § 244, 3; C. § 49, 3. — ἡγεμόνας τῶν συμμοριῶν] "the leaders of the symmoriæ," i. e. the three hundred wealthiest members (see § 171), who, according to what has already been said, were most affected by the change in question. — διδόναι] "to offer." It frequently has this meaning in the pres. and imperf. See below, § 104, fin.; also Orat. F. L., p. 293, § 183: ὧν ἡμῖν ἐδίδου ξενίων, "which he was offering us as presents." For the reference of the infin. pres. to past time, and for the contrast in the mode of representation between it and the infin. aor. (θεῖναι), see K. § 257, 1, c. — ὥστε . . . . ὑπωμοσίᾳ] "in order first of all (μάλιστα μὲν) that I should not propose this law, but if not this, that, having dropped it, I should leave it under protest"; i. e. as the connection indicates, the protest made by the prosecutor against it, which had the effect of delaying the passage of a law until the cause was decided, and, if the proposer chose to drop it at that point, prevented its passage altogether. The wealthy citizens, therefore, as Demosthenes says, would have given him almost any sum, in the first

place, not to have proposed the law, or, even after he had done this, to drop the matter when protested against by the prosecutor. *ὑπωμοσία* generally means "a petition for delaying a trial, for certain reasons given under oath." But as the *γραφὴ παρανόμων* had the effect of delaying the passage of the law against which it was brought, and as it was often resorted to for this purpose, the party who had recourse to it was required to take the same oath. Comp. Herm. Polit. Antiq. § 132, 3.

104. *συνεκκαίδεκα λειτουργεῖν*] "to perform the service by sixteens, *or* sixteen together." — *αὐτοῖς μὲν*] "themselves indeed." In the dative by attraction. — *τὸ γιγνόμενον .... συντελής*] "for each one to contribute his proportion according to his property, and he proved to be the trierarch of two galleys, who was formerly the sixteenth contributor to one."

105. *καθ' ὃ .... τὴν γραφήν*] "according to which I entered upon the charge"; so also § 103; C. § 82, 5. — *τοὺς καταλόγους*] "the lists," i. e. the parts of the respective laws which contained the principle of the assessment (*tax-rolls*). Dissen. — *νόμον τριηραρχικὸν*] I have rejected *εἰς τὸ* between these words, after Boeckh, Pub. Econ. Ath., Bk. IV., chap. 14, n. 387. One MS. is in favor of this, the whole connection, and the expression, § 312, *τὸν τριηραρχικὸν νόμον*.

106. *τὸν καλὸν*] Ironical. — *Τοὺς τριηράρχους, κ. τ. λ.*] "That sixteen trierarchs be made for each galley, out of the companies in the divisions." Wolf suggests that *λόχοι* here may mean the same as *συμμορίαι*. If so, the division into classes and companies, for the purposes of the trierarchy, was founded upon a similar division of the citizens that existed previously to this, for the purpose of other extraordinary contributions, which is probably the fact. Comp. Herm. Polit. Antiq. § 162. — *ἐπὶ ἴσον, κ. τ. λ.*] "sharing the expense equally." *χορηγία* seems to lose its technical sense here, and take the more general sense implied in it. — *Τοὺς*

τριηράρχους . . . . δέκα] "That trierarchs be chosen to each galley from property according to valuation, from ten talents as a basis." Observe the distributive use of the article with *τριήρη*. K. § 244, 5; C. § 49, 3. — *χρημάτων*] Gen. of price. — *τὴν αὐτὴν, κ. τ. λ.*] "and let it also be according to the same proportion to those to whom there is less property than the ten talents, they uniting into a company until their property amounts to ten talents."

107. *ἢ μικρὰ . . . . πλούσιοι ;*] "or do the rich appear to you that they would have spent a small amount of money for the sake of not (being compelled) to do what is just?" We see the Greek idiom here, in using the personal where we should use an impersonal verb, i. e. *δοκοῦσιν*, to be supplied from the previous line. See § 4, n. *τοῦ* refers to the clause which follows it, and is governed by *ἀναλῶσαι*, as a gen. of price. — *Οὐ τοίνυν . . . . σεμνύνομαι*] "Therefore, I glory not only in not desisting from these measures through collusion with them," i. e. the rich. *καθυφεῖναι* = *prævaricari*. See the word in Orat. pro Megalop. p. 206. — *Πάντα γὰρ . . . . ἀνάγεσθαι*] "For during the whole war, the naval expeditions being fitted out under my law, no trierarch ever lodged a petition with you as if having been wronged, nor seated himself in Munychia, nor was thrown into chains by the naval board, nor was any galley, either having been seized out of the harbor, lost to the city, nor left there, not being fit for sea." But all these things, he goes on to say, did happen under the old law. The petitions here alluded to as lodged with the people on account of injuries, were placed upon the altar in the Pnyx by the poorer members of the *syntelicæ*, praying for relief from the oppressive burdens which fell upon them according to the former law. It was the same class, too, who, for the same reason, were in the habit of seating themselves at the altar of Artemis Munychia, as suppliants. Probably this altar, situated in one of the most important ports of Athens, was the sanctuary to which those who were not able to discharge the duty

required of them by the old law fled for protection against the *apostoleis*. These officers, ten in number, constituted a kind of naval board for the enforcement of the regulations concerning the equipping of vessels, and for their inspection after they were built.

108. Τὸ δ' . . . . λειτουργεῖν] "But the cause was, the burden fell upon the poor." — βάσκανον . . . . ἀνάξιον] "while there is no public measure of mine dictated by envy, hostility, and malice, neither grovelling nor unworthy of the city," i. e. he had been governed in his policy by enlarged, high-minded, and statesman-like views, and had not been influenced by private piques and jealousies, or by low and grovelling feelings, as Æschines had.

110. τὸ γὰρ . . . . νομίζω] "for this, *that I both did the best things, and am always well disposed and zealous to promote your interests*, I think has been sufficiently shown by me by what has already been said." μοί here is employed as a dative of the agent with the perfect passive, as it often is in Greek, instead of the genitive with ὑπό. K. § 284, 3, (11); C. § 59, 11. — τὰ μέγιστά γε] The final struggle with Philip, ending in the battle of Chæronea, to which he incited his countrymen. — ὑπολαμβάνων, κ. τ. λ.] "supposing it necessary for me, in the first place, to produce in order the arguments relative to the illegality itself (i. e. of the decree of Ctesiphon), then, even though I say nothing concerning the remainder of my political acts, supposing that nevertheless there exists a consciousness of them with each one of you for me." ἐφεξῆς means "in their proper place," i. e. without digressing too far in following out his public measures. ὑμῶν takes the construction with παρά, instead of the partitive construction after ἑκάστῳ, on account of the influence of ὑπάρχειν ("there is from you each one a consciousness with me," instead of, "there is a consciousness to each one of you"). μοί is governed by συνειδὸς.

111. Τῶν μὲν οὖν . . . . διαλέξομαι] "Of the words, then,

which this man, jumbling together confusedly, spoke concerning the laws written opposite (i. e. the laws represented as violated by the decree of Ctesiphon, and hence presented before the court written out opposite to it by the accuser), I think, by the gods, that neither you see the bearing of the greater part, nor was I myself able to comprehend them; but I will reason simply and in a straightforward way concerning the justice of the cause." That is, he wishes to show that his case is justly distinguished from ordinary cases of responsibility in public officers, and hence that the laws referred to by Æschines are inapplicable. — ὧν .... πεπολίτευμαι] "for what I have passed through my hands (i. e. the money which he had had the management of), and for my public measures."

112. Ὧν μέντοι .... τύχῃ] "But, indeed, for what promising (*or* of my own accord) I have given to the people of my private property, I say — (do you hear it, Æschines?) — that I am not accountable for a single day, and that no other one is, not even if he be one of the nine archons." This is what Æschines (§ 17) calls his ἄφυκτος λόγος. It was the law at Athens, that every one who held a public office must, at the expiration of the period of his office, pass his accounts before certain officers called Logistæ, and obtain their approval of them before he could be regularly discharged. Until this was done, he was considered a state debtor, and could dispose neither of himself nor of his property, the latter being pledged to the state; neither could he be a candidate for any public office or distinction. Comp. Herm. Polit. Antiq. § 154, 14. This duty of public officers Æschines had shown very fully in his speech (p. 56), and also that Demosthenes had not been thus discharged from the offices which he held. But it so happened that Demosthenes, in both of his offices, had contributed largely to the service of the state, and on this ground he contends, as the money which he had expended for the state came from his own pocket, that he was not accountable for it to any one,

and therefore was a proper candidate for the distinction proposed, without going through the formality of having his accounts examined. — εἰς τοὺς συκοφάντας . . . . ἐφιστάναι] "to bring before sycophants, and empower these to institute a scrutiny into those things which he gave;" i. e. to put it in the power of sycophants to demand that he should give up an account of what he had thus presented to the state.

113. ἀλλ' οὗτος . . . . ὄντα] "but this calumniator, because being at that time over the theoric fund I contributed money. says, *the Senate praised him, being undischarged of his accounts.*" The Senate are said to have praised him, because they had already passed the preliminary decree to crown him. — τἀνηλωμένα] Three talents, according to the decree § 119. — Ὁ μὲν . . . . προσδεῖται] "For an account requires examination, and those who will examine it." — ὁδὶ] "this one, this friend of mine here," i. e. Ctesiphon.

114. στρατηγῶν] "while holding the office of general." Observe the force of the participle. — οὑτοσὶ] "this here." He was present, most probably. — διὰ τὴν ἀρχὴν] "on account of his magistracy, *or* office."

115. τὸν ἐπὶ τῶν ὅπλων] "the general of the heavy-armed soldiery, *or* infantry." ὅπλων here is used for ὁπλιτῶν, as is seen from the fact that the soldiers under this general are designated by the latter term, a few words after. It is often used in this way, too, by Xenophon (Anab. II. 2, 4, *et passim*), and other Greek authors. This usage is precisely the same as that of *artillery* in our language. — αὐτὰ] "themselves." In distinction from their contents, already given.

116. πρυτάνεων . . . . γνώμῃ] "the prytanes bringing it before the people with the approbation of the Senate." Callias was the author of the decree, but it was brought before the Senate by the prytanes. The name of the author is often found first, as here, in inscriptions of decrees. Dissen. — Σαλαμῖνα] According to Vömel (as quoted in the Class. Mus., No. VIII.), "the Attic Salamis, whither he was ordered, in conjunction with Diotimus, after the battle on

the Cephissus against Philip." See § 216. — θεσμοθέτας] "Thesmothetæ." A name given to the six inferior archons; so called from θεσμοί and τίθημι, having originally, perhaps, been intrusted with making laws.

117. ταὐτὰ . . . . δήπου] "for assuredly there are the same rights to me with others, concerning the same things." ταὐτὰ, it will be perceived, is for τὰ αὐτὰ, "the same," and governs ἄλλοις. In what follows in this paragraph, the orator goes on to describe the entire likeness of his case to that of the others alluded to. See a case similarly put below, § 198. — Ἦρχον] "I held a magistracy, *or* office." — Νὴ Δί', κ. τ. λ.] "Yes, by Jupiter, but I exercised my office unjustly (perhaps you will say); then, being present, when the Logistæ summoned me before them, did you not accuse me?" Before this trial came on, Demosthenes had been discharged from his offices; and, as he says, had given an account of these, though not of what he had made a present of. He therefore asks his opponent, if he had done any thing wrong in his magistracy, which would make his case different from those just cited, why he did not at the time of the examination of his accounts charge him with the wrong. This question is asked, because, at the time of a magistrate's passing his accounts before the Logistæ, any one who considered either himself, or the state, as having been defrauded by him, was expected to appear and make the charge, and he was bound to answer to it.

118. Ἵνα τοίνυν, κ. τ. λ.] "Therefore, in order that you may know that this man himself (i. e. Æschines) bears witness to me, that I have been crowned for those things for which I was not responsible, taking, read the whole decree which was proposed for me (i. e. that of Ctesiphon). For from what things of this preliminary decree he did not indict, from these he will be seen to act the part of a slanderer in those which he prosecutes." The point of the argument here is this, that Æschines, by not objecting to the preamble of the decree of Ctesiphon, in effect allowed that

he was crowned for what he had given, and was not, therefore, responsible for, since the crowning was there expressly recommended upon this ground ; and, furthermore, that the points of the decree which he had attacked, compared with those which he had not, showed him to be governed by the feelings of a slanderer.

119. ἐπέδωκε . . . . θυσίας] "presented to the theoric funds from among all the tribes (i. e. of the different tribes) a hundred minas for sacrifices." The theoric funds were by degrees diverted from their proper use, and distributed among the people or tribes for defraying the expense of various other entertainments besides those of a theatrical nature. See Boeckh, Pub. Econ. of Ath., Bk. II., chap. 13. Demosthenes contributed to the funds thus distributed the sum here named. This seems to be the interpretation, if the MS. reading be retained. But perhaps the reading θεωροῖς for θεωρικοῖς, suggested by Schäfer, and approved by Dissen and others, should be adopted. In that case, the present was made to the *sacred deputies* for sacrifices at some religious festival. This reading makes the construction of ἐκ πασῶν τῶν φυλῶν ("from all the tribes," i. e. the whole body of deputies) easier. — ἀντὶ τούτων] "in return for these things." — Τὸ λαβεῖν, κ. τ. λ.] "Acknowledging, therefore, the receiving of what has been given to be lawful, you accuse of illegality the returning a recompense for them. But a man wholly depraved and detested by the gods, and thoroughly slanderous, by the gods, what sort of a man would he be? Would he not be such an one as this?" The abrupt close here, breaking off suddenly, as if tired of pursuing so disgusting a subject, is very happy.

120. ὥστ' οὐ δύνασαι] οὐ is used here instead of μή, because the design is to render δύνασαι negative, rather than the whole sentence. See K. § 318, 2, (h), 3, (f), and R. 1. — ζῆλον] This word has both an active and a passive sense In the active sense it means "zeal," "emulation," "desire," etc., and of course in a passive sense "an object of

zeal," "emulation," "desire," etc., i. e. any thing which is esteemed desirable or valuable, and hence may be best rendered here "desirableness *or* value." — τοὺς ἀποδιδόντας τὴν χάριν] "those returning the favor." — τῶν δήμων] "of the demi *or* boroughs." — τὰς ἀναγορεύσεις . . . . δήμοις] "that they make the proclamations of the crowns among themselves, each in their own demus." ποιεῖσθαι is in the mid. to express what they were to do among themselves.

121. ψηφίσηται] "may vote," i. e. to proclaim, ἀναγορεύεσθαι being understood. Æschines (§§ 35 – 48), by a rather forced process of reasoning, as it seems to me, makes this exception apply wholly to crowns conferred by foreign states. — Τί οὖν . . . . εἰσάγων] "Why then, O wretch, do you bring this false accusation? Why do you invent statements? Why do you not purge yourself with hellebore on account of these things? But you are not even ashamed instituting a trial for envy." The orator, having thus completed the refutation of the charges contained in the indictment, breaks out upon his adversary in this contemptuous language. He represents his charges as so groundless, and his whole course in the trial so infatuated, as to indicate that he was insane; and hence advises him to take hellebore, which was the common remedy for insanity in those times, and thus confess his madness. — τοῖς γε . . . . ψηφιεῖσθαι] "at least, to those who have sworn that they will vote according to the law," i. e. the judges. ψηφιεῖσθαι is a first future middle, made after the Attic form, by dropping σ, and then inflecting it like a contract verb in έω. K. § 117, 1; C. § 35, 6.

122. ὥσπερ . . . . γιγνωσκομένους] "just as if you had let out a statue to be made upon contract, and then had received it, not having what it ought to have according to the contract or as if men of the people are known by description, and not by acts and measures"; i. e. arbitrarily setting up a standard of what a popular man ought to be, and then condemning all who fall short of it, just as he would a statue

or any thing capable of exact description. See § 168 seq. of his speech. For the construction of the participles here, see K. § 312, RR. 12 and 13.— Καὶ βοᾷς . . : . ἐμοί] "And you vociferate, calling me things decent and indecent, as if from a wagon, which epithets befit you and your race, not me." In this and the preceding sentences the orator has given a sort of running analysis of the speech of his opponent, in such a manner as to convey a most contemptuous idea of it. According to his account, he had, in the first place, instituted the trial from envy, and, having thus instituted it, had resorted to the grossest perversion and even mutilation of the laws in order to sustain his charges; that he had then subjoined some remarks upon what was requisite for a public man, and, finally, had attacked him with the foulest abuse. The expression ἐξ ἁμάξης refers to the custom prevalent at many of the festivals among the Greeks, of throwing out jests or coarse abuse from the carriages, while making the processions connected with those festivals; and hence the peculiar meaning of πομπεύειν, § 124. Comp. Müller's Hist. Lit. Greece, Vol. I. p. 291, note.

123. Καίτοι . . . . τοῦτο] "And yet even this." Often used thus in referring to some common maxim or admitted principle applicable to the case in hand. See Philip. II. § 12; also, Jelf's K. § 655, 8.— κατὰ τὴν αὐτῶν φύσιν] "according to their nature"; i. e. as Reiske says,—"seu lenis, mitis, sedata, seu atrox, vehemens, cita, impetuosa. sæva, ita probra sunt."— Οἰκοδομῆσαι . . . . πόλιν] "But I have supposed that our ancestors built these courts of justice, not that, having assembled you within them from your private business, we should utter reproaches against each other, but that we should prove it against him, if any one perchance has injured the city in any respect." For this use of ἴδιος see Dem. Olynth. II. § 16.

124. Οὐ μὴν . . . . ἀπελθεῖν] "However, not even here ought he to come off having less," i. e. than he had given. That is to say, as Æschines had taken this course, unsuit-

able as it was in a public trial, it was but just, to use a homely phrase, that he should get as good as he had sent. This is said by the orator in order to justify himself in entering upon a general criticism of the character and conduct of his opponent, both private and public; which therefore he proceeds to do, having first asked him one question. — Εἶτα οὗ . . . . κρίσεσιν] "Where then it was possible (ἦν) to obtain satisfaction from me in behalf of these (i. e. the Athenians), if I had done any thing wrong, viz. at the examination of my accounts, in the public accusations (γραφαῖς), and the other trials brought against me, you neglected it." At the examination of one's accounts, any one, as already stated, might bring a charge of malversation against him, and he was obliged to answer to it. Besides, Demosthenes, soon after the unfortunate battle of Chæronea, was several times prosecuted, in various forms, for the course which he had pursued, but, as he says a few lines below, was convicted in none of them of having done any thing wrong. These now, he reminds Æschines, were the occasions on which to have brought him to justice if he had done any thing wrong, but he had made no attempt to do so.

125. οὗ δ', κ. τ. λ.] "but where I am clear by all things, by the laws, by the time which has elapsed, by the period within which it is allowable to bring an action (προθεσμίᾳ), by my having frequently been tried before concerning all these things, by my never having been convicted of injuring you in any thing, but where it is inevitable that the city must share more or less in the glory of my public acts, there have you attacked me? Beware, lest you are an enemy of these (i. e. the Athenians) while you profess to be an enemy of me." The point which the orator wishes to establish here is that expressed in the last clause, that Æschines, while professing hostility to him alone, was in reality acting the part of an enemy to the city. The way in which this is made out is this: Æschines had neglected bringing any charge against him on the proper occasions,

when the city would have sustained no disgrace by it, but now that the proposition was to crown him for measures which he had proposed and the city adopted (and in the glory of which, therefore, they would share alike), he objected to it, thereby endeavoring not only to deprive him of the glory of his measures, but the city also. See the same subject touched again, § 207. *προθεσμίᾳ*, more definite than *χρόνῳ*, means the legal time within which it was allowable to bring an action, which in most cases was five years. Comp. Herm. Polit. Antiq. § 141, 5.

126. *Ἐπειδὴ . . . . δέδεικται*] "Since, therefore, the pious and just vote (i. e. the vote to acquit him) has been pointed out to all." Wolf supposes that the orator, at this point, saw in his judges signs of favor towards himself and of indignation towards his adversary, and hence seized the opportunity to draw this bold conclusion. Perhaps, however, it is sufficient to suppose, that he considered that he had said enough to convince them all which way they ought to vote, and therefore took it for granted that they were convinced. — *ἀντὶ . . . . αὐτοῦ*] "instead of many and false things (like Æschines), to say barely the most essential things concerning him." *αὐτὰ* here strengthens the superlative, as *self* does in English, in such expressions as "the very essence itself." K. § 303, R. 4. — *ῥᾳδίως . . . . φθέγξασθαι;*] "he so readily commences reviling, and what words (of mine) he criticizes, himself having spoken words, which who of respectable men would not have shrunk from pronouncing?" i. e. such tawdry, pompous words, as appears from what follows. For the strictures of Æschines on certain expressions of Demosthenes, see §§ 72, 166, of his speech.

127. *ἀλλὰ μὴ . . . . ἀγορᾶς*] "but not an idle babbler, a practised knave." I have translated *περίτριμμα ἀγορᾶς* (lit. "hack of the agora") according to the meaning given to it by the Scholiast on the Antigone of Sophocles, v. 320, namely, as = *ἄλημα*, or *veterator* in Latin. See *περίτριμμα*

in Lid and Scott. The ground upon which he says that the wisest and purest of men, such as Æacus, etc., would not have used such pretending language as he had, is more fully explained below, in the last part of § 128, and is briefly this: that all truly excellent men are modest, and make no display of their sympathy with what is great and good, though they really possess it. — ἐπαχθεῖς] "offensive," "disgusting," i. e. because unsuited to his character and in every way out of taste. — ὥσπερ . . . . βοῶντα] "as if in a tragedy, exclaiming." Such exclamations were common in tragedies, which are designed to exhibit the workings of strong passions. — ταῦτα . . . . λέγοντος] "for these things doubtless you heard him speaking," i. e. in the peroration of his speech (§ 260).

128. μνησθῆναι] "to mention," "to speak of." — ἧς τῶν μὲν, κ. τ. λ.] "which not one of those really having obtained would say any such thing concerning himself, but would even blush to hear another one say it, while to those destitute of it like yourself, yet pretending to it through stupidity, the result is, that they cause those to grieve who hear them laying claim to it, not that they appear to be such themselves." ὡς ἀληθῶς mean, together, "really," ὡς having the effect of strengthening the meaning of the adverb, just as it often does the superlative. K. § 343, R. 2. τοιούτοις is put in the dative to agree with the case after περίεστιν. K. § 307, 2; C. § 70, 10.

129. τοῦ πρώτου] "what first." τοῦ for ὅτου, the direct for the indirect. K. § 344, R. 1; C. § 48, 8. — τῷ πρὸς . . . . ξύλον] "who teaches school near the temple of Theseus, wearing heavy stocks and a wooden collar." The χοῖνιξ was properly a measure of capacity, and hence, as an instrument of punishment, must have been a kind of stocks or fetters into which the feet were inserted and confined. As to the ξύλον, this was a heavy collar of wood, into which the neck was inserted, so as to prevent it from all freedom of motion. These were employed as instruments of pun-

ishment, especially in the case of refractory slaves. Comp Esch. Man. § 113. — *τοῖς μεθημερινοῖς . . . . σε*] "resorting to the midday prostitutions (i. e. the most shameless prostitution) in the brothel, near the statue of the physician Hero, brought you up a pretty little doll and an accomplished actor of third parts." I think it clear that Hero is the proper name, and not Calamites, as some editions have it. See Orat. de F. L., p. 419, where the same person is called Ἥρως ἰατρός. *καλαμίτης* seems to have been a term of contempt for a physician, from the use of *κάλαμοι* for surgical purposes, = "man of the probe." The orator calls Æschines *καλὸν ἀνδριάντα*, on account of the smallness and primness of his person; or, according to Bekk. Anecd. Græc., in allusion to the caressing expression of fond mothers, "my pretty little doll." The Scholiast on the passage says, Μικρὸς γὰρ ἦν ὁ Αἰσχίνης τὸ σῶμα. By *τριταγωνιστὴν* reference is made to the former occupation of Æschines as a stage-player, and, furthermore, to the inferiority of his rank even among those of that profession. An actor of third parts was the representative of the least important personages in a drama, especially of tyrants. See Dem. F. L., § 247. For a full and clear account of the relation of the three actors in the Greek tragedy, the reader may consult Müller's History of Grecian Literature, Vol. I. p. 306. — *τριηραύλης*] "galley-piper." Perhaps her first husband.

130. *βεβίωκεν*] "has lived *or* done during his life." — Οὐδὲ γὰρ . . . . *καταρᾶται*] "For not even of so respectable parentage as he finally attained was he originally, but of such as the people execrate," i. e. probably persons of servile origin, who clandestinely got enrolled as citizens. The execration of the people, here referred to, probably, was that expressed at the opening of each assembly. See § 282. — Χθὲς *μὲν οὖν καὶ πρῴην*] This of course is to be taken in a modified sense. For *μὲν οὖν* ("or rather," "nay rather"), see K. § 316, R. — *ἐκ τοῦ . . . . τυχοῦσαν*] "having

obtained this nickname, evidently, from her doing and sub mitting to every thing." The reason of her being called Empusa on this account was, that this was an obscene spectre of the night. This was but a nickname, it will be perceived, her true name being Glaucis, which, by the addition of two syllables, as Demosthenes says, Æschines changed to Glaucothea, just as he did his father's, from Tromes to Atrometus. The names may have been changed because they were common with the lower classes; besides, the lengthened forms are more sounding, and sounding names are generally preferred by upstarts. In opposition to this account of the parentage of Æschines, see his own account of his father, Contr. Ctes. § 191.

131. διὰ τουτουσὶ] "by means of these," i. e. the Athenians. — οὐχ ὅπως] "not only not." K. § 321, 3, (c).

132. ἀποψηφισθέντα] "rejected." He had somehow, it seems, contrived to get his name enrolled as a citizen, but, upon an examination of his claims to that right, the fraud was discovered and he rejected. This was probably done at the general scrutiny of citizenship instituted in B. C. 346, which gave occasion for the speech of Dem. contr. Eub. For the mode of deciding questions of citizenship among the Greeks, see Shömann, Bk. III., chap. 3. Being enraged at this, he retired to Philip and made arrangements with him to burn the navy-yards of the Athenians, for which purpose, at the time here alluded to, he had returned to the city. — Πειραιεῖ] "the Piræus." The principal port of Athens, where the navy-yards were. — ὡς ἐν . . . . ἐποίησεν] "as if I were doing outrageous things under a democratic form of government, insulting unfortunate citizens, and entering houses without a warrant, caused him to be released." In free governments the house is always one's castle. For the partitive gen. (τῶν πολιτῶν), see § 27, n.

133. ἡ βουλὴ ἡ ἐξ Ἀρείου πάγου] "the council of the Hill of Mars *or* Areopagus." This was a venerable court at Athens, composed of the ex-archons who had filled their

office blamelessly, holding its sessions in the open air, upon an elevation of ground called the Hill of Mars, from some traditionary connection of Mars with the place. This court had the cognizance of all cases of homicide, was intrusted with the guardianship of the laws, and in the time of Demosthenes, as appears from this as well as other passages, acted as a kind of superior court of police, making it its particular business to bring to justice men who might endanger the state. Comp. Herm. Polit. Antiq. § 109. — ἐν . . . . συμβεβηκυῖαν] "having terminated in a very unfortunate result," i. e. the discharge of the person referred to. οὐ δέον means properly "something which ought not to be," i. e. something unusual, monstrous, unfortunate, or undesirable. — ἐπανήγαγεν . . . . τουτουί] "had brought him again before you, such a wretch would have been snatched away, and, escaping the penalty of his crime, would have been sent out of the country by this fine-spoken gentleman." ὡς here = πρός. It is used, however, in this way only before nouns denoting intelligent objects.

134. Τοιγαροῦν . . . . προδότην] "Accordingly, the council of Areopagus, acquainted as it was with these proceedings of this man at that time, when (ὡς) you, having, from the same thoughtlessness from which you neglect many of the public interests, chosen him advocate in the case relative to the temple in Delos, both selected it and made it arbiter of the matter, immediately rejected him as a traitor." This, I believe, expresses the proper sense of this passage. But it is worth while to observe how much more complicated the sentence becomes in English, from the necessity of introducing every clause in its strictly *logical* order, instead of placing them in the *oratorical* order, and leaving the sense to be determined from the agreement of the different words. κἀκείνην, "and it," refers for its antecedent to the council of Areopagus. The control of the temple in Delos, like that of the temple at Delphi, was a matter of the greatest political importance. The question here alluded to

was a contest with the Delians concerning its superintendence; which was finally brought before the Amphictyonic Council about B. C. 345, when Æschines was rejected as advocate on account of his supposed leaning to the interest of Philip. — καὶ ταῦτα . . . . ἔπραξε] "and this it did, giving the vote from the altar," i. e. after having taken an oath at the altar. This custom, as appears from several passages in Demosthenes (Adv. Macart. § 14) and other Greek authors, was common in the courts at Athens. The practice was probably adopted in order to give greater sacredness to their decisions, by appearing to act, as it were, under the eye of their gods. Comp. Herod. viii. 123, 2, Wess. and Valck.

135. ὑπὲρ ἁπάντων] "in behalf of all," i. e. all the court of Areopagus, these four being chosen to testify for the whole court.

136. τοῦ νεανίου] Said rather with reference to his forwardness and pertness, or, perhaps, with reference to his recent acquisition of Athenian citizenship, than to his actual age, as he was at this time full forty. — ὅμοιόν γε] "is like, I dare say." Observe the ironical force of γε, and see F. L., p. 421, § 283. — ὡς ἐν . . . . ὑπεχώρησα] "as if about to put the city to shame and show it to be in the wrong, then indeed I did not yield nor give way to Python, assuming an impudent tone and pouring forth a tide of abuse against you." πολλῷ ῥέοντι (flowing with a torrent of words); like Horace's *sulso multoque fluenti.* Sat. I. 7, 28. The individual here spoken of was one of the most eminent orators of antiquity. He was originally of Byzantium, but early enlisted in the service of Philip, by whom he was employed in various public matters, but especially on embassies. For the occasion here alluded to, on which he visited Athens accompanied by ambassadors from the allies of Philip, See Thirlw. Ch. XLV.

137. μετὰ ταῦθ' ὕστερον] "thereupon afterwards." An oratorical expansion not uncommon. See § 36: εὐθὺς, οὐκ

εἰς μακράν. — τῷ κατασκόπῳ] i. e. from Philip. Having been sent by him to observe the movements at Athens relative to liberating Eubœa and sending aid to the Hellespont. See § 79, n. Æschines (§ 224 of his speech) says that Demosthenes got up this failure of Anaxinus in order to save himself from prosecution. — τῇ φύσει] "by nature," "to all intents and purposes." — ἐπὶ τῶν στρατηγῶν] "before the generals." The generals tried cases of treason.

138. Καὶ γὰρ . . . . ἔχει] "For evidently the case is somehow as follows"; i. e. though he should proceed to enumerate ever so many of his crimes, they would be recollected but faintly and without suitable indignation. οὕτω, though commonly referring to what precedes, occasionally refers to what follows. K. § 303, 1, R. 1. — ὧν] By attraction for the acc., and governed by ὑπηρετῶν in a kind of pregnant sense, = "doing as a service." — ὑποσκελίζειν] "to trip up, to thwart." — τῆς ἐπὶ . . . . ἀνταλλαττόμενοι] "bartering away the interests of the city for the pleasure and delight there is in (listening to) revilings." ἡδονῆς is governed by ἀνταλλαττόμενοι as a gen. of price. K. § 275, 3; C. § 54, 10. — τοῖς ἐχθροῖς . . . . πολιτεύεσθαι] "to take bribes in the service of the enemy, than to manage affairs, having taken a stand in your defence."

139. δή] "quite certainly," "as is well known." Referring to the certainty and notoriety of the act. K. § 315, 1. — πρὸ τοῦ πολεμεῖν] "before the war," i. e. before the open renewal of hostilities. — Ἀλλ' ἐπειδή, κ. τ. λ.] The events spoken of in this and the following lines have been alluded to before (§§ 79, 80), and explained as being some of the preliminary steps towards the renewal of hostilities. ἐπειδή, in the first part of the passage, qualifies all the verbs as far as ὅ τι. ἄνθρωπος (i. e. ὁ ἄνθρωπος), after ἐπορεύεθ', means Philip, who is spoken of thus in contempt. ἰαμβειοφάγος means, literally, "a devourer of iambics," i. e. a wretched, mouthing actor, tragedies being written in iambics; or it may refer to his slanderous character, as iambics were used

in satire. — Εἰ δέ . . . . ὕδατι] "But if he says (there is any such decree), let him now show it during my time"; lit. "during my water," the time being measured by an instrument called the *clepsydra*. This was a glass vessel filled with water, in the bottom of which there was a small aperture, through which the water issued slowly (stealing out, as it were, and hence receiving its name, from κλέψις ὕδωρ), and fell into another vessel, by the rise of the water in which they judged of the time. This instrument was used in the Athenian courts, in most causes, to measure the time allowed to each speaker, which varied according to the nature and importance of the cause. — Καίτοι, κ. τ. λ.] "And yet there is a necessity, one of two things, either, having nothing to complain of in the measures proposed by me at that time, he does not propose others in their stead, or, being intent upon the interests of the enemy, does not bring forward any better than these." We have here an *enthymem*, or an abridged syllogism. Thus: "Proposing no decree proves one of two things; Æschines proposed no decree (as shown above), therefore one of these two things is true of him." The enthymem has all the cogency of the syllogism, without its rigidness and formality. It is much used by Demosthenes; as, §§ 24, 47, 124, 196, 217. θάτερον is a kind of adverbial acc., expressing the equivalent idea to what follows, governed by the general idea of *doing*, expressed in a modified way by the *two verbs*, γράφειν and φέρειν. Jelf's K. § 579, 4.

140. μὲν οὖν] "nay rather." See § 130, n. — Καὶ τὰ . . . . λανθάνειν] "And the city, as it seems, was able to bear other things, and this man to perform them without being detected." — περὶ οὗ . . . . πόθεν;] "concerning which he expended the many words, *or* told that long story (i. e. in his speech, §§ 107 – 135), rehearsing the decrees concerning the Amphissian Locrians, as if about to pervert the truth. But it is not of this nature (i. e. so easily perverted). how can it be?" The decrees here spoken of were the

decrees of the Amphictyons relative to the Locrians of Am phissa, the gen. being of the objective kind. K. § 265, 2, (b); C. § 56, R. 1. τοὺς πολλοὺς, "*the* many," "*those* many," the article being used as a demonstrative for what was well known or notorious. K. § 244, 6. Τὸ δ', "whereas," "but" (K. § 247, 3, a). ἀληθές is understood. For πόθεν see § 47, n. The crime of Æschines here alluded to was the getting up of an Amphictyonic war against the Amphissians, thus opening a field for the ambition of Philip.

141. ἅπαντας καὶ πάσας] ἅπαντας ("all together") seems to have been used to include both gods and goddesses in a general way, and πάσας to have been added as a sort of afterthought ("and goddesses too"). — τὸν Ἀπόλλω . . . . πόλει] "the Pythian Apollo, who is the paternal deity of the city." Apollo was originally the principal divinity of the Dorians, but was adopted by the other Grecian tribes, to a greater or less extent, and especially by the Ionians, who became at an early period the possessors of Attica. On account of this adoption of the religion of Apollo, as is supposed, Ion, the mythological father of the Ionian race, was represented in the ancient legends as the son of Apollo; and hence it was that Apollo was called the paternal deity of the city. Comp. Müller's Hist. Dorians, Vol. I. pp. 257 - 263. — εἰ μὲν . . . . δήμῳ] "if I should speak the truth to you (i. e. now), and then also immediately spoke it before the people." — εὐτυχίαν . . . . σωτηρίαν] "happiness . . . . safety," i. e. in the highest sense, as depending upon the gods. Thus perilling his soul upon the point, as in an oath. — πρὸς] "on the side of," "out of regard to." — ἀνόνητόν] "devoid of." Takes a gen. of privation. C. § 55, 7.

142. Τί οὖν . . . . σφοδρῶς;] "Why now have I imprecated these things upon myself, and why have I been so vehement?" The perf. denotes "had and still continues to have," — he still remaining under the imprecations; but the vehemence was confined to the simple utterance of the passage, and hence is properly expressed by the aor. The

preceding passage (which is alluded to by the words under consideration) is a favorable specimen of the means resorted to by Demosthenes to enliven his discourse and relieve the monotony of narration or discussion. For this purpose he often suddenly breaks off the direct line of discourse to make an appeal to the gods, to his hearers, or to his adversary; or to press by interrogations, to recapitulate what he has said, or to anticipate objections; or by pretending to shrink from the utterance of thoughts which are in his mind; by professing uncontrollable indignation, and venting his rage in a strain of invective; by supplicating, deprecating, execrating, or some of the numerous turns of thought which Cicero, taking Demosthenes as a pattern, describes as being resorted to by the perfect orator. Orat. c. 40. — *Ὅτι . . . . κείμενα*] "Because, although having documents lying in the public archives." The participle expresses a concession. K. § 312, 4, (d). — *μὴ τῶν . . . . ἐλάττων*] "lest this fellow should be thought too contemptible for the mischief done by him." *αὐτῷ*, dat. of the agent. K. § 284, 3, (11).

143. *οὗτός . . . . κακῶν*] "this fellow is the one who helped him get it up, and, as far as one man can be (or "is *the one man* who"), is the cause of all these greatest of evils." *εἷς ἀνὴρ* is employed to limit or modify *τῶν μεγίστων*. K. § 239, R. 2, (e); C. § 50, R. 5. — *οἱ μὲν . . . . συγκαθήμενοι*] "while those sitting with him by invitation," i. e. the Macedonian faction. The assemblies of the people at Athens being open for all the citizens to attend in person, great facilities were presented to such as wished to carry any measure, or to make opposition to any, to succeed, even against the true sense of the people at large, by securing the attendance of their friends, who would act with them by concert, and thus enable them to carry their point. Allusion is made to this practice in the words under consideration. See F. L. § 1.

144. *καὶ μεγάλα, κ. τ. λ.*] "and you will be greatly assisted

by it for the investigation of public affairs, and will see how great craftiness there was in Philip."

145. *ἀπαλλαγὴ*] "escape," i. e. from the contracted theatre of his country, his ports being blockaded by the Athenians (see below), and there being no way of entering Attica except as here proposed. — *ἀλλὰ . . . . κακά*] The principal Athenian generals in the time of Demosthenes were Chares, Charidemus, Diopithes, Timotheus, Chabrias, Iphicrates, Lysicles, and Phocion. Of these only Phocion was distinguished for the higher qualities of a general, while most of the others were not only inferior generals, but men of little character. The large revenue, also, which Athens had formerly received from her allies, had been mostly lost by the Social War, which had alienated the greater part of her foreign dependencies; and the rest had been absorbed by the theoric fund, for the purpose of furnishing amusement to the populace. The generals, therefore, were obliged to maintain their forces as they could, which was usually done, either by calling upon the allies of Athens, if any remained. for *benevolences*, as they were called (see Orat. de Chersoneso, § 25), or, more commonly, by making descents upon defenceless cities and tribes, and robbing them of what they wanted. This gave them more the character of adventurers than any thing else, and encouraged the business of privateering, which is but another name for piracy. This is what is alluded to by *λῃστῶν*, who were private adventurers, after the fashion of the public generals, seeking support for themselves and their attendants by pillaging, if possible, from the enemies of Athens, but if not, from her allies or those at peace with her. — *ἐκ τῆς . . . . γιγνομένων*] "proceeding from the country, *or* growing in the country."

146. *μήτε . . . . μήτε*] Used instead of *οὔτε . . . . οὔτε*, because the part. express a condition. K. § 318, 5; C. § 81, 4. — *συνέβαινε . . . . κακοπαθεῖν*] "but it happened to him, conquering in war the generals, of such character as they were (for I omit the consideration of this), whom you

sent out, to suffer from the nature of his situation and the relative advantages of the two parties," i. e. themselves and Philip. τῷ πολέμῳ is opposed to τῇ φύσει τοῦ τόπου, etc., which follows.

147. βαδίζειν ἐφ' ὑμᾶς] "to march against you." — οὐδένα] I have substituted this for οὐδέν' ἂν (which would be easily confounded with it), since the laws of the language plainly require it. K. § 255, 3. — τὰ μὲν . . . . πείσειν] "that he should carry some things by deception and others by persuasion." — πόλεμον . . . . ταραχὴν] "to excite a war for the Amphictyons and disturbance in the assembly." περὶ, "round among," "through," "in." — εἰς γὰρ, κ. τ. λ.] Philip might naturally have supposed that he would be wanted in such circumstances, from his having previously executed with great vigor and success the decree of the Amphictyons against the Phocians.

148. ἱερομνημόνων] "Hieromnemons." One class of the delegates sent to the Amphictyonic Council by the different states of Greece. There was another class of delegates, mentioned below, called *pylagoræ*. The principal object of this council or league was to defend their common sanctuaries, and especially that at Delphi. Hence, the council being religious in its nature, some have supposed the *hieromnemons* to have been priests; but there is no evidence of this that I know of. Their business at the meetings of the council seems to have been, either to prepare subjects for the consideration of the *pylagoræ*, or to execute their decrees. For a more particular account of the nature and organization of this council, see Herm. Polit. Antiq. §§ 13 and 14. — τῶν ὑπεναντίων] "his enemies."

149. προβληθεὶς] "having been brought forward, *or* nominated" (B. C. 340). — πόλεως ἀξίωμα] "dignity of the city," i. e. the office of deputy to the Amphictyonic Council. — πάντα . . . . ἐμισθώθη] "having dismissed and neglected all other things, he accomplished those things for which he was hired," i. e. by Philip. — μύθους] "legends." Referring to

the musty lore which Æschines adv. Ctesiph. § 107 seq. raked up relative to the Cirrhæan territory. This was a district lying on the Corinthian Gulf around the ancient city of Cirrha, which, before its destruction by the Amphictyons, on account of its ill-treatment of pilgrims to the temple, was the port of Delphi. After its destruction it was consecrated to Apollo and devoted to perpetual desolation. The Locrians of Amphissa, however, in violation of this decree of the Amphictyons, as it seems, had appropriated the district to themselves, and were cultivating it like common land. This crime, Æschines, on the occasion here alluded to, charged upon them; in self-defence, as he states, and in the heat of passion, as a retort upon one of the Amphissian deputies who had accused the Athenians of impiety, and as deserving to be excluded from the council; but, as Demosthenes contends, at the instigation of Philip, and for the purpose of exciting an Amphictyonic war against them, and thus opening a field for his ambition. — *ἀνθρώπους . . . . λόγων*] "men unacquainted with the tricks of speech." The *hieromnemons* are thus spoken of, according to Hermann (§ 14. 15), on account of their being chosen by lot, and hence, of course, as a general thing, being men of the common class, and of no experience in public business. — *περιελθεῖν*] "to survey," "set off." See the following decree.

150. *οὐδεμίαν . . . . ἐκεῖθεν*] "although the Locrians brought no action against us, nor even what he now falsely pretends they did. But you will see (that they did not) from this," i. e. what follows. Æschines, in his speech (§ 116), states, in justification of his attack upon the Locrians, that they were introducing a suit (*δίκην*) before the Amphictyons to fine the Athenians fifty talents, for dedicating certain shields in a new chapel dedicated to Apollo, and on his attempting to defend his countrymen, one of the Locrian deputies inveighed against them for their impiety and as deserving to be expelled from the council (*ἃ . . . .*

προφασίζεται). — Ἐπὶ .... ἀρχῆς;] "Under what administration *or* archonship?" Public documents or records, as has already been remarked, received date from such or such an archon. — κατεχρῶ] This is the second person singular of the imperfect middle of καταχράομαι.

151. μικροῦ] ὡς δεῖν being understood. K. § 341, R. 3. — εἰς ἐπιοῦσαν πυλαίαν] "to the following session." Some put a comma after this phrase and connect it with ἦλθον. Πυλαία was a general name for the meetings of the Amphictyons, from Πύλαι (Thermopylæ), one of the stated places, and probably the original place, of holding their meetings. — ἐπὶ τὸν .... ἦγον] "brought (the matter) to Philip as general." ἡγεμόνα, since the suggestion of Lambinus to that effect, has usually been considered as standing for ἡγεμονίαν; but Schäfer supposes πρᾶγμα to be understood here, and quotes an altogether parallel passage from the Third Philippic, p. 125, where it is *expressed* after ἦγον. This explanation is much the most satisfactory of the two.

152. ἢ γὰρ .... αἱρεῖσθαι] "for they said it was necessary, either that they themselves should contribute and support mercenaries and punish such as would not do this, or choose him general." — ἐῤῥῶσθαι φράσας πολλὰ] "having bid a long adieu." This infinitive means literally "to be strong," but was used like τὸ χαίρειν, in the sense of "farewell." See the same phrase, Orat. F. L. p. 419. In other places we find it with both εἰπεῖν and λέγειν, in the same sense. See Orat. de Pace, p. 62, fin. The idea conveyed in this place is, that Philip departed widely from his professed designs against the Cirrhæans and Locrians, in the act here spoken of.

153. μετέγνωσαν] "had repented *or* changed their mind." The Thebans, it will be recollected, had been associated with Philip in the war against Phocis, and were beholden to him for many favors. By the taking and garrisoning of Elatea, however, their eyes were opened to the true character of his designs. Elatea was the principal town in the

eastern part of Phocis, and so situated as to command the defiles which form the principal entrance, in that direction to Bœotia, and hence to Attica. — νῦν . . . . ἐκεῖνοι] "but as it is, *or* as the matter turned, they prevented him at least from a sudden irruption." νῦν here refers to the course which events had taken in accordance with his policy, as opposed to that desired by his adversaries. The τὸ before ἐξαίφνης refers to εἰσπεσεῖν, to be supplied from the preceding sentence, which is used as a noun with αὐτὸν accusative before it, and is governed by ἐπέσχον.

154. Ἐπὶ ἱερέως] "Under the priest." According to Hermann (§ 14. 12), the archon of Delphi (who, as he was connected with a religious establishment, would naturally be called ἱερεύς) was the Eponymus of the Amphictyons, or the magistrate from whom the year was named. — ἐαρινῆς πυλαίας] "at the spring session." The council had two sessions annually, one in the spring and one in the autumn, the former at Delphi and the latter at Thermopylæ. This is the commonly received opinion with regard to the meetings of the Amphictyons, but President Woolsey (Bib. Sac., July, 1850) makes it appear highly probable that the autumnal session was at Delphi, these words being regarded as forgeries. — συνέδροις] Hermann supposes these to be the same as the *hieromnemons.* — τῷ κοινῷ] "the commons," i. e. the body of the citizens who happened to be present from the various states belonging to the league. These, according to the author just quoted, constituted the assembly, while the two classes of deputies corresponded to the senate in a democracy. This decree, it is probable, was passed at the session at which Æschines attacked the Amphissians; that which follows, at the following session.

155. τὸ κοινὸν . . . . συνέδριον] The Amphictyonic Council was called the common council or congress of the Greeks, because it embraced nearly all the original tribes of Greece, together with their colonies. Herm. § 12. — Ἄρχων Μνησιθείδης, κ. τ. λ.] The beginning of the decree

by which Æschines was made pylagoras, which designated the year in which the above transactions took place, which was B. C. 340.

156. ὡς οὐχ . . . . Θηβαῖοι] "when the Thebans did not listen," i. e. to his proposition to unite with him against Athens. — τὰς ἀφορμὰς] "starting-points," "facilities," "means."

157. τοῖς δημιουργοῖς . . . . συνέδροις] "to the magistrates and councillors." δημιουργοί were magistrates common in the Peloponnesus. Müller, Hist. Dorians, Vol. II. p. 144. — πλημμελοῦσιν εἰς] "offend against." — λεηλατοῦσι] "plunder," "ravage." — εἰς τὴν Φωκίδα] εἰς is used on account of the previous *motion* implied in συναντᾶτε (*come* and meet). K. § 300, 3, b. — ἐνεστῶτος μηνὸς] "the present month." This is governed as a gen. of time. K. § 273, 4, (b); C. § 54, 13. There is some difficulty in making out the correspondence between the Attic month Boëdromion and the Corinthian month here named, since Panemus corresponded to the Athenian month preceding Boëdromion. But Boeckh (as cited by Dissen) supposes this to have been an intercalary year at Corinth, and this month to have been carried forward in consequence. — Τοῖς δὲ, κ. τ. λ.] The reading here adopted is that supported by the best authority, and yet no possible sense can be extracted from it. There can be no doubt that the text in this place is corrupt. Schäfer proposes, in so desperate a case, to leave out all that intervenes between χρησόμεθα and ἐπιζημίοις, which would leave a kind of sense to the passage, which is all that can be said of any of the emendations which have been suggested.

158. Μὴ τοίνυν . . . . ἀνθρώπου]. "Do not, therefore, O men of Athens, going around (i. e. walking up and down the agora, as the Athenians were wont to do, "either to tell or to hear some new thing"), say that Greece has suffered such things from one man alone," i. e. Philip.

159. μηδὲν εὐλαβηθέντα] for one "fearing nothing." — ἀλιτήριον] *homo piacularis*, i. e. "a man laden with the guilt

of," "the guilty cause."—Ὃν ὅπως .... ἀληθείας] "Whom that you did not by any possibility (ποτὲ), as soon as you saw him, turn away from in disgust, I wonder; but, as it seems, there is a certain thick darkness with you before the truth," i. e. between them and the truth. The pres. tense is employed, as expressing a general truth, implying that the Athenians were very slow in detecting rogues.

160. τούτοις ἐναντιούμενος] "opposing, *or* in opposition to these things."—τὰ ἔργα] "the realities." Opposed to τοὺς λόγους below.

161. Ὁρῶν γὰρ .... διετέλουν] "For seeing the Thebans and almost you, through the influence (ὑπὸ) of those seeking the interest of Philip, and corrupted in each state (i. e. Athens and Thebes), overlooking and not at all guarding against what was dangerous to both and deserving of much vigilance, viz. the permitting Philip to increase in strength, but on the contrary being ready for enmity and collision with each other, I continually watched that this might not be," i. e. that there might not be a rupture between Athens and Thebes, and thus Philip be permitted to gain strength by their disunion.

162. Ἀριστοφῶντα .... Εὔβουλον] Two distinguished orators at Athens, and friends of Æschines, when living; but who, as appears from what follows, were dead at the time of the delivery of this speech.—ταύτην τὴν φιλίαν] "this friendship *or* alliance," i. e. of Athens and Thebes.—ἑαυτοῖς] Used reciprocally. K. § 302, 7; C. § 48, 5.—κίναδος] "fox," i. e. an artful, knavish fellow; similar in import to another designation which he gives him, περίτριμμα ἀγορᾶς. See § 127, n.—αἰσθάνει] The more common reading, αἰσχύνῃ, is evidently incorrect, as it is inconsistent with the connection, especially the reason which is given in the following clause.—ἃ γὰρ .... δοκιμασάντων] "for in what you charge upon me concerning the Thebans, you censure them much more than me, since they approved of this alliance before I did."

163 συμπεραναμένων . . . . ἔχθραν] "while (δὲ) his other coadjutors united with him in completing the enmity against the Thebans." — ἐλθεῖν ἐφ' ἡμᾶς] "advanced against us," i. e. by suddenly turning aside from his course against Amphissa, and taking Elatea, and, as it would seem from the following decree, some other cities in the same vicinity. — καὶ εἰ μὴ . . . . ἠδυνήθημεν] "and unless we had previously roused ourselves a little (i. e. in order to effect a union between the two cities), we should not even have been able to recover ourselves." In some MSS. αὑτούς, and in others αὐτούς, is found after ἀναλαβεῖν, while in others neither form is found. This latter seems to me to be the preferable reading, since the second seems to give a wrong sense, and the first is not required by the usage of the verb. — οὕτω] This qualifies πόῤῥω, but is separated from it, as is often the case. See §§ 33, 220, n. — 'Εν οἷς, κ. τ. λ.] "But in what condition you were at that time in respect to your relations to each other, having heard these decrees and answers, you will know."

164. βουλῆς . . . . γνώμῃ] i. e., probably, "brought forward by the generals, approved by the Senate, and now passed by the people." — ἃς μὲν] Used demonstratively for τὰς μέν ; K. § 331, R. 1 ; and responded to by τινὰς δὲ, instead of ἃς δέ. — μάλιστα μὲν] "especially," "above all things." Always indicates the first choice among two or more things or courses of action. See §§ 267, 324. — πρὸς τὸ βουλεύσασθαι] "for consultation," "deliberation." — τὰς ἀνοχὰς] "the truce," "armistice." A noun used mostly in the plural, like *induciæ.*

165. πολεμάρχου] This was the title of the third archon in point of dignity. The title was given him originally on account of his acting as general in the army ; but this did not belong to his duties in later times. — ἐπειδὴ . . . . καταστῆσαι] "since Philip is endeavoring to place the Thebans in estrangement towards us, *or* to estrange the Thebans from us." — παραβαίνων . . . . συνθήκας] "violating the stipu-

lations existing to him on our part," i. e. between him and us. Referring, perhaps, to the peace so often alluded to; but, as some suppose, to another peace after the war of Byzantium. — ὅπως ἐνδεχομένως] "that as far as possible," i. e. considering the circumstances of the case. — καὶ γὰρ .... τῶν μετρίων] "for as yet they (i. e. the people) have not determined to come to the aid (i. e. to the defence of their territory and interest against Philip) in any ordinary circumstances."

166. αἵρεσιν] "choice," "feeling," "inclination." — προσκαλέσασθαι] "to entice to yourselves." — Βέλτιον .... ἱσταμένων] "But they thinking better (becoming wiser), and not wishing to yield their choice to you, but standing upon their interest." ἐφ' = "under," "in the power of." See § 215, n. — παραπέμψαντες] "having sent away," "dismissed."

167. ἀνανεοῦσθε] "you renew," "remind of." — Πρότερον] "Formerly," i. e. before he received the letter referred to. — τὰ πρὸς .... εἰρήνην] "to have sought peace with us." For the construction of ἔχειν as an auxiliary with a part., see K. § 310, 4, (k). — ἥσθην] "I was rejoiced." A first aor. pass. from ἥδομαι.

168. ὡς οὐδ' .... Θηβαίων] "as if we and the Thebans should not conspire together, even if any thing should happen," i. e. even if any such flagrant act as the taking of Elatea should be done by him. συμπνευσόντων has the same meaning as our word *conspire*, and is of precisely the same origin; meaning, like that word, literally, "to breathe together," and figuratively, "to agree *or* unite together." For its construction with ὡς ἄν, see K. § 312, 6; C. § 71, III. 1.

169. ἧκε δ' .... πρυτάνεις] "and a certain one came announcing to the prytanes." ὡς = εἰς or πρός. This has justly been considered by critics as a masterly description. The circumstances are so happily selected, and so briefly and forcibly presented, that we seem to see the tumultuous

excitement which is described. — ἐξαναστάντες . . . . ἐκάλουν] All the circumstances here mentioned are indicative of great excitement; the prytanes leaving their meal half eaten; some of them proceeding to disperse the hucksters around the agora, and to burn their sheds (or rather, perhaps, *the fagots*, see below), while others called the generals and the trumpeter. Various reasons, none of them, however, very satisfactory, have been assigned for the dispersing of the hucksters and burning their sheds; such as the design of forcing them from their employments and securing their presence in the assembly; or of clearing away all obstructions to the hurried approach of the people to the assembly. But as the people did not meet till the next morning, and as, consequently, measures might have been taken in the mean time to secure these ends without resorting to so violent acts, the conjecture of Schäfer seems more reasonable, viz. that these sheds, being of combustible materials, were ordered to be burnt as a signal, so as to call in the people from the country as extensively as possible. But more probably these γέῤῥα were not the sheds of the hucksters, but the hurdles which were used ordinarily to surround the place of assembly: or, it may be, simply bundles of fagots, kept to be burnt for signal-fires upon extraordinary occasions. The generals were summoned so as to make the necessary military preparations, and the trumpeter as a usual attendant. — Τῇ δ' . . . . ἡμέρᾳ] "On the following day early in the morning"; lit. "at the same time with the opening of day." — ὑμεῖς] "you," i. e. the people generally, in distinction from the Senate. — καὶ πρὶν . . . . καθῆτο] "and before that (the Senate) had time to deliberate and pass a preliminary decree, the whole people were seated above." This, too, was an evidence of extraordinary excitement, since ordinarily there was great difficulty in getting the people together to transact business; for which purpose a small compensation was given to those who were there promptly, and even compulsory means were resorted to, at times, to secure their attendance. But on this occasion, such was the excitement, that they all assembled before the Senate had agreed on a decree to submit to them for approval. The people are here spoken of as having taken their seats *above*, on account of the Pnyx, in which they met, being in a more elevated situation than the Senate-chamber.

170. εἰσῆλθεν ἡ βουλή] i. e. into the assembly. Not the whole Senate, but only the fifty *prytanes* and the nine *proedri*, who regularly attended the meetings of the assembly. See Grote's Hist. Greece, Vol. IV. p. 139; also § 29, n. — κἀκεῖνος . . . . οὐδείς] "and he spoke (i. e. the messenger), the crier asked, 'who wishes to harangue the people?' but no one came forward." This invitation was given at the opening of every assembly. Originally the crier called upon any of the citizens over fifty years old to speak first, and after them any others who wished. But this custom soon fell into disuse. — ἣν γὰρ . . . . ἡγεῖσθαι] "for the voice which the crier sends forth according to the laws, this it is just to consider the common voice of the country."

171. παρελθεῖν] "to have come forward," i. e. to the Bema, to harangue the people. — οἱ τριακόσιοι] "the three hundred" (arising would have advanced to the Bema). These were the three hundred richest citizens, who formed the first quarter of each of the twenty symmoriæ who were bound to discharge the duties of the trierarchy (§ 99, n), called, § 103, ἡγεμόνες τῶν συμμοριῶν. — εἰ δὲ . . . . ἐποίησαν] "but if for those being both these, viz. both well disposed towards the city and rich, they (would have come forward) who afterwards made so large contributions to the state; for they did this from their patriotism and wealth." Reference is here made to the other wealthy citizens not included in the first class, who nevertheless, in the ensuing struggle with Philip, made great sacrifices in defence of their country.

172. ἀλλὰ . . . . ἀοχῆς] "but for one having attended

closely to the course of events from the beginning." This is a phrase of precisely the same nature, and of nearly the same form, as that used by the Evangelist Luke in the first part of his Gospel, in allusion to his qualifications for such an undertaking: παρηκολουθηκότι ἄνωθεν πᾶσιν ἀκριβῶς.

173. Ἐφάνην . . . . ἐγώ] "I therefore appeared such an one on that day." For this use of οὗτος (very much like τοιοῦτος), see § 236; also Soph. Antig. v. 66. — τὴν τῆς εὐνοίας τάξιν] "the post of patriotism." — ἐξηταζόμην] "I was proved *or* found." This verb properly means "to examine," "to test," but it here expresses the *result* of a severe test or examination.

174. ὡς . . . . Φιλίππῳ] "as if the Thebans were devoted to Philip." For the part. in the gen. absolute with ὡς, see § 168, n.

175. Πλησίον . . . . βιασθῶσιν] In this passage the orator gives the reason which he supposed influenced Philip to take the step in question.

176. εἴ τι . . . . μεμνῆσθαι] "if any thing unpleasant has been done by the Thebans towards us, to call up this." δύσκολον is a softened expression for ἄδικον. — εἶτα . . . . γένησθε] "then I fear lest those (of the Thebans) now opposing, having received him, and all with one consent having united themselves to Philip, they should both advance against Attica. Nevertheless, if you will listen to me, and surrender yourselves (lit. *be*) to the consideration, not to contending about what I may say." φιλιππισάντων, literally, "Philipizing."

177. ἐπανεῖναι] "to lay aside." This is the second aorist infinitive, from ἐπανίημι. — μεταθέσθαι] "to change your view." Used absolutely. — ἔπειτ', κ. τ. λ.] Eleusis, the place here spoken of, was a town in Attica, lying towards Thebes from Athens, and therefore a desirable place as a rendezvous for the forces in order to counteract at Thebes the influence of Philip's army stationed at Elatea. The age of majority at Athens, here spoken of (ἡλικίᾳ), was

nineteen, at least as far as liability to military duty was concerned. Comp. Herm. Polit. Antiq. § 123. — *ἵνα τοῖς .... ᾖ*] "that there may be to those at Thebes preferring your cause, equally (i. e. with the faction in favor of Philip), courage to speak in defence of their rights, seeing that, as there is a force at Elatea ready to assist those selling their country to Philip, thus you are ready and will assist those who wish to contend for their liberty, if any one advances against them." The two factions at Thebes, that in favor of Philip, and that in favor of uniting with Athens against him, were very equally divided, and it was only by the most energetic and untiring efforts that Demosthenes gained the voice of the majority in favor of his measures.

178. *κελεύω*] "I direct," "I advise." — *κυρίους*] "directors." — *καὶ τοῦ .... ἐξόδου*] "both of the time when it is necessary to march thither, and of the expedition itself." Wolf considers these specifications as meaning the same thing, but Reiske justly says, in reference to the distinction between them, "De tempore modoque expeditionis, quando, et quantas numero copias, exire oporteat in castra versus Thebas." — *πῶς .... κελεύωσιν*] "how do I advise to conduct the matter? For ascertaining this give your mind very attentively to me. (I advise) not to ask any thing of the Thebans, for the occasion is disgraceful (*or* it is disgraceful to do so on such an occasion), but to offer to assist them if they urge it." The sense of the passage is this: That they should not ask aid of the Thebans, but rather offer them aid, since it would be disgraceful to appear to be seeking aid for themselves, when the Thebans were in so much more immediate danger. — *ἵν' ἐὰν .... πεπραγμένον*] "that in case they should receive these proposals, and commit themselves to us, we may both have accomplished what we desire (i. e. a measure important to Athens), and may have done it under a pretext worthy of the city (i. e. from a regard for Thebes); but if, on the contrary, it should not happen that you should gain your object (i. e succeed in

the negotiations for an alliance with Thebes), that they may reproach themselves, if in this case they fail of any thing, while nothing disgraceful or grovelling shall have been done by you."

179. οὐκ εἶπον, κ. τ. λ.] "I did not speak of these things indeed, and yet not propose them," etc. This is an instance of the climax, so called, on account of the sense rising step by step like *stairs* (κλίμαξ).

180. βούλει] This is a common form of the second person singular indicative of this verb, instead of βούλῃ. While the clerk was getting ready to read the decree just called for, the orator employs the time in rendering ridiculous, in view of his eminent services on this occasion, the nickname Batalus, given him in youth on account of his stammering (often alluded to by Æschines in his speeches, as F. L., p. 41). I am aware that a different origin has been assigned to this name, which Æschines follows in his oration against Timarchus (p. 18). But this is evidently nothing more than a play upon the word, as βάταλος, according to Passow, meant both a stammerer and an effeminate or debauched person; which latter meaning Æschines gave to it, on account of its conveying a greater reproach. Furthermore, the common tradition that Batalus, from whom the name was derived, was a flute-player, would seem to indicate that the nickname had reference to some defect in the manner of his speaking; as the blowing of wind-instruments often affects the voice, and especially gives to the performer that inflation of the cheeks which is common in mouthing and bad speakers. At all events, it seems evident that Demosthenes understood it so, from his proceeding at once to compare himself in this character with Æschines as a bad actor, — as an ἰαμβειοφάγος, or "eater of iambics." And this, by the way, is probably what is alluded to by ἐπέτριψας, "you murdered," a few lines below. — εἶναι θῶ] 'set down to be, *or* as being" — Βούλει . . . . σκηνῆς] "Do you wish (me to set down) myself to be one whom

you reviling and deriding might call Batalus, but (to set down) you as no ordinary hero, but one of the heroes of the stage," i. e. such characters as he, as an actor of third parts, had represented. — Κολυττῷ] This was the least respectable quarter of the city, lying northeast of the temple of Theseus. To have failed in such a place added to his disgrace. See Wordsworth's Athens and Attica, p. 179.

182. Ἑλληνίδας πόλεις] "Grecian cities." πόλεις is here placed in apposition with its parts, ἃς μὲν, τινὰς δὲ, and ἐνίας δὲ, instead of being in the gen. and governed by them. K. § 266, 3. The cities referred to in the text, just above, have been before mentioned (see §§ 60, 70), but it is uncertain what cities these are, unless they may be those mentioned in § 164. — οὐδὲν . . . . χρώμενος] "doing nothing abhorrent either to the spirit of his country or to his own character, and using his present fortune intemperately." The genitives πατρίδος and τρόπου are governed by ἀλλότριον. K. § 271, 3; C. § 54, 1.

183. Καὶ ἕως . . . . πλημμελεῖσθαι] "And as long as they saw him destroying barbarous cities, although their own (i. e. cities out of Greece belonging to Athens), the people of Athens considered of less importance the offence committed against itself."

184. δέδοκται] "it has pleased," or "it has been decreed." Taylor proposes to substitute δεδόχθαι instead of the indic., making it depend for government, as is usual in decrees, upon εἶπεν, near the beginning. As, however, this emendation is purely conjectural, it is better to suppose that, as the preamble had been long, its proper dependence was overlooked, and therefore a different mood adopted. — ἥρωσι] "heroes." These were mythic characters who had been deified, and were regarded as demigods and tutelary divinities by the people. — διότι . . . . ἐποιοῦντο] "that they (their ancestors) considered it of more importance." διότι = ὅτι, §§ 167, 184. K. § 338, 2. — ἐντὸς Πυλῶν] "within Thermopylæ." The object of directing a squadron to this place

was, to cut off Philip's communication with his country, and otherwise to annoy him in that quarter.

185. τὸν Φίλιππον] Governed by καταπλαγέντας. K. § 279, 5. — καὶ ὅτι . . . . ἀλλήλας] "and (to say) that the Athenians, forgetting all injuries, if formerly there has been any estrangement to the two cities towards each other," i. e. between the two cities.

186. Ἔτι δὲ . . . . ὁμοφύλῳ] "And besides, neither do the people of Athens consider the people of Thebes alien from them, on account of their relationship not only in origin but in race," i. e. they were of Grecian origin like themselves (which Philip was not), but whether any closer relationship existed between them is not certain. The whole sentence being rendered negative by οὐδὲ, the negatives (οὔτε . . . . οὔτε) in the two distributive clauses should be rendered positively in English. — καὶ γὰρ τοὺς Ἡρακλέους, κ. τ. λ.] The allusion here is to the migration of the Dorians from the northern regions into the Peloponnesus, under the name of "The Return of the Descendants of Hercules." This expedition is represented as having been undertaken by the descendants of Hercules in order to recover the right to the dominion of the Peloponnesus, of which their illustrious ancestor had been deprived by Eurystheus. Now the Athenians, as it happened, had assisted them in making good their claims; which was considered as a kindness done to the ancestors of the Thebans, because Hercules, when expelled from the Peloponnesus, was received at Thebes, and became a Theban hero. The other act of kindness here alluded to consisted in receiving Œdipus, their king, with his children, when banished from Thebes in obedience to the direction of an oracle. — This strikes me as a genuine decree of Demosthenes. For, aside from its great length, which seems to have been characteristic of his decrees (Æschin. contr. Ctes., § 100), it is characterized by his peculiar magnanimity and reverence for the past.

188. Αὕτη . . . . τούτων] "This was the beginning and

first establishment of affairs in regard to Thebes (i. e. of a good understanding with Thebes), in matters previous to these measures the cities having been drawn into hostilities, and hatred, and distrust, by means of these," i. e. Æschines and his associates.

189. Ὁ γὰρ . . . . συκοφάντης] "For the counsellor, and the malicious accuser." The difference here pointed out between these two characters is just and important. The counsellor fearlessly gives such advice as the emergency requires, and risks the consequences; but the sycophant, avoiding all responsibility by his silence on such occasions, watches only for evils flowing from the measures of others at which to carp and find fault. The distinction is very much the same as between the statesman and the mere politician.

190. Ἦν μὲν . . . . καιρὸς] "That, therefore, as I said, was the proper time." — ἐγὼ δὲ . . . . ποιοῦμαι] "I go so far." ὑπερβολὴν ποιοῦμαι is a circumlocution equivalent to ὑπερβάλλω. See F. L., p. 447, fin. — ἐνῆν] "it was possible," i. e. to choose or adopt, προαιρεῖσθαι being understood. See § 193. — Εἴ γὰρ . . . . λαθεῖν] "For if there be any measure, which any one even now has discovered, which, if taken at that time, would have been useful, I say that this ought not to have escaped my notice." λανθάνειν, though apparently intransitive in many cases, properly takes the acc. K. § 279, 4.

191. τουτουσί] "these," i. e. the Athenians.

192. ἀφεῖται] "has been put aside," and therefore "is disregarded." The orator proceeds to state in few words what a counsellor or statesman has to do, and consequently from what points of view his own measures should be judged of in the scrutiny which he calls upon his enemies to subject them to. He has not, he observes, any thing to do with the past, but only with the present and future. His own measures, therefore, should be judged of exclusively with reference to the dangers which already existed, and those

which threatened them in future. Besides, it was the *wisdom* of his measures with reference to these two points of time, and not their *issue*, which was to be considered; since the issue of all things is in the hands of the Deity, and cannot be controlled by man. — ἡ δὲ προαίρεσις αὐτὴ] "but the very aim, plan, *or* motive" (of one's policy), i. e. without reference to the results to which it had led. — διάνοιαν] "purpose," "mind," "state of mind." See § 210.

193. ἐνεστησάμην] "I instituted," "set on foot."

194. Εἰ δ' ὁ συμβὰς, κ. τ. λ.] "But if the tempest (*or* storm) that befell (i. e. the attack of Philip) has overpowered not only us, but all the other Greeks, what ought to be done? Why, just as one would do if a person should accuse of the shipwreck the owner of a ship who had done every thing for safety, and provided the vessel with every thing by which he supposed she would be secure, but which afterwards encountered a storm, when her tackling labored or even gave way altogether." ἂν refers to a suppressed predicate, to be supplied from the preceding verb, which predicate is more definitely explained by φήσειεν below, with which the particle is repeated. K. § 261, 4. ναύκληρον means the owner of the ship, or the one who fitted it out, and not the pilot or captain. For the rendering given to the participles in the latter part of the passage, see K. §§ 309, 3, (b); 312, 4, (a).

195. οὕτως . . . . πρᾶξαι] "it was fated for us to come off, *or* fare, thus." For this rendering of πρᾶξαι, see § 252, n. — ὑπὲρ οὗ . . . . φωνάς] "for which (i. e. that the Thebans might join themselves to him) he (Philip) used every argument, *or* exerted all his power of lungs." — τῆς μάχης] "the battle," i. e. of Chæronea, this being the decisive battle, in which the struggle with Philip ended. Chæronea was a city of Bœotia, as Demosthenes here states, three days' journey from Attica. — Ἆρ' οἶσθ . . . . τότε δ' —] "Do you (Æschines) know, that *now*, indeed (i. e. the counsels of Demosthenes having been followed), to stand, to assem-

ble, to regain breath, many things of what tended to the safety of the city one, two, and three days gave; *but then*" —. The consequences intended to be implied are left to the hearer's imagination. The mark of interrogation is wanting, on account of the incompleteness of the last clause. νῦν and τότε are opposed to each other: and as the former refers to the circumstances of the case alluded to, the latter must refer to what would have followed if events had taken a different course. — καὶ τὸ προβαλέσθαι . . . . συμμαχίαν] "and the placing before the city this alliance," i. e. the protecting the city by the alliance with Thebes.

196. μοι] "on my part." Ethical dat. K. § 284, 3, (10), d. — τῆς αὐτῆς . . . . ἄλλοις] "you are guilty of the same ignorance with others." ἄλλοις is governed by τῆς αὐτῆς, which is an adjective of likeness. K. § 284, 3, (4); C. § 59, 5.

197. οὐ γὰρ . . . . ἐχρῶντο] "for (had you proposed any better measures) they would not have adopted these," i. e. of mine. — ὅπερ δ' . . . . ἐξήτασαι] "but what a man of the most detestable character and most hostile to the city would have done, this you have been found doing after the results or calamities," i. e. bringing Demosthenes to trial as the other sycophants did the friends of Athens, and consequently enemies of Philip, in the other places mentioned below. The phrase ἐπὶ τοῖς συμβᾶσιν, "after the results," is introduced in opposition to εἰς ταῦτα above, in order to exhibit Æschines as maliciously active after the fate of his country was decided, but stupidly indifferent while its fate was pending.

198. Καίτοι . . . . ἀπέκειτο] "And yet, to whomsoever the misfortunes of Greece were reserved, for him to become famous by them." The peculiarity of the construction consists in the finite verb being used personally instead of impersonally. See § 4, n. — καὶ ὅτῳ . . . . ἐχθροῖς] "and to whomsoever the same times are profitable as to the enemies of the city." καί before τοῖς . . . . ἐχθροῖς makes the construc-

tion coördinate, instead of leaving this dat. to be governed by οἱ αὐτοί. K. § 284, R. 3; C. § 59, R. 2. — Δηλοῖς δὲ] "Bu. you show this," i. e. that he was no friend of his country. — Ὥσπερ . . . . κινεῖται] "As fractures and sprains, when any evil (sickness) seizes the body, then are affected." Allusion is here made to the physiological fact, that fractures and sprains, which in a healthy state of the body have not been felt for years, are discovered at once on the approach of weakness or disease. Just so, the orator says, it was with Æschines; when the body politic was in a healthy state, he took no part in public affairs; but when it had suffered injury, he at once made his appearance to censure those who had remained constantly at their posts. See the same illustration employed, Olynth. II., p. 21, to show the tendency of an invasion of a country by an enemy to discover to the people the evils of a government, to which they have been blinded by a brilliant succession of foreign campaigns.

199. Ἐπειδὴ . . . . ἔγκειται] "But since he lays much stress upon the issue *or* the calamities." — ὑπερβολὴν] "extravagance." — οὐδ' οὕτως . . . . ἦν] "not even in this case could the city have departed from these" (counsels of mine). For the construction of the verbal here, see § 58, n. — εἶχε λόγον] "had an account," "regard."

200. δοκεῖ] Used personally here. — τότε . . . . τούτου] "but in the other case, claiming to be at the head of the other (Greeks), then relinquishing this." For προεστάναι, see K. §§ 194, R. 3; 173, R. 2; C. § 39, 3. Observe also the difference between the pres. and aor. part.; the former denotes a continued claim, the latter a shrinking from her usual position at the crisis referred to. — Εἰ γὰρ . . . . πρόγονοι] "For if she had yielded this (i. e. taking the lead in this contest) without a struggle, for which there is no danger that our ancestors did not incur." ἀκονιτί is a gymnastic term, and means, literally, "without dust"; descriptive of one who retired from the palæstra without daring

to wrestle, and consequently without the dust collected by that exercise. οὐδένα κίνδυνον is for οὐδεὶς κίνδυνος, being attracted into the case of its relative. See § 16, n.

201. Τίσι δ' . . . . πεποιημένοι] "But with what eyes, by Jupiter, could we have looked upon those visiting the city (i. e. any who might visit the city, as was done by thousands, on account of its renown), if affairs had come to the pass which they have now come to, and Philip had been chosen leader and lord of all (the Greeks), while others, without us, had made the struggle that these things might not occur." The time of the tenses here is affected by εἰ and ἄν, or, perhaps it should be said, by the nature of the proposition. Butt. § 139, 10. See also Philip. I., § 1, n. For the attractions which Athens presented to visitors, see Isoc. Panegyr., pp. 49 and 50. — καὶ ταῦτα] A phrase of frequent occurrence in Greek, and corresponding precisely to our phrase "and that too." See § 282, n.

202. ἰσχυρῶν γενομένων] "having been powerful," i. e. the most powerful tribe in Greece. Alluding to the state of things after the Peloponnesian war, when the Lacedemonians enjoyed an ascendency in power over all the other tribes; which, however, as already mentioned, they lost at Leuctra in a contest with Thebes. Now, even under these circumstances, as Demosthenes says, when Athens was but a secondary power, she never would relinquish the right of taking the lead of the other tribes in all struggles affecting the interests of the Greeks generally. Reference is here made to the ἡγεμονία or *precedency*, or *leading*, of which so much is said in Athenian history. — μετὰ . . . . προεστάναι] "that this would have gladly been given to the city with many thanks, viz. to receive whatever it desired, and to retain its own possessions (if it would only submit) to perform what was commanded by another, and allow some of the other Greeks to take the precedency." We have here a kind of metathesis by which infinitives are put instead of participles, in the clause expressing the condition on which

the concession would have been made, and participles instead of infinitives in the clause stating the concession. By this arrangement, the concession is ironically presented as a privilege, since on the principles of Æschines it should be regarded as such.

204. οἳ καὶ, κ. τ. λ.] Allusion is here made to the time of the Persian war, when the Athenians, under Themistocles, made great sacrifices in behalf of Greece, and gained to themselves enduring renown.

205. τὸν τῆς . . . . περιμένει] "awaits the death of fate or natural death," i. e. does not expose himself to death voluntarily, by incurring dangers in defence of his country, but waits till some extraordinary providence, or the regular course of nature, may bring him to an end. μοίρας is understood with εἱμαρμένης.

206. Εἰ . . . . ἐπεχείρουν] Denies the fact, and is followed in the apodosis by the opt. with ἄν. K. § 339, 3, α, β. — ὡς ἄρα] "that forsooth." See § 22; also Popular Orations, VIII. § 4, note.— προήγαγον] "I incited," lit. "I led forward," "induced." Thus differing from προσάγειν, which means "to carry through to a result." — προαιρέσεις] "aims," "habits," "constant practice." — τῆς μέντοι . . . . κατηγορῶν] "but, indeed, I say that I share with you the services connected with each of the things done; but this man (Æschines) censuring all these measures," i. e. the measures taken against Philip. In this passage the orator prepares the way for what follows, viz. that in censuring him Æschines was at the same time censuring the people at large; since they had enacted and executed the measures which he had proposed. For the construction of μετεῖναι with a genitive and dative, see K. § 273, 3, (b), (a); C. § 56, 4.

207. τουδὶ] "this friend here," i. e. Ctesiphon. Ctesiphon had proposed to crown Demosthenes, on account of the high value of his public services, especially in the contest with Philip. If now he were condemned for this, it would be saying, of course, that his measures were not

wise, and consequently that they had erred in following them. — ἀγνωμοσύνῃ] "unkindness."

208. Ἀλλ' οὐκ ἔστιν, κ. τ. λ.] "But it is not possible," etc. This is a passage of great celebrity, on account of its lofty and impassioned eloquence. Longinus, in his treatise De Sublimitate (§ 16), speaking of the use of rhetorical figures, thus remarks upon it: — "Demosthenes is introducing a proof in defence of his administration; what now was the simple way of expressing it? 'You did not err, ye who engaged in the contest in defence of the liberties of Greece, and of this you have familiar examples; for neither those who fought at Marathon, nor those who fought at Salamis nor those who fought at Platæa, erred.' But when, as if suddenly inspired by a god, or possessed by Apollo, he thundered out that oath, 'It cannot be that you erred, — no by those who fought at Marathon!' he seems by one form of the figure of adjuration, which I here call apostrophe, to deify those ancestors (suggesting that it is proper to swear by those having died so gloriously, as by gods), and inspire his judges with the spirit of those heroes, while he has changed a dry proof into the transcendent sublimity, pathos, and cogency of unusual and surpassingly beautiful oaths, and at the same time lodges in the hearts of his hearers a certain consolatory and healing word; till, being elated by these encomiums, they come to esteem the battle with Philip no less glorious than the victories at Marathon and Salamis." The Athenians first met the Persians at Marathon; hence the use of προκινδυνεύσαντας. The same word is employed by Thucydides, § 73. — ὃ μὲν .... κέχρηνται] "for what was the part of brave men was performed by them all, but the fortune which the divinity allotted to each of them that they met." So, the orator would reason, has it been in the present case; we have acted the part of brave men, and ought to be honored as such, although we have not been successful.

209. ὦ .... γραμματοκύφων] 'O execrable wretch and

servile scribe!" The last of these nouns is derived from γράφω and κύπτω, from the stooping position of a scribe while writing. The idea intended to be conveyed by the term is, that he was a servile scribe, who, according to the Scripture expression, "bowed down his back always"; that he was not in possession of an honorable post, but was an inferior clerk, who was compelled to bend over his desk for a living. Allusion is here made to the former occupation of Æschines, as a secretary to the petty magistrates. See § 261. — παρὰ τουτωνὶ] "from these," i. e. the Athenians. — ὧν τίνος .... οὑτοσί;] "what one of which did the present cause need?" i. e. what did any of these military proceedings have to do with this question pertaining to civil matters? Demosthenes here alludes to the cases of victories, etc., cited by his opponent, in his speech (§ 181), from the ancient history of Athens, in order to show how sparing the Athenians had always been of public honors. But these examples, he contends, had nothing to do with the case. — 'Εμὲ δέ, ... ἔδει;] "But, O actor of third parts, assuming the spirit of whom was it proper for me, coming forward (παριόντα) as counsellor to the city concerning the precedency, to ascend the Bema?"

210. ἀπὸ τῆς αὐτῆς διανοίας] "with the same state of mind," or "from the same principles." — ἀλλὰ τὰ μέν, κ. τ. λ.] "but (it is necessary for you to judge) the common suits, examining them by private laws and facts, but public systems of policy, having reference to the renowned deeds of our ancestors. And it is necessary for you, if you would do what is worthy of them, to consider, when you enter upon the trial of public causes, that each one of you receives with the staff and the symbol the spirit of the city"; i. e. becomes, as it were, a representative of the general tone of feeling, or spirit of the city, and therefore is bound to maintain it in his decisions. In other words, the orator reminds his judges that they are bound by the nature of their office to decide public matters with reference to the

general history and spirit of the nation. With σκοπεῖν, ἐπὶ often has this meaning ("with reference to," "by"). See §§ 233, 294. ἀξιώματα, in the plural, properly has the meaning here given it. K. § 243, 3, (3); C. § 47, 7. The βακτηρία was a *staff* handed to each judge on entering the court in which he was to serve for the day, as a mark of judicial honor, and bore the number or emblem of the court. The σύμβολον was a ticket, by presenting which to the proper officer he received his fee. The tablet, on which the name of each judge was inscribed, and the number of the division to which he belonged for the year, was called πινάκιον, and consequently was quite distinct from the σύμβολον, though generally confounded with it. Comp. Herm. § 134, 17.

211. 'Αλλὰ γὰρ] "But (I must check myself) for." See Xen. Anab. III. 2, 32; also § 42, n. — ἔστιν ἃ . . . . πραχθέντων] "there are some of the decrees and public doings on that occasion which I omitted." He here returns to the point from which he diverged at the beginning of § 196. He was there speaking of his measures to secure the alliance of Thebes, the account of which he here resumes.

212. ὡς ἑτέρως] "very otherwise," i. e. adversely. See § 128, n. Æschines says these things, §§ 137, 141, 157 of his speech. — συναίτιος] "a contributory cause." Placed in opposition to μόνος αἴτιος below. Πῶς . . . . καταρατότερος;] "How could there be a more savage and execrable calumniator?"

213. ΕΠΙΣΤΟΛΗ] The letter itself is wanting, which is the case, also, with all the letters, decrees, laws, etc., from this point. See Appendix. — ἐδημηγόρουν] "they (i. e. the ambassadors of Philip and his allies) harangued the people." — Τὸ δ' . . . . 'Αττικήν] "In short, therefore, they demanded that they (i. e. the Thebans) should make a return for the favors which they had received from Philip, but that they should inflict punishment for the injuries which they had received from you in which of two ways they prefer, either by letting them (the Macedonians) pass through (i. e. through

Bœotia) against you, or by joining with them in an incursion into Attica." Τὸ δ' οὖν κεφαλαῖον is an adverbial acc. in apposition with the following sentence. K. § 279, R. 8; C. § 57, R. 9. — πεπόνθεσαν] Observe the omission of the augment in the pluperf. after a word ending in a vowel which cannot be elided. K. § 120, R. 2. — εἰς . . . . συντείνοντ'] " but all tending to the same things."

214. τὰ μὲν . . . . νομίσητε] " these things, in all their particulars, I should esteem it a recompense for a whole life to state, but I fear you, lest, since the times have passed away, just as you would if you thought there had been a general obliteration of the things, you may consider the account of these things as a useless vexation." For the effect of the eloquence of Demosthenes on the Thebans at the time here referred to, see Plutarch's Life of Demosthenes. For the grammatical resolution of ὥσπερ ἂν, see § 194, n.

215. ἐκάλουν] "they called *or* invited," i. e. to march to Thebes and unite with them against Philip. Æschines, in his speech (p. 75), states that this assistance was sent out before Demosthenes had proposed any decree on the subject. This seems to be a malicious falsehood, added by him in publishing his oration, and never uttered before the court. — οἰκείως] " cordially," i. e. by the Thebans. How cordially they were received the orator goes on to state, by saying that they were received into the bosom of their families, while their own soldiers were encamped without the walls. — τὰ τιμιώτατα] " the things most precious." A sort of comprehensive summary, referring to nothing in particular, but designed to cover every thing of the kind which had just been mentioned, like our term " whatever is most sacred *or* dear." — Καίτοι . . . . σωφροσύνης] " And, indeed, on that day the Thebans exhibited to all men three of the most honorable encomiums upon you; one for bravery, another for justice, the third for self-government, *or* continence." In the following sentences the orator proceeds to show how they exhibited these encomiums. The first and

second they exhibited, he says, in uniting themselves with them instead of Philip, and the third, by receiving them so unreservedly into the privacies of their families. — ἀμείνους] "braver." It is thus distinguished from κρείττων, which means "more powerful." See § 146; also Æsch. adv. Ctesiph., § 11, and Soph. Antig., v. 73. — καὶ . . . . δ'] "and also," "and too." K. § 322, R. 7. — ἐφ' ὑμῖν] ἐπί means here "depending upon," "in the power of," = *penes*. See Xen. Anab. III. 1, 17, 18, *et passim*.

216. κατά γ' ὑμᾶς] "at least as far as you were concerned." For the position of γέ between a preposition and its noun, see Jelf's K. § 735, Obs. 2. — οὐδεὶς . . . . ἐνεκάλεσεν] "no one accused you, not even unjustly." A genuine Demosthenian expression. — δίς τε . . . . χειμερινήν] "and twice having fought in conjunction with them the first battles, that at the river (probably the Bœotian Cephissus) and the battle of the storm." Scarcely any thing is now known of these battles, though they were doubtless familiar to those whom the orator addressed. Thus much, however, is evident from this account, that they were preliminary skirmishes with Philip previous to the decisive battle of Chæronea. That χειμερινήν cannot mean "in the winter," as some have translated it, is shown by Mr. Clinton in his Fasti Hellenici, Vol. II. pp. 352–354.

217. πῶς οὐ . . . . θεούς;] "how does he not perform outrageous, or rather impious acts, if, of what things he made the gods witnesses (i. e. by sacrifices, rejoicings, etc.), as being most desirable, these he now demands of you (the judges), who have sworn by the gods, to condemn as not being the most desirable?" Observe the inextricable dilemma in which he puts his antagonist by this enthymem. See also § 196, and compare the other enthymems referred to in § 139, n.

218. Θηβαῖοι . . . . ἐμοί] "but the Thebans, in thinking that they had been preserved by us, and it had happened to those who, on account of what these men (such as Æschines)

did, seemed to be on the point of needing assistance (i. e. the Athenians) for them to help others (the Thebans), from what you listened to me in," i. e. from his measures. — ἡ ἐμὴ συνέχεια, κ. τ. λ.] "my perseverance, etc." Demosthenes here refers to his long course of active opposition to Philip, in which he had not only proposed measures, but gone on embassies (πλάνοι), and toiled in almost every capacity. See § 237.

219. Καλλίστρατος, κ. τ. λ.] Callistratus, here referred to as renowned (ἐκεῖνος), was the orator who first incited Demosthenes to the study of eloquence, by his celebrated speech concerning Oropus. The others are often referred to by Demosthenes as famous orators of his times. See §§ 162, 251. Observe the omission of the connective before ἕτεροι. K. § 325, 1, (e). — οὐκ ἂν ἐπρέσβευσεν] "would not have gone on an embassy," or "was not accustomed to go on embassies." K. § 260, 2, (2), (β); C. § 73, 3, 2). — Ὑπέλειπε . . . . ἀναφοράν] "For each of them reserved to himself, not only leisure, but also, if any thing (adverse) happened, the liberty of excusing himself." ἀναφορά seems to be used here as ἀναφέρειν often is. See ἀνενεγκεῖν ἐπ' ἐκείνους, § 224. This use of ἅμα μέν . . . . ἅμα δέ is not uncommon in representing two things as belonging to the predicate equally at the same time. See § 219; also Xen. Anab. III. 4, 19.

220. ὥστ' οὐκ . . . . πράξειεν] "so that it did not seem to me to allow any opportunity for, or even thought of, one's own safety, but that one should be contented, if, having neglected no duty, he should do whatever the crisis demanded." The substitution of ὥραν for χώραν, made by Dissen, seems uncalled for, and, on all grounds, undesirable

221. τυχὸν] "perhaps." This meaning grows out of the use of the part. in the acc. absolute. K. § 312, 5.

222. ἀποπεφευγότα] "having escaped without censure,' or "having been acquitted." The same legal terms are not unfrequently applied by Demosthenes to things as to

persons. See F. L., p. 399, init., where this word is used of a person.

223. *πρότερον*] "formerly." For the occasion on which the decree of Aristonicus was proposed, see § 80, seq. — *οὔτε . . . . συγκατηγόρησεν*] "nor did he abet him who did prosecute them." — *Καίτοι . . . . ἕτερα*] "And yet at that time he might have prosecuted Demomeles and Hyperides, who proposed these things, if, indeed, he now brings true charges against me, with much more reason than he does this man (Ctesiphon). Why? Because it is possible for him (Ctesiphon) to appeal to them (Demomeles and Hyperides), and to the decisions of the courts (i. e. which in this and similar cases had been made in favor of Demosthenes), and to the fact that he himself (Æschines) has not accused them (Demomeles and Hyperides), who proposed the same things which this man (Ctesiphon) now has, and the fact, also, that the laws no longer permit (i. e. after a case of the same kind had been decided in his favor) to accuse on account of things thus publicly done (or "carried through," "settled"), and many other things." That is to say, as he had already been tried in a case of precisely the same kind, and received a verdict in his favor, the present trial was like putting him twice in jeopardy for the same thing, and hence was not allowed by the laws.

224. *τότε δ' . . . . προλαβεῖν*] "but at that time the cause would have been decided by itself, before it had gained any of these advantages." For *προλαβεῖν* in this sense, see § 314.

225. *οἶμαι*] Ironical, like our "I trow." Demosthenes, of course, had no doubt on the subject. It is often thus used. See § 46. — *μήτ' ἂν . . . . ῥηθῆναι*] "nor would have expected to hear spoken of at this day." — *τι λέγειν*] "to say something to the purpose." This use of *τὶ* is analogous to that of *τὶς* for *μέγας*, — the idea being that of "something weighty," "important," or "pertinent to the subject."

226. *οἱ λόγοι*] "the arguments," "proofs." — *παρ'*] "at

the same time with." See § 13, n. The action had been deferred by Æschines about six years, in order to bring it on in times more favorable to his cause. See § 19, n.

227. ὅταν . . . . λογίζησθε] "when thinking that there remains a balance of money (in your favor), you have a reckoning with some one." — καθαραὶ . . . . ψῆφοι] "clear accounts," i. e. balanced. Accounts were cast by the use of pebbles, which, to express debt and credit, were placed opposite each other on corresponding lines, a given value being always indicated by a given situation. In balancing accounts, pebbles were removed from one side for debits and from the other for credits, and if, in this way, both sides became *cleared* at the same time, the account was balanced. This sufficiently explains the expression under consideration, and also the phrase τιθεὶς ψήφους, § 229. — συγχωρεῖτε] "you yield," i. e. change your mind on this point. The sophism of Æschines, here referred to, is found in §§ 59, 60 of his speech. — σαθρὸν] "rotten."

228. ὑπαρχούσης ὑπολήψεως] "the existing opinion."

229. οὐ τιθεὶς . . . . λογισμός)] "not casting accounts (for this is not the way of estimating public measures)." See § 227, n.

230. ἀντὶ δὲ . . . . πόλεμον] "instead of pirates from Eubœa plundering us, that Attica on the side of the sea was in peace during the whole war." φέρειν καὶ ἄγειν, like *agere et fere*, mean together "to plunder," referring originally to the different kinds of property that were the objects of plunder.

231. Ἢ δεῖν . . . . κεκόμισθε] "Or that it is necessary to cancel these deeds (i. e. by what Æschines had done), and not rather to take care that they shall be preserved in memory through all times? And I do not now add, that the cruelty which may be witnessed where (ἐν οἷς) Philip became thoroughly master of any, it happened to others to experience, but that, of the kindness which he feigned, aiming at (περιβαλλόμενος) the remaining interests (i. e. the

acquisition of the states yet unsubdued), you, by the blessing of God, have enjoyed the fruit." That is to say, by holding out against Philip, in accordance with the advice of Demosthenes, they had enjoyed the advantage continually of this insinuating policy, — which was continued, indeed, even after the battle of Chæronea. For this use of *καλῶς ποιοῦντες*, see Viger's Idioms, p. 779 ; also Dem. Pop. Orat. I. 28, note.

232. *παραδείγματα*] "illustrations," "comparisons." Such as that above cited, concerning the accounts. — *πάνυ γὰρ .... Ἑλλήνων*] "for the interests of Greece (don't you see?) depend much upon this." The question gives point to the irony. Demosthenes here alludes to the strictures which Æschines (§§ 72, 166, 207, of his speech) had bestowed upon his style and manner of speaking. This, doubtless, might easily be done, since a person of such vivid ideas and intense feeling would be likely, at times, to commit some improprieties in language and gesture.

233. *ἐπ' αὐτῶν τῶν ἔργων*] "with reference to the actual realities." *ἔργων* evidently stands opposed to *ῥῆμα* and *χεῖρα* above. For this use of *ἐπί*, see § 210, n.

234. *Κέρκυρα*] "Corcyra." A large island off the coast of Epirus. This, with the other important islands here named, was formerly in a kind of dependent alliance with Athens, but had revolted from her in the Social War, which occurred shortly before the contest with Philip. See § 17, n. — *ἦν προεξειλεγμένα*] "had been collected in advance." Of course, then, he had no more to expect for the year, nor any means of making the annual assessment larger, in order to meet the emergency. — *οἰκείων*] "domestic *or* city forces." Called (§ 237) *πολιτικῶν δυνάμεων*. — *οὗτοι*] "these," i. e. Æschines and his associates. — *ἔχθρας .... ἐγγυτέρω*] "nearer enmity than friendship."

235. *παρὰ*] "excepting," "contrary to," "besides." A common meaning with an accusative. See Orat. de Chers. § 76. — *ἦρχε .... ὢν*] "he led those following him, being

himself absolute." That is to say, he was not simply a general, subject to the direction of some government which had commissioned him, nor even a prime minister, responsible to his people, but an absolute king at the head of his subjects. This of course gave him a great advantage in war, as it enabled him at all times to act with promptness and decision, without being embarrassed by the slow process of gaining the popular consent to every measure before he could enter upon it. See a parallel passage, Dem. F. L., p. 399. — εἶθ' .... ἀεί] "then these (his soldiers) always had arms in their hands," i. e. were always engaged in war, and, consequently, experienced soldiers.

236. Αὐτὸ γὰρ .... βεβουλευμένοι] "For this very right of addressing the people, in the first place, which alone I shared in (i. e. which was his only power), you extended equally to his hirelings (i. e. Philip's) and to me, and in what things these (hirelings) had the advantage of me (and these were many from the specious pretexts with which different measures were put forward), these having decided upon in favor of the enemies, you broke up the assembly." And thus they prevented him from getting his plans approved. The phrase δι' ἣν ἕκαστον τύχοι πρόφασιν means literally, "through the pretexts which each thing might find," i. e. through various specious pretexts.

237. ὅσων] By attraction instead of ὅσα. This is used, and not the simple relative, because it refers to *quantity* ("the *greatest* as," instead of "as great as.")

238. Εἰ δὲ λέγεις, κ. τ. λ.] "But if, Æschines, you speak of our rights towards the Thebans, or towards the Byzantians, or towards the Eubœans, or contend for equality now," i. e. an equal distribution of the expenses of the war among the allies, on the occasion referred to. νυνί, therefore stands opposed to πρότερον in the same line. The orator, having just spoken of the allies which he had gained for Athens in the struggle with Philip, takes occasion here to allude to an objection which Æschines had made in his speech (§ 137,

seq.) to the conditions upon which some of these allies had been received, as they were required to bear but a small portion of the expenses. This policy he justifies, first, by an appeal to the example of their forefathers at the battle of Salamis in the war with Persia, and then by stating that upon no other condition could they have been kept from joining themselves to Philip, and thus augmenting his strength. — ἐκείνων] For the position of this word between the article and its noun, see § 71, n. — τῶν ἄλλων] Governed by διπλάσια, which implies a comparison. K. § 275, 2 ; C. § 54, 1.

239. Εἶτα . . . . ἐμέ] "Then surely you show worthless favors to these (the Athenians) in accusing me." That is to say, his advice came too late to be worth any thing, — it was but a cheap wisdom, which did not come till after the event. — ἐνεδέχετο] "was possible *or* practicable." — ὁ γὰρ . . . . ἕτοιμος] "for he who was bidding against us (i. e. Philip) was ready both to receive them at once, if driven from us, and to give them money besides." Of course, then, there was no opportunity for chaffering with them, in order to see how large a proportion of the expenses they would bear ; they were to be received on their own conditions, if at all.

240. τί ἂν] ἂν here is prospective, and hence is repeated below. K. § 261, 3 ; C. § 73, 7. — ἐμοῦ . . . . ἀκριβολογουμένου] "I chaffering about these things."

241. διὰ Βυζαντίων] "by means of the Byzantians," i. e. through their influence and coöperation. The orator is still describing what his enemies would have said, if the allies in question had gone over to the interest of Philip on account of too hard conditions being required of them ; and in doing this he makes them state what he conceived would have been the consequences of such an event. He has passed, however, from the oblique to the direct form of discourse ; since he personates, as it were, the accuser, and utters his sentiments. K. § 345, R. 5.

242. τοῦτο δὲ . . . . πατρίδι ;] "but this apology for a man is a fox even by nature, never from the first having done any thing wholesome or noble, a very tragic ape, a rustic Œnomaus, a counterfeit orator. For in what does thy eloquence come to the aid of thy country?" τἀνθρώπιον (= τὸ ἀνθρώπιον) is a diminutive from ὁ ἄνθρωπος, and seems to refer to the size of Æschines. αὐτός, in αὐτοτραγικός, retains something of its exclusive meaning, = "*himself*, if there ever was one." ἐλεύθερον here = ἐλευθέριον, as it frequently is. The language in this passage is very harsh, and shows something of the Scythian blood, with which the orator was often reproached by his enemies. But it should be recollected that a most malicious attack had been made upon his reputation by an old and embittered enemy. The reader will call to mind a passage in Mr. Webster's reply to C. J. Ingersoll's strictures upon his course in making the Ashburton Treaty, of equal severity, and very similar in language and spirit.

243. Ὥσπερ ἂν] "This is altogether analogous to what he would do." See § 194, n. — ἀσθενοῦσι . . . . εἰσιὼν] "visiting the feeble laboring under disease." — τὰ νομιζόμενα] "the customary funeral rites." — τὸ καὶ τὸ] "this and that." K. § 247, 3, (b); C. § 49, R. 1. We have here a fine specimen of the happy manner of Demosthenes in summing up and condensing into a single burning illustration the scope and gist of a long argument. See, also § 198.

244. τὴν ἧτταν] "the defeat," i. e. of Chæronea. — γεγονυῖαν] "having happened," or "to have happened." A part. used in the same relation as an infin. K. § 310, 4, (b). — ἄλλοθεν οὐδαμόθεν] "from no other place whatever." Adverbs ending in θεν are much used by Demosthenes in sweeping statements. See §§ 212, 252. — τὰ τελευταῖα] "finally," "last of all." — λόγῳ] "by word," or "force of argument." This is opposed to ὅπλοις in the same line. What Philip's ambassadors had been defeated in by argument, Philip himself had subverted by arms.

245. Ταῦτ'] "This," i. e. to prevent the success of Philip's arms. — μαλακίαν] "timidity," "cowardice," i. e. in deserting his place in the ranks at the battle of Chæronea. See §§ 148, 152 of the speech of Æschines. — ἀξιῶν . . . . γενέσθαι] "demanding of me but a single individual to be superior to." This, of course, was strangely inconsistent with his charge of cowardice. — σκαιὸς] "awkward," "perverse," "inconsistent."

246. οὐ παραιτοῦμαι] "I do not beg off," "I do not shrink from it." — τὰ πράγματα ἀρχόμενα] "difficulties in their incipient state." πράγματα often has this meaning. See §§ 20, 292, *et passim.* — ἃ πολιτικὰ] "which are native *or* natural." Democracies like those of Greece are specially liable to these faults. πολιτικὰ = οἰκεῖα, as in §§ 234 and 237. — τὸ κατ' ἐμὲ] "as far as I am concerned." The article gives a substantive meaning to the preposition with its case. See § 247, fin.

247. τίσι] "by what means." — τοὺς . . . . πραγμάτων] "those intrusted with the conduct of affairs." — Καὶ μὴν . . . . πρίηται] "Besides, by not allowing myself to be bribed by money, I have conquered Philip; for as the bidder has con quered the one who receives the price, if he purchase him." For καὶ μήν, see § 14, n. The whole of this paragraph is an extremely ingenious exculpation of himself from all blame in the defeat which his country had suffered; but especially this closing sentence, in which he claims even to have conquered Philip.

248. Ἃ μὲν . . . . ἐμοῦ] "What, therefore, I contributed towards its being just for this man (Ctesiphon) to propose such things concerning me." ἐγὼ is opposed to ὑμεῖς below, which, of course, is nominative to παρέσχεσθε understood. Having stated what he had done to render such a decree as that of Ctesiphon proper, the orator proceeds in this paragraph to state what the people generally, and the judges in particular, had done to warrant it. — ἐμβεβηκώς] "having entered into," or "being in the midst." This participle

agrees with δῆμος above. — ἡνίκ' . . . . πρὸς ἐμέ] "when it were nothing remarkable for the multitude to have treated me harshly." ἄν is often omitted thus with the indicative of the historical tenses in conditioned clauses, especially in expressions denoting *duty*, *probability*, *possibility*. K. § 260, R. 3. The difference between the forms with and without ἄν seems to be something like that between *were* and *would have been*, as used for each other, to some extent, in English. — αἱ τάφροι] "the trenches," i. e. around the city. — σιτώνην] "commissioner to supply the scarcity of corn." The appointment of such commissioners, according to Hermann (§ 150, 11), was resorted to only on extraordinary occasions, there being regularly fifteen magistrates, called Sitophylaces, to regulate the corn trade.

249. συστάντων] "having conspired." Demosthenes here alludes to the attempts made by his enemies, soon after the battle of Chæronea, to procure his condemnation. For this purpose, as he goes on to state, they brought against him, not personally, but by instigating to it such persons as they would be least suspected of having in their service, every species of trial. — τὴν ἡμέραν ἑκάστην] "every single day." The article adds definiteness and emphasis. K. § 246, 6. — ἀπόνοια] "recklessness," "desperateness." This quality of the individual here mentioned, as is the case, also, with the qualities attributed to other individuals whose names follow, fitted him for the service in which he was employed; hence it is that these qualities are singled out. This passage is thus imitated by Cicero (Cat. III. 7): "Quem quidem ego quum ex urbe pellebam, hoc providebam animo, Quirites, remoto Catilinâ, nec mihi P. Lentuli somnum, nec L. Cassii adipem, nec Cethegi furiosam temeritatem pertimescendam." — τούτοις] Dative of the agent after ἀπείρατον, the verbal being equivalent to the perf. pass. part. K. § 234, 1, (i). — τοῦτο γὰρ . . . . δικαστῶν] "for this (i. e. that he had been justly acquitted) is both confirmed by facts (ἀληθές), and is for the credit of (ὑπὲρ) judges under

oath, and deciding what is in accordance with their oaths." For this meaning of *ἀληθές*, see *ἀλήθειαν* below, § 250.

250. *τὰς εὐθύνας ἐπεσημαίνεσθε*] "you approved my accounts," i. e. by signing or sealing them, after having examined them. See Boeckh's Pub. Econ. Ath. p. 193. — *τί προσῆκεν . . . . ὄνομα ;*] "what name was it proper or just that Ctesiphon should give to the things done by me?" That is to say, What ought he, under these circumstances, to have denominated them, whether good or bad? Alluding to the language of the decree, where he had affirmed that Demosthenes had always said and done what was for the good of the people. — *τὴν ἀλήθειαν . . . . βεβαιοῦσαν*] "the truth confirming *or* rendering conclusive all things." Referring to the results of these trials, and the examinations of his accounts, which had shown him to be innocent.

251. *ἀλλὰ . . . . φυγεῖν*] "but the example of Cephalus is honorable, never to have been indicted." The person here alluded to was an Athenian orator of great distinction, who flourished during the Peloponnesian war, and who, though for a long time engaged in public affairs, was never indicted. Demosthenes, having spoken of the approbation which had been bestowed upon his conduct by his having been often acquitted in previous trials relating to these matters, alludes to this example of Cephalus (cited by Æschines in his speech, § 194, as presenting a very strong contrast to that of his rival), in order to show that the contrast in this respect argued nothing against him, and indeed, that, as far as Æschines was concerned, no such contrast existed between him and Cephalus, since, whatever others might have done, he had never indicted him. — *ἐν . . . . δικαίως ;*] "should on this account justly come under censure?" — *οὐδεμίαν . . . . γραφήν*] For a personal acc. in addition to a cognate acc. see K. § 208, 1; C. § 58, 1.

252. *ἀγνωμοσύνην . . . . βασκανίαν*] "his unfairness and slanderousness." Demosthenes here alludes to the malicious remark of his adversary, that an evil fortune had

always attended him, and that nothing could prosper with which he had any thing to do. See §§ 114, 135, 158, 253, of his speech. — *ἣν γὰρ . . . . ἑτέρῳ;*] "for how is it proper to speak of or reproach another for this, which he who is persuaded that he enjoys best, and possesses in the highest degree, does not know whether it will remain such till evening?" For the meaning here given to *βέλτιστα πράττειν*, see *ἄμεινον πράττειν*, § 254. Observe, also, the difference between *νομίζων* and *οἰόμενος*, the former expressing a much higher degree of confidence than the latter. — *ἀνθρωπινώτερον*] "more humanely," "more kindly."

253. *Δωδωναῖον*] "Dodonian." An epithet of Jupiter derived from Dodona, a city of Epirus, where was a celebrated oracle dedicated to him. As this was an oracle of great authority, it was much resorted to both by individuals and states, in order to learn their destiny. It would seem, from this passage, that it had pronounced favorably upon the destiny of Athens. I have removed the brackets from *καὶ τὸν Ἀπόλλω τὸν Πύθιον*, since the reading seems to be sustained by other passages in Demosthenes. See Epist. IV. p. 1487. — *ἣ νῦν ἐπέχει*] "which now possesses them," or "prevails." Referring to the victories of Alexander.

254. *Τὸ μὲν . . . . τὴν πόλιν*] "Therefore, the choosing the most honorable course, and the coming off better than those very Greeks who thought that they should live in prosperity if they deserted us, I ascribe to the good fortune of the city; but in the want of success (*lit.* the collision *or* bringing up against something), and all things not happening to us as we desired, I think that the city has received the part of the fortune of others falling to us." *ἐπιβάλλον* is a participle, and means here "falling upon," or "happening to."

255. *ἀξιῶ*] "I think," or "judge." — *ἀγαθῆς καὶ μεγάλης*] These adjectives agree with *τύχης* understood, which, in turn, is governed by *κυριωτέραν* understood.

256. *πρὸς*] "in comparison with." A meaning similar to

that of ἐπί with σκοπεῖν. See § 210, n. — ψυχρότητα] "cold heartedness," "unfeelingness," i. e. in raking up things against Æschines for which he was not personally guilty, but which belonged to his fortune. Referring obviously to the same state of feeling implied in χαλεποῦ below. His apology, then, is, that the severity of Æschines upon him made it necessary for him to defend himself with the same weapons. — ἐκ τῶν ἐνόντων] "considering the existing materials."

257. αἰσχρὸν] "disgraceful *or* servile." Such as he represents Æschines as having been obliged to resort to for a support, on account of his poverty. — ἀκόλουθα τούτοις] "things in keeping with these," i. e. with what he had just represented himself as having done while a boy. What some of them were, the orator proceeds to state, viz. "to defray the expense of choruses employed at the public festivals and theatrical exhibitions, to be at the charge of fitting out galleys for the public service, and the contributing of money to the state." These were duties which fell by law upon the more wealthy, or were undertaken voluntarily by the more patriotic citizens, and hence were of a highly honorable nature. — καλά γ'] "honorable at least." This character, he says, not even his enemies had ever denied to his measures, though they had not been successful.

258. καὶ πόλλ' . . . . παραλείπω] "and, although I might speak many other things concerning it, I omit them." ἂν here gives to the participle ἔχων the sense of the optative, according to a familiar principle of Greek grammar, while at the same time, by another principle, the participle conveys the restrictive idea, "although." Compare § 50, n. — σεμνὸς] "dignified," "illustrious." To be taken ironically. — ἅμα . . . . προσεδρεύων] "attending with your father at the school," i. e. as a drudge, his father having been spoken of in a previous passage (§ 129) as a slave of the schoolmaster Elpias. That this was the capacity in which he was employed is evident, also, from the description which

follows of the services which he performed, such as mixing ink, cleaning the benches, and sweeping the school-room.

259, 260. ἀνὴρ δὲ . . . . νεήλατα] "but having become a man, you read for your mother, engaged in the rites of initiation, the books (containing the forms of initiation), and assisted her in performing the other rites; by night prowling around in fawn-skins, and gulping down goblets of wine, and purifying the novitiates, and rubbing them down with clay and bran, and, having caused them to rise up from the cleansing, directing them to say, 'I escaped the bad, I found the better'; priding yourself on no one's being able to shout so loud, and I certainly agree with you (for you cannot think that he speaks so magniloquently without being a magnificent shouter); and by day leading through the streets those fine troops of Bacchanals crowned with fennel and white poplar, squeezing the copper-colored snakes and holding them above your head, and crying Evoë Saboë and dancing Hyes Attes! Attes Hyes! being saluted by the old crones as guide, leader, box-bearer, basket-carrier and by such like titles, receiving as a compensation for these services sops, twists, and fresh flour-cakes." I have thought best to translate this passage entire, as it contains an unusual number of technical expressions, the meanings of which are not easily ascertained. The rites here alluded to appear to have been a strange intermixture of Phrygian and Bacchic rites, celebrated by the superstitious and vulgar. The mother of Æschines, it would seem, was employed to superintend the rites of initiation to this worship, and also to teach the forms of the worship itself to the novitiates, in which her son assisted her. As to the different parts of the ceremonies here described, it will be necessary to remark upon only a few. The ceremony of clothing the novitiates in fawn-skins had allusion to the goat-formed Satyrs by which Bacchus was represented as being attended. The formula translated, "I escaped the bad, I found the better," was one which every child at Athens, on arriving at a certain age, was made to pronounce, with certain attendant ceremonies symbolical of the thing signified, in allusion to the happy change which had taken place in their mode of living since the ancient times, when the inhabitants fed on roots and acorns. This formula also, it would seem, was pronounced by novitiates on their initiation into the mysteries of the worship of Bacchus, as implying that by these rites they were restored to the favor of their god. παρείας is supposed by some to be derived from παρειά, "a cheek," in allusion to the fulness of the cheeks of the snakes here spoken of; but see the word in Liddell and Scott. Σαβοῖ was originally the name of a Phrygian deity, but, from the similarity of the character and worship of Bacchus, the name was applied to him also by his worshippers. Ἄττης, also, was a name applied to Bacchus, and for the same reason, it having originally belonged to the Phrygian goddess Cybele; and Ὕης was an epithet which he derived from his mother Semele, who was sometimes called Ὕη. These were all forms of enthusiastic invocation to Bacchus, employed by his devotees in the frenzied excitement of their worship. In these rites Æschines is represented as having acted as leader and guide to the novitiates, bearing the basket and the box, in which were contained the image of Bacchus and other sacred symbols, and as surpassing them all in the holy shout. The articles of food, which he is said to have received as a recompense for these services, are to be regarded as choice bits presented him by the devout old women by whom he was surrounded. In conclusion, I refer the reader to Horace, B. 2, Ode 19, as throwing some light on the phraseology employed in some parts of this passage.

261. ὁπωσδήποτε] "in whatever way you please," or "in some way or other." This adverb is thrown in to suggest a doubt as to the legitimacy of his citizenship. See a similar use of the word, Olyn. III. § 7. — ἀρχιδίοις] "inferior magistrates." A diminutive from ἀρχή. — πάνθ'] "all,"

i. e. the disgraceful things. The orator here intimates that his adversary, in accusing others of crimes and scandalous things, drew from his own experience.

262. οὐδὲν τῶν προϋπηργμένων] "nothing of those things commenced in early life." The idea here intended to be conveyed is, that Æschines fully sustained in after life the bad reputation which he acquired while young. προϋπηργμένων is the perf. pass. part. of προϋπάρχω. — τοῖς . . . . ἐπικαλουμένοις] "called groaners." So called, probably, on account of their unnatural and extravagant exhibition of pathos in their representations on the stage. — ὀπωρώνης] "fruit-dealer." According to some, this is to be taken as the name of a man notorious for stealing fruit, whose example Æschines was represented as imitating. In most editions, also, πλείω, in the next line, is made to agree with τραύματα, which, in these editions, stands expressed in the sentence. But this Becker included in brackets, as of doubtful authority, and Dindorf, in his text, rejected entirely. As it stands here, πλείω must be understood as meaning "more profit," but in the other case, "more wounds," i. e. more from the owners of the fruit than from their audience, on account of the wretchedness of their acting. — δειλοὺς] "cowards." Alluding to the charge of cowardice which Æschines had made against him.

263. αὐτὰ . . . . κατηγορήματα] "I will proceed to the very (αὐτὰ) accusations of thy character *or* nature." That is to say, such accusations as refer to him personally, and not, like the preceding, to his circumstances. — λαγὼ βίον] "the life of a hare," i. e. a timid, fearful life, continually expecting, while his country was triumphant over him and his party, the punishment which he was conscious of deserving.

264. οὐ γὰρ . . . . λέγειν] "for I do not think it necessary o speak indiscriminately, all the disgraceful and reproach-ul things which I might show to pertain to this fellow."

265. βεβιωμένα] "the course of life pursued." — Ἐδίδασκες . . . . ἐσύριττον] "You taught school, I attended; you

performed the rites of initiation, I was one of the initiated; you served in the chorus, I defrayed the expense; you acted as a scribe to the assembly, I harangued it; you served as a third-rate actor, I was one of the audience; you were driven from the stage, I hissed you." This contrast between their respective courses of life is very ingeniously conducted. It is a summary of all that had previously been said of the difference between their fortunes, and is so managed as to represent Æschines as the servant and drudge, and himself as a gentleman of liberal and generous pursuits, sometimes enjoying and sometimes rewarding the drudgery of his rival, and in all cases his superior. For this meaning of ἐκπίπτειν, see § 186, fin.

266. σοὶ . . . . κινδυνεύεις δὲ] "but to you it is to seem to be a sycophant, and you have at stake." The contrast, it will be observed, is still kept up here.

267. ἀναγνῶ] "let me read." It is not to be understood, however, that he read the records in question himself, but caused them to be read, as he says below, addressing the clerk, Λέγε τὰς μαρτυρίας. — ῥήσεις ἃς ἐλυμήνω] "the lines which you murdered." Alluding to his bad pronunciation of these lines in speaking them on the stage. The first of the lines is from the Hecuba of Euripides (v. 1), and the other from an unknown source. There is, however, a couplet in Soph. Antig. (vv. 276, 277) very similar in sentiment. — καὶ κακὸν, κ. τ. λ.] "and thee, evil man, may the gods above all, and then all these judges, evilly destroy."

268. οὐδὲν ἂν εἴποιμι] "I would say nothing." The apodosis of the following clause, which is introduced by εἰ. K. § 339, 1. — τινας] i. e. prisoners of war. See F. L., p. 394. — συνεξέδωκα] "helped dower," i. e. assisted those in humble circumstances in furnishing their daughters with the requisite dower for a respectable marriage. Which was often done at Athens. See Lys. pro Bon. Aristoph. p. 659.

269. οὕτω] Refers to what follows, as in § 138. — εὖ πα-

θόντα] "having received favors." Opposed to ποιήσαντα, "having done favors," below. — μικροῦ .... ὀνειδίζειν] "is virtually to disparage them." The sentiments expressed in this passage are exceedingly elevated and refined, — every way worthy of a disciple of Plato. For the government of μικροῦ, see § 151.

270. ἀθῷος] "uninjured by." Demosthenes, almost single-handed, had resisted Philip from the beginning, and might, therefore, if any had escaped falling into his power, justly claim to have been the cause of it.

271. φοράν .... ἔδει] "a certain irresistible rush *or* course of events, and such as was out of the ordinary course of nature" (*lit.* was not necessary *or* proper). An Attic euphemism, intimating something very disastrous. See § 133, n.

272. παρὰ τουτοισὶ] "in conjunction with these" (the Athenian people). This is said to show that the people had coöperated with him, and that therefore, as he goes on to say, any blame thrown upon him was at the same time thrown also upon them. — ἦν ἂν] "it would have been proper," or "there would have been an opportunity."

273. ἐν κοινῷ .... σκοπεῖν] "and the city offered in public (i. e. to all) the liberty of considering what was for the best." That is to say, as the orator has remarked once before, all others, equally with himself, had the right of proposing and discussing public measures. — οὐ γὰρ .... τιμῶν] "for you did not out of good-will surely relinquish to me hopes (i. e. of praise and reward), and admiration, and honors." The genitives are governed by παρεχώρεις, which implies separation. K. § 271, 2; C. § 55, 5.

274. Παρὰ μὲν .... τοιαῦτα] "Among all other men, therefore, I see some such *principles as these* laid down and established." What these are, the orator proceeds to tell in an indirect way, by first stating cases of conduct, and then stating how they were usually treated. See the same figure, § 117. — ὀργὴν .... τιμωρίαν .... συγγνώμην] Governed

in the same way as τὰ τοιαῦτα, with which they are in apposition. The three degrees of delinquency described in these and the following cases correspond to what is indicated in our language by "wrongs," "errors," and "misfortunes." See § 72. — οὐ . . . . ἁπάντων] "failed of success in common with all." — συνάχθεσθαι] "to grieve with," "sympathize with."

276. αὐτὸς] "he himself," i. e. Æschines. — ἐκέλευεν] "charged you." — ὅπως μὴ] The fut. indic. after these particles definitely implies the possibility of the result referred to. K. § 330, 6. — δεινὸν . . . . σοφιστὴν] "vehement, as well as a juggler and a sophist." See Æsch. §§ 16, 207, 215. — καὶ δὴ . . . . ἔχοντα] "now that not only these things are thus," i. e. applicable to another, rather than to himself. ἔχοντα is in the acc. plur. absolute, depending upon ὡς ("as if") in the previous line. K. § 312, 6, (c).

277. δεινότητα] "vehement eloquence." This sentence, it will be perceived, is incomplete, the orator having stopped in the midst of it, at the mention of the word here quoted, as if about to retract it, since the use of it acknowledged the charge of his adversary in calling him δεινόν, — or, perhaps, from modesty, on account of the pretending character of the word. Instead of retracting it, however, after some suspense, he adds, "Yes, be it so," which is equivalent to saying, "It is the right word, I will not retract it." We can judge pretty well how he would have completed the sentence, by what he says below, at Εἰ δ' οὖν, where he resumes the point. — κυρίους] Hearers (especially judges) may be considered as the controllers of the power of speakers, since, as our author goes on to say, speakers are wholly dependent upon their approbation for their own reputation. This view of the subject must have been far more agreeable to them than that of Æschines, who, by warning them to be on their guard against the effects of the eloquence of Demosthenes, plainly implied that they were under the control of the orators. — ἐξεταζομένην] "tried," "proved." —

ἀλλὰ . . . . τούτων] "but also, if any one offended or came into collision with him in any thing, against these." τὶς, being an indefinite pronoun, and hence having a sort of general or collective sense, takes the demonstrative τούτων, referring to it, in the plural, by the construction κατὰ σύνεσιν. K. § 241, 1; C. § 52, R. 1.

278. τοὺς ὑπὲρ . . . . βεβαιοῦν] "to ask of the judges convened for causes of a public nature to confirm to him," i. e. to gratify him in. — διακείμεν'] "disposed." This participle, with the adverbs standing in connection with it, may be rendered "meekly and gently disposed," i. e. well subdued and held in check. — 'Εν τίσιν] "On what occasions." — τῶν ὅλων τι] "any of the matters of the highest interest."

279. Μηδενὸς . . . . αὐτοῦ] "But for him, having demanded punishment from me neither in behalf of the state nor of himself, there having been no public crime whatever of mine, and, I will add, no private crime either," i. e. committed against Æschines. — Τὸ δὲ . . . . κακίαν] "But, indeed, that he, having neglected to bring the trials against me myself, should now come against this one (Ctesiphon), involves the sum of all baseness." ἐμὲ αὐτόν is more emphatic than ἐμαυτόν. K. § 302, R. 6.

280. φωνασκίας] Æschines, it would seem, possessed a very powerful voice, which is often referred to by Demosthenes. See §§ 260, 291, 318. Demosthenes, on the contrary, had by nature a bad voice. By cultivation, however, he attained great power over it, and especially excelled in the variety, modulation, and piercing emphasis of his tones. See Plutarch's Life; also, Æsch. F. L., p. 49, and Contr. Ctesiph., §§ 209, 210.

281. οὐκ ἐπὶ . . . . πολλοῖς] "does not rely upon the same anchor with the multitude," i. e. does not have the same hopes, the anchor, in all languages, being regarded as the emblem of hope. This was a common figure among the Greeks, of which critics cite many instances from the ancient Greek writers. It should be further stated, that αὐτῆς

agrees with ἀγκύρας understood. — Ἐγώ] "I" (have the same hopes, etc.). — καὶ . . . . πεποίημαι] "and have performed nothing disconnected (with the interest of the city), nor of a private nature."

282. Ἄρ' οὖν . . . . πῶς;] "But did not you (i. e. do some thing aside from the public interests)? And how (can it be that you did not)?" — τὴν μάχην] "the battle," i. e. of Chæronea. — καὶ ταῦτ'] "and that, too." See § 201, n. — Τῷ δ' . . . . τοιούτῳ;] "And whom does the crier justly invoke curses upon? Is it not on such an one?" By κήρυξ here is meant the crier or herald, who opened the meetings of the assembly, by first praying, and then inviting all who had any thing to say to speak. In his prayers, he invoked curses upon such characters as Æschines is here represented to be. Comp. Smith's Dict. Antiq., Art. Ἐκκλησια, *sub. fin.* — εἰ μή] For the indic. after these particles, see K. § 318, 3, (e). — οὗτος] "this one," i. e. such as he had just described. See § 173, n.

283. ὥστ' οὐ] For the negative οὐ instead of μή, see § 120, n. — καταρώμενος] "protesting."

284. κατὰ σαυτοῦ μηνυτής] "an informer against yourself," i. e. by confessing his treachery, as Demosthenes charges him with having done, after the decisive battle of Chæronea. — ὧν . . . . εὑρήσεις] "for which you will find all to blame sooner than *me*."

285. Σημεῖον δέ] "But here is the proof of it," i. e. that the city did not forget his good deeds. — ἄρτι . . . . εἰρήνην] "recently having made the peace." Demades, who is here alluded to, was an Athenian orator of great wit and eloquence, but of loose principles, who, being taken prisoner by Philip at Chæronea, ingratiated himself with his captor. so as to be employed by him to conclude the peace with Athens which ensued. — ἔτ' ἄμεινον] "all the more zealously." See K. § 239, R. 1, (a).

286. ταῦτ'] "these things," i. e. their connection with Philip, etc., which, as stated above, Æschines had denied

before the issue of the struggle, but acknowledged afterwards; and the others, it seems, had done likewise. — ὧν . . . . ἄδειαν] "receiving freedom from fear to speak what they thought." Such could not have been friends to their country; since, had they been, they would not have concealed their thoughts till the success of the enemy made it safe for them to reveal them.

287. ἐκεῖ] "there," i. e. with the enemy. δεῦρο, "hither," a few lines below, stands opposed to it. — δ' . . . . ἀλλὰ] The one limits and the other excludes. K. § 322, 2, 6. — ὑποκρινόμενον] "acting a part," "feigning."

288. οὕτως] "thus." This word stands opposed to ἄλλως πως, a few lines below. The people at large, he says, did not act in one way towards him in this matter, and the friends of the slain in another. — δέον] "it being proper," i. e. according to established customs. An acc. absolute. See § 30, n. It was customary among the Greeks to have funeral feasts. — οἰκειοτάτῳ] "the nearest relative." ὡς, just before this word, is to be referred to it as strengthening the superlative. For its separation from the word to which it refers, see Matt. § 461. — μάλιστα διέφερεν] "it most concerned." This is used as an impersonal verb here, and governs ᾧ in the line before. — ἃ μὴ . . . . ὤφελον] "what would that they had never *suffered*." A wish that cannot be realized. K. § 259, R. 6; C. § 77, 3.

289. ἐπίγραμμα] "inscription." A short piece of poetry written as an epitaph upon the tombs or other monuments erected in honor of the dead. — Μαρνάμενοι . . . . Ψυχάς] "But, contending, they did not save their lives by bravery and courage." The genitives ἀρετῆς and δείματος depend, perhaps, upon βράβην, there being a sort of zeugma between the two sentences, = *But, contending, they did not count upon the preservation of their lives as the reward of their bravery and courage, but a common death.* But it is most probable that the reading is corrupt here. — κρίσις] "issue," i. e. death. — μοῖραν . . . . ἔπορεν] "but he (Jupiter) did not

afford them any escape from fate," i. e. those who fell in this battle.

290. αὐτῷ τούτῳ] "this very *inscription*."

291. μνησθεὶς] "having mentioned *or* spoken of." — οὐχ ὡς . . . . γνώμην] "had not the state of mind which a patriotic and just citizen would have had."

292. πολιτείας . . . . φροντίζειν] "pretending that he is concerned for the constitution." Æschines had made great pretensions to this in his speech. — καὶ μὴ . . . . τετυχθαι] "and not by his line of policy to be ranked among our enemies." κοινῶν properly means "public measures." — εἰς πράγματα] "into difficulties," "troubles." See § 246, n.

293. δι' ἐμὲ . . . . πραττομένῃ] "that, through my influence, you have resisted the power that was forming against the Greeks," i. e. the power of Philip. This, he says, would be doing too great honor to himself, while at the same time it would be doing still greater injustice to the people, by implying that they had been led into this policy contrary to their usual course. — εὖ οἶδ' ὅτι] ὅτι belongs to a predicate to be supplied from συγχωρήσαιτε. Jelf's K. § 895, 1.

294. εἴ γ' . . . . ἐμοί] "if, indeed, having laid aside misrepresentation and speaking from enmity, we should consider in face of the truth who they undoubtedly are upon whose heads all would with reason and justly place the blame of all that has happened, any one would find *them to be* such men as this fellow, in each of the cities, not such as I am."

295. ὑπάρχοντας] "existing," or "their own." The list of traitors which follows may be regarded as a kind of Black Roll, posted up for immortality.

296. αἰσχίστοις] "the basest indulgences."

297. Ταύτης . . . . ἐλευθερίας] "Of this so shameful and infamous conspiracy and baseness, rather, O men of Athens, not to speak unmeaningly, betrayal of the liberty of the Greeks."

298. καιρὸς] "opportunity." — οὐδ' ὅσα . . . . συμβεβου-

λευκα] "nor what, at any time, I have advised these (the Athenians) have I advised like you (traitors), inclining towards gain as if in a scale," i. e. from selfish, mercenary motives. — καὶ μεγίστων . . . . προστὰς] "and, as is well known (δή), having directed the most important interests of all the men of my time." κατά here is used as it is in the phrase οἱ καθ' ἑαυτούς, "those with themselves," or "their contemporaries." K. § 292, (2).

299. Τὸν δὲ τειχισμὸν] "But this repairing of the fortifications." Alluding to his services as superintendent of the repairs made upon the fortifications after the battle of Chæronea. A few lines below, the orator, playing upon the word, employs it in a figurative sense, including all that he did for the defence of Athens. — πόρρω . . . . τίθεμαι] "but I place them far below my political measures." τῶν πεπολιτευμένων is governed by πόρρω. K. § 271, 3; C. § 55, 2. — ἀμυνουμένους] Some prefer ἀμυνομένους here, — the pres. instead of the fut.

300. ἀλλ' οἱ . . . . τύχῃ] "but the generals of the allied forces, and the forces themselves, *were conquered* by fortune."

301. ἐκ δὲ . . . . ταύτῃ;] "but on the side of the places towards the Peloponnesus (to throw before the city) those dwelling near to it?" The orator, it will be perceived, speaks of the allies which he had gained as so many ramparts thrown up in different directions around the state. — παρὰ . . . . φιλίαν] "along by a country friendly in its whole extent." This region included the nations on the Hellespont, the Eubœans, etc., as corn was brought by the Greeks from the Euxine Sea. See § 73, n. For φιλίαν, without a noun, see K. § 263, a, (β); C. § 50, 3.

302. Καὶ τὰ μὲν . . . . ὑπαρχόντων] "And, on the one hand, to preserve of our existing dominions." τὰ μέν, "in part," is an adverbial acc., and is responded to by τὰ δ' below. K. § 322, 5, (a). — ὧν δ' . . . . προσθεῖναι;] "but of what things there was a lack to the city, to supply these?" The views here given are very statesmanlike and just

303. ἃ καὶ .... ἐμοῦ] "which *measures*, O men of Athens, if any one will consider them without envy, he will find to have been wisely enacted, and executed with all integrity, and that the proper time of each was neither neglected nor unperceived, nor betrayed by me." παρεθέντα and προεθέντα are both first aorist passive participles from different compounds of the same verb, ἵημι.

305. ᾤκουν] "would have inhabited." The sense is affected by ἂν in the preceding line.

306. ὧν .... περίεστι] "which, if they had been successful, O earth and gods, it would undoubtedly have been our fortune to be at the height of greatness, and justly so, too; but as they have resulted very otherwise, it still remains to enjoy a good reputation." μεγίστοις is put in the dative by attraction. See § 128.

307. οὐκ] Repeated for emphasis. — ὑποστάντα] "having undertaken." The article τὸν in the preceding line belongs to this word, which is to be understood as referring to Demosthenes himself, as the other character described in the context is to be understood as meant for Æschines. — λυπήσῃ] "may have offended *him*."

308. ἡσυχίαν] "quiet," "withdrawal from public affairs." — φυλάττει .... λέγοντος] "watches when you are full of continuous speaking," i. e. pressed with business. It was only at such times, when there appeared to be a chance for him to "make capital" out of the difficulties and troubles of others, that he came forward. It is to be observed that πηνίκα is for ὁπηνίκα, — the direct for the indirect. K. § 344, R. 1. — πολλὰ δὲ τἀνθρώπινα] "and many human things are of this kind." — συνείρει .... ἀπνευστί] "pronounces these in a continuous flow, distinctly, and without catching his breath"; i. e. in a declamatory, periodic style. — τῷ τυχόντι] "any one," "every one." The literal meaning of this participle is "one who has happened," and hence by an easy transition it comes to mean "any one," or "every one."

309 ταύτης .... επιμελείας] "of this oratorical skill and art," i. e. such as is spoken of above.

310. Τούτων .... ἐξέτασις] "For there was a test of all these things in the above-mentioned times," i. e. the times called for such services, and hence they became the test of the ability and patriotism of public men. The following sentence expresses the same idea in a different manner, and hence ἀποδείξεις means "proofs," "tests."—ἐν οἷς] "among whom." Referring for its antecedent to ἀνδρὶ καλῷ τε κἀγαθῷ. K. § 332, R. 1, (a). — οὔκουν .... ηὐξάνετο] "consequently, not among those at least by whom the country was strengthened." For οὔκουν, see § 24, n.

311. Τίς ἡ .... σοῦ;] "What civil and public relief of means (has ever been effected) by you, either for the rich or poor?" such, for instance, as he himself had effected in his revision of the laws of the trierarchy, §§ 102–109.

312. ὦ τᾶν] "my good Sir." This sentence is represented as being spoken by some one by way of obviating or palliating the charges just stated. — εἰς σωτηρίαν .... ἀργύριον] "contributed of their means to the safety (of their country), and finally Aristonicus (gave to the city) the money which he had collected for regaining his civil rank." This Aristonicus (perhaps the one mentioned § 84) had in some way, as it would seem, embezzled the public money, and consequently, according to the laws of Athens, was considered as politically disgraced until this was refunded. Having collected sufficient money to refund it, he presented it to the state. — οὐδὲ τότε οὔτε] Observe the accumulation of negatives, and see § 216; also § 24. — οὐκ ἀπορῶν] "not being destitute of means." That he was not thus destitute is shown from his having received a large amount by the will of a relative, and also from the wealthy citizens, for attacking the law of Demosthenes concerning the trierarchy. Observe that κεκληρονόμηκας takes two genitives. See C. § 54, R. 9.

313. 'Αλλ' ἵνα .... ἐκκρούσω] "But lest, speaking one

word after another, I cheat myself out of the present opportunity," i. e. by not adhering strictly to his defence. — Θεοκρίνης] An actor, or according to others an informer, who made pathetic complaints against persons.

316. οὐ μὲν . . . . ἄγειν] "nor, indeed, could any one say how great, to bring into discredit and contempt the good deeds performed in the present age."

317. βουλομένη] "aiming at." — κατ' ἐκείνους] "with them," i. e. their contemporaries, just as τοὺς καθ' αὐτόν a few lines below, means "his contemporaries." See § 293, n.

318. — ἵνα . . . . εἴπω] "that I may say nothing else," i. e. nothing worse. Alluding to the epithet which he had just applied to Æschines.

320. ἐφαμίλλου . . . . κειμένης] "patriotism for their country lying open for rivalry to all in common," i. e. all having an equal chance to show their zeal for their country. The time here alluded to is opposed to that alluded to a few lines below, when, after the ascendency of the Macedonian power, men were not judged of by their zeal for their country, but by their zeal for their masters; in which last period he freely acknowledges that he was eclipsed by Æschines and his friends. — ἐν τάξει . . . . ἱπποτρόφος] "(became) both great in rank, and a famous keeper of race-horses." A matter of great pride in Greece.

321. μέτριον πολίτην] "a respectable, frugal citizen." Opposed to the traitors, who made such a display with their ill-gotten gains. Thus also De Cherson. § 76. — ἐν μὲν . . . . διαφυλάττειν] "in favorable opportunities to maintain for the city the pursuit of honor and supremacy." — τούτου . . . . ἕτερα] "for of this, *or* of thus much, nature has the control, but of the ability and power, other things." That is to say, it was within the power of every one to have these feelings and designs towards his country, though the ability to carry them out depended upon various other things.

322. Οὐκ ἐξαιτούμενος, κ. τ. λ.] The orator here alludes

to the various ways in which he had been persecuted by his enemies, most of which have been referred to in the previous part of the Oration.

323. ἑτέρων] "of others," i. e. others besides his countrymen. — τὴν δεξιὰν . . . . οἴωμαι] "extending the hand (by way of salutation) and offering my congratulations to those whom I may expect to announce it there," i. e. in Macedonia. The orator here refers to those at Athens who were desirous of being known to the enemy as zealous advocates of their cause, and hence, on occasion of any success of the Macedonian arms, were particular to offer their congratulations to such of the Macedonian party at Athens as would be likely to report their zeal at head-quarters.

324. Μὴ δῆτ', κ. τ. λ.] This peroration is short, but exceedingly impressive. It forms a proper climax to the tone of patriotic fervor which pervades the whole Oration, and a fitting conclusion to the indignant strain of rebuke which the orator has uttered against the enemies of his country. — ἐξώλεις καὶ προώλεις . . . . ποιήσατε] "wholly destroy, and that, too, speedily" (*lit.* before their time). See Orat. F. L. p. 395, init.

APPENDIX ON THE DOCUMENTS.

The great difficulties connected with the interpretation of the decrees and other documents found in this oration seem to require a separate and more extended discussion of their character and contents than could be given in the Notes. The genuineness of these documents has long been a subject of debate, and especially, of late, has been ably discussed by Professors Boeckh and Vömel in the affirmative, and Professors Droysen and Newman in the negative. But little more will be attempted here than briefly to indicate the most important results arrived at by this discussion, so far as known to the author. The arguments against the genuineness of the documents are, —

1. The fact, that in the other orations of Demosthenes, and those of the other Attic orators, as well as in the latter half of this oration, we generally find only the bare titles of the documents. This being the fact, the question at once arises, how it could have happened. No reason can be discovered, in the nature of the case, why they should have been incorporated into the text in the first twenty-seven instances, and not in the remainder. If they were inserted by the author himself, why did he stop here? and why are they not found in his other orations, and in those of the other Attic orators?

2. Out of the fourteen documents which require the name of the archon to be mentioned during whose year of office they were enacted, only one name agrees with the received lists of archons which have come down to us. This solitary true name is that of Chærondas (§ 54), which could hardly have been mistaken by a fabricator, from its known connection with the fatal battle of Chæronea.

3. No inconsiderable difficulty is found in the *language* of the documents; such as inversions in the order of words in set phrases, unusual designations of office and duties, uncommon words and uncommon meanings.

4. Quite a number of the documents do not seem at all pertinent to the connection. The remarks of the orator by which they are introduced, or the comments which he makes upon them, seem to suppose, in several instances, something very different from what we find. This is especially true of the following documents:— 1. Philip's letter relative to his detention of the Athenian vessels (§ 77). It is introduced by the orator in order to show that Philip casts the blame of breaking the peace on others, while he exonerates him, and is commented upon as fully proving the point. But the letter found in the text does not sustain the assertion, without considerable violence in its interpretation. 2. The documents connected with his reform of the trierarchy (§§ 105, 106). They seem very deficient in fulness, and quite different from what we are led to expect from the connection and the titles by which they are designated, especially the Καταλογοι. 3. The documents concerning the relation between Athens and Thebes (§§ 164 – 167). These are introduced to show the unhappy state of feeling between the two cities, brought about by Æschines and his party. We are led to expect, therefore, decrees of mutual crimination. But the decrees found in the text both relate to Philip, and only one of them alludes to the Thebans at all. Besides, one of the letters of Philip is called a *reply to the Thebans*, while we have no decree at all from the Thebans to which he could reply.

5. Several of the decrees present very serious historical difficulties, especially the following:— 1. The decree of Demosthenes concerning the oaths (the first in the series, § 29). This decree, as found in the text, differs from the account given of it elsewhere, both by Æschines and Demosthenes, in several particulars. First, the date of it is more than a month after the *return* of the embassy which it was designed to despatch (see notes on § 30, and the Calendar). Second, it is clearly implied in the oration of Demosthenes, De F. L. (p. 376), that there were ten ambassadors on this embassy, while only five are here mentioned, and of these the name of only one (that of Æschines) agrees with the list of those known to have been upon the embassy. Third, an important particular is omitted in the decree, which is described

by Demosthenes (F. L., p. 389) as having been introduced into it, — the provision that the admiral (Proxenus) should conduct the ambassadors directly to Philip. Fourth, it speaks of the peace as having been voted at the first assembly, whereas it was voted at the second, on the 19th of Elaphebolion (Dem. F. L., p. 359); and, besides, makes no allusion to the *alliance* which was coupled with the peace in the decree referred to, as is evident even from Demosthenes (F. L., pp. 353, 354). 2. The decree of Callisthenes immediately after the submission of the Phocians to Philip (§§ 37, 38). In the first place, the date is nearly five months after the surrender of the Phocians to Philip, while Demosthenes, both in this oration (§ 36), and in the Orat. de F. L. (p. 379), states that the decree was passed *immediately* after that event. In the second place, several things are omitted here, which are described by Demosthenes (F. L., p. 379) as having been contained in the decree. 3. The second Amphictyonic decree (§ 155) purports to have been passed at the spring session, whereas it is stated by Demosthenes, in the remarks by which he introduces the decrees, that it was passed at the session following that at which the preceding decree was passed, i. e. the following autumnal session. The designation *Arcadian*, given to Cottyphus, may have arisen from confounding *Parrhasian* (an Arcadian name) with *Pharsalian*, which was his proper designation. 4. The decrees of Heropythes concerning the relation between Athens and Thebes seem to contain an obscure allusion to a second peace with Philip, after the war of Byzantium, which is highly incredible, though attested by Diodorus. There are no important difficulties in the other documents.

The counter arguments in favor of the genuineness of the documents are, briefly, as follows: —

1. It is not necessary, in order to make out their genuineness, to suppose that the orator himself incorporated them into his speech, but only *that they were actually taken from the public archives, on the supposition that they were the identical records referred to in the text, and not fabricated.* This may have been done some time after the publication of the speech; which, indeed, is the commonly received view.

2. Hence it is very easy to imagine how they came to be incomplete, since it is very conceivable that the records themselves, from a certain point, may have been lost or mislaid, or from some other cause rendered defective.

3. Hence, also, the almost uniformly wrong archons. The documents for a year were probably inclosed in a single envelope, or deposited in a single compartment, containing the name of the chief archon for the year, while those acted upon during each Prytany bore the name of the clerk for the Prytany. When, now, these documents were taken from the archives for publication, the name of the archon may have been lost or overlooked, and the name of the clerk for the Prytany mistaken for it.

4. Hence, too, the wrong document would often be introduced instead of the right one, which accounts for their want of pertinence in many cases, and the historical difficulties in others.

5. Most of the remaining difficulties may be accounted for, either by supposing corruptions in the decrees, to which they would be very liable under the circumstances supposed, or inaccuracies in the original drafts, on account of their referring to matters which their authors did not understand.

The judgment of Vömel (as given in the Class. Mus., No. VIII.), after surveying the whole question, is, that "five documents are attached to a wrong place, four are full of gaps, one perhaps imperfect, and one forged."

INDEX TO THE NOTES.

I. NAMES AND SUBJECTS.

Abuses of democracy, 143.
Accumulation of negatives, 13, 24, 216, 312.
Accusative absolute, 30.
Adverbs ending in θεν, 244.
Æschines, enmity between him and Demosthenes, 17; of small stature, 129; his character and course, 258-267; had a fine voice, 280.
Amphictyonic Council, 148; constitution and place of meeting, 151, 154, 155; — War, 149.
Ancient oratory, character of, 22.
Aposiopesis, 3, 22.
Archons, 29, 54.
Areopagus, 133.
Aristonicus, 312.
Aristophon, 162.
Asyndeton with ἕτερος, 219.
Athenian Calendar, 29.
Athens, the two parties there, 89; tribes at, 29; age of majority at, 177; assemblies of the people at, 37; number of generals at, 38; character of them during the contest with Philip, 145.
Bœotian towns, 43.
Byzantium, 87, 90.
Cephalus, 251.
Chæronea, 195.
Cirrha, 149.
Classification of Solon, 171.
Clepsydra, 139.
Climax, 179.
Colyttus, 75.
Constructio κατὰ σύνεσιν, 277, 310.
Crier at the public assemblies at Athens, 282; invitation given by him at the opening of the meetings, 170.
Dative by attraction, 128, 306.
Decelea, 96.
Demades, 285.
Demosthenes, his statesmanship, 301-303; his voice, 280; elevated sentiments, 97; severity of language, 242; happy use of illustrations, 243; repair of the walls of Athens, 299; his style, 142; his labors against Philip, 218, 237, 270, powerful summing up of topics and arguments, 86, 265.
Denial of both protasis and apodosis, 76.
Direct for indirect discourse, 241.
Divided state of the Peloponnesus, 18.
Dodonian Jupiter, 253.
Eleusis, 177.
Embassies to Philip, 17.
Enthymems, 139.
Epigram, 289.
Eubœa, its situation, 71.

Eubulus, 162.
Examination of accounts of public officers at Athens, 112, 117.
Festivals of Bacchus at Athens, 54.
Forms in υμι and ύω interchanged, 76.
Funeral feasts at Athens, 288.
Future in subordinate clauses, 26.
Generals. See *Athens*.
Harmosts, 96.
Inverted attraction, 16, 200.
Locrians of Amphissa, 149.
Logical and oratorical order of words, 134.
List of traitors in the Grecian states, 295, 296.
Neuter for masculine, 47.
Oath by the heroes of Marathon, etc., 208.
Occasion of the Oration for the Crown, 17.
Oratorical pleonasms, 21, 137.
Participial construction, 122.
Partitive genitive, instead of taking the case of the adjective, 22, 132.
Peace with Philip, 17.
Perfect and aorist dif., 142.
Perinthus, 90.
Personal instead of impersonal construction, 41, 198.
Piræus, 132.
Plural of abstract nouns, 210.
Pnyx, 55 ; its situation, 169.
Position of Athens among the states of Greece, 63.
Pregnant construction, 14, 138.
Preliminary skirmishes with Philip, 216.
Pres. in fut. sense, 21.
Published speeches of the orators different from the spoken, 215.
Relative used as an adjective pronoun, 10.
Return of the descendants of Hercules, 186.
Second Sacred War, 18.
Senate-chamber at Athens, its situation, 169.
Social War, 17, 234.
Temple of Delos, 134.
Theocrines, 313.
Theoric fund, 28, 119.
Thermopylæ, 32.
Thesmothetæ, 116.
The trierarchy, 99, 102, 104–106.
Time of the tenses in connection with εἰ and ἄν, 76, 201.
Traitors, 48, 49, 295.
Verbals, construction of, 58.
Verbs of *willing*, construction of, 11.
Vices of democracies, 143, 246.
Whole in apposition with its parts, 182.
Zeugma, 289.

II. GREEK WORDS AND PHRASES.

ἄγκυρα, 281.
ἀγωνοθέτης, 84.
ἀδικήματα, ἁμαρτήματα, ἀτυχήματα, 274.
αἰτία, διαβολή, λοιδορία, 7.
ἀκονιτί, 200.
ἀληθές, 249.
ἀλλὰ γάρ, 42, 111.
ἄλλως τε κἄν, 5.
ἅμα μέν . . . . ἅμα δέ, 219.
ἀμείνων, κρείττων, dif., 215.
ἄμεινον πράττειν, 254.
ἄν, 16, 17 ; omitted with historical tenses, 248.
ἀναλαβεῖν, construction of, 163.
ἀναφορά, 219.
ἀνήρ, with names of nations, etc., 1.

ἄνθρωπος for ὁ ἄνθρωπος, 139.
ἁπλῶς, 88.
Ἀπόλλων πατρῷος, 141.
ἀπόνοια, 249.
ἀρχιτέκτων, 28.
βακτηρία, 210.
βέλτιστα πράττειν, 252.
βλασφημεῖν, construction of, 11.
γέ, ironical, 136; between a preposition and its case, 216.
γραμματοκύφων, 209.
γραφὴ παρανόμων, 9.
γέῤῥα, 169.
δέ, ἀλλά, dif., 287.
δεινότης, 277.
δεκαρχία, 18.
δή = as is well known, 18, 139, 298.
δημιουργός, 157.
δήποτε, 21, 261.
διάνοια = state of mind, 192.
διδόναι = to offer, 103.
δυοῖν θάτερον, 139.
δύσκολον = ἀδίκον, 176.
ἐβουλόμην and ἠβουλόμην, 64.
εἰς after a verb of rest implying a previous motion, 157.
εἰσαγγελία, 13.
εἷς ἀνήρ, 143.
εἰδέναι, γιγνώσκειν, dif., 48.
ἐκεῖνος = that renowned, 219; unusual position of, 71, 238.
ἐκπίπτειν, 265.
ἑλεῖν τὴν γραφήν, 3.
ἐλεύθερος = ἐλευθέριος, 242.
ἐμὲ αὐτόν, ἐμαυτόν, dif., 13, 279.
ἐν = with, 28.
ἐξεταζόμενος, 277.
ἐξέτασις, ἐξετασμός, dif., 16.
ἐξώλης καὶ προώλης, 324.
ἐπί = under, in the power of, 166, 215; with σκοπεῖν, 210, 233.
ἐπιστάτης, 29.
ἐπιστήσας, 87.
ἕτερος without the article, 87.
ἐφεξῆς, 110.
ἡγεμονία, 202.
ἡ ἡμέρα ἑκάστη, 249.
ζῆλος, 129.
ἰαμβειοφάγος, 139, 180.
ἱπποτρόφος, 320.
καί concessive with participle, 50, 258; — μήν, 14; — . . . . δέ = and also, 215; — γάρ, 65; — ταῦτα = and that too, 282. — . . . . τε καί, 1.
καιρός, χρόνος, dif., 48.
καλαμίτης, 129.
καλοκἀγαθία, 93.
καλῶς ποιοῦντες, 231.
κατά = contemporary with, 298, 317.
καταψεύδεσθαι, construction of, 11.
κληρονομεῖν, with two genitives, 312.
κλήτορες, 55.
κοινῇ, 8.
λανθάνειν, construction of, 190.
μάλιστα μέν, 164, 267, 324; τὰ —, 21.
μέλλει with fut. infin., 8.
μὲν οὖν, 130.
Μουσῶν λείαν, 72.
νὴ Δία, concessive, 101, 117.
νομίζειν, οἴεσθαι, dif., 252.
νῦν referring to an actual course of events, τότε to a supposed course, 195, 200.
ξύλον, 129.
ὁ διώκων, 7.
οἴεσθαι ironical, like the English "trow," 225.
οἰκεῖος = πολιτικός, 234.
ὀλίγου (μικροῦ) δεῖν, 20, 151, 269.
ὀμωμοκέναι, ὀρκοῦν, ὀρκίζειν, 6.
ὁπηνίκα for εἰ, 14.
ὅπως μή with fut. indic, 276.
ὅσα for ἅ when referring to quantity.
ὃς μέν, demonstrative, 164.
ὅτι without a predicate expressed, 293.
οὐ δέον, 133, 277.
οὔκουν (οὐκοῦν), 24.
οὔτε . . . . οὔτε, 24, 186.
οὗτος nearly = τοιοῦτος, 173.
οὕτω, referring to what follows, 138, 269; separated from its word, 33, 163, 220.

οὐχ ὅπως, 131.
παρά = at the same time that, in connection with, 13, 226.
παρεία, 260.
παριέναι, προϊέναι, 303.
περί = round among, in, 147.
περιουσία, 3.
περίτριμμα ἀγορᾶς, 127.
πηνίκα for ὁπηνίκα, 308.
πινάκιον, 210.
πλὴν οὐκ, 45.
πόθεν, 47.
ποιεῖν ὑπερβολὴν = ὑπερβάλλειν, 190.
πολεμάρχος, 175.
πολιτεύεσθαι, πράττειν, ποιεῖν, 4.
πολλοῦ γε καὶ δεῖ, 47.
πομπεία, 11; πομπεύειν, 122.
πόῤῥω with genitive, 299.
πράγματα = difficulties, troubles, 246.
προάγειν, προσάγειν, dif., 206.
προαίρεσις καὶ πολιτεία, 93.
προέδροι, 29; — *non contribules*, 29.
προθεσμία, 125.
προλαβεῖν, 224.
πρός = in comparison with, 256.
πρότερος, πρότερον, 7.
πρυτανεύειν, 29.
πρῶτον, πρῶτον μέν, dif., 56.
Πύλαι, 32.
σιτώνης, 248.
σύμβολον, 210.
σύμβουλος καὶ συκοφάντης, 189.
σχήματα, 22.
σχήσειν for ἕξειν, 45.
τὰ μάλιστα, 21.
τὰ μὲν . . . . τὰ δέ, 302.
τὰ τιμιώτατα, 215.
τιθέναι ψήφους, 227.
τί κακὸν οὐχί, 48.
τιμωρία, τίμημα, τὰ ἐπιτίμια, dif., 12.
τὶς = μέγας, 225.
τὸ δ' οὖν κεφαλαῖον, 213.
τὸ καὶ τό = this and that, 243.
τὸ κατ' ἐμέ, 246.
τὸ λοιπόν, τὰ λοιπά, τοῦ λοιποῦ, dif., 78.
τὸ μὲν πρῶτον, 87.
τοῖς ὅλοις, καθ' ὅλου, 39.
τοῖς πρὸς ἐμέ, 14.
τοσοῦτος referring to what follows, 60.
τυχεῖν, 130; τυχόν = perhaps, 221.
ὑπάρχειν, 1.
ὑπάρχων, ὤν, παρών, ὑπών, dif., 17.
ὑπέρ nearly = περί, 9.
ὑπολογίζεσθαι, διαλογίζεσθαι, dif., 99.
ὑπωμοσία, 103.
φανῆναι with infin. and part., 71
φέρειν καὶ ἄγειν, 230.
φορά, 61, 271.
φυγάδες, 71.
χρηστός, ironical, 30.
χοῖνιξ, 129.
ὡς, with acc. absolute, 276; with an adverb, 85, 128, 212; = εἰς or πρός, 133, 169; — ἄρα, usage, 22, 54.
ὡς ἔοικεν, ironical, 63.
ὥστ' οὐ instead of ὥστε μή, 120, 283.
ὥσπερ ἄν referring to a suppressed predicate, 194, 214.
ὤφελον expressing a wish that cannot be realized, 288
ᾤχετο λαβών, 40.

THE END.

www.ingramcontent.com/pod-product-compliance
Lightning Source LLC
Chambersburg PA
CBHW030352270326
41926CB00009B/1069

* 9 7 8 3 3 3 7 2 7 3 2 8 6 *